#5

Rob m George

The Complete Book of Pregnancy and Childbirth

SHEILA KITZINGER

The Complete Book of Pregnancy and Childbirth

Photography by Camilla Jessel
and Nancy Durrell McKenna

Alfred A. Knopf • New York • 1993

The Complete Book of Pregnancy and Childbirth
was conceived, edited, and designed by
Dorling Kindersley Limited, 9 Henrietta Street, London WC2 8PS

For the revised edition

Editor	**Lesley Riley**
Designer	**Claudine Meissner**
Editorial Director	**Jackie Douglas**
Art Director	**Roger Bristow**

For the revised U.S. edition

Editor	**Toinette Lippe**
Consultants	**Gerrianne Griffin Bodd RN, BSN, CCE**
	Phyllis E. Maloney RN, CCE

This is a Borzoi Book published by Alfred A. Knopf, Inc.

First published in 1980
This revised edition 1989

Library of Congress Cataloging-in-Publication Data

Kitzinger, Sheila
    The complete book of pregnancy and childbirth/Sheila Kitzinger;
photography by Camilla Jessel and Nancy Durrell McKenna. — New ed.
fully rev. and expanded.
    p.   cm.
    Bibliography: p.
    Includes index.
    ISBN 0-394-58011-7
    1. Pregnancy—Popular works.   2. Childbirth—Popular works.
I. Title.
RG525.K518 1989   89—2260
618.2—dc19   CIP

Filmset in Garamond ITC by MS Filmsetting Limited, Frome, Somerset.

Printed in the United States by R. R. Donnelley & Sons

Reproduction by Spectrum Reproductions.

Published September 11, 1989

Reprinted Twice

Fourth Printing, June 1993

CONTENTS

Introduction

When I first started to teach and counsel pregnant women back in the sixties, there was little birth education around. For a small minority of women there were breathing and relaxation exercises taught by physiotherapists (who then had no training for helping women in childbirth), and talks by midwives about "what to expect".

There was a handful of books written by the pioneers: Grantly Dick-Read, Kathleen Vaughan, Minnie Randall, Helen Heardman, Vevovsky and Lamaze. Though some of them discussed the fear of childbirth, there was nothing about the socially inculcated lack of confidence we felt in our bodies and in ourselves, nor about the pressure on women by a powerful medical system to surrender themselves to it as passive patients. It seemed that all we could hope for in labor was to put on as good a performance as possible and to be told "well done".

After the birth of my first child, when I started teaching for what is now the National Childbirth Trust, I remember talking to obstetricians from the USSR who had introduced psychoprophylaxis (a system of training based on breathing techniques) into some of their bigger hospitals and were proud because "there is now no noise in the labor ward". A great achievement—to silence women!

When psychoprophylaxis was first introduced into Britain from France a woman told me that the day after a grueling labor involving drugs and the use of forceps, her childbirth educator had shown up at her bedside and commented: "You didn't do too well!" In those days, if you needed pain-killing drugs or help with the birth, you were made to feel that you had failed. The choice was between having doctors take over completely, and putting on a solo performance without support or encouragement from professionals.

Remarkable changes have taken place since then—largely due to women in the childbirth movement who have joined together internationally and across continents. It is now acknowledged, almost everywhere, that women have a right to full and accurate information about their bodies and to participate in all decisions made about them. I doubt whether this could ever have occurred if we had left doctors, nurses and midwives to challenge the system.

This new edition of *The Complete Book of Pregnancy and Childbirth* reflects the many changes that have come about because women refuse to remain ignorant of their bodies and about what doctors are doing to them. It is an expression of women's courage and growing self-confidence, and of the many ways in which we have reached out to each other to explore and understand those experiences in our lives which we share, which can reveal more about who we are, and which can help us realize our full potential as women.

◻In order to take an active part in giving birth rather than submit passively to delivery, you need to prepare yourself well in advance with an understanding of how to adapt to the work being done by your uterus, using breathing, relaxation, change of position, massage, and focused concentration to "get in tune with" the contractions. So there is a good deal of practical material in the book on how to do this. It is not just a matter of learning exercises. There is a harmony and rhythm about a natural labor: with the wave of each contraction you are swept on towards the birth of the baby, in a pattern which makes labor into a process greater than all its separate parts, and in which all the techniques you have practiced are submerged by the total satisfying experience.

The book describes the choices which are available so that you can decide how you would like to have your baby, the kind of setting and care you prefer, and how you wish your baby to be welcomed into the world. I include suggestions on talking with your doctor, how to ask about all the things that worry you, and how you can share in the decisions about yourself and your baby. The book also sets out to give a map of the route through pregnancy and labor and out the other side, explaining who does what to you and why, and what happens when things are not straightforward. In doing this I have used some of the words and phrases that you may see written on your medical chart or hear used by doctors or midwives, so that you will understand them when you meet them.

The book is threaded through with recognition of the father's importance for his partner and baby and suggestions as to how he can help most effectively during pregnancy, labor, and the time after the birth. A baby is bound to change a couple's way of life, their feelings about each other and the kind of partnership they have. The man, as well as the woman, often faces emotional challenges, and this is rarely acknowledged in our society. So another thing that I have done is to focus on the experience of childbirth for him.

Most new parents gain confidence and find it easiest to have "conversations" with their baby when there are no rules to be obeyed and no standards to live up to, when they can explore their baby, take it into bed with them, and stroke, hold, and cuddle it as much as they wish. In this book I hope to show how a couple can create the kind of setting and atmosphere for birth, whether at home or in the hospital, that nourishes relationships in the family.

Pregnancy and childbirth are normal life processes, not illnesses. You feel the incredible surge of life moving inside you, the ripening of your body heavy with fruit deep inside it, and then at last the flood of vitality as labor starts and your uterus contracts in wave after wave, bringing your baby into your arms. It is exciting, awe-inspiring and deeply satisfying. At the same time you grow up a bit, learn more about yourself and your partner, develop in understanding and awareness. I hope that this book will help you to savour the intense reality of the experience of childbearing and enjoy it to the full.

Notes to the reader

It is always difficult when writing about babies to know whether to use "he" or "she". By convention they are usually called "he", and this is often easiest in practice as it distinguishes the baby from the mother. Although I sometimes call the baby "it", I have mainly used a mixture of "he" and "she", since babies are people with their own budding personalities right from the start. I hope that the reader will not find this too awkward, and if there is a bias towards "she", note that my five babies were all girls, so it comes naturally to me.

Throughout the text references to research are marked with an asterisk (*); this indicates that the works in which the research findings have been published are given in Appendix 2, page 378, under the appropriate page number.

Author's acknowledgments

I should like to thank all those women who have helped me understand more about the experience of childbirth and how it was for them. From every couple I have taught I have learned something new or seen things in a different light. I have learned far more than I have ever taught.

My husband, Uwe, and our five daughters, Celia, Nell, Tess, Polly, and Jenny, are generous in their acceptance of my work, the time I give to couples having babies, and the inevitable phone calls punctuating family get-togethers and meals. Knowing that Uwe values what I am doing and gives me his full emotional support generates fresh strength in me to carry on when the going gets rough.

Murray Enkin, Associate Professor of Obstetrics at McMaster, read every single word of the text for the first edition of this book and looked at it from a medical point of view, but often commented too as a warm and caring human being. I have learned a great deal about human relations in the hospital from him.

Sybil del Strother proved a skilled and understanding editor in preparing the book for its first publication. Lesley Riley dealt expertly with the second edition. I know readers will enjoy the photographs by Camilla Jessel, who also studied very carefully my approach to birth so that she could express this in her work. My thanks also to Nancy Durrell McKenna, who took the photographs that appear on page 211, between pages 232 and 257 and on page 319 specially for this revised edition.

The new edition was typed by Judith Schroeder, my secretary, on whose enthusiasm and hard work I rely heavily.

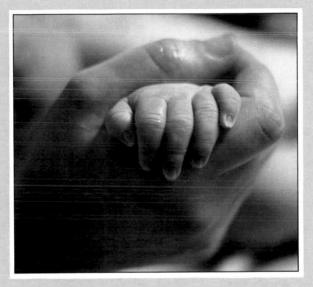

Giving birth

One birth . . . not especially difficult, nor especially easy . . . not a formula, not a blueprint . . . just some moments during a labor and the beginnings of a new life.

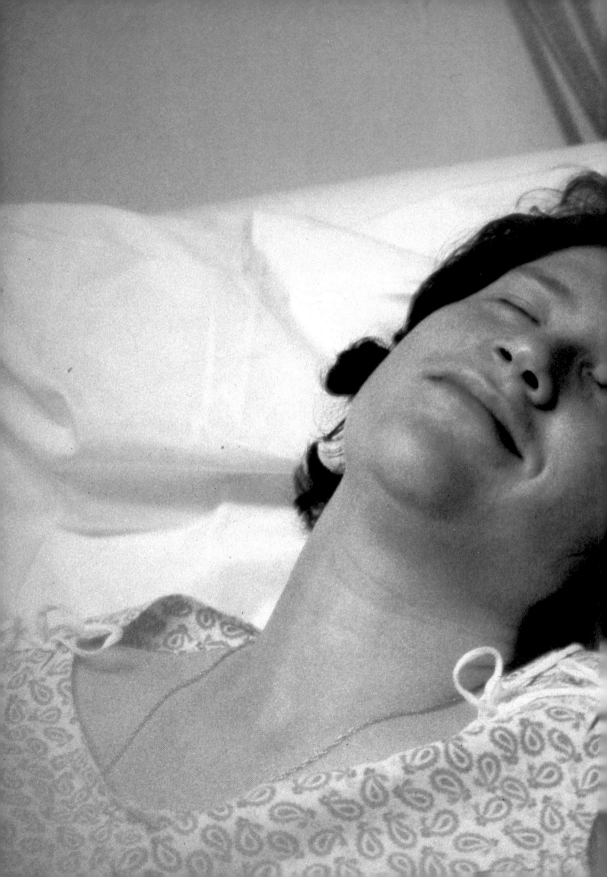

... *in the first stage the contractions of the uterus dilate the cervix* ...

... *in the second stage the head is being pressed down through the birth canal* ...

. . . then the baby's
head crowns and
slides out face down . . .

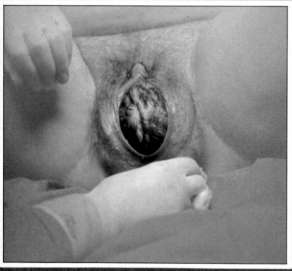

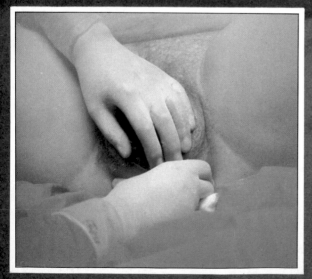

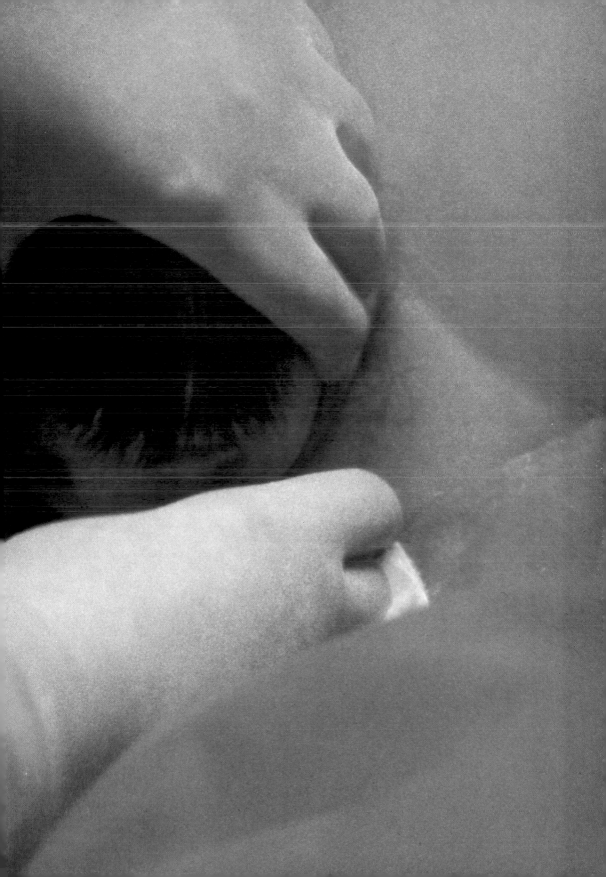

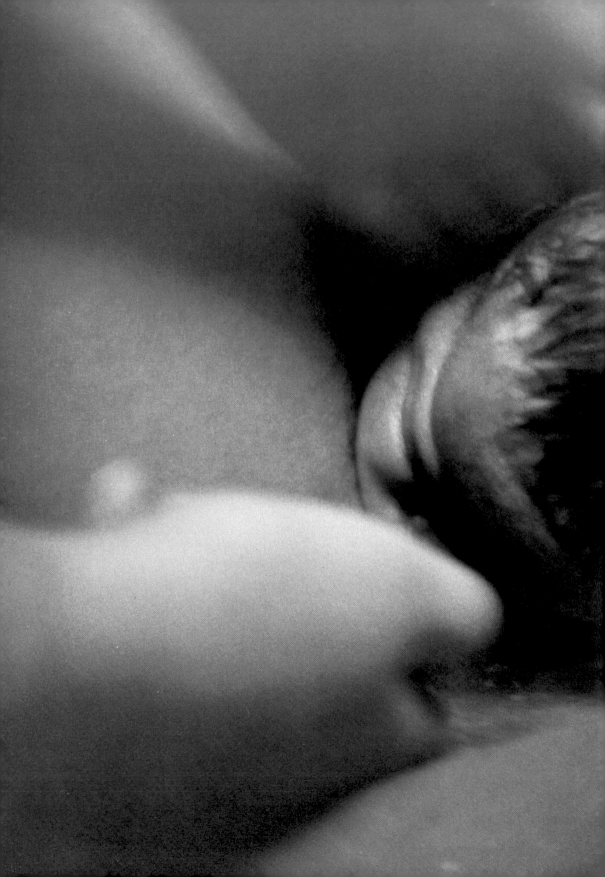

. . . the head rotates . . .

*. . . the mother reaches down
to touch her baby before
it is born . . .*

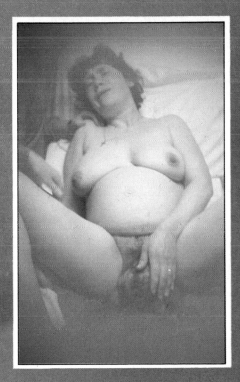

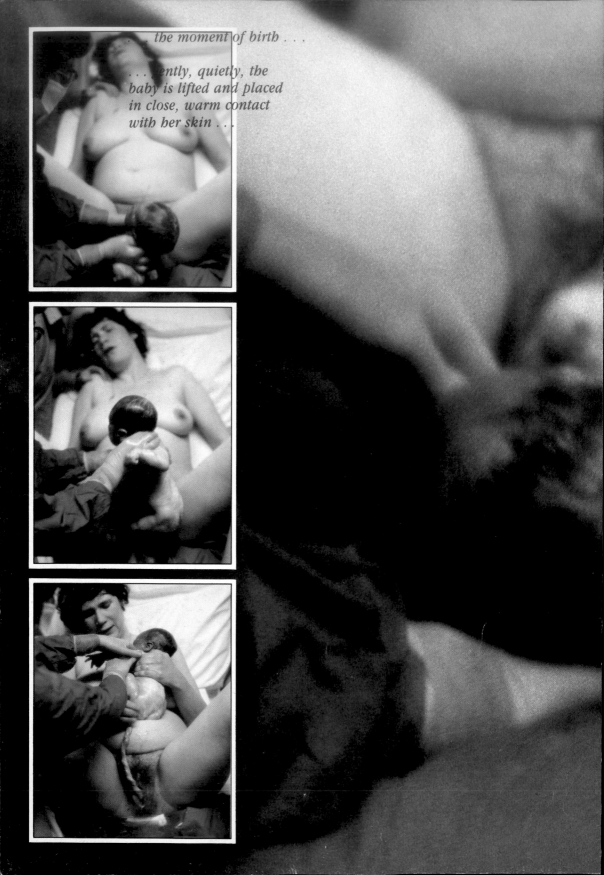

the moment of birth . . .

. . . gently, quietly, the baby is lifted and placed in close, warm contact with her skin . . .

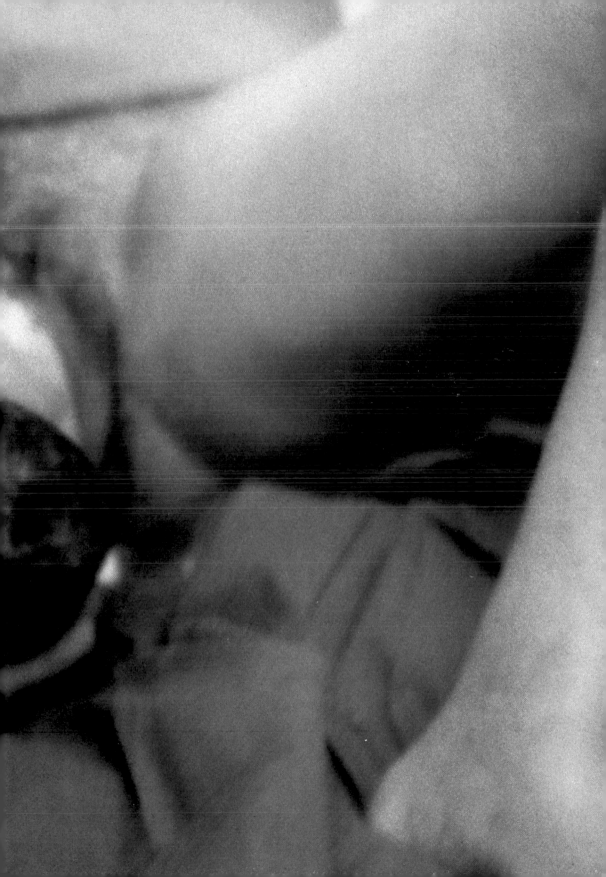

. . . she takes his hand to tell him that all
is well in this world of new sensations . . .

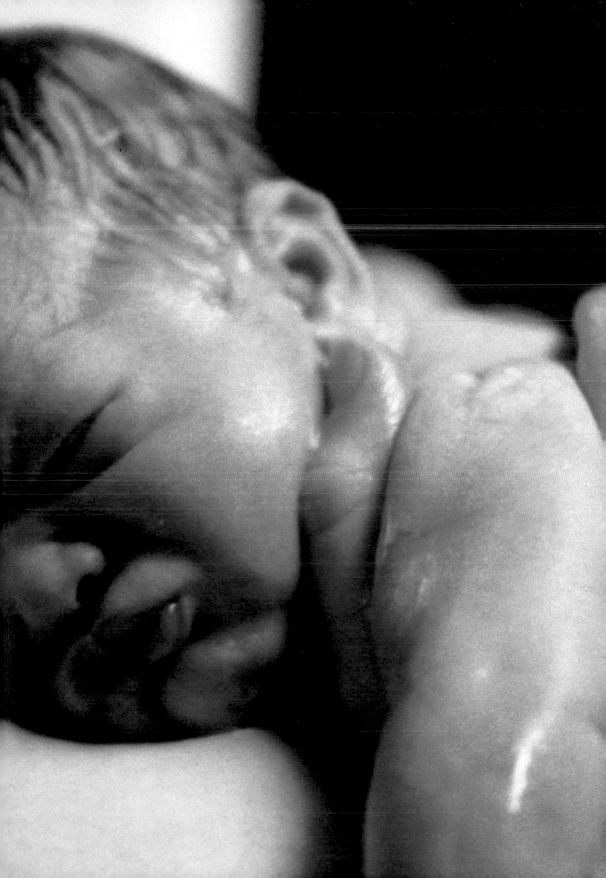

. . . now both parents are absorbed in the reality of their newborn, caressing him with their hands . . .

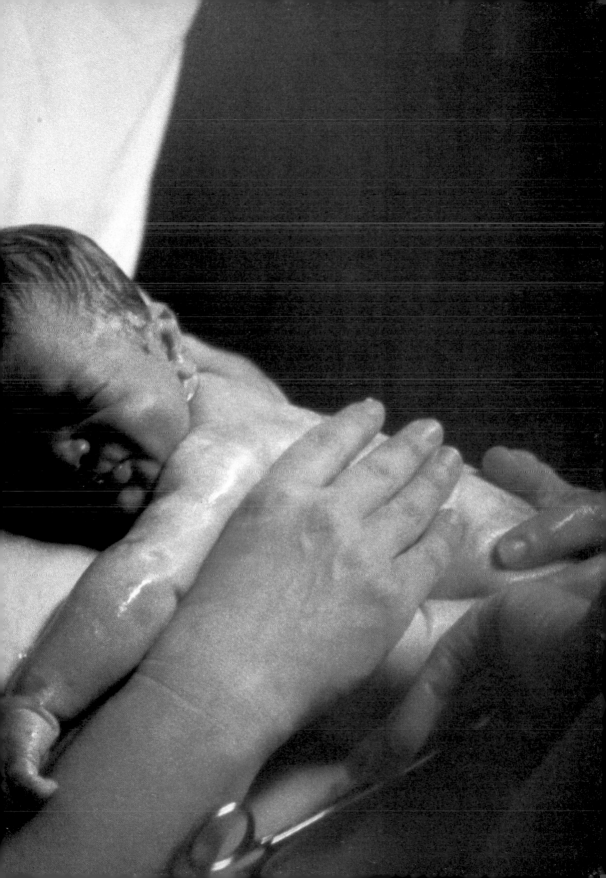

. . . when the baby is ready he will fasten on to his mother's breast . . .

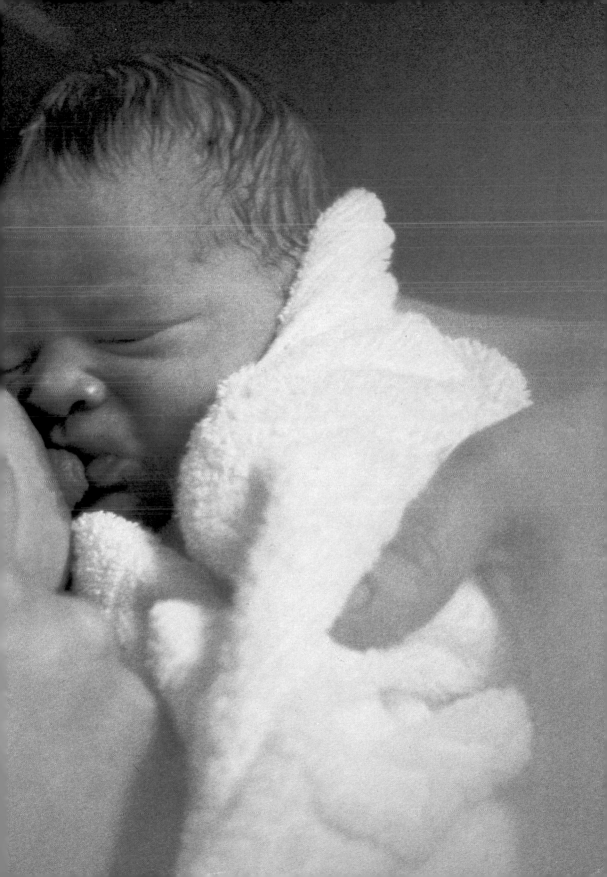

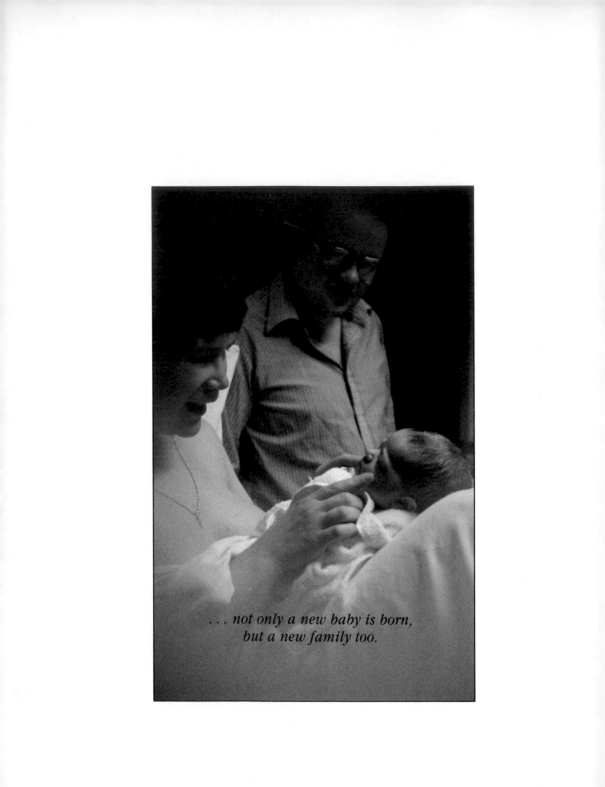

. . . not only a new baby is born,
but a new family too.

The early weeks

Finding out you are pregnant

Planning and preparation

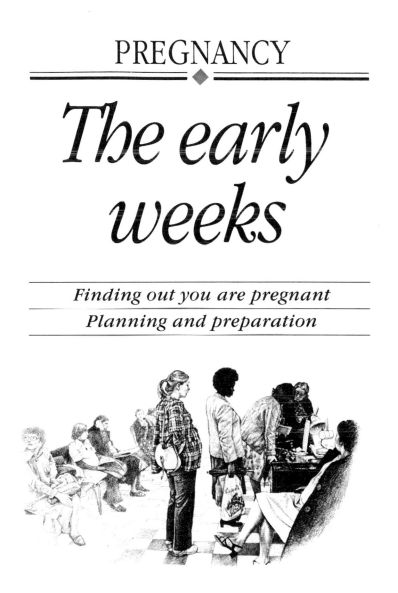

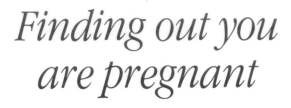

Finding out you are pregnant

You may have mixed feelings when you realize you are pregnant.

Some women are convinced that they are pregnant from the moment of conception; others have such irregular periods that a long gap in between does not alert them to the possibility of pregnancy. But for most women the first sign of pregnancy is a missed period.

Perhaps it is five days since the day when you expected it, but then you start wondering if your dates were wrong. Perhaps you usually make a note in your diary, but last time you forgot. You lie in bed, unable to sleep, trying to fix the dates firmly in your mind by finding some useful landmark, like your mother's visit or the end of a particular work assignment. Still another three days go by and the reality gradually dawns: you might be pregnant. You might not be, but it does seem quite possible that you are. When is it sensible to go to the doctor and how early can you know for certain?

When to diagnose

Until recently it was usual to visit the doctor after missing two periods. Nowadays there is a strong case for finding out if you are pregnant before two periods have been missed. It is during these few weeks, while the embryo is still no larger than a hazelnut, that the major organs of the body and the brain itself are being formed; the sooner you know that you are pregnant the sooner you can start caring for yourself and for the baby.

An early confirmation of pregnancy is also important if you take any medicines. You will want to avoid taking drugs which could harm the developing baby (see page 93). It is also useful to know early for social reasons—you may be planning to go abroad or move house at the time the baby is due.

If there is a possibility that you may want a termination (abortion) it is essential to diagnose pregnancy early: a termination at eight weeks is much safer and less upsetting than one after ten weeks.

How to diagnose

Pregnancy can now be diagnosed about two weeks after conception, on the day your period should have started if you have a regular monthly cycle, though you are likely to get more accurate results if you wait at least another four days—which can be difficult if you are feeling anxious or excited. When you are pregnant, the embryo releases the hormone human chorionic gonadotrophin (HCG) into your bloodstream. Minute traces of HCG will be present in your urine about six days after conception, but then the level builds up rapidly, doubling every two or three days until it reaches a peak about 60 days after conception—approximately 74 days after your period should have started—when it begins to decrease.

The presence of this hormone can be detected in your urine or blood. You can take a urine sample to your doctor or have him take a blood sample for analysis in the office or at a laboratory. You will need a prescription from your doctor if you go directly to a lab. Many women's centers will do a free urine test for you or you can use one of the do-it-yourself kits. Whichever method you choose, only test urine passed first thing in the morning, when you have not drunk anything during the night, since it is at this time that urine contains the highest concentration of pregnancy hormone. Store the urine in an absolutely clean jar or bottle, free from any traces of soap or detergent.

Do-it-yourself tests There are a number of different kits on the market, but they all involve mixing a drop or two of urine with the chemicals provided. If you are pregnant, the presence of HCG in your urine will, depending on the test, either prevent the mixture from coagulating (ring test), or change the color of the chemical in the test tube or on the dipstick (color test). Depending on the kit, you can use these tests when your period is between one and four days late, but you do need to be sure of when your period was due.

Occasionally a woman notices a little spotting (light bleeding) 10–12 days after fertilization. This is not really a period and the dating of pregnancy can start from your last actual period.

If the result is negative, but your period still has not come a few days later, do the test again. It is possible that you conceived later than you thought likely and that at the time of the first test there was not enough HCG in your urine to indicate that you were pregnant. If your periods are irregular or far apart, the chances of a false result are increased. After perhaps one conception in every ten, the fertilized egg does not manage to embed itself in the lining of the uterus. In this case, a pregnancy test will give you a positive result, but a second test a few days later will produce a negative result. Some packs recommend that you always wait three to five days and then re-test, and they contain two tests so that you can do this.

Going to the doctor If you take a specimen of urine with you, the doctor can have it tested and you will also be given an internal examination. He or she introduces two gloved fingers into your vagina as far as they will go, while pressing with the other hand into your abdomen where the top of the uterus lies. If it is more than six weeks since the first day of your last period the doctor can feel the already softened lower part of the uterus, which is also slightly enlarged. The neck of the uterus, or cervix, which protrudes into the vagina, is felt as firmer than the lower part of the uterus, and it is about the same consistency as the tip of your nose. The internal change is known as "Hegar's sign."

The examination may be uncomfortable but will not be painful. As the examining fingers are introduced, give a long, slow breath out through your mouth and continue breathing as slowly as you can.

Dating

Once the pregnancy is confirmed by your doctor it will be dated from the first day of your last menstrual period (LMP). If you cannot recollect this date with accuracy the doctor will probably ask you to make a guess at it. This means that from then on the length of your pregnancy is reckoned in terms of so many weeks, including the weeks from the beginning of your last period to the time when conception occurred. Since ovulation is most common midway between two periods, the usual medical way of dating pregnancy adds an extra two weeks to its length. The length of the average

Do-it-yourself pregnancy tests

There are two main kinds of test available—the ring test and the color test. Whichever you choose, be sure to follow the instructions carefully, and to test only the first urine of the day. The time when you can use these tests varies. Some kits recommend waiting until your period is at least four days late; others can be done as early as the day after your period was due, but for a reliable result you need to be certain when your period should have started.

The ring test can give a false result if you allow the tube to get hot, or shake it. Color tests are not affected by vibration, but may be affected by heat. All results are accurate only for a limited amount of time: some tests are stable for only five minutes; others remain unchanged for hours, even days.

If you get a positive result, or if you get a negative result but your period has not started after five more days, consult your doctor.

Color test

1 *Use the empty dropper tube to draw up some urine by squeezing.*

2 *Now put a few drops of urine into the test tube. Replace the stopper and shake the tube well. Wait 5 minutes.*

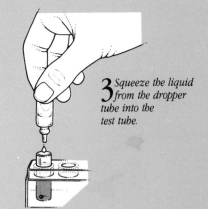

3 *Squeeze the liquid from the dropper tube into the test tube.*

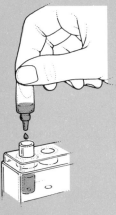

4 *Replace the test tube in its stand and leave it, away from heat, for between 5 and 15 minutes, depending on brand.*

Positive
If you are pregnant, the liquid will change color.

Negative
If you are not pregnant, the liquid will not change color.

pregnancy is some 266 days from the date of conception: your doctor will therefore arrive at your expected date of delivery (EDD) by adding 280 days, or 40 weeks, to the first day of your last period (the chart on page 31 is calculated according to this convention). You may find that pay your first visit to the doctor knowing that it is ten weeks since you conceived, but emerge three months pregnant!

But since not all women ovulate halfway between two periods, the medical convention of adding on an extra two weeks is an artificial one, and an inaccurate method of working out when a baby is due. It is wise to think of the EDD as an approximate date rather than the day when you expect to go into labor.

If you have just stopped taking the birth control pill your dates may be completely wrong. The period which immediately follows your last pill may not be followed by ovulation or you may have a

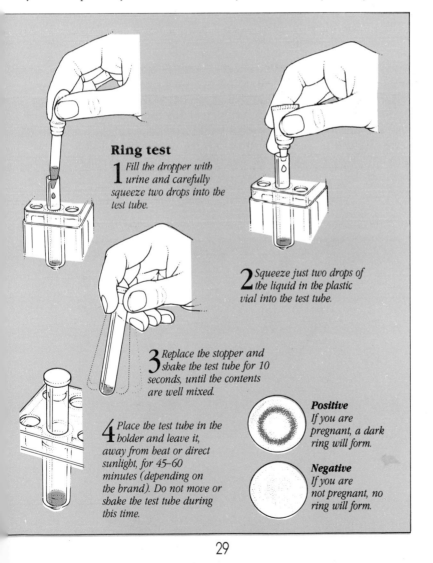

Ring test

1 Fill the dropper with urine and carefully squeeze two drops into the test tube.

2 Squeeze just two drops of the liquid in the plastic vial into the test tube.

3 Replace the stopper and shake the test tube for 10 seconds, until the contents are well mixed.

4 Place the test tube in the holder and leave it, away from heat or direct sunlight, for 45–60 minutes (depending on the brand). Do not move or shake the test tube during this time.

Positive
If you are pregnant, a dark ring will form.

Negative
If you are not pregnant, no ring will form.

slight spotting of blood which is not really a period. It may take several months to re-establish your natural cycle, and until then you cannot predict with any certainty when, or whether, you are going to ovulate. You might be a month or more out in your dates. This is obviously very important in estimating when the baby is due, especially since it could mean labor being induced unnecessarily (see page 297). It is advisable to wait for a clear three months after stopping the pill before trying to conceive; during this time you should use some other method of contraception.

Conceiving while using contraception

If you conceive with an IUD (intrauterine device or coil) still inside you, your chances of miscarrying increase. It is important to see your doctor quickly, as the IUD should be removed if possible and this can only be done early in pregnancy. Sometimes doctors advise termination. This is certainly not necessary if you want the baby: even if it is too late to remove the IUD, many women deliver the IUD with the placenta after an uneventful pregnancy and birth.

It is possible to conceive while taking the pill, if you miss one or more days when you should have been taking it, or if you have an upset stomach with vomiting so that you fail to absorb the hormones, or if you have been on antibiotics. If you do conceive but continue to take the pill for several months while pregnant, there is a slightly increased risk to the baby of congenital abnormalities. But the vast majority of women who have taken the pill while pregnant give birth to babies who are healthy and normal.

HAVING A VAGINAL EXAMINATION
You will be examined vaginally early on in your pregnancy. If you are more than 6 weeks pregnant the doctor can detect a slight softening and enlargement of the uterus. The developing embryo is well protected and cannot be dislodged by the examination.

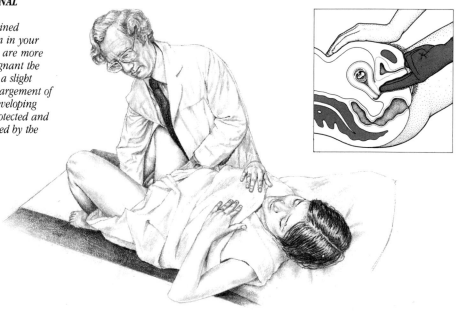

Sometimes a doctor prescribes pills containing the hormones estrogen and progestogen to discover whether or not a woman is pregnant, the idea being that you take them and if you are not pregnant your period starts. These hormone pills carry the same slight risk to the baby as the pill does: do not take them.

Pregnancy and AIDS

If you are anxious that you or your partner have been exposed to the virus that causes AIDS (acquired immune deficiency syndrome), you may decide before you get pregnant, or in very early pregnancy, that you should be screened for it. The test does not identify the virus (the human immunodeficiency virus, or HIV) itself, but reveals whether

When is your baby due?

Look down the columns of the chart at the figures set in bold type to find the first day of your last period. The date next to it is 280 days later, and is therefore your estimated date of delivery (EDD).

Jan	Oct	Feb	Nov	Mar	Dec	Apr	Jan	May	Feb	June	Mar	July	Apr	Aug	May	Sept	June	Oct	July	Nov	Aug	Dec	Sept
1	8	1	8	1	6	1	6	1	5	1	8	1	7	1	8	1	8	1	8	1	8	1	7
2	9	2	9	2	7	2	7	2	6	2	9	2	8	2	9	2	9	2	9	2	9	2	8
3	10	3	10	3	8	3	8	3	7	3	10	3	9	3	10	3	10	3	10	3	10	3	9
4	11	4	11	4	9	4	9	4	8	4	11	4	10	4	11	4	11	4	11	4	11	4	10
5	12	5	12	5	10	5	10	5	9	5	12	5	11	5	12	5	12	5	12	5	12	5	11
6	13	6	13	6	11	6	11	6	10	6	13	6	12	6	13	6	13	6	13	6	13	6	12
7	14	7	14	7	12	7	12	7	11	7	14	7	13	7	14	7	14	7	14	7	14	7	13
8	15	8	15	8	13	8	13	8	12	8	15	8	14	8	15	8	15	8	15	8	15	8	14
9	16	9	16	9	14	9	14	9	13	9	16	9	15	9	16	9	16	9	16	9	16	9	15
10	17	10	17	10	15	10	15	10	14	10	17	10	16	10	17	10	17	10	17	10	17	10	16
11	18	11	18	11	16	11	16	11	15	11	18	11	17	11	18	11	18	11	18	11	18	11	17
12	19	12	19	12	17	12	17	12	16	12	19	12	18	12	19	12	19	12	19	12	19	12	18
13	20	13	20	13	18	13	18	13	17	13	20	13	19	13	20	13	20	13	20	13	20	13	19
14	21	14	21	14	19	14	19	14	18	14	21	14	20	14	21	14	21	14	21	14	21	14	20
15	22	15	22	15	20	15	20	15	19	15	22	15	21	15	22	15	22	15	22	15	22	15	21
16	23	16	23	16	21	16	21	16	20	16	23	16	22	16	23	16	23	16	23	16	23	16	22
17	24	17	24	17	22	17	22	17	21	17	24	17	23	17	24	17	24	17	24	17	24	17	23
18	25	18	25	18	23	18	23	18	22	18	25	18	24	18	25	18	25	18	25	18	25	18	24
19	26	19	26	19	24	19	24	19	23	19	26	19	25	19	26	19	26	19	26	19	26	19	25
20	27	20	27	20	25	20	25	20	24	20	27	20	26	20	27	20	27	20	27	20	27	20	26
21	28	21	28	21	26	21	26	21	25	21	28	21	27	21	28	21	28	21	28	21	28	21	27
22	29	22	29	22	27	22	27	22	26	22	29	22	28	22	29	22	29	22	29	22	29	22	28
23	30	23	30	23	28	23	28	23	27	23	30	23	29	23	30	23	30	23	30	23	30	23	29
24	31	24	1	24	29	24	29	24	28	24	31	24	30	24	31	24	1	24	31	24	31	24	30
25	1	25	2	25	30	25	30	25	1	25	1	25	1	25	1	25	2	25	1	25	1	25	1
26	2	26	3	26	31	26	31	26	2	26	2	26	2	26	2	26	3	26	2	26	2	26	2
27	3	27	4	27	1	27	1	27	3	27	3	27	3	27	3	27	4	27	3	27	3	27	3
28	4	28	5	28	2	28	2	28	4	28	4	28	4	28	4	28	5	28	4	28	4	28	4
29	5			29	3	29	3	29	5	29	5	29	5	29	5	29	6	29	5	29	5	29	5
30	6			30	4	30	4	30	6	30	6	30	6	30	6	30	7	30	6	30	6	30	6
31	7			31	5			31	7			31	7	31	7			31	7			31	7
Jan	Nov	Feb	Dec	Mar	Jan	Apr	Feb	May	Mar	June	Apr	July	May	Aug	June	Sept	July	Oct	Aug	Nov	Sept	Dec	Oct

antibodies to it are in the bloodstream. If someone has been infected, antibodies will be present. Even though they themselves may show no symptoms of infection, they can transmit the virus to someone else. A pregnant woman can infect her unborn baby.

Before being tested you will have thought through the implications—social, emotional, and physical—of getting a positive result. As one woman carrying the virus said: "The only difference between now and before is this piece of knowledge. And it's such depressing, unhappy knowledge, I find it quite paralyzing."* According to current research, anyone who is antibody-positive has a 10 to 30 per cent chance of developing AIDS within four years. Pregnancy affects the immune system, so it may trigger AIDS in a woman who is antibody-positive but who has had no previous symptoms. It is possible that she may develop the disease during pregnancy or soon after the baby is born.

Babies born to HIV-positive mothers always have antibodies. Some types of antibody, however, can enter the baby's blood without the child becoming infected with the virus, and if an HIV-positive woman is healthy during pregnancy, there is a good chance that her baby will lose its inherited antibodies within 6 to 18 months. It may take a year, with tests every few months, to know for sure whether a baby is carrying the virus. Only about 22 per cent of antibody-positive newborn babies develop AIDS. If a woman has already given birth to an infected baby, there is a 66 per cent chance that her next baby will be infected too. If she herself has AIDS the risk is still greater. A baby infected in the uterus may have birth defects or a characteristic facial appearance with a very small head, box-shaped forehead, flat nose, blue eyeballs, widely spaced eyes, and full lips.

Antibody tests may show up negative for three months following infection. It makes sense to have a second test 12 weeks after the first if you or your partner are at high risk of contracting the virus and if you are in very early pregnancy and are sure that you would want a termination if you were antibody-positive. No test is 100 per cent free from error. The "Western blot"—which is the most widely used test in North America and Britain—is 96 per cent accurate.

Early signs of pregnancy

Breast changes Even before your pregnancy is confirmed there may be early indications other than a missed period. Breast changes, in preparation for milk production, occur in the first weeks. The brownish circles round the nipples (the areolae) become darker and the little bumps on them (Montgomery's tubercles) more prominent. If you are pink-skinned you may notice that the lacy network of blood vessels in your breasts has become much more obvious. Blue veins run over the breasts like rivers on a map. Your breasts also feel tender and heavy. Women with small breasts may note an obvious increase in size very early on, and are often delighted. If you have large breasts already you may not notice any size change at this stage.

You may notice changes in your breasts early in pregnancy, including an increase in size, a darkening of the nipples and the areolae, and extra prominence of the little bumps on the areolae known as Montgomery's tubercles.

Tiredness Enormous metabolic changes take place in pregnancy and your whole body has to adjust to the process of growing a baby. It is not surprising that you may feel tired and that you cannot carry on just as before. Many women complain of extreme tiredness in the first eight or ten weeks. But as your body adjusts to the pregnancy the fatigue vanishes and the middle months are often easy. If you are feeling tired it is only sensible to take the message from your body and go to bed early, have a rest at midday if you can, or have an early evening rest when you get in from work.

If it is your second (or third) pregnancy, you may find that you are constantly tired. Women who thoroughly enjoyed their first pregnancy say that the second one is much harder to cope with because they are exhausted by the non-stop pace of their first child's daily life. The only solution is to organize your life as well as you can; try to have at least a short time every day when you are completely free from domestic responsibilities. Even half an hour every evening when your partner attends to the child and the dishes can be relaxing if you are able to enjoy it to the full. (See page 158 for more about second and later pregnancies.)

Nausea Another common sign of pregnancy is nausea. These waves of sickness often happen early in the morning, when your blood sugar level is low, but they may also occur in the early evening, or even—more rarely—at other times of the day. Some women just feel very sick, others actually vomit. Tiredness contributes to nausea, but so does an empty stomach: small frequent snacks of bland foods like crackers or a banana may relieve the feeling. If you suffer from morning sickness, a cup of tea and a few crackers or dry toast immediately on waking may prevent the nausea, or the crackers alone may be better. A late night snack may help, too. As a general rule cut out all greasy fried foods, tobacco, and alcohol. Some women become really ill with vomiting (see page 123), although most stop feeling sick during the fourth month.

There is some evidence that women who experience pregnancy nausea are less likely than others to have miscarriages. This can be a cheering thought. But nausea does not exist in all cultures; many societies have other illnesses and disabilities or special dreams which they connect with pregnancy. Margaret Mead points out that in some societies of New Guinea boils are considered to be a typical symptom of pregnancy. Some Jamaicans do not acknowledge pregnancy until they have had a special fertility dream of ripe fruit bursting with seed. Dreams of this kind are characteristic of early pregnancy. It is as if all women need definite signs with which to link pregnancy so that they can say, "I feel this, therefore I must be expecting a baby."

You may suffer from nausea for the first time in your second or third pregnancy. This is almost certainly as a result of tiredness, and you may not relieve the nausea within three months unless you can somehow arrange to have more rest.

The first 3 months were wretched because I had continual nausea. I worried about what this might be doing to our baby—but here she is, chubby and beautiful. It doesn't seem to have affected her at all.

Emotional reactions to pregnancy

However much you want a baby, finding out that you really are pregnant can produce a flood of conflicting emotions: triumph ("We've done it!"), a sense of being trapped ("There's no going back—now what?"), fear ("Mother had an awful time having me—shall I be able to stand the pain?"), apprehension ("Will we still love each other in the same way?") and doubt ("Will he still want me once my waist starts getting thicker?"). It is surprising how many women respond to their first pregnancy with shock and feel that it has happened "too soon", even though they very much want a baby and have considered the matter carefully before stopping contraception. Confronted with the reality and the physical changes of pregnancy, they want to say: "Stop! I haven't prepared myself for this. Let's go back and start again."

If you discover that you are pregnant when you did not plan to be, you may also feel unfairly trapped. Yet, perversely, many women (for whom pregnancy is not a disaster) are aware of an odd pleasure that their fertility has triumphed over their conscious wish. Your partner may suspect that you wanted a baby all along and have not been "playing fair". Starting a baby under such circumstances can lead to conflict between you, because he may feel that you have not been open with him. Try not to go off and discuss the matter with other people as if your man were the enemy. Talk about it together: you need to understand each other.

We're over the moon! I never believed it could happen to me. I feel so pleased with myself. I know it's ridiculous, but it's as if I was the first human being ever to have a baby!

Feelings about motherhood You may have a crisis of self-confidence, feeling that you will be no good as a mother because you have no maternal instincts. But mothering is a learned activity and very little of it purely instinctive. Moreover for the first-time mother in our society, who may never have handled a newborn baby before, most of the learning goes on after the baby is born. The teacher is the baby herself. Even though you may not start off as an expert, your baby soon turns you into one.

Feelings about being on show You may feel suddenly that your most intimate relationship with the man you love is publicly displayed, not just because you are pregnant and everybody knows, but because of the physical examinations and exposure at the prenatal clinic, and the advice that people keep giving you. This sense of becoming public property may be intensified by the obvious pleasure of parents who have long been wanting you to get pregnant.

Yet your body holds life. The wonder of that cannot really be understood by anyone else. You stand naked in front of the mirror and look for changes. You rest your hand on your tummy and wonder if you can feel the tiny seed of a baby beginning to grow inside you. You think back to when you made love, wonder which time it was and if, perhaps, you really knew then that you had conceived.

Feelings about your body If you feel on bad terms with your body as it starts out on the work of early pregnancy, arrange to attend some pregnancy exercise or dance classes if these are available in your area. A list of organizations which can help you is on page 383. If these classes are not specially for pregnant women, let your teacher know that you are pregnant. Get out in the fresh air and walk. Buy a maternity swimsuit and swim regularly. Start doing the movements suggested on pages 108–109 a few times each day to pep up your circulation and increase vitality. In some countries massage is an anticipated and very pleasant part of being pregnant, so you could go to a masseuse or your partner could learn how to massage you (see page 172). This can be particularly useful if you are tense and find it difficult to release your muscles at will.

As your pregnancy progresses, you may become fascinated by your body's changing shape.

Your partner's feelings You are not the only person who has to adjust emotionally in pregnancy. Your partner needs to as well. He does not have to cope with physical changes, but the emotional impact of a first pregnancy is no less real, and the passage into fatherhood constitutes a major transition in his life. For a man this process is often delayed until several things have happened: the pregnancy has been officially confirmed; your figure has obviously changed; the baby has moved and he has felt it fluttering.

Emotions of joy, pride, and wonder may war with others which are disturbing. There may be financial problems which can cause a man to feel a sense of deep and burdensome responsibility for the woman bearing his child and for the new life that is coming. A man, too, may feel trapped by pregnancy. Perhaps his relationship with the woman was intended to remain free and untrammeled by babies (especially if the couple have not discussed pregnancy and planned for it together). His job may now assume importance not only in its own right, but because he feels an urgent need to be successful before the baby comes, as if it threatens his own powers of achievement. A man, too, may be frightened of birth and even of his partner's pregnant body, which can seem dangerous and not to be touched in case the baby is dislodged. He may feel, quite wrongly, that his own sexual desires are a terrible threat to the baby. For some men the whole pregnancy is a time of stress.

Discussing your emotions together

It does not help to bottle up these emotions. Talk about them together. If you pretend they are not there, they become destructive. What you are feeling is normal and thousands of other couples experience it too. It may be possible to work out together a sensible strategy so that some parts of your lives are left free from responsibility: you could avoid relatives until you feel better able to cope with them. You may be able to arrange prenatal appointments together, so that your partner can see what happens there, can meet the doctor or midwife and be present during the physical examination. Reading

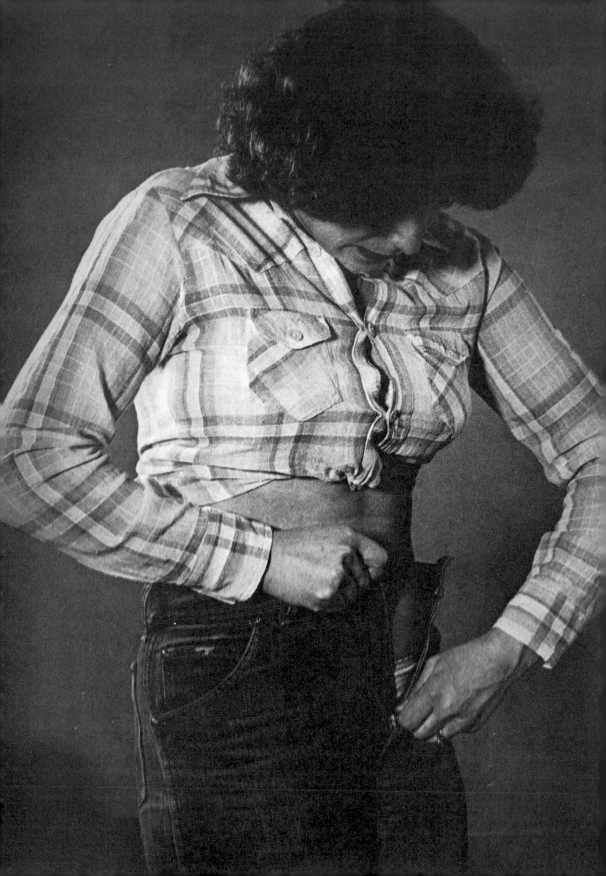

together about pregnancy and birth helps to replace ignorance with knowledge about the role a man can actively play in childbirth.

Lying together in bed, cuddling, and exploring each other's bodies is a way of communicating through loving touch and tenderness. It is a way of nourishing your partnership together, ready for the new person who is entering it. Since words often disguise your real feelings and complicate matters, find opportunities to meet each other through touch.

Pregnancy is not merely a waiting time. It is a time for working out together what you value in your relationship and what kind of world you both want to create for your child. This is not a question of making a nursery and buying things ready for the baby, but of helping each other to change from people who are responsible just for themselves into a mother and a father, with the new responsibility that parenthood brings. A man and a woman need to grow into parents. Then not only a baby, but a new family is born.

The woman alone

Pregnancy and childbirth are not easy when you do not have a partner to give you love and care. It is even more difficult once the baby is born to take complete responsibility for a new life. Yet many women have done this successfully and have reared happy, healthy children.

Talking about the single mother and the challenges she faces is in a way misleading, because women on their own bearing babies do not fall into one category any more than women with partners do. The reasons single women embark on pregnancy, and decide to go on with it, vary widely. Some women continue with a pregnancy only because they are unwilling or unable to face up to it, and drift on hoping that it may go away. Others are bearing a much-wanted child "before it is too late." Others again loved the father of the child and hoped that the relationship would continue, but then found themselves rejected and bearing a child alone. Then there are women whose men die while they are pregnant, leaving them to face the future alone.

Whatever your reasons for having a child on your own, financial problems may loom large. Trying to combine a job with rearing a child, while knowing that there is no one else to take over in time of need, can be difficult. It is important to anticipate and share the problems, and a good idea to seek counseling from people who understand them and who may be able to put you in touch with other sources of help. Contact the organizations listed on page 383 before you have your baby and see what they have to offer. These organizations are also designed to help you cope with all the practical difficulties that can crop up, such as housing, finding day care for the baby and sorting out to which benefits you are entitled.

Register for childbirth education classes (see page 164) as early as the first trimester. Many women delay until the last minute and then find that the classes are full. The International Childbirth Education

I've always had irregular periods so I didn't notice. The doctor said "Do you realize you're pregnant?" I was stunned! Alan's married you know. It was too late for an abortion.

OPPOSITE
Finding that your clothes don't fit any more may be the first time that you really believe you are pregnant.

Association and the American Society for Psychoprophylaxis in Obstetrics (addresses on page 383) can tell you about the different kinds of childbirth classes, postnatal support, and breastfeeding counseling that are available in your area.

Sometimes a man who is not your permanent partner is still willing to accept some of the responsibilities of fatherhood. It is quite common in a prenatal class to have couples who do not plan to marry or even stay together. Be frank with your childbirth educator so that she has a chance to get to know you. It may be possible for you to arrange to see her privately for a session.

Emotional support in labor

Think ahead to the birth and decide whether you would like to have a companion with you. Childbirth can feel very solitary if you do not have someone with you to encourage you and provide continuous emotional support. This person could be a good woman friend, a childbirth educator, your sister or mother, or a man friend who understands what birth is about and can give the right kind of help. Most hospitals nowadays allow a companion in labor, although they often restrict you to one person, and sometimes they state that it must be the father of the baby. Discuss the matter with your doctor and with your childbirth educator, and if necessary state your request in writing to the Chair of the Obstetrical Department or in person to the Director of Nursing.

If there is no one who can be with you in labor, discuss the subject in advance with your obstetrician. Say that you would particularly value someone as a companion to be with you throughout labor, and that you do not know anyone who can come with you; ask whether there is anyone in the hospital—preferably someone you could meet beforehand—who could be with you. The doctor may say that you will have the nurses and will not be left alone. But a labor companion is different and is simply there as a friend, to give you emotional support and to remind you of your relaxation and breathing. If you are in a teaching hospital there will almost certainly be a student nurse who can do this. If it is a midwifery training school there is usually a student midwife who can fill the same role.

But suppose that you have to be without a companion in labor. Make the nurse your friend and ask her for help. Unfortunately there is not much continuity of care in hospitals, and you may have to get to know two or three nurses, one after another—a lot to ask of someone in labor. On the other hand, sometimes a midwife will stay on duty so that she can be with you until after the delivery.

Managing alone

If your man has been unwilling to accept responsibility or perhaps even acknowledge your pregnancy, you probably feel angry and resentful. One woman, who had been told she could never have a baby but who found herself pregnant, said, "I hadn't realized just

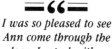

I was so pleased to see Ann come through the door. I coped with a difficult labor only because of her, and think without her I might have gone under.

how much his marriage was a going concern. Just when I most needed him I had to come to terms with the fact that he didn't want to break up his marriage and was devoted to his kids. In fact, my pregnancy was terribly embarrassing for him! I suddenly felt dreadfully on my own. I didn't hear from him through a large part of the pregnancy because it was the summer holidays and he went abroad with his family."

Another woman's husband left her when she was four months pregnant because he said he could not stand the idea of a third child. He had left her several times before for short periods and the baby was conceived during a reconciliation. Her great fear was that she would find him on the doorstep again, since she had been through so much emotional turmoil that she did not feel she could cope mentally with any more scenes and upheavals. This led to a strained and difficult pregnancy, followed by a prolonged labor and forceps delivery because of incoordinate uterine action.

A university lecturer who had decided in advance that she wanted a baby but not a man said that her colleagues accepted this but that she found it hard to tell her family: "Mother thought I was mad and said how could she ever let her friends know. I thought about them all at their coffee mornings and thought, 'Oh my God, I don't suppose she can'. I thought it would be hardest explaining to my 80-year-old grandmother but she was the one who understood best." This woman could not go home when her pregnancy became obvious because of the effect on her parents' neighbors and friends, although her parents did adjust to the idea after the baby was born and became proud grandparents.

Some women are rejected by parents, although one girl said: "In a way I rejected *them* and their values, by going ahead and having the baby." Even so, however "free" of your parents you feel and however you delight in being independent of them, cutting roots like this can be extremely painful. You may feel guilty, even if you do not accept the social conventions which thrust the feelings of guilt upon you. You may worry about imposing your views on your child, who will learn that in friends' houses there is a father as well as a mother.

Yet single mothers all stress that you do need help and must have the grace to accept it, for your child's sake as well as yours. There are the all-important questions of where you are going to live, what you are going to live on, whether you should and can go back to work, and if so when. You must also consider how you are going to retain any sort of mobility with a baby, how you will deal with the relationship between sex, motherhood, the other things you want to do and the needs you want to fulfil, and how you are going to feel when things are difficult or impossible because of the baby. Many of the difficulties confronted by single women are the same as those faced by those with partners, but intensified because the women are alone and unsupported. As one woman said, in order to go through with having a baby on your own, "you need to *really want* that child!"

Being a single parent often brings greater challenges—and rewards.

Planning & preparation

Throughout history most babies were born at home. Maternity hospitals were first started for homeless women and were really extensions of the poor-houses. Many of the babies born in these hospitals were then put in foundling institutions. These first maternity hospitals were convenient centers for medical students to learn and practice obstetrics, but infection was rampant, as doctors conveyed bacteria on their hands from one patient to another, and many babies and mothers died. They were the most dangerous places in which women could possibly give birth.

Today, modern hospitals are no longer dangerous places to have a baby. Yet, despite extremely rapid advances, and the tendency for most doctors to recommend a hospital birth, many women still feel that a home birth would be the most appropriate for them.

Where would you like to have your baby?

Home! Definitely home! I want to do it my way.

Even before you become pregnant, it is worth thinking about whether you would like to have your baby at home or in a hospital and discussing it with your doctor. You may have decided, for example, that you would prefer to have your baby at home, yet discover that your doctor is unwilling or unable to attend you. If there are no specific medical reasons for this, you might want to change your doctor before you start a pregnancy. Whether you want to have a home, hospital, or birth center birth, it is important to inform your doctor as early in your pregnancy as possible, as it is often difficult to change your mind once wheels have been set in motion. It is a good idea to make a list of things that are really important to you about the birth and the time immediately after and to decide which environment best meets your requirements, home, hospital, or birth center.

HOSPITAL BIRTH

OPPOSITE
Once you know you are pregnant, find out all you can about childbirth so that you know what to ask for and who can help.

Most women who decide to have their babies in the hospital do so primarily because they are convinced it is the safest place. They want to be sure that all the skills and equipment of modern obstetrics are at hand for their babies' sake. For some women, especially those having their first child, giving birth is a frightening experience, a step in the dark, and they feel more secure in the knowledge that they are in the hands of people who have been specially trained to cope with any possible emergency. Often a woman who fears that her labor will be painful opts for a hospital delivery, knowing that certain pain-killers are available only in a hospital and not wanting to take the chance of finding herself at home without necessary relief from pain when it is too late to do anything about it.

Sometimes a woman may know and trust a particular obstetrician and want to be cared for by this person, while another wants to go to a hospital because she feels she would benefit from a period of release from the pressures of home and family. Occasionally a woman's partner wants her to go to a hospital because he is very worried about birth at home. He may just be frightened of being involved, but more often he is afraid he might have to deliver the baby himself.

Medical reasons for hospital birth

As well as those women who would prefer the security of a hospital birth, there are those for whom it is advisable to give birth in a hospital whatever their personal preferences. It is wise to consider hospital care if you have diabetes, a heart or kidney condition, or if you smoke cigarettes regularly (see page 94). Your doctor will send you to a hospital if you get severe pre-eclampsia (see page 126) or if you go into labor three weeks or more before the baby is due; you will probably be advised against home delivery if your baby is breech, since it may need help with breathing immediately after birth (see page 334). There are really no absolutes, but there are certain things which make childbirth a little more risky.

If you are to be a first-time mother over 35 for instance, labor *may* be longer than if you were younger and many doctors would advise you to be in a hospital so that you can have labor speeded up or help with the delivery. Some doctors believe that all first-time mothers (primigravida) should give birth in a hospital because, they say, a labor is only normal in retrospect and there is always a small chance that even after a perfectly normal pregnancy you may have complications which will entail you being moved to the hospital at the last minute for specialist care.

If you have had a hemorrhage with a previous labor, either before or after the delivery, it is wise to choose a hospital birth because you may need a quick blood transfusion if it happens again. The same goes for a retained placenta or a delayed third stage in a previous labor. If you are very short, under 5 ft 2 in (1·55 m), your pelvis may be a tight fit for the baby to get through, though many short women do give birth easily. Any other indications of disproportion, because of the way the baby is lying, for example, should also make you plan for a hospital birth.

Three or more miscarriages are another reason for having the baby in a hospital, because previous problems of this kind *may* mean that labor will present problems (though often everything is straightforward). Obviously, if you have lost a baby because of a difficult birth, you are unlikely to take the small but real additional risk of a home birth and will want to know that, if the baby should need it, intensive care is available at the hospital where you are giving birth. Doctors also advise mothers of twins to give birth in a hospital, partly because they may come early and be of low birthweight and partly because the second twin can get stuck (see pages 80–85).

Choices in hospital care

There are two main kinds of hospital obstetrical care: private and clinic. In addition, many hospitals are beginning to offer a certified nurse midwife program. If you have decided that a hospital birth is right for you, you will need to think about the alternatives available to you within the hospital system.

The private obstetrician Most women choose a private obstetrician who is affiliated with a hospital near their home. This may be convenient, but it is even more important to find an obstetrician whom you like and who understands the kind of birth for which you hope and is prepared to help you have it. Finding a private obstetrician with whom you have a good relationship can be difficult. Most obstetricians in the United States are men and may not see your point of view about birth. Go to the first visit with a list of questions such as the following so that you can make your decision on a practical basis.

What is your policy on induction?

When do you recommend induction?

What percentage of your patients had a natural unmedicated birth last year?

Do you usually order medications, intravenous drips (IV), enemas, monitors, or do you judge each situation individually?

What position do most of the women you deliver adopt for the second stage?

Are they encouraged to try different positions?

Do these include kneeling, being on all fours, and squatting?

Do you usually perform an episiotomy?

Do you usually hand the naked baby straight to the mother?

Can the mother lift the baby out herself if she wishes?

Are you willing to wait until the cord has stopped pulsating before clamping it?

How much time do the mother and baby normally have skin contact following delivery?

Can the baby be put to the breast on the delivery table?

Are you willing to dim the lights when the baby is born?

Do you routinely suction the baby at delivery?

If the baby is breathing well would you be willing to wait and see whether this is needed?

If the baby requires special care can both parents visit the intensive care unit and touch and hold their baby if it is well enough?

Can the mother breastfeed the baby in the intensive care unit if it is well enough?

What percentage of your patients breastfed last year?

Do you encourage family centered care?

If yes: How do you see this working in practical terms?

The hospital's marvelous! They explain everything; I nearly always see the same obstetrician and this morning after examining me he said "Wonderful growth!" and patted my tum. I'm really looking forward to having it there.

Try to get to know as many of the midwives as possible since you do not know who will be available when you go into labor.

Obviously, the higher the proportion of women in this doctor's care who have had the type of birth experience you hope for, the greater the probability that the doctor will help you realize your hopes. Remember that the private obstetrician can write orders for anything you agree together, whether or not it is considered to be routine practice in that particular hospital.

The obstetrical clinic Most obstetrical clinics are located within large metropolitan teaching hospitals. As the name suggests, in exchange for the low cost or free care, the patient serves as "teaching material" for the medical students and resident physicians. Thus there is a higher risk of having unnecessary procedures performed on your body. Teaching hospitals tend to have a great deal of technologically advanced machinery and may be justified for the mother and baby "at risk", when there is a higher than average chance of something going wrong. These hospitals also have neo-natal intensive care units where sophisticated technology and a specially skilled staff will be available to treat the high risk baby immediately after birth.

Certified nurse midwife care This type of maternity care is not yet widely available throughout the United States. For information on the availability in your area, contact the American College of Nurse Midwives (see page 383).

The typical hospital nurse midwife practices in a group, backed by one or more obstetricians. The certified nurse midwife has been specifically trained to deal with normal pregnancy, normal birth, and normal post partum. She cares for the well woman at all stages but if any abnormality develops must refer the patient to an obstetrician. Even if this happens, the nurse midwife usually stays with the patient, offering her emotional support.

No matter what type of hospital care you choose, be sure to tour the hospital before you make a definite decision. If this is not the usual practice in the hospital, contact the Head Nurse of Obstetrics and ask for the name of the childbirth educator. Another source of information about the hospital, obstetricians, midwives, clinics and such is your local childbirth education association (see page 383 for a list of organizations to contact). If there is no childbirth education association near you, contact your local women's organization; they should be able to tell you what you need to know.

I had a traumatic experience in the hospital last time, so we've decided to have it at home.

HOME BIRTH

At the same time that hospital birth becomes more and more the standard way to have a baby there is a small but steady increase in the number of women who decide to have their babies at home.

Most women who have a baby at home after a previous hospital birth say that they enjoyed it much more and feel that it must have been pleasanter for the baby. Some opt for home births because they want to give birth in a familiar, comfortable, nonmedical environment, surrounded by their own things, in the home they have created with their partner. They want to be able to make their own decisions, to give birth in their own way and behave spontaneously, without being forced into the role of patient and having to conform to hospital rules and regulations. They also want to avoid having to change rooms and move from a bed to a delivery room, and to be able to adopt any position they find comfortable. At home you are in charge and the doctor and midwife are familiar and welcome guests in your home. For some, this continuous relationship and co-operation with just a few helpers is important.

Some women say that since birth is an act of love, personal and intimate, it should take place in one's own environment, without unnecessary observers, among friends in a loving atmosphere. They want to know that the father of the baby or a close friend can be present throughout, can take an active part, and can give emotional support through the labor. Some would like the father to "catch" the baby himself. Most hospitals allow fathers to be present for labor and delivery nowadays, but they are still sent out for a wide range of minor procedures and examinations, often just when the laboring woman feels she needs her partner most. Often a woman would like to ensure that her baby has a "gentle birth" and is welcomed into the world tenderly, without the machinery and bright lights that are almost inevitable in hospitals.

Of course, I'll go to the hospital if it looks as if the baby is at risk, and I'm quite prepared to move there in strong labor if need be, because then I'll know things haven't worked out, and it would be silly to take unnecessary risks. But I want the chance to have a natural birth. And I don't think I'll get it in a hospital.

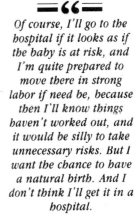

The importance of bonding

Evidence of research on bonding between mother, father, and baby points to the importance of the time immediately following birth for the couple to get to know their baby and feel it belongs to them and they to it. In many hospitals separation is still arbitrarily imposed on new parents, time for cuddling is either restricted or denied and routines take precedence over the emotional unfolding which heralds the birth of a family. Many women suspect that medical intervention is often unnecessary and that they will have a better chance of giving birth naturally and without drugs at home. They believe that full awareness of what is happening to them is a valuable experience and that drugs can harm their unborn babies. After a previous difficult hospital birth, one pregnant woman said: "I was determined to have a natural birth this time. Last time I had the whole works, and finished up with an epidural and a forceps delivery. I can't help thinking that if I let things take their own time and keep walking around and can relax and use my breathing and feel comfortable in my own home, with the people I love around me, my body will know what to do."

If you already have other children, you may be concerned that they should see birth as a normal, happy part of life and not, instead, as a surgical operation that entails you going off to a hospital. Birth is a

As your toddler helps you to sort out clothes for the new baby, it may be hard to believe that he ever wore them himself...

family affair and the baby should belong to the whole family. Some women hope that the other child or children can be involved in the labor and some would like them present at the birth. This is impossible to arrange in most hospitals. Mothers of toddlers often worry that separation from them will lead to emotional and behavioral problems in the older child, and this just at a time when the new baby puts in an appearance. And there are those mothers who just find it impossible to get someone to look after their family while they are away in the hospital. It is sometimes stated that women having their fourth or subsequent babies should always give birth in a hospital, but if all your previous pregnancies and labors have been straightforward, there is no additional risk with a fourth or fifth birth and some definite advantage in giving birth at home where the other children can also be involved.

Some doctors are reluctant to give their approval to a home birth once you are actually pregnant, even though they have seemed flexible earlier. For example, one woman said that her doctor had agreed to a home birth for her third child "in principle" before the pregnancy but then "did her best to change our minds. She did not really understand that there was absolutely no one who could come to look after the other children, and that I would not have my husband with me if the baby was not born at home. . . . There were many occasions when I was reduced to tears on my arrival home. Had I been less determined, or without my husband's support, I should have given in."

If you would like to give birth at home and your doctor is unsympathetic, contact the organizations listed on page 383.

Responsibilities of parents choosing home births

Since home birth is not the standard in the United States, a pregnant woman takes on additional responsibilities when she chooses to deliver at home. It is vital to consider whether or not you are willing to meet them. They include:

The selection of a competent birth attendant This may be a physician, certified nurse midwife or well-trained lay midwife. Be sure to ask for and check references carefully.

Starting prenatal care early in the pregnancy Screening for maternal and fetal abnormalities must continue throughout.

Particular attention to nutrition There is a significant relationship between the mother's diet in pregnancy and the health of her baby at birth and after.

Preparation for childbirth Mothers planning a home birth need an especially clear understanding of how their bodies function in labor and delivery.

Education for breastfeeding Breastfeeding after birth helps the uterus contract, making use of oxytoxic drugs less necessary.

Attendance at home birth classes, if available.

Obtaining supplies, as requested by the birth attendant.

Preparing for postpartum needs of mother and baby Planning ahead for the household simplifies life after birth.

Birth centers

A third option is the freestanding birth center. A birth center provides midwifery care in a pleasant, homelike setting in which couples and families participate fully in their own prenatal care, attend preparation for birth classes, and give birth and have uninterrupted time together afterward in the same setting. Birth centers tend to be staffed by certified nurse midwives, backed up by obstetricians. Women are very carefully screened to assure they are low risk and return to their own homes within twenty-four hours of giving birth. But some birth centers do have high transfer rates to hospital, and it is worth asking what the transfer rate during labor is. You can contact the National Association of Childbearing Centers for a list of those near you.

I like being with all the other pregnant women. I thought "We're all growing babies!" And everyone is so friendly and they explain everything. I revel in it.

CHILDBIRTH EDUCATION

One ingredient of a happy birth is good prenatal care, so that you are confident that you are healthy and the baby starts life under the best possible conditions. But the care you give yourself is probably more important than the care you receive from professionals. It also

Even if a visit to the clinic means a long wait you do have the opportunity of meeting other expectant mothers.

includes learning how to cope with stress in everyday life, and understanding how to work with your body. You do not need to attend classes until you are about five months pregnant, but it is worth thinking about the different classes available and perhaps beginning a few exercises earlier than this.

Prenatal care has developed piecemeal since the nineteenth century and we do not really know which elements in the package are valuable for all women, which are best kept for those at special risk, and which might be discarded altogether. Much of it is not very effective in producing reliable results. It is common for confusion to occur about whether a baby is growing well inside the uterus, for

Understanding your medical record

Para 0	The mother has had no previous birth.
Para 1 (or 2)	The mother has had one (or two) previous births.
Para 2 + 1	The mother has had two previous births plus a miscarriage (or termination) before 28 weeks.
LMP	Last menstrual period.
EDD/EDC	Expected date of delivery or expected date of confinement.
Alb	Albumin in urine. Your urine is analyzed for the presence of sugar, which is a sign of diabetes, and albumin (protein), which can be a sign of toxemia. Another name for toxemia is preeclampsia or metabolic toxemia of later pregnancy (MTLP for short). When sugar is present, it is noted as a percentage. Two per cent is a large amount. Ideally albumin should not be present at all.
MTLP	Metabolic toxemia of later pregnancy (or preeclampsia), another name for toxemia.
Hb	Hemoglobin, an oxygen-carrying substance present in red blood cells. If your hemoglobin level is lower than 10·5 per cent, you are considered to be anemic and will be prescribed iron. Because of the greater quantity of circulating blood, most pregnant women have reduced hemoglobin.
Fe	Iron. This means that you have been prescribed iron.
BP	Blood pressure. This is the pressure inside the arteries as the blood is pumped from the heart. The pressure built up every time the heart beats is called *systolic* pressure. Between beats the heart muscle relaxes and the pressure drops. This lower level is called *diastolic* pressure. The systolic pressure is the upper figure on your card, the diastolic pressure is the lower one. The lower figure is more significant than the upper one. A woman is considered to have high blood pressure, hypertension, if it exceeds 140/90 when measured on more than one occasion (see page 126).
FH	Fetal heart.

example, and many women are told that there is intra-uterine growth retardation when, in fact, it turns out that everything is fine. In spite of this, good medical care during pregnancy can every now and then make all the difference between life and death for the baby—and even, very occasionally, for you too.*

Unfortunately, whether you choose private or clinic care, waiting for appointments is usually a fact of life. Take a good book or needlework or make friends with another expectant mother going to the same doctor or clinic and you can keep each other company.

Some couples come together (a few doctors and clinics actually encourage fathers to be there) but usually this is not expected and

H/NH	Heard or not heard, usually referring to the fetal heart. In the last weeks of pregnancy the actual heart rate is often written in.
Edema	Swelling. Part of your weight gain is due to water retention, causing puffiness in the feet and ankles, face and vulva. A great deal of fluid retention may be a sign of preeclampsia, but it can be perfectly normal.
Fundus	The top of the uterus. As the baby grows, the fundus is pushed up to just above your navel at 22 weeks and under your ribs at 36 weeks. But when the baby drops down into the bony pelvis ready for birth the fundus is lower again (see page 69). You can find your own fundus and chart its position week by week through your pregnancy. Lie on your back, tummy bare and, with the sides and palms of your hands, feel around the hard top of your uterus, pressing against what feels like a wall of muscle
Cervix	The neck of the uterus, which shortens and opens to let the baby out.
PP	The presenting part of the baby. This is the part which is down at the bottom of the uterus and likely to be the first to press through the opening cervix if you are at the end of pregnancy. In the last few weeks the doctor may note the presentation more precisely, so that you can get an idea of exactly what part of the baby is in the cervix.
Vx/Vtx	Vertex. This indicates that the baby's position is head down, as it should be.
Ceph	Cephalic. This also indicates that the baby's position is head down.
Brim	The inlet of your pelvis.
Long L	Longitudinal lie. The baby is lying parallel to your spine.
LOA LOP ROA ROP	Left occipito anterior. These terms all refer to the position (anterior Left occipito posterior. or posterior) of the crown of the baby's head Right occipito anterior. (occiput) in relation to your body (right or Right occipito posterior. left). Therefore ROP means that the back of the baby's head is to your right and back.
RSA	Right sacrum anterior. This is the most common breech presentation.
Eng/E	Engaged. This is written on your card when the baby's head has dropped down into your pelvis, which can happen any time from about six weeks before you go into labor until after you have actually started.
T	Term. The doctor writes this on your card when it is estimated that you are right at the end of your pregnancy and the baby is ready to be born.

fathers may be asked to remain in the waiting room. If, however, it is important to you that you both talk to the doctor and that your partner is involved in the pregnancy, not only the birth, it is worthwhile being quietly but firmly persistent to get what you want. Think through beforehand any questions or worries you may have. Many women find it easier to write down their questions so that they will not forget to ask in the rush. If there is anything you particularly hope for about the way in which you have your baby, ask the obstetrician or nurse midwife if it can be noted on your record.

Routine tests

Most women see their doctor or nurse midwife once a month until they are 32 weeks pregnant. At this stage you will be seen every two weeks and in your final month will be given weekly appointments.

During a typical visit you may be weighed before you see the doctor. While the baby is growing, you will probably be putting on weight fairly steadily (see page 87).

Your blood group is determined at your first visit and a test is done to check whether the baby might develop Rhesus disease (see page 103). Your blood is automatically tested for syphilis, and you may be offered amniocentesis (see page 206). At each visit your blood pressure, complete blood count, and urine will be tested and your weight, the height of the fundus, and the fetal heart beat (as soon as it is audible) will also be checked.

An ultrasound scan (see page 202) may be indicated at any time during the pregnancy. The use of ultrasound has become routine. In late pregnancy a single scan can show the size of the baby's head in relation to your pelvic outlet. If you have a series of scans at different sessions, an estimate can be made of the baby's rate of growth and expected date of delivery.

At the first prenatal visit you will probably have an internal examination (see page 27). At most subsequent visits the uterus and baby will be felt by abdominal palpation. As this is done, you should give a long breath out and release your tummy completely, then go on breathing slowly, releasing more on each breath out. This makes it easier to feel how the baby is lying and is much more comfortable for you than if you are tense.

The examining hands feel first for the distance between your pubic bone and the baby and then the top of the uterus. This is called fundal palpation. The hands move down the sides of the baby so that the back and limbs are discovered. The part of the baby that is over the cervix is said to be "presenting". The doctor or midwife turns to face your feet and presses the hands downward and from side to side to determine whether the baby's head, buttocks, or any other part, is presenting. The next maneuver tends to be uncomfortable but is quickly performed. Facing you again, the doctor spreads one hand wide and presses in above your pubic bone to feel the exact position of the presenting part in relation to the pelvis.

In late pregnancy, take the opportunity to find out how your baby is lying and discuss anything that worries you. Notice fetal movements and report any pronounced change in their frequency or type. The best way of monitoring a pregnancy is for the obstetrician, nurse midwife, and the expectant mother to work together.

TALKING TO DOCTORS

Some people have doctors with whom they quickly feel at ease, and experience little difficulty in finding out the medical alternatives open to them in pregnancy and discussing their requirements with their doctors. However, the expectant mother and her doctor are likely to meet in a system in which time is at a premium and sometimes one or both of them finds it difficult to break out from a formal doctor-patient relationship with all that this implies of authority and subordination.

Being pregnant is a physiological process. It also involves a kind of emotional journey into being a patient. And as if all this were not enough, it propels you into new kinds of social relationships. Some of these are with the professionals you encounter during your pregnancy. So, as well as having to understand the changes taking place in your body and your emotions, you may have to develop new social skills which help you to create a satisfactory dialogue with those who care for you and your baby. This is especially the case where you meet different doctors at each clinic visit and others again when in labor. The lack of continuity in care is one of the main criticisms that women make about childbirth in a hospital today.*

Some women also feel very vulnerable emotionally when pregnant and cannot help crying under stress, even though (or perhaps because) it is the last thing they *want* to do. You are in no way abnormal if you feel surges of emotion which are difficult or impossible to control, but it means that you may feel at a disadvantage in an interview with a doctor when you want to ask for something or talk about a kind of birth you hope for.

This possibility is a good reason for having your partner or a close friend or relative with you on such occasions. It is important, of course, that you discuss your wishes thoroughly with this person first. You may find it useful for him or her to play "the devil's advocate" and act out an imagined encounter so that you have some practice in discussing the subject and develop a strategy. Do not make the mistake of anticipating opposition from the hospital staff; you will probably be pleasantly surprised. But do be prepared to give carefully thought-out reasons for what you want.

See that you are well briefed about the matters you want to discuss. There is now a good deal of published research on emotional and sociological aspects of maternity care, for example, and many papers on the technology of modern obstetrics and the active management of labor (see page 290) which are published in medical journals. It

The obstetrician was very pleasant. He told me they'd just had a baby 3 months ago. That made a lot of difference.

will help if you have a clear idea of some of the most important statements. If you are attending childbirth education classes, ask your teacher to help. The International Childbirth Education Association produces booklets and sells relevant books,* and there are other organizations which may be able to give advice (see page 383).

Preparing your questions

Since questions may go out of your head when you actually have a chance to ask them (pregnancy amnesia is a well-known phenomenon), and because some doctors seem to concentrate exclusively on the lower end of your body to the exclusion of interest in you as a person, it is a good idea to jot down subjects you want to discuss. Different treatments are done routinely in different hospitals. You may not want some or all of these, and it is best to state your preferences as early as possible. On the other hand, you may want a treatment which would not usually be given in your hospital but is probably available if you make a special request. Your list could include questions about the doctor's attitude toward induction of labor, routinely giving enemas or suppositories, the use of intravenous drips, toward electronic fetal monitoring, episiotomy, and the use of forceps (see pages 290–307). You could also ask about the availability of epidurals (see page 286) and whether or not you will be able to keep your baby with you day and night. It may also be important for you to know whether there will be much help with breastfeeding. Be specific in your requests, to avoid misunderstandings later on.

If you have not made an appointment with a discussion in mind, sometimes the office or clinic is so crowded that you feel reluctant to take up anybody's time. Even so, it is probably worth saying that you have made a note of things you would like to discuss and ask whether it is convenient that day, or, if not, whether you can arrange to have some time to talk at the next visit. There is no need to be apologetic about wanting further information or asking for the doctor's help to achieve the kind of birth you would like. After all, you are not just a baby-producing machine!

During the interview sit in a relaxed way, check that fingers and toes are unclenched, and breathe out just before speaking for the first time. Make eye contact and address the doctor by name or ask his or her name if you do not know it.

When a woman is nervous, she tends to pitch her voice too high. Modulate it so that it does not sound too demanding. You might smile nervously without realizing it. This can be confusing for the doctor, who may think that you are happy about something when you are not. Or it may be that the doctor unconsciously smiles because he or she is concerned to get you to accept another point of view and is sugaring the pill; your spontaneous reaction may then be to smile back, perhaps giving the doctor the idea that you are content when in fact you are not.

I had to sit in a little cubicle for ages feeling cut off from the world.

OPPOSITE

Regular medical check-ups will help you keep track of your baby's growth and development.

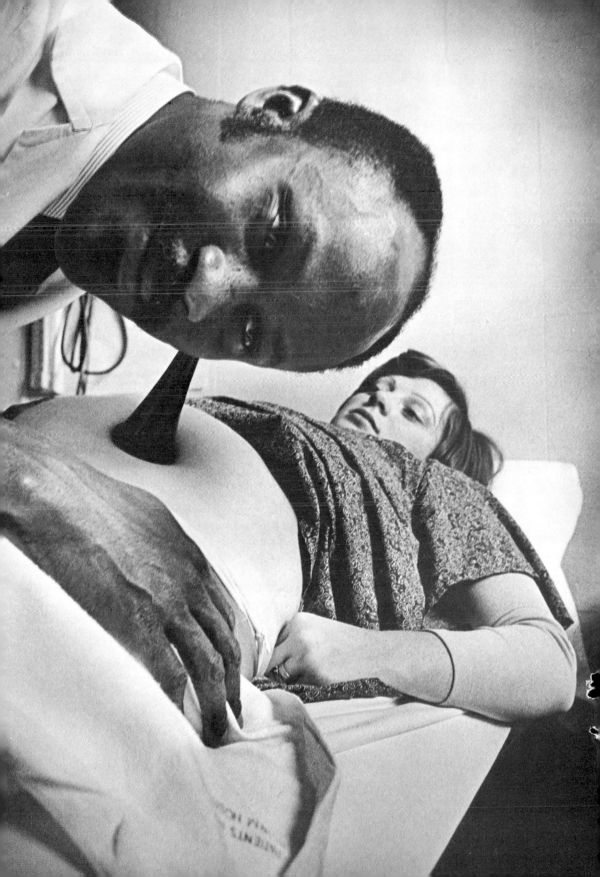

Avoid aggression and state your requests clearly and concisely. If you lose your temper, you may be classified as difficult or neurotic. If you encounter opposition or are made to feel that you cannot know what is in your best interests, restate your wishes firmly and give the reasons for them. It is a good idea to include requests that are not top priority, so that there is a possibility of compromise on some matters. Belligerence only provokes further opposition. Tell the doctor instead how unhappy or disappointed you are.

You may want to take notes of the conversation. You can always say: "I'd like to think more about that; may I just make a note of it?" Be careful not to imply that you are cross-examining the doctor and writing down any answers in preparation for a later attack. Listen to the doctor with concentration and make it clear that you are listening by "playing back" the important statements: "Do you mean . . .?" "So you are saying that . . .?" and rephrase whatever has been said as accurately as you can. You can sometimes add to your remark the *implications* that you think such a statement entails. By clarifying a point in this way you may be working toward modifying it. For example, if the doctor says, "I never allow husbands to remain if I have to give the patient a vaginal examination or do a forceps delivery because they only get in the way", you might ask: "Are you saying that it is dangerous for a husband to stay because he might affect your judgment?" Not many experienced obstetricians would say that the presence of a husband could affect their professional judgment, and the doctor might reply by telling you a story about men who have fainted. You might then say: "I take it you feel happier about a man who stays calm and who gives emotional support to his wife?"

If your interview has gone badly, you can consider changing your doctor or, if there is more than one hospital in your area, the hospital where you give birth. But give yourself a few days to simmer down and think it over calmly. You can write a letter to the doctor politely explaining your reasons for seeking other care; it is a good idea to send copies to the Medical Director and the Chair of the Obstetrical Department if it concerns a hospital.

But such drastic measures are often unnecessary and you will find that you have opened up the possibility of getting the kind of childbirth you want. Good communication with your doctor means that, if for medical reasons you do not get all you had hoped for, you can at least take an active part in the decision-making.

On one occasion I waited 3 hours before being seen. I felt sorry for moms with toddlers. No provision was made for them except a broken rocking horse.

◆

Physical and emotional changes

Life in the uterus

In the first days of pregnancy life is budding in cells far smaller than a pin-head. Because everything is happening on such a minute scale, it can be difficult to accept the reality of a baby growing deep inside you. Even when you begin to believe in your pregnancy, other people remain unaware of it. It can seem as if an explosion has taken place without anybody noticing, or as if all the colors have become more brilliant but everyone else is carrying on as usual. The chance meeting of one out of four hundred million sperm with a ripe and waiting egg has resulted in a dramatic series of events, conducted on a scale so miniature that you cannot feel the astonishing life process unfolding inside you, even though you know it is happening.

Fertilization

At birth the ovaries of every baby girl contain almost 500,000 potential single-cell eggs, but they do not ripen until the menstrual periods begin. Each cell that ripens into an egg is nourished by nearly 5000 others that will never themselves ripen. From your first period until the menopause, when your periods stop, you may carry up to 4000 ripe eggs; each month between 100 and 150 begin to ripen, but usually only one a month reaches full maturity and is capable of being fertilized. The frequency with which eggs are produced and released is determined by hormones, which interact regularly in a system known as the menstrual cycle.

This cycle lasts for about a month, and begins when a hormone released by the pituitary gland stimulates an ovary to start ripening an egg. As the egg matures, the ovary releases estrogen into the bloodstream. The estrogen stops the pituitary gland producing its hormone, so no more eggs are stimulated into ripening. It also makes the uterine lining change and thicken in anticipation of the egg, which bursts out of the follicle (a capsule bulging on the surface of the ovary) about midway through each menstrual cycle. It is then drawn by the fingered tentacles of the fallopian tube into its long canal, which is about the thickness of a ballpoint refill.

The egg itself is a minute speck. It is barely visible to the naked eye, yet when it meets with a still more minuscule sperm it has the potential to develop into a human being. The follicle (also known as the corpus luteum) that held the egg begins to produce progesterone, which carries on the work that the estrogen has been doing. If the egg is not fertilized within a few days, the follicle dries up and the progesterone level falls dramatically. As a result the uterine lining decomposes, and a menstrual period occurs.

Even while bleeding is going on, the menstrual cycle renews itself: the pituitary gland is stimulating the ovary into ripening a new egg.

OPPOSITE

Sperm meets egg and dissolves . . . the two nuclei will then fuse.

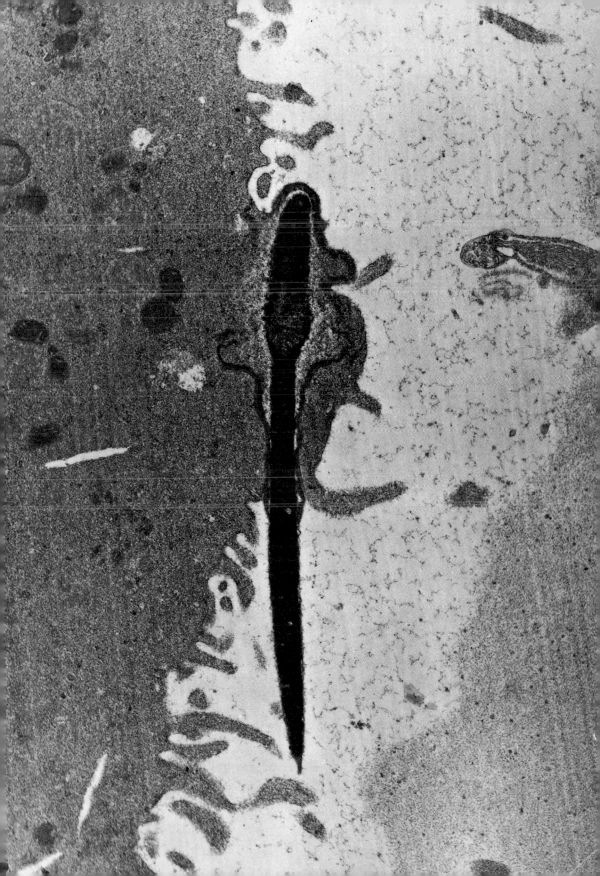

The menstrual cycle

While a follicle is developing in the ovary, the uterus is building up a lining composed mainly of coiled arteries and glands. If the ripe egg released from the ovary is not fertilized, the uterus sheds the top layer of this lining (menstruation) and the process begins again.

This diagram shows an external view of the ovary of a fully grown woman.

This diagram of a section through an ovary shows the stages of development of the follicle during any one menstrual cycle.

OVULATION CYCLE

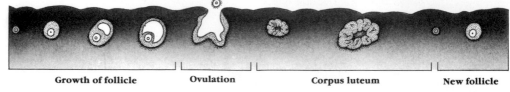

| Growth of follicle | Ovulation | Corpus luteum | New follicle |

Days

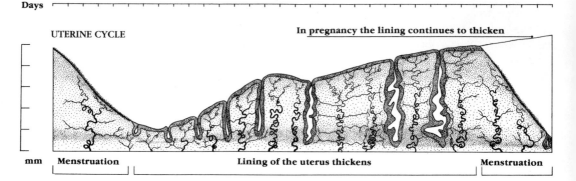

UTERINE CYCLE

In pregnancy the lining continues to thicken

mm | Menstruation | Lining of the uterus thickens | Menstruation |

But if the egg is fertilized, the follicle does not shrivel up, the progesterone level does not drop and the uterine lining continues to thicken, so that you do not have a period.

The usual pattern is that the ovary on one side releases an egg one month, the one on the other side the next. Sometimes one ovary becomes especially active for a few months. Occasionally only one ovary is functioning: if part of a fallopian tube or an ovary has been surgically removed the other one usually takes on the work of both.

Sperm are so tiny that 30,000 of them placed side by side would only just stretch across a beer bottle top. A man ejaculates hundreds of millions of sperm every time he has an orgasm. After intercourse, a mere 2000 of these survive the journey up the vagina, to the fallopian tubes, and only one can fertilize a ripe egg, which immediately puts up a chemical barrier to keep all others out.

Each sperm is shaped like a tadpole with a long, lashing tail which makes it highly mobile. The head is rounded and holds the gene-carrying nucleus. When a sperm meets the egg it burrows deep into it and its nucleus fuses with the nucleus of the egg. It is at this moment that the genes, or units of inheritance, of the parents first meet.

GENETICS

Inside the nucleus of every body cell—with two exceptions—there are 46 chromosomes, making 23 pairs. The two exceptions are the egg cell and the sperm cell, which have 23 chromosomes each instead of 46. Chromosomes are rodlike structures shaped like Egyptian hieroglyphs, each containing thousands of genes.

When the nucleus of the sperm cell fuses with the nucleus of the egg, each chromosome—and each gene inside each chromosome—unites with its opposite number. The newly fertilized cell now contains 46 chromosomes, like every other human cell. The physical characteristics of the future person are determined, and the cell can start to develop into a human being.

Boy or girl?

Out of the 23 pairs of chromosomes in every human cell one pair determines the person's sex. The two sex chromosomes in a female cell are known as XX, and the two in a male cell as XY. Since the egg and the sperm cell contain half the usual number of chromosomes, every egg cell contains 22 chromosomes plus one sex chromosome, which is an X. Every sperm cell contains 22 chromosomes plus one sex chromosome, which can be either an X or a Y.

The sex of the baby depends on these differences between sperm cells. If the egg is fertilized by a sperm with an X chromosome, the union of the two sex chromosomes will result in XX, a girl. If the egg is fertilized by a sperm with a Y chromosome, the union of the two sex chromosomes will result in XY, a boy. There is usually a 50/50 chance that a boy or a girl will be conceived; statistically it appears

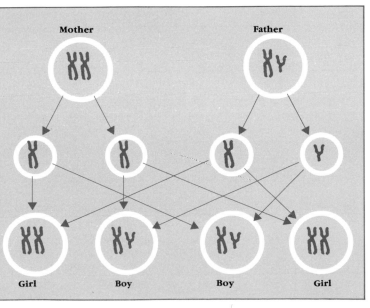

Your baby's sex
A woman's egg cells and a man's sperm cells each contain 23 single chromosomes, which are not paired until they meet their opposite number. Of the 23 single chromosomes, one is always a sex chromosome. Each egg always has an X (female) sex chromosome but the sex chromosome present in any sperm can be either X or Y. Since a Y chromosome is dominant, the egg that is fertilized by a sperm carrying a Y chromosome will result in a boy, while the egg fertilized by a sperm carrying an X chromosome develops into a girl.

Mother   Father

Girl   Boy   Boy   Girl

The female reproductive organs

When a woman ovulates, the released egg from one of the two ovaries is immediately drawn into a fallopian tube where, if intercourse has taken place, it may be fertilized by a sperm. The fertilized egg embeds itself in the lining of the uterus. If the egg is not fertilized, it is shed, along with the lining of the uterus, down through the opening in the cervix and out of the vagina: this is menstruation.

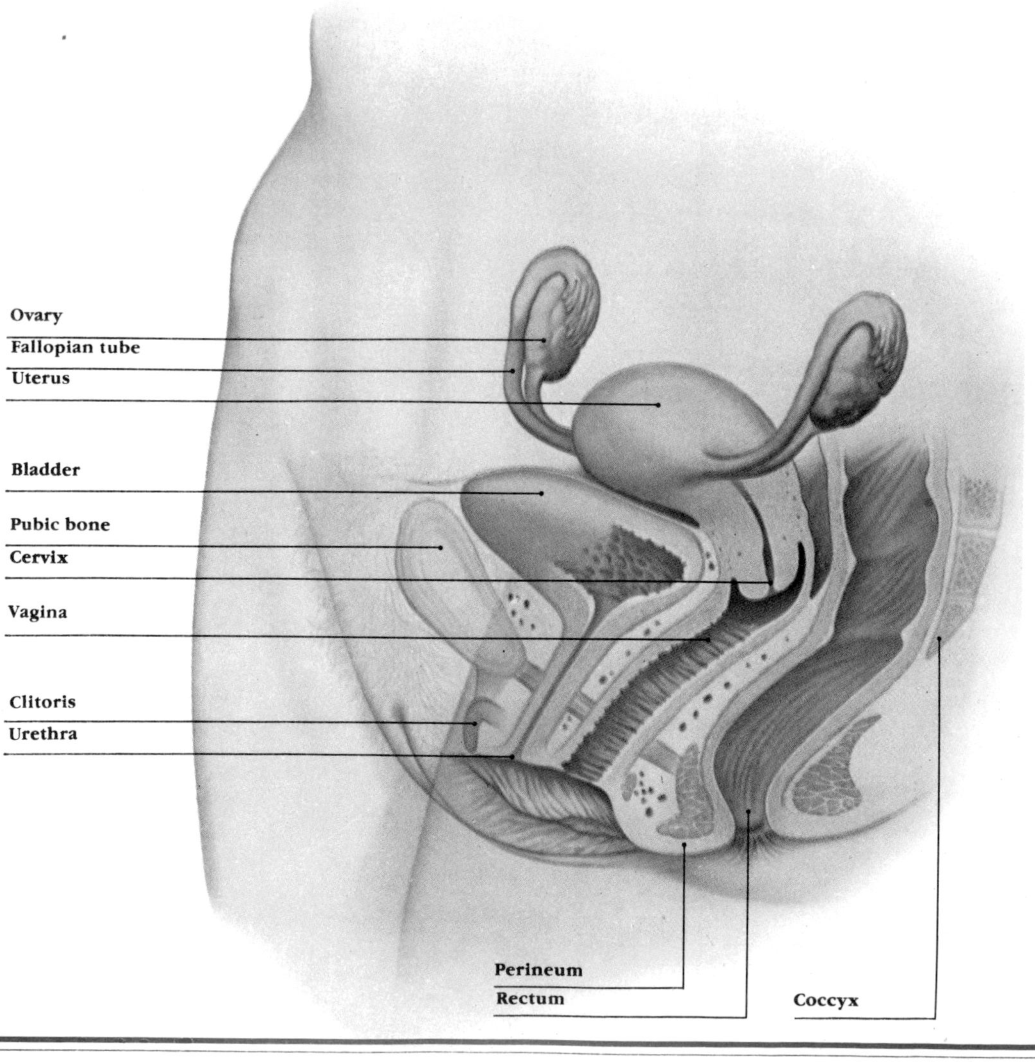

Ovary

Fallopian tube

Uterus

Bladder

Pubic bone

Cervix

Vagina

Clitoris

Urethra

Perineum

Rectum

Coccyx

The male reproductive organs

Sperm mature in both testes, which are enclosed within the scrotum. They travel up through each vas deferens, where they are stored temporarily. When a man is sexually aroused, his penis becomes erect and the outlet from the bladder into the ejaculatory duct is closed, leaving it free for the sperm. The sperm entering the ejaculatory duct are accompanied by secretions from the seminal vesicles, Cowper's glands, and the prostate gland. About a teaspoonful of the fluid (semen), containing millions of sperm, is ejaculated from the urethra at orgasm.

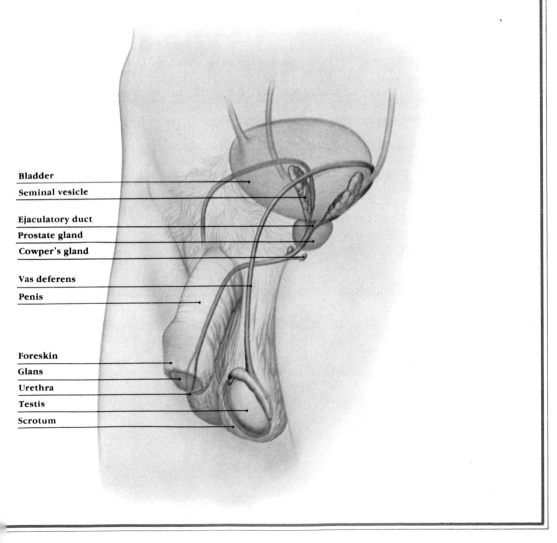

Bladder

Seminal vesicle

Ejaculatory duct

Prostate gland

Cowper's gland

Vas deferens

Penis

Foreskin

Glans

Urethra

Testis

Scrotum

that as women grow older and also as they bear more children, the chance of having a girl is slightly increased.

Although the baby's sex is determined by the sex chromosome carried by the sperm, it is also partly a consequence of the environment into which that sperm is received. Natural alkalinity or acidity of the secretions in your reproductive tract makes it easier for some sperm to survive their long journey than for others. Traditionally an acid medium has been thought to increase the chances of having a male child, and an alkaline medium a female child; because of this people have douched with acid or alkaline solutions before intercourse, but there is little evidence that this significantly affects your chances of producing one sex or the other.

Dominant and recessive genes

When a Y chromosome meets an X chromosome, the Y chromosome dominates to produce a boy. Similarly, when a gene encounters its opposite number one always takes precedence. A baby receives half of its genes from each parent. If a gene for brown eyes from one parent meets a gene for blue eyes from the other, the gene for brown eyes will always prevail. This does not mean that a child of one

Dominant and recessive genes

Since the gene for blond hair is recessive, the blond-haired grandparents in this family group must possess two blond-haired genes, one of which has to be passed on to each of their children. This means that the dark-haired mother and father in the group must each have a recessive gene for blond hair, giving them a one-in-four chance of producing a blond child.

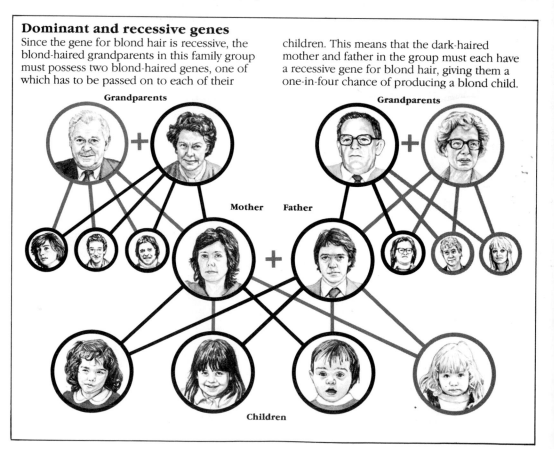

Grandparents   Grandparents

Mother   Father

Children

brown-eyed and one blue-eyed parent will always have brown eyes. But the gene for brown eyes is known as *dominant*, the one for blue eyes as *recessive*. So someone with brown eyes who has received a gene for blue eyes from one parent retains the blue-eye gene as a recessive gene. If he or she should have a child by another brown-eyed person also with a recessive gene for blue eyes, there is a one in four chance that both parents will pass on their recessive genes for blue eyes to produce a blue-eyed child. This ability of two brown-eyed parents to have a blue-eyed child is a simple example of the way in which heredity introduces diversification with each generation.

Defective genes

Occasionally genes are defective, but since healthy genes are usually dominant over faulty ones, your baby's normal development is almost always assured. Some defective genes are carried by the sex chromosomes, and then the children of one sex only are affected. Color-blindness, for instance, is carried by some women in one of their two X chromosomes; since the normal gene in their other X chromosome is dominant over the faulty one they do not suffer from color-blindness. But if a boy inherits an X chromosome with a faulty gene he has no other X chromosome with a healthy gene to dominate it, so he is color-blind. This is how color-blindness is transmitted through alternating generations of affected boys and carrier mothers. Hemophilia is passed on in the same way.

If you are anxious about the possibility of your children inheriting any diseases or handicaps from your family or your partner's, tell your doctor before you become pregnant, if possible. Failing that, as soon as your pregnancy is confirmed ask to talk to a genetic counselor. There is a skilled genetic counselor in every teaching hospital who can tell you the mathematical chances of your bearing a defective child and about the tests that can be carried out (see page 202). If it is discovered that you are carrying an abnormal child, your pregnancy can be terminated *if you wish*. Nobody has to agree to termination of pregnancy even if bearing a handicapped child.

THE BEGINNINGS OF PREGNANCY

The genetic make-up of the future child is decided at the moment of fertilization. But conception is a process, not a split-second event. Immediately after it has been penetrated, the egg starts to divide. It divides repeatedly as it is swept along the fallopian tube to the uterus, which it reaches seven days after leaving the ovary. By this time it is a clustered ball of cells, called a blastocyst, like a tiny blackberry but hollow in the center. The blastocyst floats in the cavity of the uterus until about the tenth day, when it succeeds in embedding itself into the uterine lining.

Some blastocysts (estimates range from one in ten to as many as one in three) do not manage to root themselves into the wall of the uterus, and are swept out with the next menstrual period. Conception is complete only when the blastocyst has successfully nested into the wall of the uterus. You have not yet missed a period.

Implantation

The cells now number several hundred. The blastocyst releases enzymes which penetrate the lining of the uterus, causing the tissues to distintegrate and the blood and cells—on which the blastocyst can feed—to seep out. They make a kind of nourishing soup, whose quality depends on the preparatory state of the uterine lining. Sometimes this is not rich enough to maintain the pregnancy and there is a miscarriage, which just resembles a late and rather heavy period, without your ever realizing that you have been pregnant. An inadequately nourishing uterine lining is one cause of infertility.

Early development

During the second week of the fertilized egg's life, the cells become differentiated. One set becomes the amniotic sac, an envelope of salty water in which the baby will later grow. Another cluster develops into the yolk sac out of which the embryo can make blood corpuscles. Yet another group becomes the placenta (see page 66). In between these structures are other rapidly developing cells which will form the baby. These cells are at first just an embryonic disk, but they grow lengthways in the third week until there is clearly a head and a tail end, with the yolk sac attached by a stalk to the middle of the disk.

At this point you are about one week past the date when you expected your period to come. Although you are not sure, perhaps you suspect that you might be pregnant.

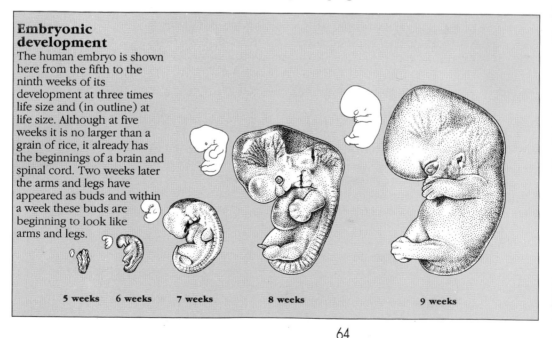

Embryonic development

The human embryo is shown here from the fifth to the ninth weeks of its development at three times life size and (in outline) at life size. Although at five weeks it is no larger than a grain of rice, it already has the beginnings of a brain and spinal cord. Two weeks later the arms and legs have appeared as buds and within a week these buds are beginning to look like arms and legs.

5 weeks   6 weeks   7 weeks   8 weeks   9 weeks

64

Six weeks pregnant It is three or four weeks after the meeting of sperm and egg, and about two weeks since you missed your period. According to the medical method of dating pregnancy (see page 28), you are about five or six weeks pregnant. The cluster of living cells has now developed into an embryo: there is a head and a neck with rudimentary eyes and ears, a brain, and a heart which is already beating, although it has only two chambers instead of the four which will develop shortly. There is a bloodstream and a digestive system, kidneys and a liver, and tiny buds which will become arms and legs.

A rod of cells develops—the notochord—which later becomes the spine. The embryo develops from the head end down, so that at this stage the lower part of its back is as yet barely formed and looks more like a tail. In fact, while now the size of a coffee bean, the embryo closely resembles a miniature sea horse.

Seven weeks pregnant A week later the embryo is about the size of a baby lima bean. Its body has plumped out into a baby shape, even though the head is at a strange angle in relation to the body. It has visible nostrils, lips, and tongue, and even the buds of its first teeth. Four chambers have developed in the heart. The limb buds have grown into arms and legs, although as yet the hands and feet are no more than ridges.

Eight weeks pregnant The baby is still smaller than your little toe. It floats in the amniotic sac like an astronaut in space, attached to its life-support system. The heart has started the vigorous pumping of blood which will continue for a lifetime. The brain glimmers through skin as thin as waxed paper, revealing every tiny branching blood vessel beneath. The jaw is not yet fully formed and the ears are slung low and have not yet been molded into their correct position. The eyes are covered by an intact skin, which will eventually split to become the eyelids. The head of the embryo is huge in relation to its body. The limbs elongate and elbows and knees appear. Even now the baby is trying out some gentle kicking, though you cannot feel any movement inside you.

All the organs and features of the embryo are completed in the course of the next month. The face grows from the top, and as the lower parts form the neck is elongated and a chin develops. The nose and outer ears are completely formed. Fingers and toes are visible, though webbing stretches between them.

By the time you are 12 weeks pregnant the basic physical equipment of the embryo is in working order. The head is still big for the body and the limbs small; few muscles are working yet. All the internal organs have formed and some of them are functioning. The genitals have developed, but it is not yet easy to tell what sex the baby is. The umbilical cord has started to circulate blood between the embryo and the group of membranes attached to the wall of the uterus. It is at this stage that the embryo begins to rely on these

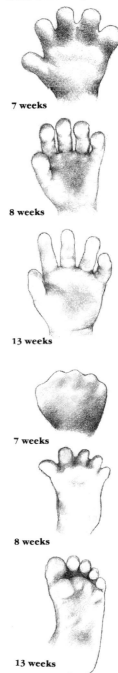

HANDS AND FEET
These develop at a slightly different rate, the feet being about a week behind the hands until the 13th week.

7 weeks

8 weeks

13 weeks

7 weeks

8 weeks

13 weeks

membranes for nourishment and the placenta starts to function. From now on the baby is known as a fetus and the rest of its time in the uterus is spent on growth and maturation.

THE PLACENTA

In the early weeks of pregnancy one cluster of cells begins to develop into the placenta, which is an organ grown especially to nourish the baby and to excrete its waste products. The outside layer of this cell cluster develops into a membrane with hundreds of tiny roots which penetrate the uterine tissues.

Your blood does not flow directly into the baby at any stage of pregnancy. It passes across the tissues on the maternal side of the placenta and the baby's blood passes back across the tissues on the other side. The two bloodstreams are separated by the membrane; chemical substances can be diffused from one bloodstream to the other through the membrane, but the bloodstreams themselves normally never mix. (Some fetal blood cells do cross the placenta, but usually without any significant effect.) The baby can thus have a different blood group from yours, while still taking its nourishment from your blood. In just the same way the baby's waste products are passed back through the placenta into your bloodstream, to be filtered and excreted by your kidneys.

Although the baby makes breathing movements, it does not breathe inside you: it takes its oxygen from your blood and passes back carbon dioxide. The oxygen diffuses through the membrane into its blood in the same way that oxygen from the air passes through the lining of your lungs. The placenta therefore works rather like a coffee filter: the coffee grains never enter the pot, but substances from them filter into it. Changes in your blood as a result of stress, illness, or toxic substances that you imbibe will affect the quality of the substances which flow through the membrane.

Blood takes only half a minute to flow from the baby's heart to the placenta and back again to the baby's heart. The flow of blood through the placenta in the fourth month of pregnancy is about 8 gallons (27.5 liters) a day and by the end of pregnancy 100 gallons (330 liters) of blood are passing through each day.

As the placenta starts to function, it gradually takes over responsibility for production of a range of hormones, including estrogen and progesterone, from the glands which normally secrete these hormones. Estrogen and progesterone control most of the changes in your body during pregnancy. The estrogen stimulates the growth of the uterus and the development of new uterine blood vessels, and also causes the milk glands in your breasts to develop so that you can feed the baby. The progesterone prevents the uterus from contracting strongly and endangering the baby during pregnancy, and thus holds off the start of labor until term. When the baby is ready to be born, the progesterone level drops. By this time the uterus has become exquisitely sensitive to the level of estrogen in the blood, so that when the placenta reduces its output of progesterone, the estrogen takes over: it initiates labor and ensures that the uterus contracts strongly right through to the end of the third stage.

THE GROWING BABY

At 12 weeks The fetus has a large head and small, rounded rump; the sex organs are distinguishable though as yet incomplete; the eyes are closed, the retina showing dark and round through translucent skin. Toes and fingers are formed; the arms are the right length in proportion to the body and the nails are beginning to grow. The ribs and spine are just starting to harden into bone and the baby is moving vigorously. You cannot yet feel these movements, but it is kicking, curling its toes up and down, rotating its feet and wrists, clenching and unclenching its fists, pressing its lips together, frowning and making other facial expressions. The baby is also swallowing the amniotic fluid, gurgling it from its mouth or passing it out through its bladder. There is still plenty of room in the uterus, so the fetus can swoop and undulate in its own enclosed sea.

Fetal circulation

This simplified diagram shows how blood circulates around the fetus. The blood that travels along the umbilical cord toward the fetus has received oxygen from its mother through the placenta. Before reaching the fetal heart, it mixes with some of the de-oxygenated blood that has already circulated through the fetus. This mixture travels through the heart and is pumped up into the head and around the body, becoming, as it does so, less oxygenated. To obtain more oxygen, it returns to the placenta via the heart again, most of it bypassing the lungs. At birth the blood vessels around the baby's navel are automatically sealed off and the baby's circulation rapidly adapts to self-survival, with the lungs taking over the function of oxygenating the blood.

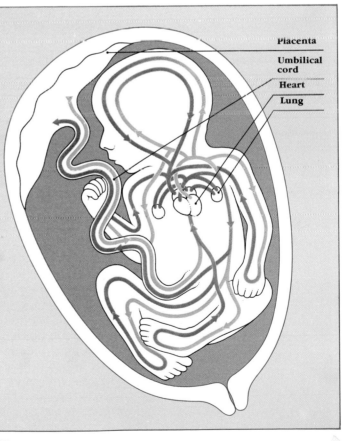

Placenta

Umbilical cord

Heart

Lung

KEY

Oxygenated blood

De-oxygenated blood

At 16 weeks Although the baby is growing rapidly, it could still nestle easily into a teacup. Its face is developing specifically human features, though the chin is still small and the mouth wide in comparison. The eyes are huge, closed, and spaced far apart. The baby is covered with a fine down, called lanugo. This is the earliest stage at which you may first become aware of its movements. At first these feel like butterflies or little fish zigzagging about in bursts of activity, but soon they are unmistakably the kicking and lunging movements of a live being deep inside your body.

At 20 weeks The baby is half as long as it will be at delivery and about as heavy as a medium-sized Spanish onion (8 oz or 250 g). You could still hold it in the palm of your hand. The closed eyes are bulbous, because the face has not yet plumped out. Hair on the head is starting to grow and there are delicate eyebrows. The baby's movements are becoming more complex and it may be sucking its thumb.

You will probably notice that there are times when your baby seems to be asleep and times when it moves very actively (often when you have just settled down to go to sleep yourself). This seems to be partly because when you lie down it is easier for the baby to move. When moving around you also automatically rock the baby in your pelvis, so when you are busiest the baby is often asleep.

At 24 weeks The baby is about the length of your telephone receiver (13 in or 32 cm). It is covered with vernix, a creamy substance which protects its skin inside the uterus and prevents it from becoming waterlogged. This vernix sticks to hairy parts and many babies are born still coated with it. You may notice that your baby responds to loud noises and to music, especially to the brass section of an orchestra. If you are practicing relaxation, you may feel the baby become remarkably active and begin to leap around energetically.

At 28 weeks The fetus is now legally viable; if it is born it must be registered as a birth. If it dies it is considered to be a stillbirth rather than a miscarriage. With modern intensive care a baby at this stage has a 60–70 per cent chance of survival—even higher in some units. The main problem encountered is usually that the baby's lungs have not yet developed bubbles of surfactant, the substance which prevents the complete collapse of the lungs between each breath. There is also still very little fat under the baby's skin, so its temperature control mechanisms cannot yet work efficiently.

The baby has virtually filled all the available space in the uterus. Most babies turn upside down at some point during the seventh month and then seem to fit more comfortably. By now you may be able to distinguish the baby's bottom from a foot or a knee. When you lie in the bath you can enjoy watching the baby swivel from one side of your abdomen to the other. Foot and knee movements are more jerky than whole-body movements and hands produce soft flutters

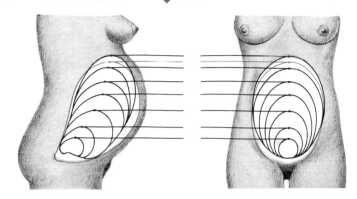

THE CHANGING UTERUS
Although the uterus is expanding throughout pregnancy, this increase in size is not usually visible until the fourth month, when it is too large to stay hidden in the pelvis. From the 12th week the uterus enlarges at a regular rate until the 36th week, when the fundus (the top of the uterus) reaches to just below the breastbone. In women having their first child, the baby sometimes engages in the pelvis at about this date, so that the fundus descends slightly, even though the uterus has not shrunk.

like sea anemones moving. Other people may now be able to feel the baby kicking when they place a hand on your abdomen.

Throughout later pregnancy you can often anticipate the periods of most hectic movement; many babies are at their most energetic between eight and eleven pm.

At 32 weeks By the eighth month the baby lacks only some lung surfactant and a good layer of insulating fat before it is ready to be born. Movements are vigorous: the prods coming from the feet are so energetic that they may make you catch your breath. Every now and again the baby may jerk spasmodically in what can be a rather alarming manner; some women worry that their babies are having seizures. But it is usually an attack of hiccups, brought on perhaps because the baby has been gulping amniotic fluid.

At 36 weeks At some point between 36 weeks and term (which is 40 weeks from the first day of your last menstrual period) the baby will probably descend into the pelvis with its head firmly fixed like an egg in an eggcup. It is then said to be "engaged"; this is a good sign and one indication that the baby can pass through the pelvic cavity without difficulty. Once your baby has engaged you are slung lower and can often feel the head like a coconut hanging between your legs. It is uncomfortable to sit down fast on a hard chair and you may also experience peculiar sensations in your vagina like mild electric shocks (see page 209).

After the baby has engaged, its larger body movements tend to be limited; you will probably feel only the kicking of legs and feet, the action of the head as it uses the pelvic floor as a trampoline and the fainter movements of the arms. But although the movements change in type no day should pass without some lively indications from the baby of its presence (see page 218).

The last weeks may be tiring and involve tedious inaction. The baby is three times heavier at delivery than it was at 28 weeks, weighs anything from $5\frac{1}{2}$ to 11 lbs (2·5–5 kg) and is between 18 and 22 in long (44–55 cm). It is now ready for its extraordinary journey to life.

Forty weeks of life

The next ten pages show different stages of the development of a baby from the moment of conception to its last week in the uterus. The illustration below shows the journey of the egg along the fallopian tube, where it is fertilized, to the uterus. During this five-day journey, the single-cell egg divides into over a hundred cells.

One of the sperm that have arrived in the fallopian tube penetrates the ripe egg.

The head of the sperm separates from the tail and approaches the egg's nucleus.

The chromosomes of the two nuclei pair off to create a two-cell egg.

The two cells divide as the egg continues its journey along the fallopian tube.

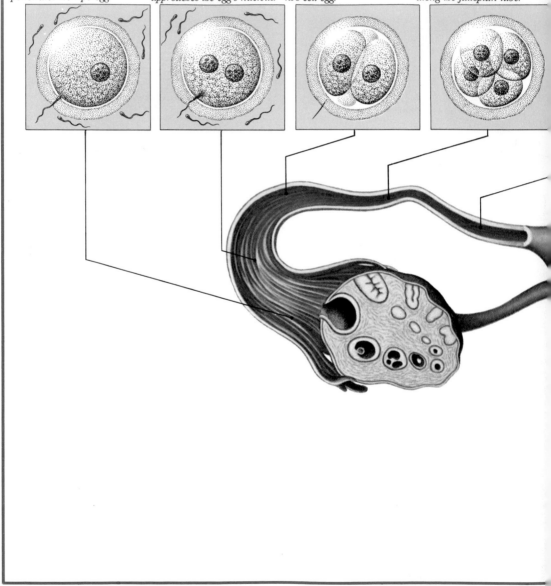

As the cells continue to divide they gradually get smaller and smaller.

On about the fifth day the egg reaches the uterus and loses its jellylike coating.

Six or seven days after fertilization the egg embeds itself in the uterine lining.

Eight weeks pregnant

The baby is just under 1 in (2·5 cm) long. The bones of its arms and legs start to harden and the baby makes slight movements, still too feather-light for the mother to notice. The baby's face is developing. Some time during this week the baby starts to open its mouth and the upper palate forms. The lower jaw is taking shape, with muscles which will enable the baby to suck and chew. The sound-perceiving mechanism of the ear has now developed.

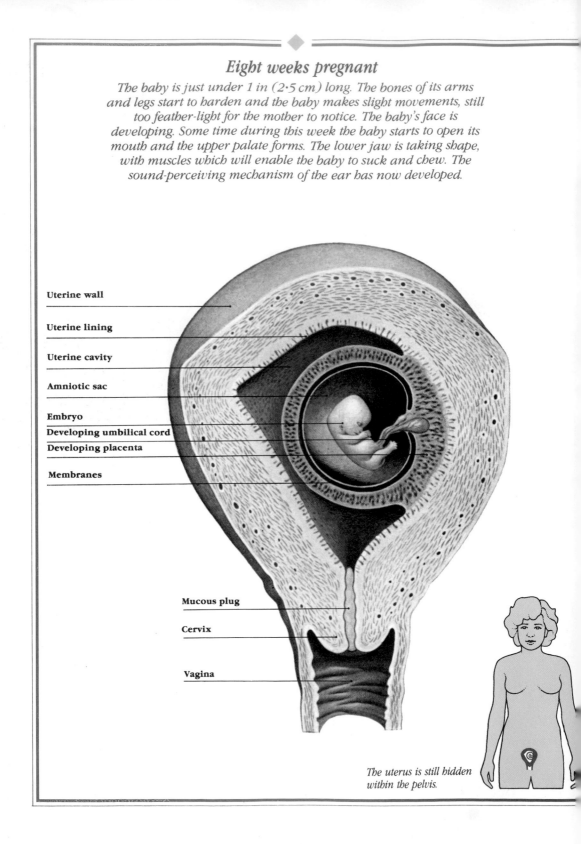

Uterine wall

Uterine lining

Uterine cavity

Amniotic sac

Embryo

Developing umbilical cord

Developing placenta

Membranes

Mucous plug

Cervix

Vagina

The uterus is still hidden within the pelvis.

Twelve weeks pregnant

The baby is now just over 2 in (5 cm) long. Its head is more rounded and is no longer so top-heavy: it is about two-thirds the size of the body. The eyes are widely separated in a broad face. The jaws have 32 permanent tooth buds and the baby is starting to suck. It is already exercising the muscles that will be used in breathing after birth.

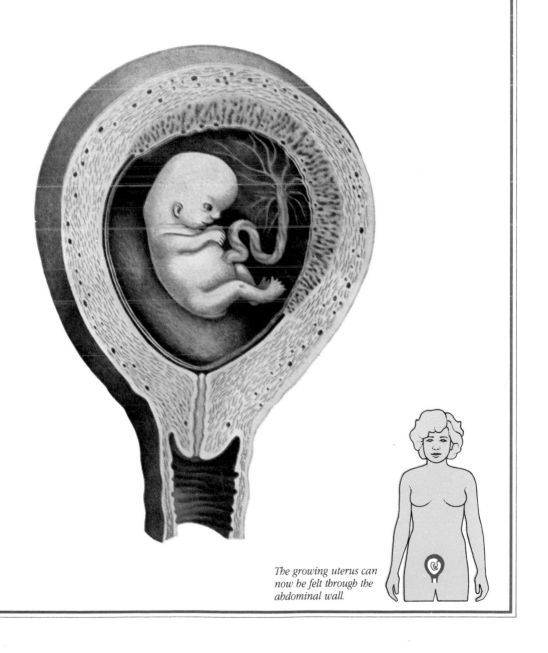

The growing uterus can now be felt through the abdominal wall.

Twenty weeks pregnant

The baby's rate of growth, which has been very rapid, slows down a little at this stage. It is about 10 in (25 cm) long. Legs are now the right length in proportion to the body and there are miniature nails on the toes. The mother feels movement, at first faint then growing stronger. Hair on the baby's head and delicately etched eyebrows have appeared and there is a fine downy hair called lanugo over much of the body.

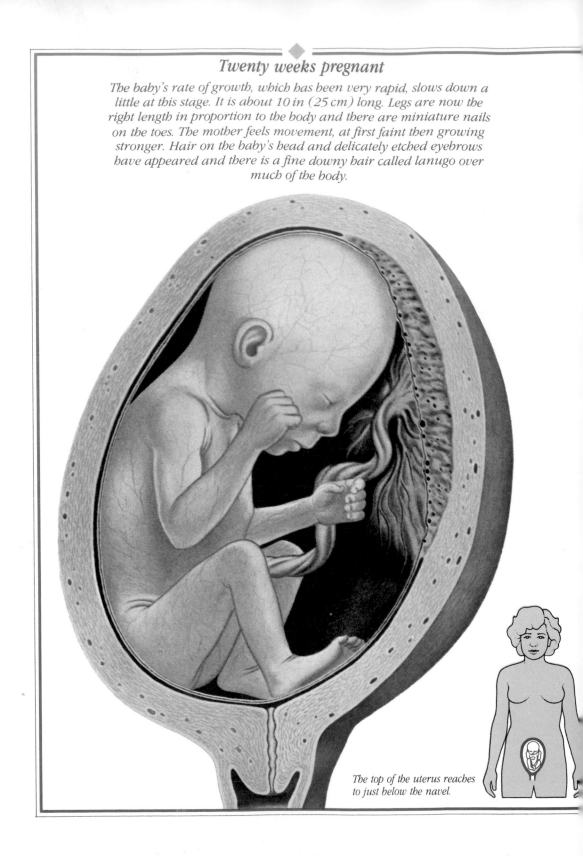

The top of the uterus reaches to just below the navel.

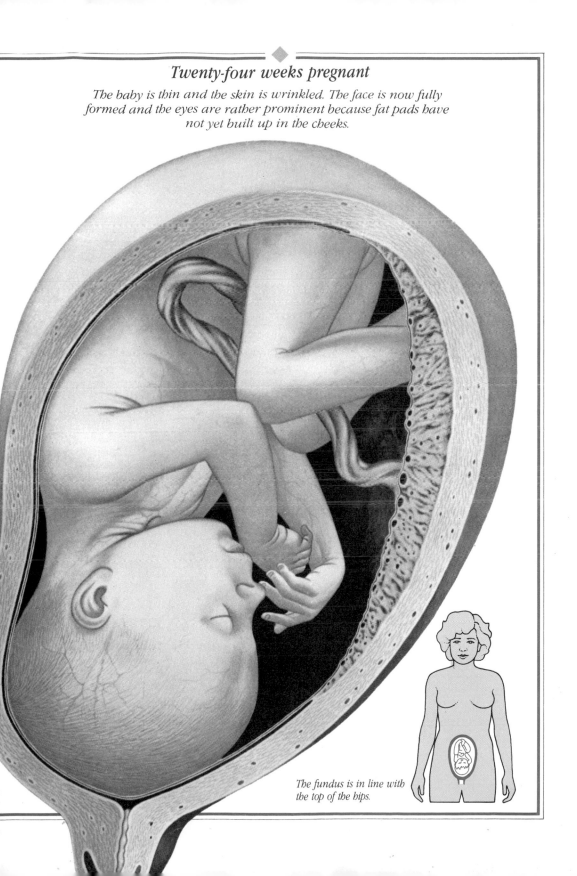

Twenty-four weeks pregnant

The baby is thin and the skin is wrinkled. The face is now fully formed and the eyes are rather prominent because fat pads have not yet built up in the cheeks.

The fundus is in line with the top of the hips.

Thirty-six weeks pregnant

There is no longer enough room in the uterus for the baby to move about freely. It has settled into one position and the main movements the mother feels are jabs from the arms and legs. By now the skin is smooth and peachlike and the body has plumped out. When the baby is awake, the eyes are open and it is aware of strong light flowing through the tissues of its mother's abdominal wall. If it is born at this time, the baby has an excellent chance of survival.

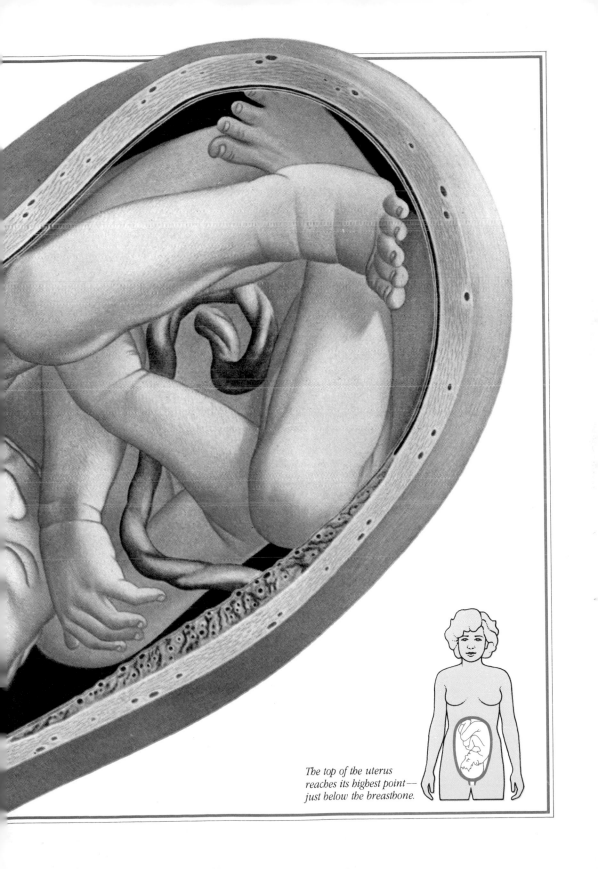

The top of the uterus reaches its highest point — just below the breastbone.

Forty weeks pregnant

The baby is now about eight times bigger than it was at three months, when all its vital organs were formed, and has increased in weight approximately 600 times. Most of the lanugo has dropped off, though there may still be some down the center of the back, in front of the ears and low on the forehead. The fingernails extend beyond the fingers and may need cutting at birth so that the baby does not scratch its face.

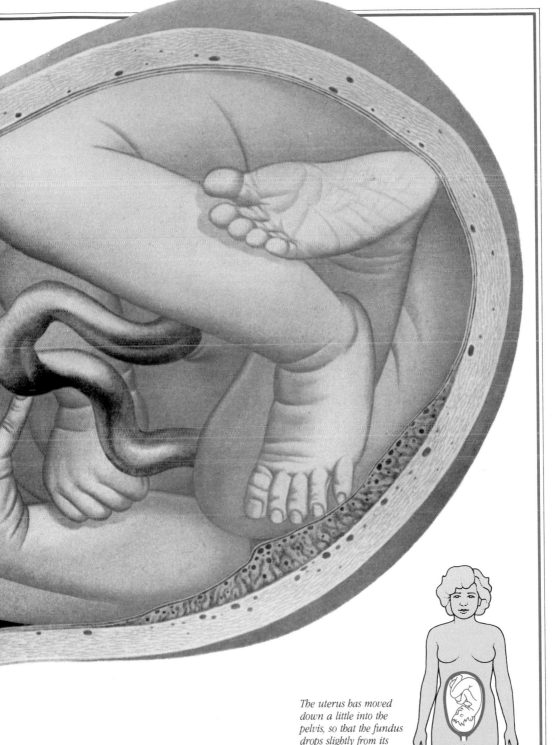

The uterus has moved
down a little into the
pelvis, so that the fundus
drops slightly from its
highest point.

Expecting twins

Finding out that you are going to have twins usually comes as a shock. Some women suspect quite early in their pregnancy that this will be the case, especially if they have already had a singleton pregnancy with which they can compare this one. If you are a fraternal twin (see below), you are about twice as likely to give birth to twins yourself as are other women, so you may be on the lookout for any confirmation of your suspicions. The chances of having fraternal twins depend on heredity, age, race, and the number of children you have already had. Although fraternal twins often skip a generation, the chances of them occurring in successive generations are high. The frequency of identical twins seems independent of these variables.

Mixed feelings

However, if nothing has led you to suspect that you are carrying more than one baby, it can be very upsetting to be told, after an ultrasound

How twins are conceived

Normally conception occurs when one egg released from a woman's ovary is fertilized by one male sperm. Seven out of ten pairs of twins result from the woman releasing two eggs, which are then fertilized independently by two sperm (fraternal twins). Usually the two eggs then implant and develop separately in the uterus. Less commonly, one egg fertilized by one sperm divides, resulting in two developing babies with the same inherited characteristics (identical twins). Often this division occurs after implantation in the uterus.

IDENTICAL TWINS
Identical twinning occurs after, rather than at, fertilization, and often after implantation in the uterus. As a result the twins almost always share a placenta although each has its own cord and bag of water.

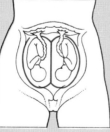

FRATERNAL TWINS
Fraternal twins have separate water bags and cords, and separate placentas. Occasionally the two eggs implant close together in the uterus, so that the placentas become fused and it looks as if there is only one.

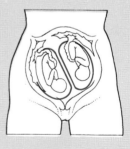

Monozygotic (one-egg) or identical twins

Dizygotic (two-egg) or fraternal twins

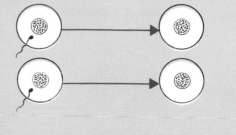

scan or a prenatal visit (see page 50), that suddenly all your expectations of birth and the time afterward need re-adjusting.

If you are to be a mother for the first time, the natural apprehension you originally felt about the labor and how you would cope with a new baby is greatly increased. Added to this you wonder how you will manage two babies at the same time in all their noisy reality— two mouths to feed, two diapers to change each time, two babies to bathe, two loads of clothes to wash, two budding personalities who will need your love and attention.

One woman, who was dismayed on hearing that she was expecting twins, said that she never really veered from this attitude throughout the rest of her pregnancy. During a hospital stay in her eighth month of pregnancy, she took the opportunity of watching mothers who had recently given birth to twins, and felt that all her worries were justified, since they seemed to have such trouble in managing two babies. However, shortly after her twins were born, she was able to comment on the "totally unexpected delight of being able to breast-feed both, often simultaneously". She did admit, though, that it was hard work at first and that "the intense joy and delight the babies now give has only come as we have got to know them."

=**66**=
I heard that I was expecting twins when I was about 29 weeks pregnant, spent two days weeping intermittently, and didn't really whip up much enthusiasm about the idea right to the end of the pregnancy.
=**99**=

Positions of twins in the uterus

Twins fill the available space in the uterus more quickly than a single baby, so they may adopt the positions in which they will be born at an earlier stage.

The pictures below show fraternal twins (with two placentas), but the same positions apply to identical twins (with a single placenta).

This presentation, with both twins in the cephalic or head down position, is the most common. It is also the most straightforward: birth should present no special complication.

When one twin is head down and the other head up the breech baby is often born second. The first baby opens up the birth canal so that the breech baby can usually be born vaginally without difficulty.

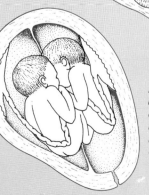

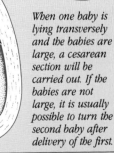

If both babies are breech the risk of complications will be evaluated in advance. A cesarean section may be performed in preference to a vaginal delivery.

When one baby is lying transversely and the babies are large, a cesarean section will be carried out. If the babies are not large, it is usually possible to turn the second baby after delivery of the first.

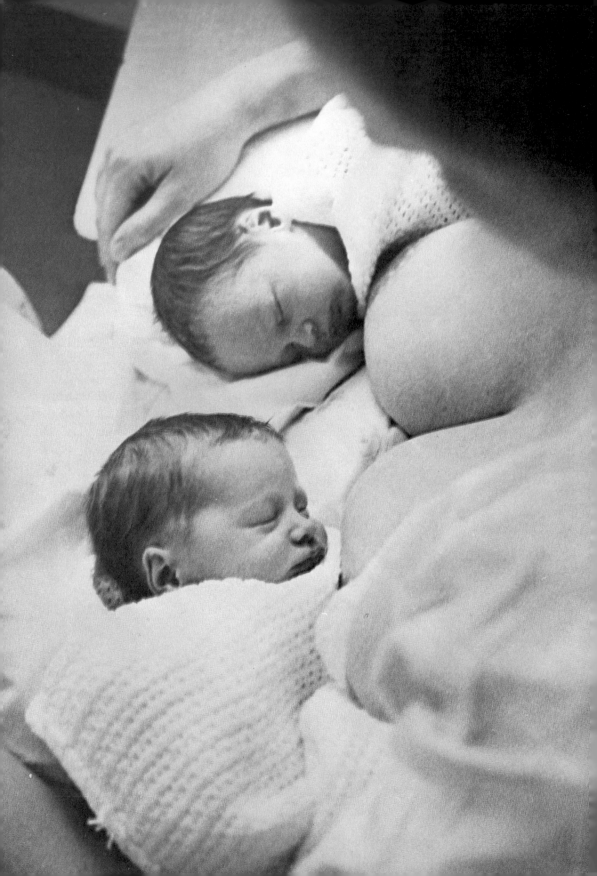

Sometimes a woman is unhappy to discover that she is expecting twins because she has been planning for a home birth and this may no longer be possible. Doctors usually advise hospital birth for twins, since the chances of a complicated delivery, especially for the second twin, are increased and it is possible that the babies will be premature and underweight.

Alternatively a woman may be overjoyed to find that she is going to have twins. Perhaps she had wanted more than one child, but was not particularly enjoying her pregnancy and certainly not looking forward to another. Suddenly she discovers that she can have two children for the price of one pregnancy and labor!

Rest

The first thing to accept is that a pregnancy with two babies tumbling about inside can be more of a strain than an ordinary pregnancy. The risk of developing preeclampsia (see page 126) is higher; since the babies are more likely to be born prematurely, they may not be so strong. Because they have to share the space in the uterus and the nutrition available through the placenta, twins are often of low birthweight. To help avoid extra strain, you need regular rest times and frequent early nights. If you already have other children, it is worth making an effort to find some motherly (or fatherly) person who can look after them for an hour or so each day so that you can relax without feeling that you will be needed in a minute.

In late pregnancy a baby who has not been growing well in the uterus invariably grows better if the mother has more rest and actually stays in bed (lying down in a darkened room for three hours every afternoon is ideal). This is why many obstetricians move you into the hospital for a compulsory rest. But if you are able to plan ahead and make other arrangements, you may avoid any anxiety about the babies' growth and be able to convince your doctor that you can reorganize your life well enough to take adequate rest at home.

There is no need to be an invalid. But if you think about the extra demands made on your body by a multiple pregnancy you will realize that your whole system has to adjust to the babies' needs. Such an adjustment involves widespread metabolic changes; there is also extra pressure put on your digestive organs and on your diaphragm and lungs, as well as stress on bones (on your lower ribs, which tend to splay out, and on your spine, for example). Your muscles, too, cope with much of the stress of a twin pregnancy, especially your tummy muscles, your pelvic floor, and the muscles of legs, feet, arms, shoulders and back, which have to support the extra weight and do the work of lifting and coping with your body mechanics. Above all this a general crowding out may make you feel very full and heavy.

So rest is good for you and will help your body adjust to the increased demands made on it by a multiple pregnancy. And the rest that helps most is rest taken *before* you become exhausted and irritable and *before* you feel that you cannot carry on a minute longer.

We didn't find out until the eighth month that we were expecting twins, and then we were delighted. The initial shock of the news left me feeling physically a bit weak at the knees, but there was never any question about our joy at the prospect.

OPPOSITE
The prospect of twins may come as a shock, but the reality may more than compensate.

Comfort

You may find it very uncomfortable to lie flat. The heavy uterus is pressing on major blood vessels in that position too, so, both for your own comfort and for the blood supply to the babies, lie either well propped up or in a three-quarters-over position (see page 118). Prop your breasts with one pillow and put two under your upper knee if this feels good. Even more so than with a singleton pregnancy, special back supports may be needed in the last few weeks. A large bean bag may be comfortable; so might a contour pillow with other pillows, two firm foam wedges, or the kind of cushion that is sold for reading in bed. Whatever you choose, try to get something solid which will support the exaggerated curve of your lower spine.

BACK SUPPORT
If you are carrying twins you are most likely to feel the strain caused by the extra weight in the small of your back. A large bean bag or firm floor cushion or a contour pillow (far right) will give you the support you need.

Exercise

Sensible body mechanics are also more important when you are expecting more than one baby (see pages 115–119). Learn how to counteract the effect of the enlarged and heavy uterus by standing straight and tall, with tail tucked in. Aim to balance on the balls of your feet rather than being flatfooted and waddling like a duck, which is only too easy to do when you are overtired. Above all, learn how to get up from a lying-down position by rolling over, if necessary kicking off with your foot and hand against solid objects, and then rising on to all fours (see page 113).

Pelvic-floor exercises (see page 107) are important throughout, whether you are carrying one baby or two; with twins they will be especially vital after the birth, as the muscles around the vagina have been stretched by the extra weight of two babies. It is a good idea in any case to do these exercises from early pregnancy, before there is any appreciable change in weight, as muscle tone is really best built up before there is any particular stress on the muscles. If your pelvic-floor muscles are under a great deal of strain, you should do these exercises while lying on the floor with your lower legs raised on a chair. In this position weight is not pressing on the pelvic muscles, and it is easier to feel what is happening there, even in advanced pregnancy when the babies may be very low down.

You will probably be aware of the babies moving a great deal inside you. Your abdomen feels like a basket full of puppies. It can be difficult to sleep, and you are often awakened by all the internal activity. Practicing release from tension and deliberately letting muscles relax all over your body can help enormously (see page 172).

Some mothers worry in case the babies are harming each other. They can certainly shuffle each other up a bit, but each one is sealed off in its own bag of waters, and this also means that each baby bobs around like a cork in a glass of water. The water cushions them from shock and allows free movement until the very last weeks of pregnancy when the pelvic girdle cradles the babies so closely that you may feel only small movements.

Diet

For a detailed discussion of diet in pregnancy see page 86. The demands made on your body by a twin pregnancy require an even more careful attention to diet than is necessary in a singleton pregnancy. Aim for a nutritious diet with plenty of salads and fruit and only those foods which are of positive value to yourself and the babies. Cut out the ice creams, flabby slices of bread, sickly doughnuts, and cookies. The easiest way to do this is to convince yourself how awful they are and to think instead of rich golden hunks of cheese, glowing fruit salad, a peach that melts in the mouth, jade-green watercress, rosy apples and a luscious, long glass of milk.

To save laboring over a hot stove have at least one raw food meal a day, which will give you a good supply of vitamins. You may like to buy some new cookbooks that concentrate on salads and fruit and stimulate your imagination. If you normally eat white bread and cereals, now is the time to switch to wholewheat bread and flour, brown rice, and whole grains. Eating like this will help you after the babies come, too, as you cannot feel full of vitality if you are poorly nourished and weighed down with "junk" foods.

The more tired you become the more you may feel that you cannot be bothered about preparing meals and shopping for food. But your health depends on your having a good diet and not skimping on protein, vitamins, and minerals. Is there any chance of getting help with marketing? Could someone else shop for you? Or could you and your partner or a friend do it together in bulk, loading up a car? (But do not lift boxes and bags into the trunk yourself or attempt to unload them!) If you have to shop unaided, use a wheeled shopping cart and avoid carrying bags. There is probably a store in your area which will deliver provided that you order enough at one time. If you live in the country, a village store may do this when they know you are expecting twins. Or could your partner take a neighbor who has no car to the supermarket, so that she can help him do your marketing?

Your baby's wellbeing

Looking after yourself in pregnancy, from the very first weeks, is probably more important for the welfare of your baby than anything else you can do. It ensures that you provide the best possible environment for the developing baby—and, equally important, it gives you the best chance of being healthy and full of vitality, ready for the birthday and the first stages of motherhood.

NUTRITION

Your baby depends on what you eat and drink for adequate nourishment in the uterus. In the sixties it was thought that provided the expectant mother had a "sensible" diet there was no need to give her any advice about what she should eat, because the fetus would always take what it needed. There were certain "do nots", the most important of which was "do not eat for two." But such a vague instruction led to large numbers of women going through pregnancy on inadequate diets.

Weighing yourself gives an indication of the progress of your pregnancy, but it should not become an obsession.

Then, in the seventies, research revealed that when pregnant women have an inadequate diet, their babies may die or be born in poor health, and women may have difficult pregnancies and labors, as well as subsequent illness*. If a woman is nutritionally deprived, her baby is deprived too; she is more likely to have a miscarriage and, if the pregnancy is maintained, her baby is more likely either to be born prematurely or to be of low birthweight because it has not received sufficient nourishment in the uterus. The research also revealed that poor nutrition in the later part of pregnancy can affect the child's brain development*.

Weight gain in pregnancy

Your total weight gain in pregnancy is made up as follows:

Weight of baby	38%
Weight of placenta	9%
Weight of amniotic fluid	11%
Increase in weight of uterus and breasts	20%
Increase in weight of blood	22%
Total weight gain	100%

However much weight you gain during your pregnancy, you will gain it at approximately the following rate:

0–12 weeks	0%
12–20 weeks	25%
20–30 weeks	50%
30–36 weeks	25%
36–40 weeks	0%

So, as a rough guide, you can assume that if—for instance—you are 30 weeks pregnant, the weight you have gained since the beginning of your pregnancy will be about 75% of your total weight gain.

However, recent research has shown that sometimes too much emphasis has been placed on having huge quantities of food and a great deal of animal protein. Metabolic changes in pregnancy mean that most women can make better use of the food they eat, and this increased efficiency extends into the period of breastfeeding, too*. So there is no need to worry too much about whether you are having the right diet, routinely taking vitamin pills and mineral supplements, or to feel you ought to be eating foods you dislike just because you are told they are good for the baby.

Weight gain

It is normal to put on between 20 and 30 lbs in pregnancy (9–13·5 kg). Some women put on more, with no ill effects. It is wrong to assume that because your baby will weigh only $6\frac{1}{4}$ to $8\frac{1}{2}$ lbs (3–4 kg) at birth, all the rest of the weight that you put on is fat. You must consider the weight of the placenta, the membranes, and the amniotic fluid, as well as the increase in size of the uterus and breasts, and the increase in volume of your blood. Fluid retention also accounts for a substantial weight gain in some women (see page 92). All these things return to normal after the birth.

Since different women gain weight at different rates it is impossible to be dogmatic about how much weight you should put on. Responsible medical opinion now is that "arbitrary weight restriction is potentially harmful to both mother and baby"*. If you start off your pregnancy underweight you and your baby may benefit from a bigger weight gain than the woman who begins pregnancy already overweight. It is certainly most unwise for any woman to try to remain slim during pregnancy, and an attempt to keep your figure might result in the eventual loss of your baby. On the other hand, if you start pregnancy overweight, you are likely to put on more weight than a woman who is not fat at the onset of pregnancy, and you are more likely to suffer from high blood pressure and urinary tract infection*.

One way of checking to see whether you are putting on superfluous fat, which you will be left with after the birth, is to measure your upper thighs each week, keeping a record of the measurement. This is a way of recording the increase in your own body fat as distinct from the weight you gain as a result of the pregnancy. The measurement should stay about the same, although fluid retention may increase it slightly in the last weeks of pregnancy.

Your upper thighs should stay about the same size throughout pregnancy.

Protein

Women who are not pregnant are recommended to have $1\frac{1}{2}$ oz (46 g) of protein a day for optimum health. When you are pregnant you may need about twice as much. The foods rich in protein are lean meat, fish, beans, nuts, brewer's yeast, milk, yogurt, all the various cheeses and the other dairy products.

All proteins are made up of chemical substances—called amino acids—in different combinations. Animal or "first-class" proteins contain all the amino acids necessary for the protein to do its body-building work; vegetable proteins, which used to be called "second-class", contain only some of these amino acids, and therefore they should be eaten either with a small quantity of animal protein or in different combinations. If you are a vegetarian who eats no animal products, combine beans with a wheat product at the same meal—say, beans with wholegrain flour pastry, chickpeas with pasta, or lentils with wholewheat bread*.

You will obtain adequate protein if every day you have one dish from each of the following categories: a) one helping of meat or fish, two eggs, a cup of peanuts or cashew nuts; b) 4 oz (100 g) of hard cheese, 8 oz (200 g) cottage cheese or 1 quart of milk (substitute soy, nut milk, or tofu); c) four slices of wholewheat bread, a helping of brown rice or wholegrain pasta, or one large potato baked in its jacket. If you are a vegan and do not eat any animal products, you will obviously not want cheese and milk, and should have a good helping of legumes instead.

Protein becomes particularly important if you are ill or fighting an infection, or if you feel overtaxed and exhausted. If you cannot face proper meals, protein and other essential foods can be obtained in the form of a drink. Try the following high-energy cocktail:

High-protein shake

1 cup of low fat milk
$\frac{1}{3}$ cup of instant nonfat dry milk powder
4 tablespoons of soy powder (available from health food stores)
1 cup of chopped fruit (strawberries, banana, pears, apricots, etc.)
1 tablespoon of honey
4 ice cubes

Blend all the ingredients on high speed until smooth. You can either drink the shake (try chilling it for an hour or so first), or freeze the mixture until slushy before eating it with a spoon.

Carbohydrates

You need carbohydrates for energy. They are found in sugar, and in the foods you eat in bulk, such as bread, flour, cereals, and root vegetables. Most foods containing carbohydrates have other valuable nutrients too; potatoes—especially if you eat them in their jackets—can contribute protein and vitamin C as well as carbohydrate, and wholewheat bread provides B vitamins, iron, and the fiber which helps to prevent constipation. If you eat small quantities of these foods daily, you should need no other carbohydrates. But if foods rich in carbohydrates are the foods you enjoy most, you may put on unnecessary weight.

A high-protein, low-fat refresher can give you an instant lift when you are feeling weary.

If you are overweight before starting pregnancy, or if you are putting on a lot of superfluous fat (see page 87 for a method of checking this), it is a good idea to cut out all white flour and sugar, and all products containing them. Cakes, desserts, and cookies do not do much to help your unborn baby's health. If you like sugar in tea and coffee, train yourself to enjoy both of these without it.

Fats

Your body's need for fat is minimal. You can deliberately reduce your intake by trimming fat off meat, by using less butter, by boiling or steaming foods rather than frying or sautéing them, and by cutting out rich sauces. You will find that cottage or curd cheese and yogurt are both useful ingredients of low fat sauces, and that you can make fatfree sauces with puréed vegetables.

Milk and dairy products

Milk is usually recommended for the pregnant woman, but unless your diet is grossly inadequate in protein you do not need more than 1 quart a day. Consumed in large quantities milk is fattening, and if you fill yourself up with milk drinks you are likely to dampen your appetite for other foods you and your baby need. Some women do not like milk or are allergic to it. You can have fatfree milk or take cheese or yogurt instead; if it is simply a matter of taste, disguise the milk in sauces or dishes where you are not aware of it.

Vitamins

It is important that most of your vitamin intake should come from food. Trying to get the right dosage of vitamins, and the right balance between different vitamins, from supplements is unwise. The chart on page 90 tells you which vitamins are in which foods, what they are for and whether it is ever advisable to take a supplement.

Minerals

Minerals and trace elements are a vital part of your diet, but if you are eating plenty of food rich in protein and vitamins you are unlikely to suffer from a mineral deficiency. Iron, calcium, and zinc are probably the only minerals about which you need to be especially concerned.

Iron is necessary for the formation of red blood cells. Red blood cells contain a substance known as hemoglobin; if your blood contains insufficient hemoglobin not enough oxygen is carried to your baby and you become very tired. Vitamin C helps your body to absorb iron, whereas antacid medicines stop you from benefiting fully from it. Liver is a good source of iron, as are dark molasses, egg yolk, whole grains, legumes, all dark green leafy vegetables such as watercress, raisins, prunes, brewer's yeast, and nuts.

Extra iron is often prescribed in pregnancy. If you eat plenty of foods rich in iron, you should have good reserves stored in your liver,

Vitamins in pregnancy

Vitamin	What it does	Foods it is in	Increase needed in pregnancy	Supplement needed
Vitamin A	Maintains skin, body tissues, vision; helps your body to resist infection.	Mainly green and orange vegetables, liver. Also dairy foods.	None.	None.
B VITAMINS B₁ Thiamine	Maintains brains, heart and nerves. Enables your body to make use of carbohydrate.	Most foods, but especially whole grains and yeast products. Lost in over-cooking.	None.	None.
B₂ Riboflavin	Helps tissue growth and regeneration, especially skin and eyes. Allows your body to use carbo-hydrate, fat, and protein.	Mainly yeast, legumes, and green vegetables. Also milk, eggs, brains, kidneys, and liver. Often lost if exposed to light.	None.	None.
B₆ Pyridoxine	Allows your body to make use of protein. Ensures cell division.	Most foods, but especially meat, fish, dried vegetables, whole grains, potatoes, bananas.	None.	None. In fact it is wise to avoid a supplement as large amounts can suppress lactation and some cases of "rebound" deficiency have been reported in babies whose mothers took enormous doses during pregnancy.
B₁₂ Cyano-cobalamin	Helps to form hemo-globin and the baby's central nervous system. Allows your body to make use of protein, folic acid, and fatty acids.	Meat and fish, especially liver.	None.	A capsule might be advisable for vegetarians.
Niacin	Helps to keep tissues healthy and allows your body to use protein.	Meat, fish, peanuts, legumes, eggs, milk.	None.	None.
Pantothenic acid	Maintains nerves and red blood cells. Essential for breakdown of fat and carbohydrate.	Most foods, especially meat, eggs, cheese, whole grains, peanuts, and some green vegetables.	90%—nearly double the normal intake.	None.
Folic acid	Aids cell division and the development of the baby's central nervous system.	Liver, green leafy vegetables.	100%—double the normal intake.	Often prescribed at the same time as iron.
Vitamin C	Helps form connective tissue and assists absorption of iron. Maintains blood vessel walls, helping to prevent hemorrhage; assists healing and the formation of bones.	Fresh vegetables and fresh fruit, especially citrus fruit.	None.	Occasionally prescribed to help the absorption of iron.
Vitamin D	Helps form and maintain bones.	Liver and fish liver oils. Butter, egg yolk, milk.	None.	None.
Vitamin E	Helps to protect cells from damage and degeneration.	Most foods, especially wheatgerm.	None.	None.
Vitamin K	Plays vital part in process leading to blood coagulation.	Manufactured in human colon. Also in green leafy vegetables.	None.	None.

and not need to take extra. The fetus draws on these reserves, so that it can store enough in its own liver to last for several months after birth—a vital need, since milk contains almost no iron. But if you are iron-deficient (slightly anemic) before embarking on pregnancy (and many women are, without realizing it), a supplement is probably advisable.

You probably need about twice as much iron when you are pregnant as you do before conception.

Calcium is necessary for the formation of strong bones and teeth. It enables blood to clot and your muscles to work smoothly. The oxalic acid in spinach and cocoa reduces the absorption of calcium: do not depend on a chocolate milk drink for your calcium intake.

Your baby's teeth start to bud very early on in pregnancy, so your calcium intake in the first four months matters a great deal. Milk is a useful source, as are other dairy foods. Calcium is also present in leafy vegetables, sea vegetables, whole grains, legumes, carrot juice, and nuts. You need almost twice as much when you are pregnant.

Zinc deficiency may result in miscarriage, growth retardation in the uterus, stillbirth, or congenital handicap*. There is also some evidence that zinc is necessary for muscles to contract well and, though it is difficult to measure accurately the concentration of zinc in human tissues, that shortage of zinc is one cause of long labor*. Taking an iron supplement can interfere with the absorption of zinc. High fiber foods—especially bran—contain zinc, as do brazil nuts, Parmesan and other hard cheeses, seeds, herring, and meat.

Women at risk

Certain women are at "nutritional risk" and need to pay special attention to diet; for them vitamin and mineral supplements may be useful. The ones who may be at risk are those pregnant during adolescence (while they are still growing themselves), women who are underweight when they become pregnant, women who are overweight because of excess consumption of carbohydrates and fats, those living on a very restricted range of foods like a macrobiotic diet, women who have lost a baby from miscarriage or stillbirth before, and women who have had three pregnancies within two years. Also included in this category are women suffering from some chronic diseases involving the regular use of drugs, women who smoke, heavy drinkers, and those with multiple pregnancies*.

Research* suggests that if a woman who has previously given birth to a baby with a neural tube defect (spina bifida or anencephaly) takes a multivitamin preparation for at least one month *before conception* and up to the second missed period, the chance of having another handicapped baby is much reduced. The woman is well nourished both at the time of conception and during the crucial early stages, when the baby's spinal cord is being formed and a neural tube defect could occur. The research was carried out with mothers who already had one baby with a neural tube defect and whose chances of producing a second child with a similar handicap were therefore much higher than average. Only one such baby was born to 178 women who took the vitamins. Thirteen handicapped babies were born to 260 women who did not take the vitamins.

What we cannot conclude from this research is that because women at high risk benefit from multivitamins then *all* women should have them. Some researchers suspect that, in some cases, high doses of vitamin supplements may prove to have a mild teratogenic effect and lead to babies being born with handicaps.

Salt and fluid retention

It used to be thought that salt was dangerous in pregnancy and was one cause of preeclampsia (see page 126). It has now been established that salt is necessary for a normal pregnancy. When a group of expectant mothers had no-salt diets they had *more* pre-eclampsia than a control group of women who had as much salt as they wished*. Cutting out salt can also cause cramp in hot weather. Since you tend to retain more fluid when you are pregnant, you will only maintain the usual level of saltiness in all your body fluids by having as much salt as your appetite dictates*.

Occasionally special diets are prescribed for pregnant women in order to reduce fluid retention, which used to be thought dangerous in itself. But these special diets can harm the unborn baby. Women with mild fluid retention (edema) usually produce babies in just as good a condition as those who have no signs of it at all. Ankle, foot, and leg swelling on very hot days, when you have been on a plane trip or after you have been standing for a long time, is therefore nothing to worry about. If your skin is looking very puffy, take more rest and look at your diet to see if you should increase your protein intake (see page 87); if your fingers and face become swollen you should mention it to the doctor, as it is a sign that your kidneys are not coping well with the excretion of waste products from your body. This in turn may mean that your placenta is not working efficiently.

You cannot prevent edema by cutting down on fluids, so drink as much as you want. Four or five glasses of water a day will help your kidneys to function well throughout pregnancy.

Eating a balanced diet

I'm taking the opportunity of reforming Chris's eating habits. It's all salads and wholewheat bread and food that's good for you.

Bear in mind that you are providing nutrition for three distinct but interdependent biological entities: your own body, the developing baby, and the placenta*. This triple nutritional task demands a good, high-protein diet rich in vitamins and minerals.

A salad a day is a must, but remember that you can use finely chopped cabbage when lettuce and other greens are hard to find, and that it makes a nice change. Experiment with salads and try mixing fruit and vegetables. Apples go with most savory things. A baked

◆

potato with cheese and a cabbage-based salad are a good source of protein, Vitamin C, and calcium. If you can spare time to bake your own wholegrain bread, add extra wheat germ or soy flour and you have added to your diet another valuable source of protein, iron, B vitamins, and fiber.

Eating well does not always mean eating expensively. Some women save money by avoiding unnecessary foods such as carbonated drinks, coffee, packaged desserts and soups, bakery and candy store items, and starchy sugary puddings. Milk and cheese are relatively cheap, and a delicious main course can be made from a selection of vegetables in season covered with a white sauce and topped with a layer of grated cheese browned under the grill.

DRUGS

The full range of substances to which the embryo and fetus may be vulnerable is not yet known. It is wise to take the fewest possible medicines of any kind during pregnancy, especially in the first few weeks when the embryo is forming and when the placenta is only just starting to be active. (You should therefore take care during the second half of the menstrual cycle if there is any chance that you might be pregnant.) It used to be thought that the placenta acted as an effective barrier to all poisons in the maternal bloodstream. But it is now known that many drugs—including nicotine and alcohol— can cross the placenta and may affect the baby*.

If you think of how the fertilized egg has to segment, travel along the fallopian tube, embed itself into the lining of the uterus, and develop into a baby, you can imagine how such delicate and complex processes can be interfered with by chemicals which have been introduced into your bloodstream.

The liver and the kidneys are the organs of your body which deal with drugs and turn them into material which can be excreted in the urine. In an unborn—and even a newborn—baby these organs are still immature. The fetus is therefore not able to excrete many of the drugs which may reach it through the placenta. Instead, such drugs can accumulate in its body in toxic quantities. It is vital to remember, when taking any drug, that a dosage which may be right for you is far in excess of that which is suitable for your tiny baby.

Everyone remembers the thalidomide disaster*, when a sedative which was thought to be mild and safe was prescribed for women in early pregnancy. As a result of this sedative more than five thousand babies were born with badly deformed limbs, or none at all. Thalidomide is an extreme example of the effect that a drug can have on the development of an unborn baby. But all drugs are potentially harmful if misused. You should think carefully before taking any drug when pregnant, especially in the early weeks. The word *drug* here includes not only prescribed drugs, but also nicotine, alcohol, and medicines bought over the counter such as laxatives or aspirin.

═ ❝ ═

Everything you read in the papers about drugs in early pregnancy, it's so terrifying! I can't remember what I took in those 8 weeks and it's haunting me.

═ ❞ ═

Drugs which are known to cause abnormalities of any kind are said to be "teratogenic". In the very early stages of a pregnancy any toxic or teratogenic drugs would probably prevent the egg from ever settling firmly in the uterus, so that you would not even realize that you were pregnant but would just have a delayed period; if you were to take the same drug slightly later, you would probably miscarry. At a later stage still, the pregnancy might continue, but there would be a risk of the baby being damaged by the drug.

Weighing the different risks

Clearly some pregnant women need drugs, and may be very ill without them. Illness in the mother can also affect the developing baby. For instance running a very high temperature (see page 102) seems to be teratogenic at certain phases of pregnancy, so it may be safer to take aspirin to get your temperature down than to try and cope without any medicines. It is always a question of balancing the risks to the baby against your need and the stress which may be caused to you by not having drug treatment.

Since the thalidomide disaster there has been acute awareness of the need to screen all new drugs before they are prescribed to pregnant women, and doctors are being increasingly careful. But drugs which have been in use a long time remain on the market without being tested. And it is difficult to be certain about any drugs, because animal experiments may produce damage in one species, yet not in another. This can work either way: rats may be affected, but not human babies, or babies may be affected when rats are not.

People are often ignorant about the chemical substances they introduce into their bodies. Antacids for the relief of indigestion, cough medicines, sleeping pills (barbiturates), antihistamines used in the treatment of hay fever, and antibiotics are just some commonly used drugs which alter the body's chemical balance. A great many pregnant women take over-the-counter as well as prescribed drugs of one kind or another in the first weeks of pregnancy, and no one has much idea of the possible risks. There are other substances which you may not think of as being drugs, including cigarettes and alcohol. Even tea and coffee have been researched for harmful effects, though normal use (half a dozen cups a day) seems to be fine*.

Smoking

There are positive steps you can take to give your baby the best start in life and other things which you should avoid since they are known to be detrimental. First and foremost among the dangers is smoking. Whether or not you inhale, nicotine passes into your bloodstream and from there into the baby's. It makes the fetal heart speed up and interrupts the baby's respiratory movements which are a rehearsal for breathing. In effect, the baby coughs and splutters.

Smoking interferes with the efficiency of the placenta and is the most widespread and efficient way of pumping a powerful poison into an unborn baby's bloodstream. Nicotine makes the blood vessels in the placenta constrict so that less oxygen and fewer nutritional substances reach the baby.

Mothers who smoke bear babies who weigh less than babies of mothers who do not smoke and the baby's weight drops in direct relation to the number of cigarettes consumed*. This does not mean that some smokers do not have good-sized babies but that statistically babies of smokers can be shown to be deprived of the best possible nutrition in the uterus. The reason for this is not just that a woman who smokes tends to eat less. Cigarettes have a direct effect on the growth of the baby*. It could be that some women make the mistake of thinking that labor will be easier if their babies are lighter in weight. Labor with a tiny, underweight baby is no easier or shorter than labor with a good-sized baby, and your baby is much more likely to be healthy and easy to care for if you have not smoked.

Smoking after the fourth month of pregnancy is a major cause of prematurity and the birth of underweight babies who, although they have had the full time in the uterus, are stunted in development and may have to be cared for in a special care baby unit. Smoking also increases the chances of bleeding during pregnancy, miscarriage (women who smoke are twice as likely to miscarry as those who do not), premature rupture of the membranes, premature separation of the placenta, hemorrhage before or early in labor, hemorrhage after delivery, congenital abnormality, stillbirth, and death of the baby in the week following delivery*. The more a woman smokes, the more likely these things are to happen.

I really get scared when someone lights up. I think, "Why should my baby have that poison in its bloodstream?" I can get quite rude about it!

How to give it up If you are a heavy smoker and dependent on cigarettes to get through the day it may be very difficult to give them up, even for the sake of your baby. Fortunately, the nausea of early pregnancy or just a sudden dislike of cigarettes prompts many women to cut them out. Even if this does not happen spontaneously you can use the techniques of aversion therapy to condition yourself to break the habit. Every time you feel queasy or vomit make yourself think "cigarette" and use the association between vividly picturing the act of smoking and the overwhelming sensations of nausea to train yourself to develop a dislike of cigarettes.

How to cut down If you are past the nauseous stage of pregnancy or feel perfectly fit throughout, as many women do, you should still try to reduce your cigarettes to at least half of the usual number. Ask your partner to help by cutting down his consumption in the same way; if the two of you are making the same effort, your determination is strengthened. Also, recent studies suggest that even being in a smoky room for a long time—being a "passive" smoker—should be avoided. The more you can both cut down the better.

You may be feeling terribly guilty about smoking while still unable to give it up. You might feel like a murderer, but the guiltier you become the more you want a cigarette to help you calm down. It is certain that guilt and emotional stress can also affect your metabolism adversely, including your heart rate, blood pressure, breathing, muscle tone, and the adrenalin in your bloodstream. The question then arises as to how much stress you should tolerate in trying to give up smoking. If you know how to release tension you may be able to cope by smoking each cigarette only halfway down and still find that it helps you enough to "unwind".

This is where your own judgment of the relative importance to you of smoking or not smoking in pregnancy is essential. Every pregnant woman has the right to be fully informed of the risks of smoking and also to make her own decision on the subject. No one can *make* you stop smoking, however many dire warnings they give: you decide.

On the other hand, your baby cannot choose whether or not to smoke. A mother chooses for her child.

Alcohol

Alcohol is as much a drug as anything you may take in the form of a pill. The safe minimal dose in pregnancy is not yet known, but because alcohol is socially accepted it is easy to forget that its use should be restricted. Fortunately, many women develop an aversion to it in any form.

Some women's metabolisms are unable to break alcohol down into harmless substances and it passes straight through the placenta to the fetus in its poisonous form. If you are one of these women, you should not drink at all. You can have a blood test after drinking to discover how well you are able to metabolize alcohol, but this is not done routinely. There is no reason why you should not ask your doctor to do this simple test before you even start a pregnancy.

The less well you metabolize alcohol the more careful you should be. Even if you metabolize it normally, there is evidence that a single "binge" during pregnancy may affect some babies, depending on the stage of development they have reached. So although common sense would indicate that you can drink in moderation and still have a perfect baby, unfortunately you cannot assume that this is the case. Limit your intake of alcohol to an occasional glass of wine.

Being careful about drugs

Think about any drugs you may be taking when you intend to conceive, and ask your doctor's advice. Do not wait until your first prenatal visit or even—if possible—until you are sure you are pregnant. If there is any chance that you might be pregnant, avoid taking any drugs which are not absolutely essential to your health.

If a doctor other than your obstetrician is treating you, especially in the early months of pregnancy before it is obvious that you are having a baby, make sure that he or she realizes that you are pregnant before prescribing. This may be particularly relevant if you are ill when away from home and have to consult a different doctor.

Go through your medicine chest when you stop using contraception. Make a list of the contents and ask your doctor whether there are any which are likely to be unsafe during pregnancy. Throw away, by flushing down the toilet, any drugs which were not prescribed for you or which are out of date, in addition to those which your doctor advises you to get rid of.

Mood changing drugs

Because so little is known about the effect of mood changing drugs it is wise to limit their use or cut them out altogether. Marijuana or Valium may help you to relax on an occasion when you cannot easily "switch off". But explore other ways of releasing tension. The effects of disciplined relaxation (see page 172) are likely to help your unborn baby more than anything you can take in through your mouth. They are positive things you can do for yourself and your baby, ways of tuning in to your body rather than making an attempt to escape from it or deaden its sensations.

Cannabis Little is known of the effects of cannabis on the baby. Its strength varies widely, and its immediate effects on the user vary with expectation, the company in which it is taken, and previous experience of it. Claims have been made that it can be teratogenic, but this is still being investigated.

Cocaine Whether the drug is taken by inhaling a powder (snorting), smoking it (crack) or injecting it (freebasing), a woman using cocaine is very likely to have a baby who is small for dates or premature, and who is addicted to the drug. These babies tend to be irritable and jumpy, and it is difficult to calm them down so that they take a satisfying feeding*.

Read the labels on all medications, including over-the-counter ones, and keep a list of anything you take right from the beginning of pregnancy.

Mild tranquilizers are often prescribed during pregnancy and do not seem to be harmful. Diazepam (Valium) is sometimes used in treating preeclampsia (see page 126) to bring blood pressure down. But it is best to stop taking even a mild tranquilizer as you approach the time when you expect to go into labor. Valium taken just before labor starts or during the course of labor can result in the baby having a low Apgar score (see page 328) at birth and breathing difficulties. The baby may also take a long time to start feeding properly, as well as become chilled more easily than usual*.

Powerful tranquilizers such as chlorpromazine (Thorazine) and haloperidol (Haldol) should not be used in pregnancy. If you think you might have conceived, change to a milder tranquilizer and see if it is sufficient to control your anxiety and reduce tension. The strong tranquilizers can affect the development of the baby's nervous system. In particular, Thorazine taken over a prolonged period of pregnancy can damage the baby's eyes*.

Sleeping pills

These include tranquilizers, antihistamines (see opposite) and hypnotics. Hypnotics are of two different kinds. Some are barbiturates, which are highly addictive even over a short period and now almost never prescribed: phenobarbital (Luminal), amobarbital (Amytal), pentobarbital (Nembutal), and secobarbital (Seconal). Others are not barbiturates: chloral hydrate, flurazepam (Dalmane), and glutethimide (Doriden). Non-barbiturates also seem to be addictive if taken over a long period. Not enough is known about the effect of hypnotics on the unborn baby, but they are cumulative. The drug concentrates in the mother's fatty tissues. Certainly large doses of barbiturates can cause respiratory depression at birth and feeding difficulties. The baby is doped along with the mother. Over-the-counter sleeping pills have not been tested for safety in pregnancy. The best solution is to try to do without sleeping pills; try to overcome insomnia by making time for more relaxation and exercise in the open air.

Painkillers

Aspirin The most widely used painkiller is aspirin (salicylate) and its derivatives. If you have a headache or other pain, try to get rid of it by resting in a quiet, darkened room. If rest is not an effective remedy, a few aspirin are unlikely to be harmful. But never dose yourself repeatedly: a recurring headache should be discussed with your doctor. If taken regularly (say every four to six hours) during the few days before you go into labor, aspirin can produce difficulties in blood clotting in the newborn baby and neonatal jaundice; sometimes it can damage the baby's central nervous system.

It is possible, however, that aspirin assists the circulation of blood through the placenta, and trials are currently taking place to see whether a low daily dose of aspirin can help in those pregnancies where there is inadequate flow of blood to the baby.

Codeine is addictive: the baby whose mother has been taking several pills daily throughout pregnancy may be born dependent, have severe withdrawal symptoms, and even die. Use it sparingly.

Acetaminophen (Tylenol) can cause liver and kidney damage if taken in large doses. Use it with caution in pregnancy, since the baby's liver and kidneys can suffer from relatively small doses.

Ibuprofen (Advil, Nupren, Motrin) has not been shown to be safe for the developing fetus. There is some evidence that it impedes the fetal circulation and may cause cardiac malformations.

Drugs to treat migraine can cause the uterus to contract during pregnancy, thus endangering the fetus.

Antinausea drugs

Drugs for nausea and vomiting are of three different kinds: anti-cholinergic drugs, antihistamines, and phenothiazines*. They can all have side effects.

The first category treats nausea by acting on your nervous system; it reduces secretions, including stomach acid, and relieves muscle spasm. No one can be sure whether these drugs are completely safe for the fetus. Antihistamines, which include Benadryl, Dramamine, and Chlor-Trimeton, block the action of histamine (a substance to which some people are allergic) and may cause drowsiness. They are best not used in pregnancy as high dosage may cause fetal abnormalities. The last category, the phenothiazines, are major tranquilizers, and are therefore inadvisable in pregnancy: the fetus may suffer the same adverse effects as from Thorazine (see page 97).

It seems then that drugs to control pregnancy sickness should not be used unless specifically prescribed by a doctor who knows you are pregnant, and then only when you have weighed up together the advantages and disadvantages of taking the drug. Do not take any pills for travel sickness if you think you may be pregnant.

Antibiotics

Antibiotics may be prescribed in pregnancy; obviously their use is sometimes necessary and any disadvantages to the baby are outweighed. Never use antibiotics left in a bottle which were prescribed for a previous infection, even if you have exactly the same kind of infection. Tell your doctor that you may be pregnant, or remind him or her that you are pregnant, when you ask for a prescription.

Penicillin appears to be a safe antibiotic to take at any time during the period of pregnancy.

Sulphonamides (which are not really antibiotics but effective antibacterials) are used to treat urinary infections. If you need to have sulphonamide treatment you should stop a week or so before the baby is due, to let it out of your system before you go into labor. Otherwise the newborn baby's kidneys may not be able to cope with excreting the drug and the baby may develop jaundice which can damage its central nervous system.

Tetracycline, a wide spectrum antibiotic, is deposited in the unborn baby's teeth and may cause yellow mottling and staining. It can also stop the growth of the baby's bones during the period when it is taken, so should not be used during pregnancy.

Streptomycin, another wide spectrum antibiotic, should never be taken in pregnancy. One of the drugs used to treat tuberculosis, it can cause deafness in the baby.

When I decided to get pregnant, I cleared the medicine chest and threw out all the half-used drugs and old bottles.

Drugs to treat constipation

Stool bulk producers, such as Colace, do no harm provided that they are used in moderation.

Stimulant laxatives, which include senna-based laxatives such as Senokot, cascara, Dorbane and Dulcolax, seem to be safe for the fetus, but they may cause you to lose excessive amounts of fluid. Make sure that you drink plenty of liquids if you are taking any of these preparations.

Saline laxatives, including milk of magnesia and magnesium sulfate (Epsom salts), can also cause dehydration if you do not drink plenty of fluids, but otherwise they do not appear to harm the fetus.

Various types of oil lubricate the bowels. But avoid liquid paraffin which reduces the absorption of Vitamins A, D, and K. A lack of Vitamin K may lead to disorders of blood clotting in the baby. Extra fluids alone may cure your constipation, especially if you adjust your diet to include a regular intake of bran. (See page 121 for more advice and information about constipation.)

Drugs to reduce fluid retention

Diuretics increase the excretion of salt and water from the body, and in so doing make your kidneys work very hard. They are used in the prevention and treatment of preeclampsia (see page 126). Since there is no proof that reducing fluid retention does prevent pre-eclampsia, it is best to avoid taking diuretics altogether*. Discuss the matter with your doctor.

Steroids

Steroids are used for the treatment of asthma or hay fever, for eczema and other skin disorders, and for rheumatism and arthritis. They affect the salt and water balance of the body, as well as sugar, carbohydrate, protein, fat, and calcium metabolism. Steroids may cause fetal abnormalities with prolonged use through pregnancy (although this is by no means always the case). But some women cannot avoid using them—women, for example, with severe asthma. If you are on steroids and plan to become pregnant, let your doctor know. It may be possible for you to change to a milder drug before starting the pregnancy.

Since steroids are often used in the form of skin ointments, do not use any cream or preparation prescribed for skin irritation when you are pregnant unless there is real need for it.

Drugs to treat thyroid conditions

You may need to take drugs for an under- or over-active thyroid, but be aware that such drugs can have an effect on the baby's thyroid. Propylthiouracil should be used only in low doses during pregnancy.

You should stop using it four or five weeks before the expected date of delivery, to allow the baby time to produce an adequate number of its own thyroid hormones, which the drug destroys. Discuss the drugs you are taking with your doctor, if possible before embarking on a pregnancy.

Anticoagulants

These drugs are prescribed for deep vein thrombosis or for a pulmonary embolism—both serious conditions caused by blood clots. Anticoagulants can cause hemorrhage in the baby and some, such as Coumadin, should not be taken in the last three months of pregnancy. If an anticoagulant needs to be given towards the end of the pregnancy, Heparin by injection is the safest. Any adverse effects on the fetus can be reversed in some cases by small doses of Vitamin K given to the baby after delivery*.

Drugs to treat diabetes

Drugs which are taken by mouth to reduce blood sugar should not be used during pregnancy*. They can cause miscarriage or fetal abnormalities. Injections of insulin, however, are safe. If you are diabetic and want to get pregnant, let your doctor know and discuss in advance how the pregnancy will be managed (see page 127).

Anticonvulsants

If you normally take anticonvulsants or antiepileptic drugs, discuss the possibility with your doctor of modifying your treatment before you conceive. These drugs may cause cleft palate in the baby.

General anesthetics

There are times when a general anesthetic may be necessary during pregnancy; but if possible such anesthetics should be avoided because the baby becomes anesthetized too. Make sure that if your doctor or dentist recommends general anesthesia for anything he or she knows you are pregnant.

OTHER HARMFUL INFLUENCES
X-rays

In pregnancy it is wise to cut down the use of X-rays to the minimum, because there is no safe threshold for radiation, and hence no minimum level at which you can be assured that X-rays are safe for your unborn child. So avoid X-rays during pregnancy if possible, or in the second half of the menstrual cycle if there is a chance that you might be pregnant.

Radiation can partially destroy the genetic material which acts as the blueprint for the normal development of each cell of the body. A damaged cell is called a mutation. Radiation can have the greatest effects on an embryo which is in the initial stages of development, and a badly affected embryo is likely to be aborted spontaneously. But X-rays taken in pregnancy can also have an effect after birth*: there is evidence that X-rays are associated with a higher than usual chance of developing diseases of the respiratory system, blood disorders, and infectious illnesses in childhood.

There are some cases in which diagnostic X-rays are important and the only means of discovering certain disorders. If a doctor or a dentist advises X-rays, take professional advice, but always check first to ensure that they really are essential. Your abdomen and thyroid should be protected by a lead shield.

High temperature

=**"**=

I had some sort of virus, with a high temperature, sore throat, and everything. And it scared me stiff. In fact, it haunted me right through the pregnancy, wondering if the baby was normal. And she's gorgeous.

=**"**=

If you find you are running a temperature, go to bed, drink plenty of fluids and sponge yourself down with cold water, or have cool baths or showers to lower your body temperature. Do not just let your temperature rise. There is a slight chance that a very high temperature—say, over 102°F—in the first four months of pregnancy can damage a baby*. The most crucial time is during the third and fourth weeks after conception. This is a horrifying thing to learn in late pregnancy if you know you had flu earlier on, but most babies are born whole and healthy even when the mother has run a high temperature. Nevertheless, it is sensible to avoid becoming run down, and so more susceptible to infection, if you think you may be pregnant. Keep up a high intake of protein and Vitamin C in your diet so that you reduce the risk of contracting an infection. As far as we know, there does not seem to be any risk of serious damage to the fetus from a high temperature after the 16th week of pregnancy.

Hot saunas and hot baths lasting for a long time can also produce a temperature high enough to harm a developing baby, so it makes sense to keep the temperatures down in pregnancy. Your own comfort is probably the best guide.

Vaccination

Vaccinations are not recommended during the first four months of pregnancy, during which time there is a small risk of damage to the fetus. In the later months, most vaccinations (apart from rubella; see below) are considered harmless, although you should avoid small-pox vaccination throughout pregnancy, especially if you have never been vaccinated against smallpox before. If you are traveling to a country which still insists on smallpox vaccination, you can obtain exemption with a certificate of pregnancy from your doctor.

Rubella (German measles) is such a mild disease that many people have it in childhood without knowing it. Unfortunately, if you contract rubella when you are pregnant, the virus may cross the placenta and in the first 20 weeks of pregnancy it can have a serious effect on the baby. It is therefore sensible to have a blood test before you even become pregnant: if the test shows that you have never had rubella you can be vaccinated against it. Alternatively, if you are already pregnant when you discover that you are not immune, you can be vaccinated immediately after the birth of your baby.

The protection afforded by rubella vaccination lasts at least seven years, and probably much longer. After you have been vaccinated, be very careful about contraception for the next three months, since you should not conceive until you have had time to build up immunity to the virus in your system. Never have a rubella vaccination if you think you might be pregnant.

If you did not have a rubella vaccination before you started your pregnancy and have never had the disease, avoid all contact with children who might possibly have it. If you think you have been in contact with rubella, get in touch with your doctor immediately. He or she will offer you an injection of gamma globulin, but the chances of the baby being damaged by rubella in the first three months of pregnancy are high, especially in the first eight weeks; if you contract the disease you may want to consider an abortion.

The Rhesus negative woman

All blood is either Rhesus positive or Rhesus negative. Some 86 per cent of people are Rhesus positive, which means that their blood contains something known as the Rhesus factor. This factor is tested for early on in your pregnancy as part of your routine blood test. Its presence or absence is noted, but is only important in one combination of circumstances: if you are Rhesus negative and the baby's father is Rhesus positive. There is no problem if the baby is Rhesus negative, but 40 per cent of all Rhesus positive babies of Rhesus negative mothers become anemic, and if this is untreated the baby may die before or after birth.

If you are a Rhesus negative mother bearing a Rhesus positive baby, the danger arises when some of the baby's red blood cells leak into your circulation. This is particularly likely after an accidental hemorrhage in late pregnancy and at delivery, or if you have miscarried or had an abortion. Your body then responds to the Rhesus factor present in the baby's cells as if to an invader, and begins to manufacture antibodies against it. If some of these antibodies leak back from your circulation into the baby's they proceed to destroy large numbers of the baby's own red blood cells.

The flow of red blood cells each way across the placenta is not usually substantial enough during a first pregnancy to cause your body to develop such antibodies. But when your first baby is born, some of its blood may flow from the placenta into your circulation. This triggers the creation of antibodies to the Rhesus factor in your blood. From then on you produce antibodies to the Rhesus factor, and the next time you are pregnant with a Rhesus positive baby your antibodies may attack the baby's blood vigorously. It may get jaundice, its brain can be damaged, severe anemia may develop and, in the worst cases, it may not even survive.

There are several things that can be done about this. The first and simplest is an injection (Rhogam), given to the Rhesus negative mother immediately after the birth of her first baby. It consists of a serum which stops her biological defense mechanisms acting against foreign Rhesus substances. A fresh injection of this serum is given after each subsequent delivery. The same routine is followed after a miscarriage or a termination of pregnancy too, since it is possible that the fetus was Rhesus positive and that some of its blood entered the mother's bloodstream.

It is no good giving this serum *after* a woman's body has already produced antibodies. If a high proportion of antibodies is detected in your blood during a second or subsequent pregnancy, and your baby is known to be at risk, amniocentesis may be performed (see page

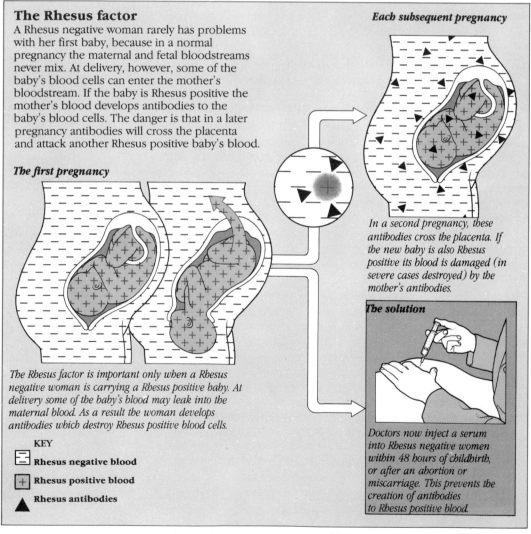

The Rhesus factor

A Rhesus negative woman rarely has problems with her first baby, because in a normal pregnancy the maternal and fetal bloodstreams never mix. At delivery, however, some of the baby's blood cells can enter the mother's bloodstream. If the baby is Rhesus positive the mother's blood develops antibodies to the baby's blood cells. The danger is that in a later pregnancy antibodies will cross the placenta and attack another Rhesus positive baby's blood.

Each subsequent pregnancy

The first pregnancy

In a second pregnancy, these antibodies cross the placenta. If the new baby is also Rhesus positive its blood is damaged (in severe cases destroyed) by the mother's antibodies.

The Rhesus factor is important only when a Rhesus negative woman is carrying a Rhesus positive baby. At delivery some of the baby's blood may leak into the maternal blood. As a result the woman develops antibodies which destroy Rhesus positive blood cells.

The solution

Doctors now inject a serum into Rhesus negative women within 48 hours of childbirth, or after an abortion or miscarriage. This prevents the creation of antibodies to Rhesus positive blood.

KEY

⊟	**Rhesus negative blood**
⊞	**Rhesus positive blood**
▲	**Rhesus antibodies**

206) and the amniotic fluid analyzed for the presence of bilirubin (bile pigment). An anemic fetus excretes into the fluid large amounts of bilirubin from destroyed red blood cells.

A woman who is Rhesus negative and whose partner is Rhesus positive is tested for Rhesus antibodies every two to three weeks. If there are antibodies, a blood test is done on the baby in the uterus, using ultrasound to guide the needle into the umbilical cord. If necessary, the baby can be given one or more transfusions before birth, again using ultrasound to guide the needle. If the baby is sufficiently mature to face life outside, labor may be induced early, If necessary, the baby can be treated immediately after delivery and given a complete blood transfusion to eradicate all the antibodies from its bloodstream.

Fortunately, as more and more Rhesus negative women are routinely immunized after delivery, this situation is increasingly rare.

An "incompetent" cervix

Occasionally a woman's cervix may be torn from a previous difficult labor or mid-pregnancy termination, or is damaged by a cone biopsy. She would not find this out until her next pregnancy, when she might lose her baby after the fourth month as a result of "cervical incompetence" (see page 340). The term "incompetent" is an unfortunate one and makes women feel as if they have failed to reach some standard of reproductive ability.

An obstetrician may recommend cervical cerclage—sewing the cervix closed for the duration of any subsequent pregnancy. This is a relatively simple procedure: once the pregnancy is established, a suture is inserted under anesthesia and is threaded through and around the cervix like the drawstring of a purse. The suture is removed at about the 36th week of pregnancy or later. Some obstetricians like to induce labor at this point because they say it is simpler, since contractions often start shortly after the removal of the suture anyway. You are not compelled to have labor induced, however, and should decide whether this is what you want in such circumstances. A random trial of cervical cerclage, conducted on women at high risk of giving birth prematurely, produced no evidence of its benefit*.

A generation ago some pregnant women were prescribed a drug called diethystilbesterol (DES) to prevent miscarriage. The sons born to these women had a much greater incidence of genitourinary malformations and infertility. The daughters had higher rates of vaginal cancer and cervical malformations. Some of these women with malformed cervixes need cervical cerclage and some do not.

Your physical wellbeing

To get the most out of the experience of being pregnant, you should ensure that your body is in good condition. Remember that healthy activity can be pleasurable in itself as well as being an excellent preparation for labor. Sometimes books on pregnancy and even childbirth educators give the impression that childbirth is an athletic event for which you have to train like a marathon runner, a kind of examination for which you must study assiduously, or even an ordeal with which you are unlikely to cope but which will be quickly forgotten afterward. No wonder expectant mothers become anxious! No mention is made of the excitement, joy, and sheer pleasure that many women experience in childbirth.

I've never been fitter. The doctor says I'm not a very interesting case. I don't really know I'm pregnant!

Most women look forward to childbirth with excited anticipation. They know that there is a slight chance of something going wrong but that the better they have prepared themselves by doing bodytoning movements and exercises, the more likely they are to be able to handle any emergencies.

GETTING TO KNOW YOUR BODY

Before beginning exercises, it is useful to gain an awareness early in pregnancy of how your body works and what is taking place in your reproductive organs. One way of doing this is to have a closer look at your genitals. For a clear view, you can kneel or squat over a mirror. A flashlight might help you to see the area better.

The perineum

The perineum is the tissue around your vagina and between your vagina and anus. Just before delivery it begins to bulge and its tissues fan out and open up as the ball of the baby's head presses through it.

The vagina

Your vagina is the soft, cushioned canal which holds the penis during sexual intercourse; it is also the passage through which the baby is delivered. The outer part of the vagina is the vulva, consisting of layers of outer and inner lips (labia) constructed like the overlapping petals of a rose. During pregnancy they change in color from red to violet, the effect of the pregnancy hormones which have also darkened your nipples, maybe your face, and other parts of your skin.

Insert one or two fingers into your vagina and feel around the stretchy folds inside. Though the sides of the vagina are normally touching each other and there is no hollow space, notice how readily they spread apart. They open like an accordion when the baby is pressing down through them to be born, and the action of hormones that are released into your bloodstream will make them become even softer and more flexible during the last few weeks of pregnancy.

The clitoris

Your clitoris is like a bud rising from the inner lips at the upper (front) end of your vagina. Its base and the inner lips around it are very sensitive, and pressure on or stroking of these parts produces sexual excitement. As you touch its root, you may notice that it swells up. You will feel that there is a hood or fold of skin surrounding the clitoris and that this connects up with the inner lips. So anything in your vagina which stretches the inner lips apart will also pull on this hood and the clitoris will be stimulated in this way, too.

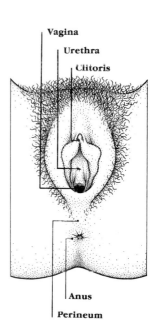

Vagina

Urethra

Clitoris

A woman's genitals vary as much as a man's. Just as penises are different sizes, for example, the clitoris may be the size and shape of a small pea or more like the curved center of an orchid. Women's labia vary too. Some are firm, some soft, some large and fleshy, others smaller. A woman may worry that masturbation might have changed the shape of her labia or clitoris, but these organs are so flexible that pulling, pressing, or rubbing them does not produce permanent structural changes. Doctors and midwives cannot tell anything about your sexual habits by examining your vulva, though many women harbor a secret fear that they can.

At delivery the baby presses against this whole area that you are examining, easing forward the tissues so that they open up like elastic, and then slides out with a rush of liquid. After the baby is born these flexible tissues spring back again; at first they will not be as firm as they were before, but they will gradually gain in tone.

Anus

Perineum

The cervix

Now introduce your longest finger deep inside your vagina and you meet the rounded, firm cervix (the neck of the womb), the part of the uterus that will open (dilate) when you are in labor. Early in pregnancy it will feel like the tip of your nose. You may notice a little dip in the middle, like the dimple in the centre of a buttoned cushion. This is where the mucous plug is situated, and this plug, like the cork in a bottle, seals off the uterus from the outside. At the end of pregnancy the cervix will have softened and, when you touch it with your finger, it will feel more like your mouth when it is soft and relaxed than like your nose. This is one of the signs that you are ready to go into labor. The cervix is "ripe".

The pelvic floor

The muscles which support everything inside the pelvic cavity (including the uterus, the bladder, and the rectum) form the pelvic floor. They have special significance for your health, whatever age you are and whether or not you are pregnant. The upright position that humans have adopted in preference to the all-fours stance puts an extra stress on these muscle layers in pregnancy.

Keeping fit during pregnancy

While you are pregnant it is easy to allow muscles that were previously firm and elastic to sag. You are putting on weight, your figure is changing and you may assume that sagging muscles are an inevitable accompaniment to these changes. However, gentle toning exercises, aimed at firming up your abdominal muscles and avoiding back strain, can do you and your baby nothing but good.

Pelvic rocking

Lie on a flat surface, your head and shoulders supported by pillows and your knees bent with the feet flat. Experiment with pressing the small of your back against the floor or bed and then releasing it so that you produce a gentle, rhythmic, rocking movement. Then roll your hips around in a slow, circular, hulahoop movement.

1 *Keeping your upper back pressed firmly down, slightly raise your hips and buttocks and rock them gently to and fro.*

2 *Roll your pelvis around—as if you were doing a slow languorous belly dance while lying down.*

Wrong

Although double-leg raising and sit-ups are exercises often recommended for pregnant women, they do not in fact strengthen the abdominal muscles. These muscles do not work to lift the legs but to stabilize the lower back. If they are not strong to start with, they cannot cope with the effort involved when the legs or trunk are raised, and the result is back strain or torn abdominal muscles.

Double-leg raising is rarely effective in toning abdominal muscles and should never be done in pregnancy or in the 4 weeks following birth.

Sit-ups can cause harm in pregnancy. They should never be done with straight knees or back if you are pregnant or in the first 6 weeks after childbirth.

Leg sliding

Leg sliding is a gentle exercise that allows you to tone up your tummy muscles efficiently without straining them. Do it five or six times at first and gradually build up until you can do it comfortably 10 or 15 times. If at any point you feel your back aching, stop. Leg sliding is best done lying on your back on a firm surface with a pillow under your head and shoulders

1 *Keeping the small of your back pressed down, bend your knees so that your feet are flat on the floor.*

2 *Slowly extend both legs until they are straight.*

3 *Draw one knee back up, then the other, without lifting the small of your back off the floor.*

Testing for separation of the rectus muscle

If you are starting exercises in the last months of pregnancy, find out whether you have already damaged your rectus muscle. You will need to be careful when doing exercises for toning up your abdomen if this muscle has separated (see page 111).

1 *Lying on your back with your knees bent, slowly raise your head and shoulders about 8 in (20 cm), stretching your arms out in front of you.*

2 *Place your hands on your tummy. A small soft bulge like a marshmallow in the middle below your navel means the rectus muscle has probably separated.*

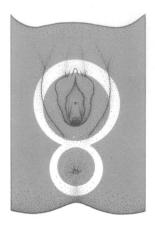

The pelvic floor muscles form a figure-8 around the vagina and anus. Learning to contract and release these muscles efficiently during pregnancy will help you both during labor and after your baby is born.

Though these muscles form a co-ordinated working structure, they are not really a "floor" at all. They are slanted at different angles and levels and can be held with varying degrees of firmness. The easiest way to find these muscles, of which some women are not aware, is to interrupt a stream of urine, since you bring all of the pelvic floor muscles into play when you do this. Or you can think of them as forming a figure of eight around the vagina and anus. In the middle of the eight is a horizontal bar, the transverse perineal muscle. When the muscles of the pelvic floor are contracted, the circular shapes of the eight change to almond shapes and the transverse perineal muscle is pulled up and over towards the pubic bone (the firm ridge of bone just above the clitoris) like the opening lid of a roll-top desk. You can feel this happening from both inside and outside if you put one finger inside the vagina and a thumb over the pubis.

Your pelvic floor muscles contract spontaneously during love-making, increasing your sensations of pleasure and those of your partner. Awareness and control of these muscles are important in labor too, when you will need to be able to release them as you press the baby down the birth canal.

Some people can hold their pelvic muscles contracted much longer than others, and you may notice, when you first try to contract these muscles, that they tire and tremble. To exercise your pelvic floor muscles gradually, you can pretend that this area is an elevator which you are taking up to the second floor. You hold it there, then move on to the third floor, and so on until the muscles are fully contracted. Then release them gradually to the ground floor. Finally end with a toning movement by drawing the muscles up to the second floor again. If you do this between 20 and 30 times a day you will be able to hold them firm for longer periods, building up to a count of eight or nine without holding your breath or tightening up your shoulders. But always alternate tightening movements with resting spaces to allow the muscles to be reoxygenated in the intervals between activity.

TONING YOUR ABDOMINAL MUSCLES

The human backbone is curved, not straight as in many four-legged animals. In some people it is almost S-shaped. Because of the forward load produced by pregnancy, strain is put on the spine, especially in the small of the back, and the upper spine may be pushed into the wrong position to compensate.

The abdominal muscles

Four-legged mammals take the extra weight of pregnancy on their abdominal muscles slung evenly between the front and back limbs. Despite their upright stance, human beings also need well-toned abdominal muscles for comfortable pregnancy because, if these are flabby, the back muscles are forced to take on too much work to support the spine. When this happens, the vertebrae of the lower spine are forced into an unnatural position and the disks between them are subjected to great pressure. They may slide and become displaced. This leads to exhausting backache. Girdles cannot help much; they just take over some of the work that healthy muscles should be doing. The best girdle is composed of your own tummy and buttock muscles, and both sets need to be toned to provide mutual support.

To understand what will benefit your abdominal muscles and what might be harmful to them, it is useful to know how this girdle of muscles is constructed and how it works.

The muscle running from top to bottom down the front is called the rectus muscle and it bears much of the load of late pregnancy. It is separated into two halves by a line down the center which is like a seam. When you are about halfway through your pregnancy, this may show as a dark line in your skin from your navel down to your pubic-hair line, although it does not occur in all women. You can see the same line as an indentation about the width of a pencil in photo-graphs of Mr. Universe flexing his muscles and caving in his abdomen. The two sides of the rectus muscle can be pulled apart if the muscle is subjected to too great a stress and then the muscle "unzips". Constipation and straining on the toilet can sometimes cause this muscle to separate.

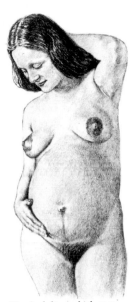

The dark line which may appear on your skin from your navel down to your pubis is a sign that the rectus muscle is being stretched.

You can test yourself to find out if there is any separation of the rectus muscle. Lying on your back with a pillow under your head, knees bent, rest your hands on your tummy and *very slowly* lift your head and shoulders with your chin tucked in. If you can feel a soft bulging area the width of a finger or more the muscle has separated. If this is the case, you can rehabilitate the muscle after the baby is born (see page 351). Meanwhile concentrate on leg sliding (see page 109).

Some exercises that are intended to strengthen the abdominal muscles can also cause the rectus muscle to separate. You should never try double-leg raising exercises while you are pregnant, or even single-leg raising unless the muscles are already in very good condition. Nor should you do exercises that entail putting your feet under heavy furniture and then raising the upper body or any kind of sit-ups without using your hands. Not only can these exercises damage the abdominal muscles, they can also strain the back.

Exploring pelvic movement

The bones that form the pelvis are like a cradle for the baby growing inside you, a cradle that can rock in all directions. Feel your pelvic bone with your fingers. Start with your hip bones. Press in over their upper ridges and then walk your fingers round and down into the small of your back where your hip girdle joins your spine. The point at which it does so is the sacrum, the bone which forms the back of the pelvis and the outlet through which the baby descends.

Posture and balance

Good posture is essential to your physical wellbeing during pregnancy. This means not only learning to stand and walk in the best way, so that your baby is cradled in the pelvis in a position that is comfortable for both of you, but also performing other everyday movements, such as getting out of bed, in a way calculated to avoid unnecessary strain. To achieve good posture you need to improve the tone of your muscles and to learn how to use only those muscles necessary for whatever you are doing. If you are looking good and walking with a spring in your step, you will probably also feel much better.

Maintaining good posture

Make a point of tucking in your buttock muscles, and feel your tummy muscles working to straighten out your spine. Keep your shoulders dropped. Now imagine a string is pulling your head straight up, and notice the back of your neck lengthening.

Wrong

If the weight of your uterus makes you stand back on your heels, with your bottom stuck out and your shoulders back, your spine hollows and you get low backache.

Tailor sitting

Tailor sitting is an ideal way of rounding out the lower back. As long as you take care not to slouch over, it can be one of the most comfortable positions for sitting during pregnancy.

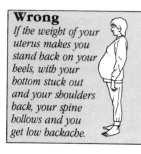

Bridging

In late pregnancy your tummy muscles can feel so stretched that it might be difficult to exercise them consciously. If this is the case, it helps to tighten your buttock muscles, since this means that you pull in your tummy muscles too. Bridging improves the tone of your buttock muscles and helps the circulation in your legs.

1 *Lie on the floor with your heels raised on a low table or stool.*

2 *Tighten your buttock and abdominal muscles and lift your bottom up off the floor, keeping your back straight.*

3 *Hold this position for several seconds, then slowly lower your hips.*

The rocking-chair exercise

This exercise encourages good posture by allowing you to press out the small of your back while keeping the rest of your body aligned. You become like a rocking chair that rocks to and fro, and you need a partner to set you in motion and provide the firm surface against which you press your lower back. Avoid hollowing your back at any time.

1 *Your partner stands in front of you with his hands on your hips.*

2 *You rock your pelvis gently backward and forward between his hands several times.*

3 *Now he stands at your side and puts one hand on the small of your back and the other over your lower tummy.*

4 *You continue rocking, pushing against his hand with the small of your back then moving away from it.*

Getting up from lying down

If you sit up suddenly after you have been lying on your back, you put great pressure on your tummy muscles, especially in advanced pregnancy. The method below is a way of avoiding strain on these muscles, and since it involves changing from a horizontal to an upright position in gentle stages, it is also good for the circulation.

1 *Roll over on to one side, swinging your shoulders around and drawing up your knees.*

2 *Push yourself up with your upper arm while swiveling your legs from the hips over to the edge of the bed.*

3 *Tighten your buttocks and swing your legs over the side of the bed in a smooth, coordinated movement.*

Now walk the fingers round again to the big bones at the side, then down into the groin and around the front till they meet at your pubic bone. This forms the front of the pelvis and the baby dips down under this bridge of bone just before delivery. Notice that your pubis is much lower than your sacrum. The human pelvis is tilted. Once you have found exactly where these bones are and have a clear picture of them, get your partner to feel them too. Guide his hands so that he is able to track your pelvis accurately.

Pelvic rocking

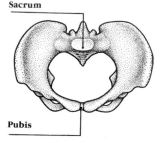

Sacrum

Pubis

Lie on any flat surface (it can be a firm bed), with your head and shoulders supported by two pillows and your knees bent with the feet flat. Explore the capacity for movement in your pelvis. Experiment with gentle, rhythmic rocking. Then try rolling the cradle around as if you were doing a very slow hula hoop movement. This is a kind of belly dancing while lying down, in which you tighten your tummy muscles while pressing your buttocks together. As you do so, notice how the different sets of muscles are alternately tightened and released and the way in which tummy and buttock muscles work together in a coordinated fashion.

Now combine this movement with controlled breathing. Each time you pull your tummy muscles *in* and press your buttocks together, give a strong breath *out* through your mouth. Then, as you release the muscles and rock your pelvis gently forward (it is a very slight movement), allow your lungs to fill up with air, breathing in through your nose. Do it at your own pace, emphasizing the breath out and letting the breath in take care of itself. This movement done in early pregnancy is a good way of toning abdominal muscles for the work they must do later.

Now rest your fingers on the big bones at the front of the pelvis on either side. Continue the movement with the breathing and notice the swing up and down of these bones. This is the distance the bony cradle rocks as you walk and move around in pregnancy. The baby is accustomed to these movements during its intrauterine existence, and it is not surprising that rocking a newborn baby quiets and soothes it. Research shows that a baby being rocked is most likely to be comforted by a swing of 3 in (7·5 cm) to either side*. This corresponds exactly with the arc of the pelvic rock.

A position with firm support for your spine is best for practicing this pelvic rocking. Other positions allow you to hollow your back in an exaggerated way, which can be harmful, especially in advanced pregnancy, because it puts stress on the sacroiliac joint, which is situated at the top of your buttocks. Such strain is particularly bad for you when you are pregnant because your ligaments are already softened by hormones released into the blood during pregnancy to make the vagina and cervix more flexible in preparation for the birth. Once these ligaments have softened, any form of pelvic rocking which involves back *hollowing* can cause more backache.

EXERCISES IN PREGNANCY

Exercises to help you cope with the stresses of pregnancy should be matched by others designed to help your adjustment after childbirth, since this is the time when the speediest and most dramatic physical changes are happening to you. Postnatal exercises are simply a modification of the ones you learn in pregnancy, so there is no need for you to learn completely new ones after the birth. In this book postnatal exercises are described on pages 352–353.

Posture and balance

Good posture maintained every day is more important than pregnancy gymnastics. As the weight load changes you should give conscious thought to balance and body mechanics, something that is usually taken for granted. It is not just a matter of "standing straight, head up" like the girl who walks with a book on her head, but of understanding how to economize on muscle work and use only those muscles that are needed for any task. This always results in more graceful and comfortable movement without straining and effort.

Standing To achieve good posture, you should stand with your back to a wall, heels far enough away from it for your seat and shoulders just to touch it. Press the small of your back toward the wall and you will feel your seat tucking under and your tummy muscles working to straighten out your spine. Make sure that you do not tighten your shoulders. Keep them dropped. Now imagine that a string is pulling your head up from the center at the top and notice the back of your neck lengthening. Relax your jaw. (Your jaw muscles cannot force your head up!) Walk a few paces away from the wall. You will find that you are in a stiff, exaggerated stance like a soldier on duty. Let the muscles settle into a more comfortable state. The rocking chair exercise (see page 113) encourages good posture, and can be done with the help of your partner.

Walking Whenever possible, walk rather than stand. The healthiest, most rhythmic and natural all around exercise is walking. If you have to stand around, exercise your feet while you do so, even if only by screwing up and extending your toes, going up onto the ball of the foot and down again and shifting weight from one foot to the other. Muscles in the feet and legs pump blood back to the heart, so movement is important to maintain good circulation in the legs.

You can also increase the tone of your buttock muscles and help the circulation in your legs by bridging (see page 112)*.

Sitting Sit back on your chair and see that your spine is well supported. If necessary, put a small cushion in the small of the back. In the last few weeks of your pregnancy you may need more support than this; try sitting well back against a large bean bag or a firm floor

Aches and pains

In late pregnancy you are carrying more weight which, instead of being evenly distributed, is centered in one area and so affects your balance. This extra weight alone can cause aches and pains by straining muscles and causing you to adopt an unnatural stance, leading to further strain. The way the baby is lying can also cause discomfort and occasionally sharp shooting pain when the baby is pressing against a nerve.

Foot exercises

Foot exercises discourage varicose veins in the legs by stimulating the blood flow back to the heart. When you are sitting down or having a rest, practice drawing the alphabet with your feet, one foot at a time, keeping your legs still. You will find that you can easily read or do some work at the same time.

At any time when you are sitting comfortably, draw letters or even whole words, moving only your feet and ankles.

The angry cat

However many exercises you do with your back supported, it feels good to get the weight of the baby off your spine occasionally. You can do this by going on to all fours and rocking your pelvis, an exercise sometimes known as "the angry cat". This is a kind of pelvic rocking reversed.

1 *Get on to all fours, keeping the small of your back flat, not hollowed.*

2 *Without moving your elbows or knees, tighten your tummy muscles and hump up your lower back. Relax back to the flat position after a few seconds.*

Wrong

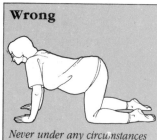

Never under any circumstances allow the lower back to cave in.

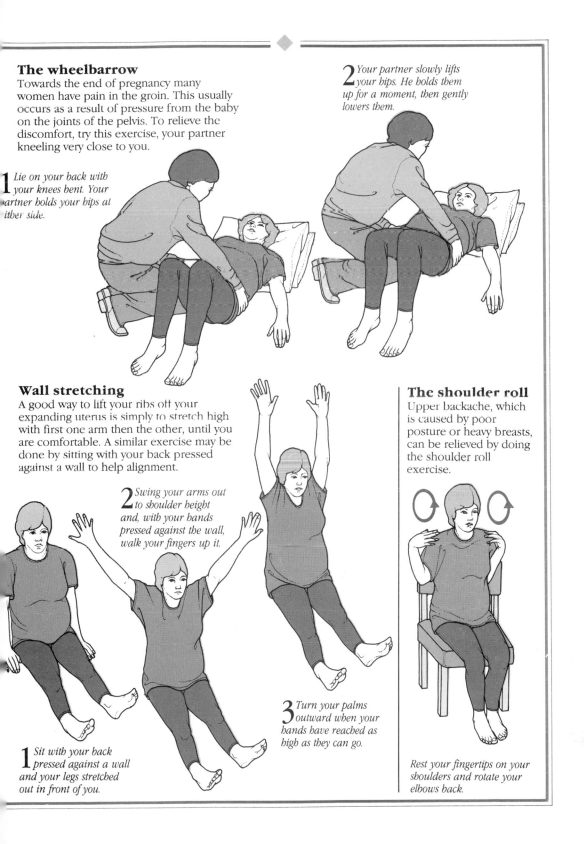

The wheelbarrow

Towards the end of pregnancy many women have pain in the groin. This usually occurs as a result of pressure from the baby on the joints of the pelvis. To relieve the discomfort, try this exercise, your partner kneeling very close to you.

1 *Lie on your back with your knees bent. Your partner holds your hips at either side.*

2 *Your partner slowly lifts your hips. He holds them up for a moment, then gently lowers them.*

Wall stretching

A good way to lift your ribs off your expanding uterus is simply to stretch high with first one arm then the other, until you are comfortable. A similar exercise may be done by sitting with your back pressed against a wall to help alignment.

2 *Swing your arms out to shoulder height and, with your hands pressed against the wall, walk your fingers up it.*

3 *Turn your palms outward when your hands have reached as high as they can go.*

1 *Sit with your back pressed against a wall and your legs stretched out in front of you.*

The shoulder roll

Upper backache, which is caused by poor posture or heavy breasts, can be relieved by doing the shoulder roll exercise.

Rest your fingertips on your shoulders and rotate your elbows back.

cushion. If you have to write or type at a desk or table for any length of time, remember to rest your head down on it occasionally and gently stretch the back of your neck.

Bending and lifting Use your legs, not your back, when you reach down for anything. This means that, whenever possible, you should bend your knees and get right down to the load. Kneel or squat when you are working low down, cleaning the bath or making a low bed, for example. Avoid misusing your spine as if it were a crane. For some jobs, such as wiping or polishing a floor, it is most comfortable to get onto all fours. This takes the weight of the baby off your spine and is surprisingly comfortable, especially if you do have backache.

Lying down and getting up The front-lateral or "three-quarters-over" position is often the most comfortable when you are lying in bed. It may help to put a pillow under your upper knee. Allow good space between your legs. Avoid hollowing your back when you are lying down, too. This is likely to happen if you have a soft mattress and like to lie on your front. If necessary, put a small pillow under your hips so that your back does not cave in.

Whenever you get up from lying on your back, roll over onto one side first, swinging your shoulders round, and push with your upper arm, drawing up your knees at the same time till you are in a kneeling position; tighten your buttocks and then rise from that position (see page 113). This movement will avoid unnecessary strain on your abdominal muscles. It may sound complicated but it can come to be a beautifully smooth, coordinated movement, making you feel like Cleopatra rising from her barge.

Squat or kneel down to pick up a toddler, rather than using your back like a crane.

Aches and pains

Although bad posture is often responsible for aches and pains during pregnancy, you may have other aches and pains that are just the result of being pregnant. If this is the case all you can do to relieve them is concentrate on relaxation and experiment with different positions in which you feel more comfortable.

Low backache In late pregnancy, if the baby is facing toward your front and engages as a posterior (see page 257) with the back of its head pressing against your sacrum, you may develop backache. Rest in positions in which the weight of the baby is tilted off the spine, and take every opportunity to get onto all fours. Scrubbing a kitchen floor can provide extraordinary relief from backache. The angry cat (see page 116) is an exercise that combines this position with pelvic rocking to relieve your spine of the baby's weight.

The front lateral or three-quarters-over position is often comfortable for resting.

Upper backache This occurs when you try to compensate for the weight of your pregnancy dragging you forward, by flinging your shoulders back and tightening the muscles in the upper back. To relieve it, roll your shoulders backward whenever you have the opportunity and do the shoulder roll exercise (see page 117).

Tingling and numbness You may sometimes feel a tingling and numbness in your hand. This is known as the carpal tunnel syndrome. It results from pressure on the nerves and tendons caused by swelling of the hand and wrist. You will be most aware of it in the morning after your wrists have accumulated fluid during the night. To relieve the sensations of discomfort, try the shoulder roll exercise or hold your hand above your head for a few minutes and flex and gradually extend the fingers upward.

Pain under the ribs You may experience pain below the ribs at either side when the top of the uterus (the fundus) is high after 30 weeks (see page 69). This pain tends to come on whichever side the baby is lying.

You will discover that you are only comfortable when sitting straight on a rather high chair and will not want to slump down onto your uterus. In spite of folklore about the dangers of an expectant mother lifting her arms above her head, you will find that it helps to stretch upward so that your whole rib cage is lifted off the uterus. You can also do stretching exercises while sitting with your back against a wall for support (see page 117).

Lifting your arms above your head may help if you have a tingling sensation in your hands.

Pain in the groin In late pregnancy it is common to have pain around the pubic area, where the pelvic joints have softened in readiness for labor. Avoid standing for long periods, and even when sitting change position often. Symptoms can be relieved by doing the wheelbarrow exercise (see page 117). Some women get a stitch in the side because the round ligament at either side of the uterus is stretched. If you are lying down, you may find it easier to get up if you roll over slowly and sit up gently while supporting your sides with your hands (see page 113).

Cramp in the leg A few pregnant women get cramps because they are trying to go on a saltfree diet. Eating something salty before you go to bed may make the cramp disappear. However, most cramps are probably caused by a calcium deficiency and, if you are plagued by recurring cramps, you will be prescribed calcium tablets. Avoid curling your toes under. Use a duvet or make up the bed loosely so that your toes are not pressed down by the bedlinen overnight.

Lifting your feet above the level of your heart will also help circulation and hence relieve cramps. However, in advanced pregnancy this may give you indigestion, so you are left with a choice between two discomforts. While you are lying with your feet up, roll them round in circles from the ankles to help stretch the calf muscles, or practice drawing the letters of the alphabet, one foot at a time, keeping your legs still. If you do get a cramp, ask your partner to grip

your heel and push your foot up while pressing down on your knee with the other hand. It is a useful precaution to do this regularly about ten times before you settle down for the night.

COMMON PROBLEMS DURING PREGNANCY

Although your baby can grow inside you without your having to think consciously or do anything about it, this growth affects your whole body and every system in it. You may worry about these disconcerting changes taking place in your system if you do not understand what they are and why they have occurred.

Varicose veins

The valves which help direct the blood through the veins back to the heart may soften in pregnancy and become unable to propel the increased amount of blood through the legs.

Avoid all positions which allow pooling of blood in the legs: sitting with your legs crossed or with your thighs pressing against the edge of your chair, for example. Foot exercises will help keep the blood moving. If you are advised to wear elastic stockings, choose semi- or full-support styles and put them on *before* you get up in the morning. Bend a knee, put one leg on and wriggle it up; then do the same with the other.

Vaginal varicose veins Sometimes a woman develops varicose veins in her vagina. The discomfort may be relieved by wrapping some ice chips in a clean handkerchief, knotting it, and packing it against the sore and tender areas. Obviously you cannot walk around like this, but it is a good excuse to lie down for a while, so offering a position in which the whole weight of your uterus is not pressing down on the swollen veins. Sometimes Vitamin B6 (pyridoxine) can help, and you should take prenatal vitamins which contain B6.

Hemorrhoids (also known as piles) are varicose veins of the rectum and can be caused by constipation. If you have piles avoid any straining on the toilet. This condition should be treated as quickly as possible because the hemorrhoids can become prolapsed (protrude through the anus) causing extreme pain. Your doctor may give you a prescription for a painrelieving cream. Alternatively a lint pad soaked in witchhazel can also bring relief.

Constipation

You are more likely to be constipated during pregnancy because some of the extra hormones produced while you are pregnant cause the intestine to relax and become less efficient. First of all ensure that you are eating the right kinds of food (see page 86). Eat plenty of fruit, vegetables, fiber, and whole grains and drink as much water as

═ 66 ═

I feel enormous and old and exhausted. I used to be a ballet dancer—and this is the end! I never imagined I could be so gross.

═ 99 ═

OPPOSITE
Swimming when you are pregnant is a good way of maintaining a state of physical wellbeing.

you can. When you are on the toilet, allow your pelvic floor to be fully released and bulging down. Take your time over emptying the bowels, and take a brisk walk every day if possible.

Bladder control and infections

In the first three months or so of your pregnancy the developing baby and enlarging uterus are pressing against your bladder, while the extra progesterone flowing through your bloodstream softens the tissues. So it is quite normal for a pregnant woman to have to urinate very often. This may be even more noticeable at the very end of pregnancy when the baby has gone down into your pelvis.

Cystitis Pressure and engorgement of blood vessels in the pelvic area mean that a pregnant woman is more exposed to the risk of urinary infection. If you notice a stinging, burning feeling when you urinate, this usually indicates that you have developed cystitis. If left untreated, cystitis rapidly becomes very uncomfortable.

If you suspect that you have cystitis, go to your doctor, who will probably prescribe a course of antibiotics. It is sensible to seek help when you first notice the symptoms as delay can mean that the infection takes hold more firmly. As a general treatment, drink plenty of liquid. Drink a glass of water every time you have used the toilet. Drinking cranberry, orange, lemon or grapefruit juice can help, or try an alkaline-based drink such as a mixture of sodium bicarbonate and sodium citrate. One natural remedy is marshmallow tea.

Wear cotton briefs and avoid any clothing that is tight on the crotch. If you wear pantihose, get some that have a cotton panel or air holes between the legs. Spend time on the toilet to empty your bladder as completely as possible. When the baby is pressing against your bladder in late pregnancy, you will be able to shift position so that the baby moves a little, allowing you to void some more.

Pyelitis If you have a temperature and low back pain, and if it hurts when you apply pressure over your kidneys, on one or both sides, you may have pyelitis (a kidney infection). Sometimes the infection causes nausea and vomiting too. Seek treatment immediately, since this is not only painful for you, but can affect the functioning of the placenta. Antibiotics are effective, but all the measures suggested for coping with cystitis are also helpful and you will probably appreciate a hot water bottle against the painful area. Women with pyelitis are often admitted to the hospital to allow a proper diagnosis. The right drugs usually clear up the problem within two weeks.

Yeast growths

It is normal to have an increased vaginal discharge in pregnancy, but if your vulva becomes itchy and your vagina is red, sore, and burning, you probably have thrush ("candida" or "monilia"). Vaginal suppositories are usually prescribed. Cut out sugar and white flour and try a diet based on whole grains, fruit, vegetables and protein. Painting gentian violet (which you can get from a drug store without a prescription) over the affected area works well but is messy. If you try this method, wear a sanitary pad to stop staining.

Breast tenderness

The normal breast tenderness of the early weeks of pregnancy can be acutely painful for some women, and they walk about with stiff arms to protect themselves in case anyone brushes against them. A good supporting bra (see page 130) is important even if you do not normally wear one, since if the breasts are increasing in size, as they usually are at this stage, their own weight can be uncomfortable. If your breasts become extra-sensitive like this, you will not enjoy your partner's most gentle touch until about the middle of pregnancy.

Inverted nipples

Some women have one or both nipples shaped like dimples. These are called "inverted" nipples. If you have a nipple like this but can press it out, or if it projects when you are sexually excited, the baby will be able to get hold of the nipple well and draw it out further. Otherwise you may find it more difficult to fix the baby on to the breast with a good mouthful. However, if you do manage to start the

Usual nipple shape

Shape of inverted nipple

Plastic nipple shell

WEARING A NIPPLE SHIELD
Using a dome-shaped plastic nipple shield under your bra in the last 2 months of pregnancy may help an inverted nipple into an easier shape for the baby. The pressure of the shield on the breast coaxes the nipple through the hole in the middle.

baby off, he or she will suck the nipple into a good projecting shape. It is a fallacy to think that you have to have prominent nipples in order to nurse successfully.

Vomiting

For some women the nausea and vomiting that is very common in the first three months of pregnancy (see page 33) goes on much longer, and this prolonged sickness is known by the medical term of hyperemesis. A woman with hyperemesis is really ill because she cannot take any food by mouth. Surprisingly, the cure may simply be admission to the hospital and often no further treatment is necessary. This is why some psychiatrists and obstetricians have suggested that hyperemesis is a symptom of disturbed relationships and that, if the woman has a chance to get away from the relentless day-to-day contact with a partner, mother, mother-in-law, or anyone who is part of the stress to which she is reacting, the vomiting will ease.

If you find that you are vomiting at all hours of the day, cannot be sure of keeping any meal down and are feeling really wretched, it is worth trying to get away, preferably among people you know only slightly or not at all, and who will not fuss over you. If this gives you the opportunity to do something you have never done before (not hang-gliding!) or see something you have never had the chance of seeing before, so much the better. There is a phrase that is sometimes used about a person who is "run down": "she needs taking out of herself." A woman who is vomiting almost without interruption may need to be taken "out" of herself and her usual relationships until she can cope emotionally, and then, when her pregnancy has settled down, she can come back "into" herself with new strength.

Nasal congestion

Sinusitis The mucous membrane inside the nostrils and sinuses often swells up during pregnancy because of the action of hormones liberated in the bloodstream which are also, fortunately, softening up your vagina and cervix. Some women seem to have a permanent cold in late pregnancy for this reason. It does not interfere with your breathing during labor, so there is no need to worry about this, though you may be more comfortable breathing through your mouth than through your nose. This means that you will need to take frequent sips of water or have a small plant spray filled with ice water to spray into your mouth between contractions and lip salve to smooth on your lips. The symptoms will go after delivery.

In three pregnancies I had slight bleeding in the first 10 weeks each time. After that it was plain sailing. The births went fine and the babies were perfect.

Nosebleeds are very common in pregnancy. These, too, are associated with higher hormone levels and congestion. A tiny blob of vaseline in the nostril will usually stop a nosebleed, and you should avoid blowing your nose hard.

Vaginal bleeding in early pregnancy

Bleeding from the vagina at any stage of pregnancy is always worrying. In early pregnancy it may be that the level of your pregnancy hormones is not sufficiently high to avoid breakthrough spotting. There is no way you can stop this without possibly affecting the developing baby, but it is sensible to take it as a message from the body that you need rest. Go to bed and stay there till the bleeding stops. Cut out unnecessary exertion and, if the bleeding started at a time when your period would normally have been due, take life especially gently then and see if you can manage a few days in bed. Practice deep relaxation every day. There is further information about how to deal with a threatened miscarriage on page 339.

Vaginal bleeding in late pregnancy

If you notice bleeding in late pregnancy it may be a sign that labor is about to start. It is usually blood from around the cervix and, except in those cases where there is a polyp in the cervix that has started to bleed, shows that thinning out and some dilatation is taking place. If your baby is due within a month and the bleeding looks like the beginning of a period, a blood-stained mucous discharge (a "show", see page 228), accept it as a normal sign that your body is in working order for labor and that you may start within a week or two.

Bright red bleeding, which flows as if you were at the height of a period, is another matter. It is called antepartum hemorrhage (APH) and, although quite rare, is serious. If you start to hemorrhage, you should call your doctor or go to the hospital immediately

Placenta previa Sometimes blood flows from the placental site when it is too low-lying and partly in front of the baby's head. Intermittent APH from 27 weeks onward is a typical symptom of this condition, known as placenta previa. Placenta previa occurs in about one in every 200 births and it almost certainly means that delivery will be by cesarean section. During a vaginal birth, as the lower segment of the uterus thinned out, the placenta would be torn away from its roots, depriving the baby of nourishment and oxygen. If you start to bleed when you are as much as 37 weeks pregnant, or thereabouts, you will be admitted to the hospital and, if bleeding continues, will be advised to stay there until the baby is mature enough to be born.

In fact, ultrasound at 16 weeks often reveals that the placenta is lying in the lower part of the uterus. Although this tends to be taken by some obstetricians as an indication of the need for cesarean section, it is normal in early pregnancy and, by the end of pregnancy, when the wall of the uterus has stretched and enlarged, the placenta is usually in the right place in the upper part.

Abruptio placenta APH can also mean that a tiny part of the placenta, situated in the upper part of the uterus as it should be, has peeled away. This is called accidental hemorrhage (accidental in that the hemorrhage has occurred by chance) or abruptio placenta. The severity of accidental hemorrhage depends entirely on how large a portion of the placenta has separated from the lining of the uterus, but it is always a potentially serious problem, and the doctor should be informed at once. You will be advised to go to the hospital for bedrest and, if the bleeding stops and all is well with the baby, will be discharged after four to five days. It is probably wise to avoid intercourse and orgasm until after the baby is born.

Blood pressure

Every time you go for a prenatal visit your blood pressure is checked (see page 50). This is because, although slight fluctuations are normal during pregnancy, any significant rise may be an indication of preeclampsia (see page 126). If the diastolic figure in your blood pressure reading rises by as much as 15, you are considered to have hypertension—high blood pressure. Hypertension can be a signal of preeclampsia, which reduces the efficiency of the placenta. Bedrest will be prescribed, since the placenta will begin to work more efficiently if you stay in bed.

Preeclampsia

The full name of this condition is *preeclamptic toxemia*, but it is usually known as preeclampsia, *toxemia* or sometimes just as *MTLP* (metabolic toxemia of late pregnancy). The Australian name for it is *hypertensive disease of pregnancy* or *HDP*, and it is also called *pregnancy induced hypertension* or *PIH*, even *gestosis*. All these names reflect the uncertainty as to the cause of the illness. One doctor in the nineteenth century called it "the disease of theories" and this remains true today.

Preeclampsia affects between 5 and 10 per cent of all pregnant women, but rarely occurs in the early part of pregnancy, unless a woman has been malnourished for years.

Symptoms Your blood pressure rises, the level of uric acid in your blood goes up, and you retain a lot of fluid. A rise in blood pressure alone does not mean that you have preeclampsia, and neither does an increase in fluid retention. The two symptoms in combination, however, indicate the need for some form of treatment. If mild pre-eclampsia goes untreated, eventually protein appears in the urine. Babies of mothers with a high proportion of protein in their urine may be born prematurely; once a woman is excreting a lot of protein pregnancy is unlikely to continue longer than two more weeks*.

The danger of preeclampsia is not so much to you as to the unborn baby. If the condition is allowed to progress, clots and fatty acids build up in the placenta, blocking the arteries and causing the placenta to fail. This means that labor occurs prematurely, before the baby is necessarily mature enough to survive. In its severest form preeclampsia becomes eclampsia, and then it can seriously affect you as well as the baby, causing convulsions and possibly a state of coma. The following symptoms can be signs of eclampsia: headache, flashing lights, nausea, vomiting, and pain in the abdomen. Don't make the mistake of thinking that you have the flu if this happens to you in late pregnancy. Get in touch with your doctor immediately.

Causes No one is certain what causes the disorder, but research at Oxford, England, indicates that it may be because the blood vessels in the placenta are thinner than usual. The problem starts between the 6th and 18th week of pregnancy, when placental cells do not infiltrate arteries in the uterus deeply enough to make the blood vessels expand so that they can nourish the baby (see page 66).

There is another element in preeclampsia, too; it seems to be a process similar to graft rejection. It is as if the baby is a transplant in the mother's body, and her immune system recognizes it and produces cells in order to expel the intruder.

The risk of preeclampsia is highest in the first pregnancy. But it also has something to do with the man; if the woman has a new partner for a subsequent pregnancy, the chances of her developing pre-eclampsia are about the same as if it were her first baby.

Poor nutrition may play an important part in preeclampsia. You may be able to avoid the disorder by eating well, ensuring you have adequate protein throughout pregnancy (see page 87). If you have had preeclampsia in a previous pregnancy, start out on a programme of good nutrition *before* you conceive again.

You are more likely to develop preeclampsia if any of the following apply: you have diabetes or kidney disease; you have high blood pressure anyway (140/90 or higher); you are having twins or more; members of your family have high blood pressure or have had preeclampsia; you are still in your teens or are over 40; you are under 5 ft 3 in (1·6 m); you have had preeclampsia with a previous pregnancy (in which case there is a one in ten chance of it recurring); you suffer from migraine.

Treatment Many doctors think that staying in bed at the first signs may avoid further developments. Certainly bedrest coupled with relaxation of body and mind will reduce your blood pressure and improve the blood flow to the baby. Don't lie flat on your back in bed, but on your side or well propped up.

If you have high blood pressure with protein in your urine, or high blood pressure alone above 170/110, your doctor will probably admit you to the hospital the same day. You will be kept in bed and your blood pressure and urine will be checked every four hours. Sedatives are sometimes prescribed. After a couple of days you will be allowed up for short periods: if your blood pressure falls below 90 and stays there, and if there is no longer any protein in your urine, you will probably be allowed home after three or four days.

Many women feel trapped in the hospital when they have pre-eclampsia, because they may not feel at all ill. In these circumstances, knowing what is happening to you and why means that you can help to care for yourself rather than just put up with having things done *to* you. Ask questions: find out about your condition and its progress, and understand the reasons for the treatment you are receiving.

Eclampsia If your preeclampsia has developed into eclampsia an intravenous drip will be set up through which a drug is introduced into your blood to prevent convulsions; injections will lower your blood pressure. Your baby may be delivered by cesarean section.

Sugar in the urine

Your urine is tested whenever you go for a prenatal visit (see page 50). If more sugar than usual is detected in your urine, you may have a tendency to be diabetic which has remained hidden until pregnancy. Nearly all women at some time during pregnancy produce sugar in their urine. They are not diabetics. The diagnosis of diabetes is more likely to be correct if you have not previously had a highly sugared meal or snack, if you have a parent who is diabetic, or if you have already had a baby weighing 9 lb or more at birth.

When you are pregnant, the amount of blood in your system rises and so does the amount of blood sugar to be dealt with by your kidneys. You may be able to reduce the sugar level by modifying your diet and cutting out all sugar, cakes, sodas, ice cream, desserts, candy, and chocolate. The accumulation of glucose in a diabetic woman who is pregnant is absorbed by the fetus, which then grows very fast. The obstetrician may recommend induction of labor before the baby grows too big to pass easily through your pelvic outlet. Although large, the baby will not be mature and may need special care after birth. Some babies of diabetic mothers are delivered by cesarean section because the mother's cervix is not soft and ready to open.

If you become diabetic during pregnancy, the diabetes may be controlled by insulin and will probably disappear after delivery. It is now possible for a woman to monitor her blood sugar levels at home using a glucose meter; when linked to a computer at the hospital, the meter provides details of the levels of blood sugar in the average day, so that the woman can adjust her sugar intake as necessary.

There is no reason why a diabetic woman should not breastfeed, and many diabetics do so successfully.

Anemia

When you are anemic (see page 89), you tend to feel very tired, easily become exhausted when you do anything vigorous and may also have dizzy spells and be short of breath. If you have vomited a great deal during early pregnancy, are having a baby within two years of the previous birth, have had a number of babies in quick succession and are on an inadequate diet, or are pregnant with more than one baby, you are most at risk of being anemic. Women who suffer from anemia in pregnancy are less able to cope with any heavy bleeding at the time of the birth and are more likely to have an infection. The baby suffers because less oxygen is carried by the mother's blood to the placenta and premature labor often results. Adjust your diet so that you get more iron-rich foods, protein, Vitamin B, especially B12, Vitamin C and a folic acid supplement which your doctor will prescribe (see page 90). All are necessary to ensure that your blood can carry enough oxygen to all the tissues. Your doctor will also prescribe iron tablets. If they make you constipated, ask for another kind. If you have a low hemoglobin level (see page 48) after 30 weeks, injections of iron may be prescribed.*

Headache

There is no reason why you should have more headaches when you are pregnant than when you are not pregnant. In fact, some women who usually suffer from migraine find that it disappears throughout pregnancy. You can have tension headaches while you are carrying a baby just as at any other time. If your pregnancy is fraught with anxiety, or you are taking on more than you can handle, you will probably be prone to headaches. Decode the messages from your body, modify your life style and, if you are worried about labor, find out how you can help yourself (see page 135).

A sharp, blinding headache that affects your eyesight in late pregnancy should be reported to your doctor as it could be associated with toxemia.

Digestive disturbances

Indigestion and heartburn are problems of the last three or four months of pregnancy. There seems to be so little room in your abdomen and it feels as if all your organs are being crushed.

It is better to have many small snacks than several larger meals a day, and it is sensible to avoid fried or rich, spicy foods. Some people find that they cannot digest bread or products containing yeast and that, by cutting out these foods, they can eliminate heartburn. Many women discover they cannot drink during a meal and that meals have to be taken dry. You need to experiment with different combinations of food and liquid to find the kind of diet that suits you personally. There is no perfect diet that is right for everyone.

Since heartburn results from acid normally present in your stomach flowing back into the esophagus, try to find positions for sitting and sleeping in which the upper part of your uterus is not pressing against your stomach. You will probably prefer upright chairs and at night will feel better if you sleep well propped up with pillows. Make sure jeans, trousers, and skirts are comfortably loose at the waist if you want to avoid indigestion.

Shortness of breath

When the baby is high, after about 34 weeks and before it drops into your pelvis, you will probably find that you are short of breath whenever you exert yourself or even just climb the stairs. Your uterus is putting pressure on your lungs, and your diaphragm may be shifted out of place by as much as 1 in. Again, sitting straight and sleeping propped up can help and you will probably discover that you have to take life rather more slowly in order not to get breathless. There is a rhythm to everything in nature, and this is a phase of pregnancy when your body is telling you to slow down.

DAILY CARE AND COMFORT

When you are pregnant you find that you carry round your own very efficient central heating system. You do not need to dress as warmly as usual and in hot weather you will probably feel more comfortable in cotton dresses, skirts, and so on and should avoid synthetic materials. Many pregnant women suffer from varicose veins in the

Toward the end of pregnancy you may find you are short of breath when climbing stairs or doing anything energetic.

◆

legs, rectum, or vagina (see page 121). Boots should not grip so tightly that circulation is impeded. If you wear jeans or trousers, make sure that they do not interfere with the circulation in the groin.

Shoes

Shoes should allow the feet to keep their normal shape and should not be so high that your weight is thrown forward onto the balls of your feet. In late pregnancy you may find that your feet are wider than usual and so need a wider-fitting shoe or a half size larger. Although oxfords give good support to the arches, you may not be able to tie them easily in late pregnancy. For the same reason slip-on sandals are better than shoes that have elaborate buckles.

Bras

Since breast changes and enlargement occur from the first days of pregnancy, you will need a bra which gives good support and, if you are heavy-breasted, choose one with straps sufficiently wide not to dig into your shoulders.

Heavy breasts, allowed to hang without support, may develop stretch marks (see opposite), which will leave you with silvery streaks after the pregnancy. A woman with large breasts may prefer to wear a lightweight bra at night too during pregnancy.

WHAT SORT OF BRA?
Bras you wear in pregnancy should have a band around their lower margin and wide straps over the shoulders, adjusted to provide firm support for your breasts. The cotton bra (right) can be adjusted at the back for girth, but opens at the front: it is suitable for nursing as well as pregnancy.

Teeth

Although the baby needs calcium to grow strong teeth, your own teeth are no more likely to fall out in pregnancy than at any other time. However, as your gums soften and become spongier along with other tissues in the body as the result of the action of pregnancy hormones in your bloodstream, you may be liable to a gum infection. Good nutrition (see page 86) is the first line of defense against this. Mouth hygiene is also important, with regular tooth brushing, especially after breakfast and before you go to bed at night. Arrange a dental examination and cleaning but not X-rays when you know you are pregnant and again for mid-pregnancy. Since it may be difficult to fit in appointments immediately after the baby is born, arrange another shortly before the baby is due. The dentist's waiting room is an excellent place to practice your relaxation for labor, and slow, full abdominal breathing in the dentist's chair works wonders.

Skin pigmentation

For many women pregnancy is better than a beauty treatment: skin improves, eyes shine, and hair is in better condition. But some women develop patches of darkened (pigmented) skin on the face, and this can be distressing. The technical term is "chloasma", but it is also called "the mask of pregnancy." It is a result of the high level of pregnancy hormones and also occurs in some women taking oral contraceptives. It is made worse by exposure to sunlight. The kind of cosmetic cream sold for minimizing birthmarks often disguises it effectively. The mask usually disappears once the baby is born.

You will notice that other parts of the body that are already pigmented become darker, for example the circles around your nipples and the skin of your labia. You may also develop a dark line down the middle of your tummy from your navel, and this is where the rectus muscle is being stretched (see page 111). It is particularly obvious in dark-haired women. All these colorations should disappear once the baby is born.

Stretch marks

Stretch marks (striae) may appear over your tummy, buttocks, and breasts. They are dark streaks and are a sign that the skin has been stretched from underneath. They never disappear completely but, after the birth, they change from being brown or deep violet to a silvery shade, rather like the marks on some fine, gauze-like fabric that has not been properly ironed. Many women use a rich cream or oil to "feed" the skin, and there are even some on the market especially for stretch marks. However, these are expensive and any cream that is readily absorbed, or even vegetable oil, will do. If your skin is very stretched, and especially if you are having twins, it is marked like this because of pressure on the layers underneath which cannot be reached by anything applied from outside. Still, it can feel good and be relaxing for you to stroke your tummy; even though you may still have stretch marks, there is nothing to be lost and some pleasure to be gained from regular gentle massage with a rich, slippery cream applied by you or your partner.

Sport

Any sport you do well is probably fine during pregnancy: if you are really good at something, you do not waste muscular energy and your movements are smoothly coordinated. As pregnancy advances, you will notice your balance changing as the centre of gravity is concentrated in your tummy. This will almost certainly limit your activities, although I heard of a tightrope walker who practiced daily on the high wire until she went into labor—an exceptional woman! Swimming is splendid exercise during pregnancy, and dancing too, provided you are not in a stuffy room. Cycling is also beneficial although, if you can avoid heavy traffic, it is kinder on both you and your baby.

I've always been very active physically and was determined I wasn't going to give up because I was pregnant. So I've cycled everywhere and gone on with my yoga and swum every day.

Travel

Travel in pregnancy is usually quite safe, but the exhaustion which may result from it is not. It is important to divide up long journeys into short, manageable sections if you can; rest in between. Do not sit immobilized in a car, train, or plane for longer than two hours at most without getting up and walking around for five minutes. Sitting for long periods reduces the circulation of blood in the pelvic area. Also remember to empty your bladder regularly as you are more likely to get a bladder infection during pregnancy (see page 122).

Travel in loose, comfortable clothing, and in shoes that allow for a little expansion. Soft slipper-socks are usually the most comfortable. Take any opportunity of dropping off to sleep. Pack an eye shade made of soft material to block out lights.

Flying On an airplane drink water or fruit juice; avoid alcoholic drinks, as air travel is dehydrating, and alcohol will dehydrate you further. If you are over 25 weeks pregnant, most airlines will require a letter from your doctor saying that it is all right for you to travel. Your doctor will probably agree to write such a letter as long as the risk of your going into labor on board a plane is slight. It would be reasonable of your doctor to refuse consent if, for instance, your blood pressure was high, or if you had suffered a threatened miscarriage in early pregnancy. In such cases a change in altitude could bring on premature labor. Similarly, it is unwise to fly in a small unpressurized plane, as the supply of oxygen to the fetus can sometimes be drastically diminished.

You might also bear in mind, if you are thinking of flying a long distance, the strain caused to you by jet lag.

Driving is perfectly safe if you do not find it exhausting and if you are not subject to dizzy spells. Bear in mind that if you drive in city traffic you are almost certainly breathing in exhaust fumes. This does not do your baby any good, so try to avoid the rush hour. If you have a heavy standard shift, the sheer hard work of changing gear can cause discomfort in the later months. An automatic car makes lighter work of driving. Make sure your seat belt is strapped under your belly and the shoulder harness is used properly, not so tight as to interfere with breathing or digestion.

Rest and sleep

During the first and last three months of pregnancy you will probably feel much more tired than usual, and it is advisable to rest as much as possible, rather than trying to fight off the tiredness. Toward the end of your pregnancy there may be several reasons why you cannot sleep as much as you would like.

Nearly every pregnant woman goes through a period when she either cannot drop off to sleep or wakes in the night because the baby

If you are finding it hard to sleep in late pregnancy the traditional methods of dealing with insomnia are probably the most reliable.

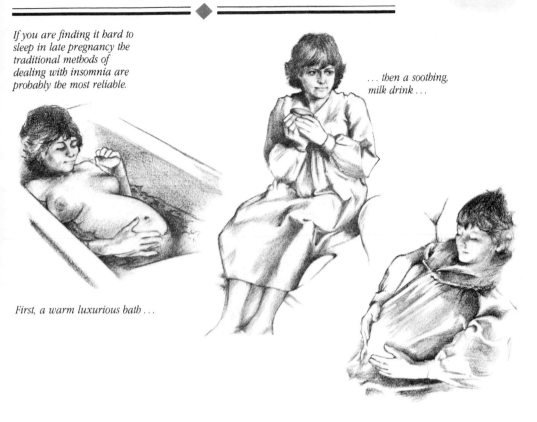

... then a soothing, milk drink ...

First, a warm luxurious bath ...

is kicking her, she needs to empty her bladder, or she has been awakened by a violent and disturbing dream and cannot get back to sleep. Sometimes the insomnia occurs because she is lying worrying and in the darkness her fears gain the upper hand.

... and finally deep, relaxing breathing, all the while concentrating on the new life within you.

If you have recently given up work, you may feel that your pregnancy has become a time of passive waiting and is stretching out longer and longer, so that you cannot see an end to it. You probably cannot sleep because you need action, and sometimes vigorous exercise during the day can be a remedy for this problem. You could also try the traditional remedies for sleeplessness, such as a hot milk drink after a luxurious warm bath at bedtime.

The stillness of the middle of the night actually provides a marvelous opportunity for practicing your relaxation and breathing. Use the time to center down into your body and become more aware of the developing life inside you. Allow your breathing to flow right down to where the baby nestles deep inside you. Cup your hands over the lower curve of your abdomen and breathe so that the wave of the inhaled breath presses your hands up and, as you give a long breath out, you sink on the receding wave.

Relax and enjoy lying there with your baby. Once you have begun to lose yourself in these feelings, you will probably find that your deep breathing has relaxed you back into sleep.

Emotional challenges in pregnancy

Many expectant mothers look and feel radiant. A healthy woman who is looking forward to a much-wanted baby, who has a loving and secure relationship with a considerate partner, and some knowledge about childbirth and what she can do to help herself, often revels in her pregnancy. Many women say "I feel fitter than I ever have before" or "I'm really enjoying being pregnant" and are surprised at the vitality and sense of inner fulfillment which they experience.

Yet probably all of us are assailed by darker thoughts at times when we are overtired or under some special stress. Some of the more negative feelings that women experience in early pregnancy have been discussed on page 34. But as your pregnancy advances, more specific anxieties may preoccupy you at times. Anxiety may grip you in the middle of the night when the baby has kicked you awake or when you have had to get up to empty your bladder and cannot get back to sleep again. Every fear is magnified in the darkness as you lie trying to sleep and unable to relax.

Worries about the birth

Labor can be an intensely pleasurable, all-absorbing and deeply satisfying activity which it is really possible to enjoy. But just as some people do not like climbing a mountain, even though the view at the summit is magnificent and the climb exciting, and just as some feel that sex is overrated and not worth the effort, whereas others think it is one of the best experiences life offers, different women have very different attitudes toward childbirth. This is not just a matter of what happens physiologically or how you are treated in the hospital, but also depends on what kind of person you are. Anxiety can cast a shadow over childbirth and produces the speeded-up heart rate, high blood pressure, muscle tension, and other physical results of stress which actually make birth more difficult. It is important to think through it and to understand why you are anxious.

Anxiety about labor is probably best dealt with first of all by finding out more about it, not just its mechanics, but the physical and emotional sensations of each phase, and the relaxation, breathing and focused concentration which can help you to work with your body instead of against it. The simple process of sharing fears also often results in women feeling much more lighthearted, so that they begin to enjoy their pregnancies. A good childbirth class where discussion is encouraged and women can talk freely about their apprehensions as well as about their hopes is often effective in

OPPOSITE
There are bound to be doubts and anxieties, but for many women there is also a new-found serenity and a sense of inner fulfillment.

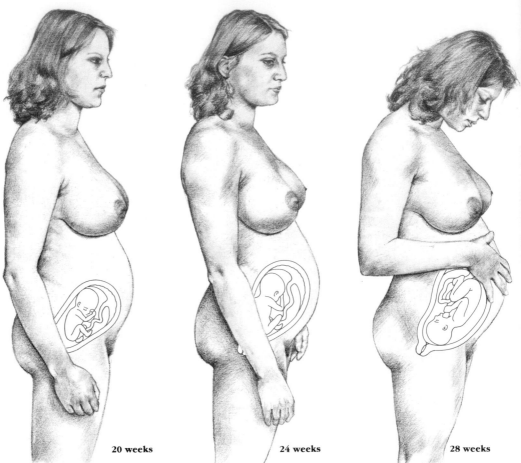

20 weeks   24 weeks   28 weeks

YOUR CHANGING SHAPE
Some women delight in the physical changes brought about by pregnancy. Others feel threatened by the inevitability of the process. Taking pleasure in your expanding form is good preparation for working with and expressing yourself through your body in labor.

developing self-confidence and helping you to look forward to labor as a peak experience which brings delight and fulfillment, not just an ordeal to be endured.

Pain A woman having her first baby often thinks "I have never had anything really painful. How shall I stand up to the pain of labor?" and since she has no idea what that pain is like or what contractions feel like, the thought can bring terror. Learning about labor, about how contractions work and how they may feel at different stages of labor, is the most effective way of coming face to face with this anxiety and doing something about it. There is a whole chapter in this book about pain and pain relief (pages 278–288), but the important thing to understand is that for most women the pain of labor is quite different from the pain of injury. Some women describe it as "positive pain" or "pain with a purpose."

Loss of control For many women anxieties about labor are linked with a dread of losing control. For your whole life you have been

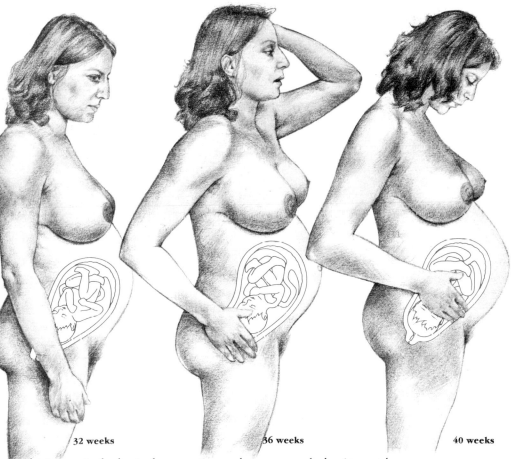

32 weeks   36 weeks   40 weeks

taught to control physical processes and your own behavior, and suddenly something is about to happen which clearly cannot be controlled and which is about to take over your body. You are told that you may cry out or groan, for example, that you may lose inhibitions, be impatient or irritable with your partner or whoever is helping you in labor, and swear and say things you never meant to, and are horrified to hear that during labor you may involuntarily empty your bowels or your bladder.

You also learn that the waters may break suddenly. In any group of women discussing the events of labor, first-time mothers nearly always ask those who have already had babies when the waters broke, whether it was sudden, and if so where it was; they express keen anxiety that they may break in the supermarket or on a bus. What these women are saying is that they are fearful of letting their bodies function freely because of the embarrassment and social stigma attached. It is as if degrading physical processes, above all dirty ones which involve getting rid of waste products from the body, are taking place in public.

Think through why you find the thought of the waters breaking in public so upsetting. You are having a baby and it is perfectly obvious that you are going to give birth soon. If the waters do break in public, is it really so very terrible? You will attract interest and sympathy, but not disgust. You may see it as a kind of sexual act in front of other people. You are quite right, and understanding this can help you in labor. Birth, just like lovemaking, is a sexual process. If you can go *with* your labor instead of fighting it the experience can be fulfilling in a strangely pleasurable way. Prepare the way to this through body awareness and relaxation. Touch relaxation (see page 173) is a special kind of release which teaches you to flow toward sensations of pressure and heat. It will help a lot in labor.

Loss of dignity and failure An anxiety closely connected with loss of control is the fear of making a fool of yourself. Some women think doctors and nurses will laugh at them if they find themselves making uncontrollable noises, for instance. You may feel that you are on public display in labor and approach it as a test of endurance. You may also be anxious about "letting down" a partner who puts great faith in your ability to cope, or even of "failing" a keen childbirth teacher. Some men who participate in classes and the other preparations for the birth become so enthusiastic and obsessional that they are in effect "trainers", rather like athletic coaches. The woman then feels that she is expected to put on a performance and must excel in it. Childbirth classes which are geared exclusively to techniques used in labor rather than focusing on wider aspects of the total experience can reinforce this feeling.

Just as the elaborate techniques performed to "ensure" satisfaction in lovemaking can sometimes disturb the spontaneous rhythm of sex and interfere with the intense feeling and play of emotion between the couple, so breathing exercises and "distraction" techniques can sometimes intrude on the experience of labor. Exercises need to become "second nature" and be made a part of yourself. It is like learning to play the piano: there is a vast difference between laborious scales and playing a sonata. The exercises are important because they prepare you for playing music. But the eventual aim is to let the music flow through you, rather than to superimpose tricks and techniques onto it. Such a physical and emotional surrender is simple in labor because of its intensity. Birth involves mind and body working together in a completely absorbing, exciting, and passionate way. There is no success or failure in labor. You cannot make a fool of yourself, let anyone down or flunk an examination in birth.

Fear of managing alone Some women approach labor as a medical incident like having an appendectomy, an unwelcome interruption of normal life rather than an experience which can be satisfying in itself. They feel totally dependent on the technology provided by the hospital and worry about whether they will get there on time, or whether the right people will be present to deliver the baby. Such women's dependence is reinforced by contemporary obstetrics and by every programme on television which illustrates the latest marvel of science applied to childbearing. The impression is readily given that women must depend on lifesaving machines, and that without them it is not safe to have a baby.

The fact is that although these machines can be extremely useful in diagnosing difficulties when a baby is at risk or when special problems are met in pregnancy or labor, the majority of women can give birth perfectly well without them.

It is not advances in medicine but improved conditions, better food and general health which have made childbirth much safer for mothers and babies today than it was 100 years ago. The rate of stillbirths and deaths in the first week of life is directly related to a country's gross national product and to the position of the mother in the social class structure.

It is a disturbing thought that it is twice as safe for a woman in the professional classes to bear a child than it is for an unsupported mother at the bottom of the social scale. The challenge is to find out which mothers and babies are at risk, to offer them everything possible which can make birth safer, but to let those who are at no special risk give birth naturally if they can.

Loss of autonomy Another frequent anxiety is that of being denied the right to function as an adult and fear of being under the control of doctors, nurses, and even machines. Many pregnant women resent the feeling that they cannot make their own decisions. Increasing numbers feel that they do not want to hand their bodies over to professional care-givers in pregnancy and childbirth, and are seeking maternity care in which they can take an active part, sharing the decision-making with their advisers.

I can still remember when I had my tonsils out when I was 7. I can't bear hospitals.

If you are not sure whether your doctor is being quite open with you, or whether the hospital will really let you do the things in labor which you have asked to do, the uncertainty can produce a sick fear in the pit of the stomach. Too often pregnant women are treated like children or as patients in categories of "high risk", "low risk", "primigravida", "multigravida", "MTLP" and so on, who have to be processed through the hospital system, passive receivers of care rather than active birthgivers.

Fear of hospitals For many women hospitals are threatening places. People usually go to a hospital when they are ill. This may be the first time that you have been a patient in a hospital and the sights, sounds and even smells of hospitals may alarm you. Society has given little thought so far to designing and decorating maternity units so that they look more like home, or at least a good hotel. Hospitals are still places with long green painted corridors and white tiles and instrument carts. Delivery rooms in otherwise splendid modern

hospitals can be windowless boxes, and prenatal clinics, your first introduction to the hospital, are often forbidding places without pictures and with backache-inducing chairs set in rows. Even more important than the physical surroundings are the attitudes of members of hospital staff and the way in which they interact with patients. If you meet cool indifference, rigid authoritarianism, or obvious hostility, you may dread going to the prenatal clinic, and this anxiety can color your whole approach to labor.

There is a certain kind of emotional climate in which anxieties flourish and unfortunately it is one which our society provides for many pregnant women. If there is no one readily available of whom you can ask questions and be answered in terms you can understand, the seeds of anxiety are often sown. They are nourished by the insecurity of seeing different members of staff in the prenatal clinic at each visit.

Women often feel apologetic about anxiety, about not being "sensible", as if they were revealing some shameful lack of emotional stamina. They are sometimes regarded as having something psychologically wrong with them if they show anxiety. But many of the fears you have during your pregnancy are not the result of inadequacy but a response to stresses caused by an environment which is alien and unfriendly and by care which is impersonal. In such a situation anxiety is *realistic*.

Although you may not be able to eradicate anxiety about the birth itself, it is sensible to tackle it directly. Ask to see around the labor and delivery rooms, including the machinery which may be used; attend childbirth classes at the hospital so that you can get to know at least some of the staff, and talk with your doctor about the style of childbirth which you would like if possible; ask him or her to note down any particular request on your chart. Read the section in this book on talking to doctors (pages 51–54) before you go.

Loss of attractiveness Some pregnant women are deeply concerned that their sexual attractiveness may be completely destroyed by childbearing. They are frightened of losing their figures; they may also be anxious that the vagina will be slack and changed in shape, and that as a result they will not be able to make love with their partners in a mutually satisfying way.

The fear of a tear or a cut (see page 294) often discussed in childbirth education classes is not so much about pain resulting from stitches, although it is often dealt with by the childbirth teacher in terms of coping with discomfort after the birth. It is really anxiety about genital mutilation.

Episiotomy In many hospitals episiotomy is routinely used for all women having their first babies and for a large percentage of those having second and subsequent babies. Now this is changing fast. Women are questioning the need for what amounts to surgical

All the coming and going and the noise makes me feel really het up. I can practically feel my blood pressure rising.

OPPOSITE

Finding time to concentrate on yourself when an older child is constantly present creates its own particular challenge.

intervention in normal birth and the creation of an artificial wound. Obstetricians are asking why this intervention has become so widely used without any proper evaluation.

Women are often more anxious about episiotomy than any other invasive procedure. The thought of being surgically cut, or injured, in such a sensitive place is horrifying, and some women feel as if they are being punished for enjoying sex. Many worry that childbirth will so damage them that they will never be the same again.

There are various ways in which you can prepare your body and the tissues of your perineum—the area between your vagina and your anus—to become soft and supple, so that you enter labor fully confident that you can give birth without injury.

Pelvic floor exercises (see page 107) can help create the sensitive awareness, coordination and control which help you in the second stage of labor, preparing you to open your body for the baby to be born, and reducing stress on the pelvic muscles and perineal tissues. Many women find that massage with vegetable oil also helps. Certainly getting in touch, literally, with this part of your body and feeling how flexible the tissues are, will give you confidence that your vagina and perineum are able to fan out and open wide. Since in late pregnancy it can be quite difficult to reach your perineum and exert firm pressure, you may want to ask a loving partner to help with this massage. It feels especially good if the oil is warmed first.

If you are concerned to avoid an episiotomy, discuss the subject with your midwife or doctor in advance. Say that you would like help at the delivery so that you can breathe the baby out rather than push it out, and ask for this to be noted on your chart. It is wrong to think that a woman who is anxious about episiotomy is in any way "neurotic", though doctors sometimes assume this.

Sometimes episiotomy must be performed for the baby's safety, so that he or she can be born quickly, or to avoid a large tear. It can help you to understand the healing process afterward if you know what has happened, and exactly where. Exploring the vagina with your fingers during pregnancy (see page 106) and after the birth, and looking at it in a mirror, helps you to feel that it belongs to you; you can then rehabilitate the area through gentle pelvic floor movements.

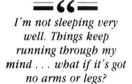

I'm not sleeping very well. Things keep running through my mind . . . what if it's got no arms or legs?

Worries about the baby

Almost every woman wonders at some stage of her pregnancy whether her baby is normal. Fear of producing a handicapped child is often connected with anxiety about not being able to live up to standards set by somebody else, usually either or both of the woman's own parents. You may feel it almost impossible that you could produce from the dark interior of your body anything which is perfect. This is probably the most persistent, gnawing fear of all, and the only way of coming to terms with it is to develop self confidence, a process which, not surprisingly, takes time. This is where regular attendance at childbirth education classes which encourage you to

If you are pregnant for the first time and maybe living in a different area, make the effort to meet other people with young families. You will build a new set of social relationships which will stand you in good stead after your own baby is born ...

have trust in your body and in your ability to give birth, rather than depend on others to get the baby born for you, can help enormously.

One woman who had disappointed her parents academically became pregnant outside marriage, in a desperate effort to show them that at least there was *something* she could do. She now lay awake wondering if her baby was deformed. Talking about this fear in a childbirth discussion group led her to reveal that she was having awful dreams. It then emerged that five out of the twelve women in the group were having very vivid dreams, and that even some of those who had not admitted to any worry about whether the baby would be "all right" were having dreams in which the baby was disposed of because it was not "good enough", or was taken away and looked after by other people because *they*, the mothers, were not themselves good enough. Dreams can often reveal emotional tangles which cause great distress in pregnancy until they are brought out into the open.

Most women who fear bearing an abnormal baby have little reason to expect that the baby will not be perfect. The minority of women who are aware of the possibility of inherited diseases or handicaps in their or their partners' families, or who are pregnant after the age of 40, will realize that they can seek genetic counseling and can have alphafetoprotein (AFP) screening (see page 205) and, if necessary, amniocentesis performed (see page 206).

Worries about the future

Loneliness Many women having their first babies move away from their own homes during pregnancy, often to a larger apartment or house, so that they find themselves in an area where they know nobody at all. They stop work in late pregnancy and no longer even have the daily contacts with friends and colleagues at work. At home and alone for the first time, they are initially delighted, but often quickly become bored and depressed.

If you are in this position plan to take up some activity which brings social contacts; learn something new; join a club of some kind; attend childbirth education classes; track down interesting places in the locality to which you have moved, and invite people to your home. If you do not know anyone with young children and would like to discover more about what babies are like, seek out your nearest playgroup or nursery school and go when parents are meeting their children, or go to your community center and say that you want to get to know somebody who has a baby. Your doctor or midwife may be able to tell you about other pregnant women or mothers with new babies who live near you. It is worth investigating the possibilities while you are still pregnant. When you are busy with a baby it may be more difficult to make new friends, especially during the winter months, so take the opportunity of making them now.

Change When a woman expresses anxiety about "things never being the same again", it helps to think through what exactly this means for her. If things are irrevocably altered, what might happen? One couple who had a deeply satisfying relationship saw the pregnancy and the upset connected with the birth as an "interruption." "We don't want to change our lives for a child," the woman said, "to be swamped by it. How long will it take before we get back to normal again? Sometimes I'm frightened we'll *never* get back to normal." When I asked what she found frightening about this, after some thought she explained that she did not want to become the same kind of woman as her mother and did not see herself as bound to babies and a home. Most of all she was afraid that because of the pregnancy her partner would not love her any more and that she would be desexed by maternity.

Social expectations Another woman said that her pregnancy made her feel that at last she was fulfilling a socially acceptable role and that her own mother was proud of her for the first time in her life. In a way, she resented this. Other women acted as if they knew how she felt and what she thought and wanted. The doctors at the hospital expected her to be a "good patient" and be processed through the busy prenatal clinic like all the others with their swelling bumps. She suddenly felt miles away from her former colleagues and the others with whom she had worked, separated from them by the inescapable fact of her pregnancy. But by the end she felt guilty that she had resented the baby at the beginning of her pregnancy. At night as it moved inside her she lay thinking whether she would ever be a good mother. She said, "I sometimes feel so sorry for the little thing in there that I end up crying."

In a prenatal discussion group both of these women had the chance to talk about their disturbing feelings. It emerged that several of the others were also lying awake at night thinking and worrying about much the same things. What had seemed personal handicaps proved to be an experience shared by a number of women.

If you realize that you are not all alone with your fears, and are not being "odd" or neurotic, the anxieties usually become much less disturbing. Thinking about inevitable change may worry you in different ways: you may be afraid that the relationship with your partner will deteriorate; that you have no maternal instincts and will be no good as a mother; that the loss of a job and the money and sense of freedom associated with getting out of the house and earning your own living may bring a real deprivation. You may wonder if you will be able to tolerate being at home all day with a "screaming brat", and whether you will miss all the interesting people at work.

Although such anxiety is realistic in the sense that these changes are dramatic and demanding for many women, most expectant mothers are more aware of anxieties about labor and the baby than they are of how they will cope after the birth. Many take the unknown "afterward" more or less for granted. It is as if they can only see as far as the birth, which dominates the horizon. The postpartum experience may then come as a shock for which they are not prepared. So some anxiety about life after the baby arrives is a healthy sign, and indicates that the emotional work is taking place which prepares a couple not only for the birth but for parenthood.

Many anxieties during pregnancy, both for the woman and the man, offer clues to the challenges confronting the couple. It is a waste of emotional energy to try to "forget" them or put them to the back of your mind. They are there to be worked with. It is often the man and woman who are determined to take it all in their stride and carry on as usual, and who do not acknowledge feelings of apprehension on the threshold of the unknown, who are likely to face the most shattering crises, both in the experience of birth and also when they have a baby in the house.

The discomfort anxiety produces can force you to think through the meaning for you of the coming of a child into your lives. Without stress and challenge of this kind emotional preparation for birth and parenthood may be overlooked. Fears and anxieties are an important element in the emotional changes necessary if you are to face up to the reality of birth and then to the astonishing reality of the new baby.

Becoming a father

Becoming a father is a major step in a man's life. It can also be a daunting one. Yet it is an experience usually treated as insignificant in comparison with that of becoming a mother. As a result the emotional upheavals and stresses of the future father are little understood and men are not prepared for the impact of pregnancy. If people do notice that a man is finding the going difficult they tend to laugh rather than sympathize. In fact the nervousness and anxiety of the father-to-be are favorite subjects of jokes and anecdotes, ranging from the picture postcard variety—showing a man wide-eyed and desperate in the hospital corridor as his wife produces triplets— to those amused tales about male ignorance and incompetence shared between women over coffee.

In childbirth classes and hospital lectures for parents-to-be a man is often discussed only in terms of how he can help his partner, and his own profound emotional needs are neglected. One result of this is to make him feel isolated and resentful, finding it difficult to reach out and give his partner the support she needs. She is the fairy princess going to the ball and he feels a bit like the back legs of a pantomime horse.

An expectant father may feel jealous of all the attention given to the future mother, absurdly envious of her reproductive powers and sometimes even jealous of the coming baby. Then he feels guilty about succumbing to these emotions and decides to concentrate on his work—because that at least is one thing he can do properly. And the more he immerses himself in his own preoccupations, the more isolated and left out of the pregnancy he feels.

Some men become really depressed during pregnancy or experience violent mood swings similar to those that a pregnant woman may go through. A few even walk out of the relationship because the stress is too great for them to handle. So it is important to remember that usually there are *two* people having a baby and that the man also goes through a transitional period of stress when very deep emotions may be stirred and his behavior may be difficult to understand.

Reacting to fatherhood

The sheer responsibility of having a baby can be frightening. The woman may be going to give up work outside the home for a time, or even for good, and the man is expected to support the family. The financial burden alone may be too great for some men to shoulder without anxiety. But for many men money problems constitute a rationalization, a socially acceptable explanation for anxiety, without getting to the root of what they find disturbing. In fact, some men find that the prospect of becoming a father brings with it a crisis of identity. Although it is a common occurrence and one which in due course brings about creative change, it is nevertheless still a crisis.

The changing relationship One element in this crisis involves grieving over a relationship that is bound to change. The easy ways, the lack of routine, the spontaneity of the early stage of the relationship, all have to give way to an existence centered around a baby. Some men see their partners as their mothers. When the woman becomes pregnant it is as if the man is losing a mother and is being replaced in her love by a new baby. As she becomes more involved in the pregnancy and the coming baby he feels increasingly rejected and finds this inevitable shift of focus very threatening.

The changing woman Some men acquire a woman as a show-piece, proof of their success in hunting down and possessing a desirable sexual object, or evidence of their social success, a demonstration and symbol of a life style which embodies achievement. Delighted as such a man may be to be fathering a child, he may find it difficult to cope with his partner's new concentration on the pregnancy rather than on him. He feels that the physical changes in his partner's body are upsetting as conventional attractiveness is replaced by a very different body—no longer the outline of a neat figure but a melon-shaped abdomen and heavy, swelling breasts covered with a network of tiny blue veins. A man who has valued a woman as a status or sex symbol may feel that he is being cheated.

I'm deeply moved by this baby growing inside her. I feel we're very close in a new way.

The developing baby It is sometimes difficult initially for a man, who does not have the baby growing inside his body, to feel its reality. He often begins to become more aware of the child at about the time when he feels it bump and kick at night. Some men find this sensation not only astonishing and exciting but rather eerie, and they take a while to adjust to the idea of another being living and growing inside the body of the woman they know so well.

The future grandparents When a couple have a first baby they may have to work through a painful transitional period in which they forge a new adult relationship with their own parents, which allows for the responsibility and commitment they have to the child they are bearing. This may produce stresses with the future grand-parents, and a man may get caught up in a difficult relationship with his own mother just as a woman may with hers. When a man's mother is fearful that she is losing her son she becomes demanding. He may feel the pull of her possessive love drawing attention away from the needs of his wife and baby. Sometimes a woman sees this, whereas the man is completely unaware of it. It is important to understand that the older women, the exmothers, are being replaced, and they may feel hurt and unwanted. If there is a problem of this kind, the couple should talk about it together and be honest about their feelings.

The father's new role

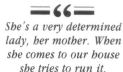

Having a baby used to be solely the concern of the woman, with her mother standing in the background giving advice. Nowadays it is much more something for woman and man to share.

There are still some men who say they do not want to get involved in "women's things" and who feel that their manliness is being threatened. They have the uneasy suspicion that learning about childbirth means that they will no longer be potent, virile males. Some imagine that it is expected that they will hand the woman over to the experts and retire from the scene. They believe that the professional must know so much more than they do that they are bound to be in the way and have no function in the delivery room.

Thirty years ago some midwives and obstetricians looked askance at men who became involved in the process of childbirth, as if they were slightly odd. Go back fifty years or so and men kept well away from anything to do with birth; pregnancy was a "certain condition" which a man pretended he knew nothing about. My mother told me that my father felt embarrassed to go out with her in advanced pregnancy, so that walks they took had to be after dark, with her enveloped in a wraparound coat. And as for a father wheeling a stroller, or changing a diaper—it was unheard of; even a man who might have liked to try his hand at such things rarely got the chance. This was partly because there used to be what one perceptive psychoanalyst called a male "taboo on tenderness." Men were frightened that to become involved with women's activities would humiliate them in the eyes of other men. And childbirth was the epitome of all feminine mysteries. Both women and men were prevented by these rules from discovering their full potential.

Many modern men are determined to share as much as they can in pregnancy and birth. They enjoy the woman's changing shape and the reality of the baby kicking against their hand. But a man often still feels a novice at fatherhood. He wonders just how much he can do, since the baby is growing in her body, not his. In a way, the partnership between the mother and her unborn child is complete. And pregnancy often seems to be so carefully managed by the obstetric team that a man can feel an intruder.

But a woman depends on her partner's support and needs the special relationship with him, which is quite different from any others that she has. She may not realize just how much her partner is sharing in the pregnancy emotionally and the heights and depths of his own feelings about it. There is no longer any need for a man to square his shoulders and pretend he is not stirred by what is happening. Take the opportunity to talk together about your feelings.

Feelings about being present at the birth

Most expectant fathers today approach childbirth with curiosity and interest and in a very different spirit from that thought suitable by their fathers and grandfathers. Though they may wonder whether they are going to make fools of themselves while playing an unfamiliar part, and may be nervous of unpleasant procedures involved in labor, they want to understand what is going on and to help and support their partners. They realize that hospital staff are usually extremely busy and working with more than one patient at a time. It is therefore impossible for other people to give the constant companionship and loving care which a woman craves as she is swept through the powerful physical and emotional experiences of labor; and the very unfamiliarity of the surroundings can make the most courageous woman apprehensive. She needs her partner or someone else who loves her. She needs someone who is there not simply as an onlooker but as a companion, who has studied what happens in childbirth, who knows what the prenatal preparation has been like, and who is able to help her in labor. (For more about the father's part in the birth, see pages 267–277.)

The man who fully involves himself in the birth shares in an experience which is exciting, challenging, intensely moving, and deeply satisfying. It is not only a question of helping his partner have their baby but of an often surprising encounter with his own emotions and a discovery that he is swept into a peak experience which is bigger than anything he anticipated. There may be an astonishing, an incredible joy and wonder at having been close to the beating center of life. In a very direct way, love is made flesh.

BEING SUPPORTIVE ABOUT PRENATAL CARE
The prenatal clinic

Pregnancy can be a time of great emotional upheaval as a woman adapts psychologically to the extraordinary things happening inside her body. She has to go through all sorts of manipulations and physical examinations that are not always conducted in a warm, sympathetic way. It is clear that many women are made anxious by the kind of prenatal care they receive.

Some men find this difficult to understand. They say that they find the sophisticated technology which is used today reassuring and fascinating. But if the man imagines something happening inside his own testicles or penis, he may find it easier to comprehend. How would he feel if his testicles started to swell up and change shape dramatically, forcing him to visit a doctor regularly and be prodded, poked, and examined by strangers who seemed concerned only with the lower end of his body? He might find it impossible to get information about what was happening to him, knowing only that he faced an ordeal at the end of nine months when whatever was occurring must be terminated and the thing inside him somehow got out. How would he like lying flat on a high table, sometimes with his legs up high and wide apart in metal stirrups, while various women in white coats peered at him with little lights and probed his body with special machines? Out of the corner of his eye he could see them writing up case notes full of technical terms and abbreviations apparently suggesting a disease.

A man has to go to the doctor's office only once to get an idea of how intimidating it can be. In the rushed atmosphere of a busy doctor's office women often feel that they have become part of a factory process for producing babies. Questions about treatment or requests for advice go out of their heads, or else seem to interrupt the smooth running of the office and mean that other women waiting their turn have still longer to wait. All too often a woman returns from the doctor depressed and anxious. If her partner can get away from work to attend occasionally and to meet the doctor, he can give her moral support and build the foundation for a good working relationship with those who will be caring for her during labor.

Even if this is not possible, he can still help his partner by providing comfort and security if this is what she needs, and by talking to her about the things that ought to be discussed with the doctor. It is helpful to write questions down and keep a notebook for this purpose, as well as for any instructions given during pregnancy.

Childbirth education classes

When a woman starts attending classes in preparation for the birth there is usually an opportunity for her partner to share in some or all of the meetings. He can then learn a good deal about the physiological process and emotional changes of labor, can understand his own part in it, and often has the chance to see films of birth where women are using techniques similar to those learned in classes.

Everyday help

In the last three months a man can help his partner by seeing that she takes more rest and lies down for a nap every afternoon or evening. Sometimes extra labor-saving equipment, additional help in the house, or the use of services like a laundry, can ensure that she does not get worn out. She should not be carrying heavy shopping so he may take over supermarket duty, or come as well to load the boxes into the car. If there are jobs in the house which entail moving furniture, these are his now. And if the woman cannot get down to bathe the toddler or strip the bed and make it again the man can take over these chores too while she does some of the easier tasks. On the other hand the woman does not need to be treated like an invalid, and the couple can enjoy going out together, especially at the end of pregnancy when time may seem to pass very slowly and she feels she has been pregnant forever.

A man can also protect his partner from all the well-meaning advice, often very contradictory and confusing, that comes from other people both before and after the birth. He can support her in doing things the way they have both decided.

Practical help is important, especially in the last few months.

OPPOSITE

With a new baby on the way, a father helps by becoming more involved in the older child's daily routine.

Your changing relationship

Pregnant women are not only obstetrical patients or even just future mothers. They are also usually in a loving relationship with a man. Pregnancy can be a time of great opportunity for both partners in the relationship to discover things about themselves and each other. However two people feel about each other, the emotional changes of pregnancy are bound to affect them. If they do not communicate easily it can be a time when small irritants turn into major crises.

The couple under stress

There are some couples who find the transition period of pregnancy an especially stressful time. It can put stress on the couple who have an informal, even casual, relationship and who have not attached particular importance to getting married, but who perhaps marry when a baby is on the way. It can put equal stress on a couple who both enjoyed their careers and never saw themselves as parents, but who nonetheless decide to continue with the pregnancy when the woman conceives by mistake. It can bristle with challenges, too, when a woman has been on the pill, stops taking it because the couple think it might be a good idea to have a baby, and then immediately becomes pregnant before she has had time to switch her mind to the possibility of motherhood. In these situations rapid adjustment is necessary, and either or both parents may feel trapped, at the same time that they are feeling delighted.

As soon as they tell other people about the pregnancy they may feel that a social machine has swung into action. Some couples say that they felt strong disapproval from relatives, especially their parents, when they put off having a baby; then when the woman eventually did become pregnant they were overwhelmed by the relief and pleasure these people expressed, as if at last they were doing the socially acceptable thing. In some ways the reactions feel like a public intrusion on their intimate and personal relationship with each other.

Sharing the problems

When a pregnancy starts, a man and a woman often begin inhabiting different worlds. He may think that she becomes psychologically unpredictable and vulnerable. In her turn she may see him as unsympathetic, unloving, and crude. He may feel he can no longer talk to her about "rational" matters, and that she has lost interest in everything except the coming baby. He may even feel pushed out into the cold, as if he were living with a different woman. Because they are often isolated from other couples facing similar difficulties, they may be under the impression that such problems are unique to them. Talking to other couples expecting babies can help them to see the social pressures on prospective parents and the cultural style of childbirth in modern Western societies which often creates emotional stress. Attending classes together can provide a bridge between the different socially assigned gender roles of a man and woman, and can help draw them closer.

Talking in a group

At one prenatal group couples discussed together the effect of pregnancy on their relationship. One woman, who was feeling that she had lost her individuality in the universal category of expectant motherhood, remarked that she was frightened of what this was doing to her relationship with her husband. Would they, she worried, become just "Mom and Dad" and cease being lovers? Her concern about this was even making her resent the baby at times.

In discussion the members of the group found that other couples too were experiencing these pressures and the same kinds of anxiety. Some of them felt strongly that they wanted to be different kinds of parents from their own parents and to have a happier marriage than their parents had. It was agreed that it was important for a couple to share these thoughts with each other and to discuss not just the practical arrangements for preparing for the baby, but their ideas about the kind of parents they hoped to be, and what they thought about their partners as prospective parents too.

Becoming a mother involves emotional "growing pains" which can be no less disturbing than those of adolescence. A similar psychological process often occurs in a man too, but he usually feels he has even less justification to talk about it because *he* is not pregnant. Yet to be able to nurture their young, both the man and the woman have to change and become different kinds of people.

Another couple, who had been through this process with an earlier pregnancy, said that talking about it had helped them understand each other better and that they came to like their changed roles. At first the parts of "Mommy" and "Daddy" were merely playacting, but then they found they were good at them. The new roles made each see qualities they had never imagined the other possessed.

One of the things to emerge from that discussion was that becoming parents is not just a matter of physical changes but also of learning. The adjustment and adaptation take time, and pregnancy is the ideal time to start this process of growing up.

Developing confidence

Many couples have a funny name for the unborn child, and talk about it as if it were a friend whom they know well but have never met. When doctors prod and poke and the hospital takes the woman over at the prenatal clinic or when she goes into labor, the couple can feel as if a very personal and intimate relationship between the three of them has been invaded. "Our" baby has become "the" baby, or even "the hospital's" baby. A woman needs to feel that the baby really belongs to her. This may be important in pregnancy, and is vital after the birth, if she is to have a chance to fall in love with her baby.

Other couples have problems in family relationships (especially with their in-laws), which they imagine to be peculiarly their own and which they do not realize are shared by many others. Each partner may be resenting the other for his or her insensitivity and ineptitude at handling these situations, or for being overdependent on parents. In a childbirth education class there is a chance to talk through these problems, to discuss the future grandparents' feelings and any other situations which are causing stress. The very fact of finding that they are not alone with such difficulties may help a couple.

Parents can start to get to know their baby even before it is born, and this knowledge may give added depth to their own relationship.

Growing through the experience

Many couples have their babies before they are really emotionally ready for them. As a result, some babies come into the world in spite of, rather than because of, what their parents feel about each other. When a woman decides to continue with an unplanned pregnancy, the accidental product of an impermanent relationship, she needs special emotional support. Even if a man has nothing else to offer a woman he can give her this. It is bound to be painful for them both if they decide to part with the baby, but the experience can be important for both of them and can help them to grow in understanding. In fact, when a couple are unhappy together, there is an even more compelling reason to use the time of pregnancy for joint preparation for the birth of their child, if only because the task can in itself bring a new perceptiveness and sensitivity to the other's needs.

So, in all circumstances, preparation for birth is not merely the acquisition by the woman of a set of instructions and exercises, but a process in which two people start out together on a shared enterprise. It provides opportunities for increased understanding of each other's needs and enrichment of their whole relationship. For both parents pregnancy can be a time of growing up. If a man and woman can understand what the pregnancy means to the other partner they are well on the way to growing up *together.*

The emotional changes of pregnancy exist for *all* couples expecting a baby, and it helps to realize that others share these experiences and find them challenging. Sharing brings relief from anxiety and a new understanding of the emotions involved.

SEX IN PREGNANCY

It is important for your sense of wellbeing that you are physically loved in pregnancy, whether or not this involves sexual intercourse. Stroking, massage, loving touch, and sexual pleasuring are all part of this physical expression of the relationship.

Attitudes to sex

Many couples make love right through pregnancy. At the beginning nausea and vomiting can mean that the last thing you want to do is to make love, but usually by the middle months lovemaking is enjoyable and satisfying, sometimes for the first time. Pregnancy is a good time for you to learn more about how your body works. A woman who begins to learn about her uterus, vagina, and pelvic floor muscles may become sensitively responsive to this part of her body when she was not before. Some women have their first experience of orgasm during pregnancy. Many do not realize the function of the pelvic floor muscles (see page 107) in active lovemaking and some have never looked at or explored the way in which the vagina, labia, and clitoris are constructed.

But this is not just a matter of intellectual information and diagrams of the female genitals. Some women dislike and have a general and profound distrust of their bodies. For the first time in pregnancy they can learn to know and be comfortable with themselves. If you have never before allowed feelings to sweep through you, you may find that preparation for the intensely emotional experience of labor, with its storms and currents, and the extraordinarily powerful drama of delivery, unlocks a capacity for "letting go" which can apply to lovemaking also.

But some couples (especially in the later months) feel that they do not have the doctor's approval about lovemaking. You may have guilty feelings and be anxious that you are somehow harming your unborn baby. This is one of the subjects that expectant parents often talk about in childbirth education classes. Couples say that they often find sex a very difficult subject to discuss with their doctor.

Sex? I can barely remember what that is!

Positions for lovemaking

The conventional "missionary" position (with the man lying on top of the woman) is rarely comfortable, unless the man gets on all fours and puts no weight on the woman. It is worth experimenting with some other positions in which she is uppermost or in which entry is from the side or from behind (see page 156). No harm will come to the baby: the bag of waters cushions it and a seal is provided by the mucous plug, which is rather like a stopper in a bottle. Even when your abdomen is bumped hard the only effect on the baby is that it bobs like a cork in a glass of water.

Can orgasm start labor?

Although the female orgasm involves contractions of the uterus, it will not trigger off labor unless everything is ready to start anyway. But it is quite natural after intercourse to feel uterine contractions, which usually die down after a few minutes. The uterus is an active organ and contracts regularly from the time of a girl's first period right through to the menopause. It is especially active in pregnancy and the contractions (known as Braxton Hicks contractions) which you feel in the last months are rehearsals for the labor. If you have had a premature labor before, notice spotting of blood or if the mucous plug has already gone (the show—see page 228), it is wise not to have intercourse. Once the cervical mucus has been disturbed by contractions (and this *can* happen in the last four to five weeks), ascending infection is a possibility.

I love her luscious, pregnant curves!

Using sex to induce labor

If you are "due", especially if induction of labor has been suggested by your doctor, lovemaking is one of the ways in which you might be able to start things off naturally. Some women are thought to be especially sensitive to prostaglandins in the semen. (Prostaglandins cause the uterus to contract, and semen has a higher proportion of them than any other body substance.) It is best to choose a position— such as the woman lying on her back with her legs raised on the man's hips—in which semen is deposited right up against the cervix. But since such a position may be very uncomfortable at this late stage of pregnancy, it should be done gently.

Breast stimulation in late pregnancy also sometimes produces a strongly contracting uterus. This worries some people, but unless

Lovemaking in pregnancy

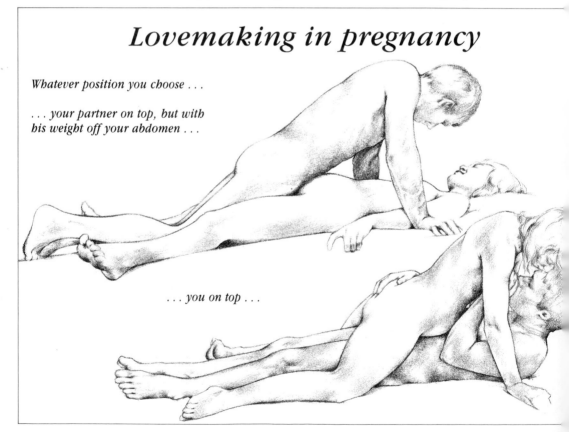

Whatever position you choose . . .

. . . your partner on top, but with his weight off your abdomen . . .

. . . you on top . . .

you have reason to think that the baby may come too early it is equally harmless, and may actually be a good thing, because the Braxton Hicks contractions which result (see page 229) help to prepare the way for labor, softening and drawing up the cervix, and—just before the baby is due—dilating it a little even before labor begins.

Nipple stimulation during labor

It has been discovered that stimulation of the nipples can reactivate a labor that has come to a halt. Some doctors have tried using it in place of the oxytocin drip (see page 298) to augment a slow labor. Unfortunately they have discovered that it does not always work. It may be that its success depends on how the stimulation is provided: perhaps someone you love may be more effective than simply using a breast pump. The midwife and doctor may agree to go out for a while and leave you to it. Though there may be a few raised eyebrows, it makes sense to try the natural way of stimulating the uterus first.

The emotions you have as lovers are not in conflict with the feelings of compassion and tenderness everyone agrees it is right to have about a baby. The sexual excitement felt by two people bound in love and caring for *each other* is a good basis for becoming parents able to give love to their baby and growing child.

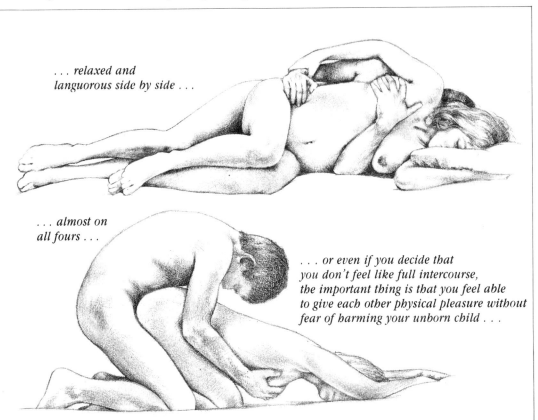

. . . relaxed and languorous side by side . . .

. . . almost on all fours . . .

. . . or even if you decide that you don't feel like full intercourse, the important thing is that you feel able to give each other physical pleasure without fear of harming your unborn child . . .

Pregnant again

Pregnancy the second or third time round is a new experience. It will not be exactly like the first time. It holds different challenges. Coping with them involves flexibility and resourcefulness on the part of both parents. In some ways things are much easier because you know what to expect and have probably developed self confidence in your role as a childbearer. You may sail through the pregnancy with style and thoroughly enjoy it. But there may be difficulties which come as a surprise because you thought it would be simple this time.

Reactions to another pregnancy

Other people's reactions The first problem you may encounter is the reaction of other people to a new pregnancy. Whereas your first was greeted with delight, friends and relatives are usually far less interested in the next pregnancy and may even raise their eyebrows and criticize you if you already have three children or if you are pregnant again after a very short interval. They can make you feel that what you are doing is not very public-spirited and even socially harmful. Some women say they were asked "Do you want it?" or "Don't you think you've had enough?", others that sympathy was offered by well-meaning friends, "How ever will you manage?" Being prepared for this reaction will help you cope with it.

Your partner's reaction You may find that your partner is not so excited about the next pregnancy. He may be busy and preoccupied and even seem totally uninvolved. Many men feel an extra burden of responsibility and financial anxiety when a second or subsequent baby is on the way. One baby was fun but now he feels "trapped" into having to provide for a growing family for years to come. Some women are desperately disappointed at their partners' reactions to later pregnancies and feel that they are missing out on all the joy of the first baby and the companionship that drew them close together the first time around. Talk about your feelings together so that you can come to appreciate what the experience means to each of you.

Finding time to relax

When you already have a lively two- or three-year-old or a group of energetic youngsters to look after, pregnancy can be very tiring. The first time around you were able to look after yourself and luxuriate in afternoon rests, with time for thinking, planning, and dreaming. Caught up in the hustle and bustle of family life, ferrying children to and from school, coping with the enormous meals they can consume and facing the everyday battle with egg on the stairs, tricycles in the hall, crumbs on the carpet, and dishes in the sink, you may have to

relegate pregnancy to the back of your mind. You simply do not have time for it. This may result in your neglecting yourself, your nutrition, your relaxation, and also missing out on times when you can just "center down" and focus your thoughts on the baby and yourself.

When you realize this, in the short intervals between your commitments as wife, mother, nurse, psychotherapist, teacher, hostess, house cleaner, chief cook and bottle washer, the chances are that you will feel guilty. You begin to feel apologetic to the little baby growing inside you, and perhaps also fearful that you cannot give him or her the time or even the love that you have devoted to the others. This feeling may be intensified after the birth, when to some extent the new baby has to be fitted into family life rather than your own activities being modified to the baby's needs. If you are sitting a two-year-old on the potty, or calming down three children in the bath having a very splashy game which threatens to submerge the toddler, it is difficult at the same moment to fix the new baby comfortably on the breast and to enjoy the release of milk.

Talk about these feelings of inadequacy with other women who are facing the same problems. If you do feel guilty, the only solution is to try to organize your life so that every day you have at least some time to think about and plan for the coming baby, or, once the new baby has been born, to give him or her your whole concentration. It is certainly difficult to find even a short space of time for such attention; but you may be able to find someone who is willing to take your other children for a walk some afternoons or your partner might bathe them and put them to bed every evening, giving you a time when you will be able to concentrate on yourself and your new baby.

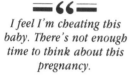

I feel I'm cheating this baby. There's not enough time to think about this pregnancy.

Taking care of yourself

A new pregnancy may produce aches and discomforts which you have not experienced before. Lifting bigger children and the inevitable clearing and cleaning may contribute to backache associated with bad posture. This is accentuated by fatigue and doing things in a rush. If your child still wakes in the night, doesn't like the idea of an afternoon nap, *ever*, or wakes very early in the morning and, because he or she is still too young to read quietly, comes jumping into your bed and remains during the hours after dawn, a restless bundle, you may be running short of sleep and long for a solid uninterrupted 10 or 12 hours. Perhaps it is possible to arrange this when your partner is at home on the weekend.

The chances are that you look and feel more pregnant with this baby too, partly as a result of poor posture and tiredness, but also as a consequence of the stretching your uterus has had during previous pregnancies. This may mean that you don't feel at all happy about your body; such a lack of pleasure in yourself is then expressed automatically in the way you stand, walk and sit. It is a vicious circle.

Ask your childbirth educator to help you firm up your abdominal muscles. Use buttock and leg muscles to help support your spine and

Try to set aside a small part of every day when you can relax completely and focus your thoughts on yourself and the coming baby.

Preparing your first child

Borrow a friend's baby for a few hours so that your child can discover what babies are really like . . .

. . . let your child feel the baby moving inside you . . .

. . . make a book showing pictures of your first child when she was a baby so that she can see how babies change and grow . . .

. . . and let father take responsibility for some of your child's daily routine before the new baby arrives.

tummy and do a few rhythmic exercises each day (see pages 108–109). Your older child may enjoy doing them with you. Then make an opportunity to cherish yourself a bit. Ask your partner to give you a massage session. Think about what would cheer you up.

Preparing the older child

Some parents worry a great deal about how to prepare the older child for the new baby. This problem can seem almost insurmountable if the older one is clinging and still very dependent. Some childbirth educators* have come up with the idea of making a book for such a child, illustrated with photographs of himself and starting with a simple description of how a baby grows inside its mother, illustrated with line drawings and a photograph of the mother when she was pregnant. You could show preparations for the birth, and then your child as a newborn baby, being suckled or bathed. These pictures could be followed by a series of photographs of the older child showing him eating, drinking, playing, helping in the house and garden. Perhaps the last page of the book can be left blank for a photograph of the new baby. All this helps the older child to prepare for the new baby and to realize that he was once just as small and incapable as it will be.

If possible borrow a baby for a few hours or have a mother and her small baby in the house for half a day or so. This will help your child to understand the reality of a baby and also how a mother holds and cares for it. Many older children expect a new baby to be either a passive bundle that can be handled like a doll or a playmate who can join in their games immediately.

If you are moving the older child from a crib to a bed, do so several months before the birth, so that it does not seem a consequence of the baby's arrival. And, if you are going to have extra help after the birth, encourage the helper to become friends with the older child well before the advent of the new baby.

When another baby is on the way, the relationship between the father and the older child is of great importance. It is a time when the two can draw closer together and enjoy each other's company for longer periods, something that will help you a great deal after the birth when you are busy with the new baby.

Toward the end of pregnancy take your older children with you to the doctor. Ask if they can listen with a fetoscope to the fetal heart, or help measure your tummy.

Anticipating the birth

In tune with your body for labor

Windows into the uterus

The last few weeks

In tune with your body for labor

Part of preparation for birth is doing exercises, but it is even more important to *think* about labor in a constructive way. Give yourself time to imagine what is going to happen in your body and what you may feel, and so build up a picture that has meaning for you. This picture will be quite different from illustrations in obstetric text-books: it is vital that it relates to *feelings* and is not just built up of intellectual information. Only then can the subjective sensations you experience in labor fit into a pattern that makes sense to you and that can help you adjust to each challenge as it comes.

So during pregnancy take time to imagine the birth of your baby. Think of different kinds of labor (see page 257) and how you might cope with them. Avoid restricting your fantasies to only one kind of labor when it may turn out that the labor you have is very different.

Childbirth education

If you are having a baby without having had instruction in childbirth, your body will probably respond naturally. However, education for birth helps you to know more about your body and so feel happy with it during pregnancy. You learn how to prepare yourself so that when you are in labor you can work *with* your body instead of fighting it, so that you can understand the activity of the uterus, and so that, through relaxation, breathing, and focused concentration, you can gradually come to achieve harmony with the birth process.

CHOOSING A PRENATAL CLASS

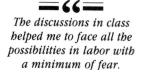

The discussions in class helped me to face all the possibilities in labor with a minimum of fear.

Once you have booked into a prenatal clinic (see page 46), it is time to think about arranging prenatal classes, so that you and your partner can learn about the physiological changes of pregnancy and labor and the possible emotional impact of the stresses likely to be involved. It pays to shop around for classes and discover the different ones available in your area. You would not dream of walking into any hairdresser's and asking them to cut and style your hair without first finding out what sort of work they did. Learning your task in childbirth is even more important, and so you should approach childbirth education classes with the same discrimination. For teaching to improve, more critical, informed consumers are needed. Any prenatal teacher worth her salt learns from her students, and continues to modify her teaching on the basis of the feedback she receives from them and the ideas they share with her.

Finding out about classes

When you inquire about classes, do not assume that they are successful only if those who have attended them have had easy labors and births. If you have to have a forceps delivery or a cesarean section it does not mean that you have "failed" in applying what you have learned. Having a baby is not like passing an exam or winning a race. You are not expected to come out "on top" with a two-hour labor, or no painrelieving drugs or whatever. It is much more a question of learning how to adapt your responses—mainly those of breathing and relaxation—to the particular challenges of your own labor. So it can be useful to talk also to women who have had labors that were not straightforward, and to find out from them if attending classes helped them at all.

Even though women all the world over have babies in much the same way, birth can be a vastly different experience for different women; just as, even though sexual intercourse involves certain mechanical and physiological processes which are the same everywhere, what people feel about it, exactly what they do and the meaning the total experience has for them, varies with the individual and the occasion. Childbirth is not primarily a medical process, but a psychosexual experience. It is not surprising that adapting your responses to the stimuli it presents should involve a subtle and delicate working together of mind and body.

When asking about classes, ask a woman whether she found the techniques that she learned in class helpful when she was actually in labor, and whether she felt confident and as if she understood exactly what was going on. If she says "Nothing helped", implies that the classes did not relate in any way to the reality of labor, or says that she was absolutely terrified from beginning to end, it sounds as if the classes did not help her, even though she may have enjoyed getting to know the other expectant mothers.

Your local hospital may have prenatal classes, although frequently they focus on routines and procedures you may expect to have done in that hospital, rather than choices or methods. Your doctor or midwife may know of classes. Alternatively, if you write to the International Childbirth Education Association (ICEA), the American Society for Psychoprophylaxis in Obstetrics (ASPO), or the American Academy of Husband-Coached Childbirth (AAHCC—addresses for all of these are given on page 383), they will let you know where classes are held by their teachers, or put you in contact with the organizer of a childbirth group in your area.

I didn't realize how scared I was till I went to classes and then it hit me. I'd been kidding myself. But after a few classes I started to feel a new confidence.

What makes a good prenatal class?

Good classes are progressive in the sense that you learn a little more each time; you should not feel at the third or fourth lesson that you have sat through it all before. There should be opportunities for you to ask questions, discuss freely and practice the exercises rather than

simply listen to a formal lecture. Breathing and relaxation exercises which can be of practical use in labor should be included. Their relevance to labor should be specifically described, and why and how they are used. Relaxation is not as simple as it might sound. It is not just a question of flopping in front of the TV screen or of lying down with a bar of chocolate and a good book, but of learning complete awareness and control of muscle groups all over the body so that they can be contracted or relaxed at will, including muscles you may not even know you possess. Relaxation also means learning how to relax *under stress*, not just lying in a deck chair on a sunny day or in a classroom while a cool voice tells you that a contraction is beginning, continuing, and then fading away.

It helps to learn different patterns and rhythms of breathing for the different phases of labor (see page 187). So when you are asking about classes inquire of any woman who has been to them whether she learned breathing in detail.

An effective teacher helps her students realize something of what labor feels like, and the reality and power of its challenge. She also explains things fully, without fear that she is burdening her students' minds, and does so honestly and clearly. In some classes there is far too much talking down to pregnant women. You have a right to understand what is happening to your own body and what people are proposing to do to you. A good teacher does not answer a query with "Oh you don't have to bother about that", or imply that everyone will do what is best for you and your baby, and that all you need to do is trust your birth attendants. Discussion should be a real exchange of ideas, not simply a few questions to which answers are given without recognition of the apprehension and the sometimes nightmarish fears that can lie behind them.

You can see from this that a good deal depends on the personality of the teacher. It is not so much "the method" that is good or inadequate as the quality of the teaching itself, and perhaps most of all the relationship that the teacher has with her students. I have seen teaching in different countries—including Western Europe, the USA, and beyond the Iron Curtain—which seemed woefully inadequate or mechanized, or which involved learning a number of rather irrelevant physical exercises, and yet, because of the personality and attitude of the teacher, the women participated joyfully in their labors.

The Dick-Read method

There are different approaches to childbirth education and the names associated with them can be confusing for expectant mothers. The Dick-Read method is named after Dr Grantly Dick-Read;* it is the oldest method and is usually associated with "relaxation classes". The philosophy behind this approach is that ignorance produces fear, which leads to tension, which in turn quickly produces pain. So teachers concentrate on overcoming fear by teaching deep relaxation and the breathing that accompanies it, along with providing full

Now I've had the baby I do miss the classes! It was such fun meeting every week.

OPPOSITE
Learning to relax for labor can benefit both of you and be enjoyable too. . . .

and accurate information about the childbearing process, exercises to keep you supple and poised, and discussion of breastfeeding.

Psychoprophylaxis

Psychoprophylaxis is a highly systematized training centered on techniques of breathing rather than relaxation. This method originated in the USSR, was developed in Paris, and then adapted in the United States by Elisabeth Bing. Psychoprophylaxis classes start by deconditioning the women from their fear and doubts about childbirth, and then recondition them to respond to labor contractions as helpful stimuli and not as pains. Exercises are taught both for limbering up and for use in labor. Full information is given about the anatomy and physiology of pregnancy and labor. This system is taught by the American Society for Psychoprophylaxis in Obstetrics teachers and is one of a range of approaches taught by International Childbirth Education Association teachers.

Here, women know psychoprophylaxis as "prepared childbirth" or by the name of its French originator, Lamaze, whereas in France itself it is often called *accouchement sans douleur* (labor without pain). This name is misleading and might make any woman having pain in labor feel that something is going wrong. For most women who have been to classes the pain of labor is not the most important thing about the experience and is a side effect with which many, helped by techniques of adjustment and by emotional support and guidance at the time, can cope well without pharmacological aids. Others want some additional pain relief, and should have it.

In North America and Britain, psychoprophylaxis methods have changed radically since they were first introduced. Dogma has disappeared, breathing is no longer regimented, and the whole approach has become more relaxed. Many teachers have learned skills in group dynamics and psychological counseling, and, from psychoprophylaxis, several people have evolved their own approaches to childbirth education.

The Bradley method

An American obstetrician, Robert Bradley, has created "husband-coached" childbirth, in which the man acts as the woman's teacher and supporter in pregnancy and labor, breathing is slow and full, obstetric intervention is kept to the minimum, and painrelieving drugs are not used. Many Bradley enthusiasts opt for home birth. The American Academy of Husband-Coached Childbirth can refer you to a Bradley instructor nearby (see page 383).

The autogenic method

On the European continent, a system of training based on Schulz's methods of relaxation and breathing is taught in many hospital classes. A woman learns to relax by conceptualizing warmth and weight in different parts of the body; breathing is slow and relaxed.

A typical delivery room

It is a good idea to have a look at a delivery room in the hospital where you are going to have your baby. Many hospitals arrange tours of labor wards and delivery rooms so that expectant mothers can see them well in advance of labor. Some of the equipment can seem rather daunting until it has been explained to you.

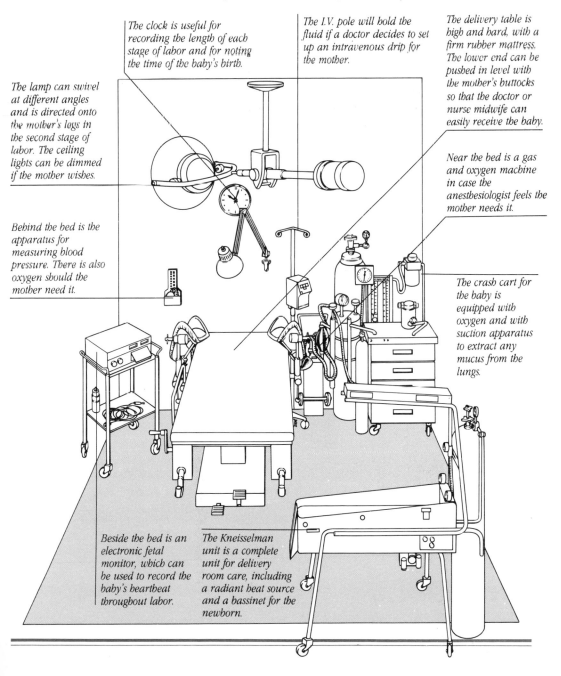

The clock is useful for recording the length of each stage of labor and for noting the time of the baby's birth.

The I.V. pole will hold the fluid if a doctor decides to set up an intravenous drip for the mother.

The delivery table is high and hard, with a firm rubber mattress. The lower end can be pushed in level with the mother's buttocks so that the doctor or nurse midwife can easily receive the baby.

The lamp can swivel at different angles and is directed onto the mother's legs in the second stage of labor. The ceiling lights can be dimmed if the mother wishes.

Near the bed is a gas and oxygen machine in case the anesthesiologist feels the mother needs it.

Behind the bed is the apparatus for measuring blood pressure. There is also oxygen should the mother need it.

The crash cart for the baby is equipped with oxygen and with suction apparatus to extract any mucus from the lungs.

Beside the bed is an electronic fetal monitor, which can be used to record the baby's heartbeat throughout labor.

The Kneisselman unit is a complete unit for delivery room care, including a radiant heat source and a bassinet for the newborn.

Active birth

Janet Balaskas has developed a method of preparing for birth based on hatha yoga, with the focus on moving around and changing position throughout labor, and giving birth squatting, kneeling, or on all fours. To be able to do this freely and with comfort, "stretching" exercises are important beforehand, and a woman learns how to adopt "open" positions with help from her partner.*

Methods of preparation for active birth are now often incorporated into other classes, and Janet Balaskas's great achievement is that in many hospitals all over the world she has succeeded in getting women down from the labor bed and delivery table onto the floor.

The Odent approach

Although a surgeon, Dr. Michel Odent perceives that childbirth is very different from surgery. For him, the most important thing is to provide an environment that facilitates a spontaneous psychophysiological process in which the woman who is left undisturbed will feel as if "on another planet".

Instead of childbirth classes, Odent organized singing get-togethers in which new parents, pregnant women, and their partners, midwives, doctors, and little children all joined. He has rediscovered the use of water in birth, offering the woman a deep bath of warm water in which she can float in a peaceful, darkened room. For delivery, he favors the standing squat, with the woman supported from behind by her partner or a female helper.

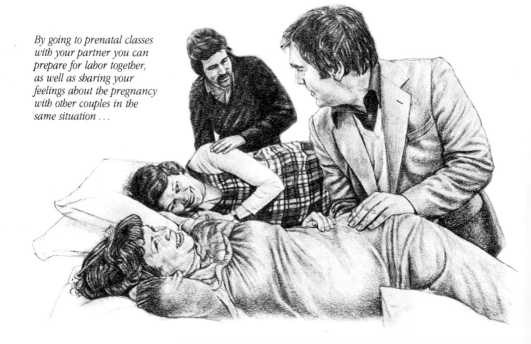

By going to prenatal classes with your partner you can prepare for labor together, as well as sharing your feelings about the pregnancy with other couples in the same situation . . .

Michel Odent's ideas have been incorporated into many classes run by birth centers, by midwives, and by other childbirth educators.

The Kitzinger psychosexual approach

My own "psychosexual approach" originally grew out of both the Dick-Read and psychoprophylaxis systems and now incorporates many active birth positions and movements. It is based on the idea that the woman is an active birthgiver rather than a passive patient. It focuses on birth as experience rather than as a series of exercises in breathing and relaxation.

Psychology and social anthropology have contributed much to my own approach, and especially my observations of how women behave in and feel about labor in many different cultures. I have learned most from women themselves. Labor involves often barely glimpsed feelings about ourselves which have developed through the formative years of childhood: attitudes to and fantasies about our bodies, feelings about the relative size and positions of organs and orifices, and concepts of cleanliness and pollution, beauty and ugliness. All of these are partly social in origin, products of our upbringing and family relationships.

Labor is a social situation, not just a physiological or even a private emotional experience. Because it involves human relation-ships at a sometimes tense and demanding time, it helps to know how to talk with the different people assisting at the birth and how to understand what may be in the doctors' and midwives' minds. All prenatal teachers agree that students require plenty of information about how their bodies work and what goes on in hospitals. Most classes include a visit to the hospital and a tour of the delivery room (see page 169). But it is not just a question of knowing what will happen to you when you are giving birth, but of learning how to negotiate to get the kind of birth you want.

The aims of childbirth education classes

So you will see that there is wide variation in exactly what is taught and how, although there is general agreement that six sessions of one and a half to two hours each are the minimum required. The aim is not to retreat from contractions but to adjust to them and respond actively. There is more and more emphasis on a woman being in the kind of setting and having the loving emotional support which enables her to be confident in her own powers and to behave spontaneously, without having to do "exercises" or wondering whether her performance is good enough. Classes for fathers should also be offered, so that they can learn how to help in pregnancy and labor and understand something about the feelings involved in becoming a father. Many teachers offer couples classes where the whole of preparation for birth is shared. If you are offered less than this in the classes you attend, you will probably feel the need to supplement them with other classes, reading, or extra private tuition.

When to start classes

Whatever method you finally opt for, do not leave registration for classes or your reading till the last moment. Start finding out what is available and begin your course of reading four or five months before the baby is due, even though classes may not be offered till the last nine weeks or so. Where teachers run classes only for those in the last two or three months of pregnancy there is often an opportunity to meet the teacher earlier. This is an excellent idea, although some teachers of psychoprophylaxis believe that students get bored if they start too soon. Even if you do not start to practice any breathing techniques till the last weeks, it can only be beneficial to learn good posture in early pregnancy, something about how the baby develops inside you and how to cope with any minor discomforts of pregnancy. It is also an advantage at any time, whether or not you are pregnant (and for men as well as women), to know how deep relaxation can help you get to sleep.

Whatever approach you select, provided you are happy with your teacher and develop confidence in yourself through the instruction, the teaching will be right for you, and you will find that you have a variety of suitable tools with which to adapt to contractions in labor. Labor need not be an ordeal to be feared, but a positive, rewarding experience, and a really *happy birthday.*

RELAXATION AND MASSAGE

Relaxation is the art of letting go and allowing peace to flow through you. The skill is in being able to release your muscles at will and not only when you are in a special mood to relax. It is not just an exercise, but as necessary a partner to—and interlude in—strenuous activity as the breath out to the breath in.

The importance of relaxation

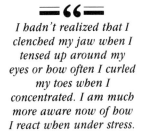

I hadn't realized that I clenched my jaw when I tensed up around my eyes or how often I curled my toes when I concentrated. I am much more aware now of how I react when under stress.

Relaxation is vital for labor. If you cannot relax you are likely to become exhausted as a result of tightening up muscles all over your body in reaction to the challenging stress of contractions. By tensing muscles unnecessarily you are wasting energy, and if you are exhausted any pain experienced will be felt more keenly and your ability to control it is bound to be diminished.

Generalized tension and anxiety can sometimes affect the way the uterus contracts, producing incoordinate uterine action, which means that the contractions are painful but are not very effective in pulling open the cervix. Because it alters your whole body chemistry, marked tension lasting a long time can also reduce the oxygen supply to the baby. Just as the smooth coordination of the digestive system, the beating of your heart and your breathing are all affected by acute tension, so stress and anxiety can slow down the unfolding process of childbirth and make it more difficult.

When you know how to relax you can adjust to your labor with special ways of breathing, positions, and other techniques. Relaxation helps keep your mind clear so that you are able to understand what is happening and can respond to it purposefully and creatively.

Centering down

To explore the skills of relaxation, you need to be able to "center down", to use an old Quaker term, and be still and enjoy peace of body and mind.

Lie on your back, well propped up with plenty of pillows, or sit in a comfortable chair with cushions supporting all of your back, including the back of your neck. You may also like a cushion under each arm or under your thighs. If you prefer, lie on your side, back rounded, head and shoulders forward, legs and arms bent. Before starting any exercises spend time thinking of the journey the baby makes to be born. Read page 246 and then focus your thoughts on that part of your body. Feel muscles and flesh heavy and released.

Touch relaxation

With touch relaxation, a partner gives you a message of touch to say, in effect, "release here." You respond to the pressure and warmth of the hands with immediate relaxation. If you learn to respond to your partner's touch in this way during pregnancy, it will be a spontaneous reaction when you are in labor. In effect, your partner will be able to draw the tension out of you.

To practice the technique, you contract different sets of muscles one set at a time. Your partner then rests his or her hands over the area that feels tight, and as soon as you feel the touch, you release, as if you are flowing toward it. Sometimes it helps if the touch develops into a gentle massage over the part of the body that is tense. This massage should be very slow; a partner who is worried or excited may massage in fast, jerky movements and this has the effect of communicating tension rather than relieving it. Whenever massage is done against bare skin, it is a good idea to use a little powder or warm oil, so that the hands glide smoothly and you do not feel itchy.

Between each exercise it is important to discuss whether it feels right for you—whether you want the touch firmer, lighter, or in a slightly different place. During labor, too, you can talk together

We are enjoying it a lot. We do it each night when we go to bed and to tell you the truth we like the massage and everything so much that we don't always get around to finishing the exercises!

Settle into a truly comfortable position for a while each day; make sure that there are no distractions to prevent you concentrating on your baby's presence inside you . . .

between contractions so that your helper understands exactly what you want. Some examples of touch relaxation for different parts of the body are given on pages 178–186.

In childbirth, touch can be enormously comforting. It helps you release all the muscles you do not need to use in order to have the baby. It relieves psychological stress, too, because you are able to feel secure and nurtured.

On the other hand, some women find that the experience of giving birth is so total, so overwhelming, that touch would be superfluous. While touch relaxation can be an important part of preparing for the birth, when you are in actual labor you may come to a phase when you do not want to be touched at all. If so, simply tell your partner this. It is vital that you have the kind of support *you* want and that your partner is willing to stand back and let you do things your way.

Release of tension By practicing relaxation with you like this, your partner becomes aware of any tensions in your body, and when you are in labor will be able to notice if there is a build-up of tension long before anyone who does not know you well realizes what is happening. All that is needed is to reach out a hand with the message: relax! If your shoulders are getting tense, for example, a firm hand is rested on your shoulder. If your legs are tense, loving hands stroke your legs firmly.

One great advantage of this is that it does not involve giving directions and "coaching" in labor. There may be times—especially at the very end of the first stage—when positive guidance is invaluable, but there is no place at all for bullying a woman in childbirth. Through learning touch relaxation, your partner will have the self assurance to give you just the kind of help you need.

Responding to the doctor or midwife Experiencing touch re- laxation together also means that you are preparing yourself to respond to the touch you receive when the doctor or midwife examines you. Instead of feeling threatened, tensing up, and pulling away from their touch like a snail drawing in its horns, you will be able to relax. This makes having your tummy palpated and pelvic examination much easier and more comfortable.

Pressure from the uterus During childbirth the stimulus coming from the uterus is remarkably like a strong, intense kind of touch radiating from inside. As the uterus contracts it squeezes tightly. A powerful pressure builds up and there is a sensation of heat. When the cervix is being opened and pulled wider, still more pressure is exerted. Then, as the baby moves down through the cervix, pressure is produced by the ball of its head. It feels as if a grapefruit were being pressed down first against the anus and then through the vagina. To all these stimuli a woman may respond either by tightening up, or by releasing her muscles.

Learning to flow with a contraction Now imagine that you are in labor and that the pressure of the uterus is building up with each contraction. Visualize the pressure of the baby's head, too, then release and flow towards these sensations. Some women feel each contraction as warmth building up to heat and then dying down again. One woman told me that every contraction was like an oven door swinging wide open; at its peak she received the full blast of the heat and then the oven door closed again.

When the baby's head is on your perineum and coming through the vagina, all the tissues are fanned out like the petals of a flower. As they open you may feel a warm, tingling sensation, as if the whole area is flooded with heat. If you have learned always to relax in response to the pressure and warmth from your partner's hands, you will be able to respond to these messages from *inside* your body too, not by pulling back, but by releasing and *flowing toward* them. In this way the sensations you get from within your body can guide you in labor.

Puppet-strings relaxation

Of course you do not always have someone to help you with relaxation. You can practice relaxation by yourself, using a method that I call the puppet-on-a-string method.

Lie in whatever position you usually sleep. Make yourself really comfortable, well supported by pillows, and give a long, sighing breath out and relax. Imagine that strings are attached to all your joints. Think of one fixed to your elbow, being tightened gradually so that your elbow is pulled up with the string. Depending on the position in which you are lying, your elbow may be moved a lot or a little. Then let it go. Notice the different feelings. Now the angle of the string is different, so feel the pull in a different direction. It lifts your elbow higher and higher. Now the string is released. It may take a little practice, but try not to allow any parts other than those operated by the string to move. The hand hangs limp at the wrist. The shoulder is not lifted. Only the elbow is activated.

Now do the same thing with an imaginary string attached to the other elbow. Let it be pulled in various directions. Continue as if a string were fixed to one big toe, then the other one, the back of one ankle, then the other, the left knee, the right knee, the left wrist, the right wrist, the index finger, the middle joint of a finger, one shoulder, the other shoulder, your left hip, your right hip.

Then imagine two strings, attached to your right elbow and right wrist, for example, tightening one after the other till both are drawn taut; first the wrist string is released, then the elbow string. Experiment with the strings working in a different order. Keep your mind focused on the tightening string rather than on the muscle you are contracting. Only when the invisible string is taut should you turn your mind to analyzing which muscles are tightened.

Imagine one string fixed to the top of your head, another to the base of your skull. First one is pulled, then the other. One goes slack, then the other. You will find that you can make the strings pull in different directions and at varying angles. This saves it from becoming a repetitive exercise that you do just from habit, without focusing on what your body is doing. It is important that any body movements you do bring awareness, an increased sense of working *with* your body. Mechanical exercises have no place in learning to relax.

Stanislavsky relaxation

There are acting techniques for increasing body awareness and learning which muscles contract and work together. The precise combination of muscles working together varies with each individual and the nature of the task, the angle at which you tackle it, the weight, dimensions, and even the texture of the tools used. You will find that tasks you perform, even ordinary, everyday tasks, often cause you to change your breathing, and sometimes you hold your breath altogether. You may discover too that you tense up muscles that you do not need to use because you tackle a job in the wrong way or overwork at it, or because you are emotionally keyed up about what you are doing. All this is a valuable process of self discovery and you can gradually learn more and more about yourself.

The method of relaxation based on Stanislavsky acting techniques explores different sets of muscles in the body that naturally function together and the way they work in response to different imagined activities and tasks and even thoughts and feelings. You think of certain situations—things you might be doing with your body—and mentally involve yourself in these situations as if you were actually performing them. Notice which muscles have become tense. Once the observation is made, switch off the picture in your mind and deliberately release those muscles.

Start by sitting or lying against a firm support and let the pillows take your whole weight. Listen to the sound of your own breathing. Breathe so that you can just hear yourself—in through your nose, and out through your mouth. Allow the breathing to flow through your mouth, letting the breath out be long and slow. The sound is like a little sigh as you breathe out. You may notice that there is a slight pause after you breathe in as if you have reached the crest of a wave. Enjoy that slight pause. Then give a long breath out. And with each breath out, relax a little more.

Suggested exercises for Stanislavsky relaxation

The jaw Imagine that you have some very sticky taffy in your mouth, and chew it well. It is sticking to your teeth. Work this great hunk of taffy out of your teeth. Notice what is happening. Then rest and drop your jaw. Let it relax, quite soft and loose. Notice the different feeling of complete release of the jaw muscles.

The eyes We do not usually notice when our eye muscles become tense. Imagine that there is a fireman climbing a ladder to rescue a little dog stranded at the top of a house. Focus on the fireman as he climbs all the way up. Observe the feeling in the muscles behind and around your eyes. Follow him with your eyes—up and up—until he is at the top. He has the little dog under his arm and is bringing it down and down. Now he is at the bottom. Relax your eyes, and if you want to, let them close. Notice how different they feel.

The feet Imagine that you are on the seashore standing on a very pebbly beach with no shoes on. Making very slight movements, imagine that you are walking on the beach with the sharp pebbles underfoot, and really feel them under your bare feet. Pick your way carefully over them. Oh! That was a sharp one! Observe the tension in your feet. Now go on to the soft sand. Really feel the difference. Then imagine that you lie down and let your feet relax completely.

The hands Can you recollect the feeling of making a snowball? Imagine that you are picking up snow and are patting the hard cold mass into a firm snowball. You are hurrying so that you can throw it at someone. As you quickly make your snowball, notice the tension in your hands. Then drop them and let them relax beside your body on the bed or floor again and notice how warm, soft, and loose they feel.

Taste Imagine that you are sipping some water. Place the glass to your lips. It is sharp, neat lemon juice! Really taste it. Notice what is happening in your mouth and the tension that is spontaneously produced. Now it is gone. Let the muscles of the mouth soften.

Now you have a large, ripe peach. Take a good bite of it. It is very juicy and the juice is dribbling down. You need to suck it and draw in the juice. Smell it, too. Chew it, swallow it. Now it has gone. Notice the very different feeling in your mouth. Relax completely and think through what happened to the muscle inside your mouth and nose and the other facial muscles as you imagined you ate the peach.

Smell Muscles around the nostrils, in the cheeks and the mouth work together as we smell and taste things. Imagine that you have in your hand a bottle of liquid. Take out the stopper and take a good sniff—it is ammonia! Notice how you have become stiff down the back of your neck. Then relax. Breathe fresh, pure, clean air. Let yourself breathe easily.

Here is another bottle. Do the same with this one. It is perfume this time: lily of the valley. You will find yourself drawing in the scent of lily of the valley in long, slow breaths, holding the fragrance as if it were suffused behind the surface of your face. Now the fragrance has gone and you are just breathing air. Relax.

Stanislavsky relaxation gives you a greater awareness of how your body works.

Go on from this to recreate in your imagination actions that you usually perform without thinking, simple things like writing a shopping list, tying shoe laces, or unlocking a door, and discover exactly how you use your body.

Touch relaxation

Tension makes childbirth unnecessarily painful. Learn how to relax to your partner's touch, so that this will be a spontaneous reaction in labor. To practice touch relaxation, first sit on the floor, well propped with cushions, and with legs and arms bent and spread a little. Give a long breath out through a soft, relaxed mouth. Now you are going to contract different sets of muscles—especially those you tend to tighten under stress—noticing how you feel when they are tight. Your partner will watch carefully, and then will rest one or both hands over the area you have tightened. As soon as you feel the touch you should relax and allow yourself to feel as if you were flowing out toward the touch.

The abdomen

Pull the muscles of your abdomen toward your spine. You will find that you have also tightened muscles at the bottom of your back and that your breathing is affected, too. Now your partner rests both hands gently over the lower curve of your tummy. Relax as soon as you feel the warmth and pressure of the hands. Then they can be slowly lifted away.

This touch can be comforting during contractions in the first stage of labor.

Light massage just above your pubic bone, where the pull of the dilating cervix often feels painful, usually helps too. The massage should be very light, as if stroking the baby's head. And it must be slow.

Sitting or kneeling at your side, your partner can massage with both hands in a continuous, flowing movement, one hand following on the other, and stroking slowly and evenly from the groin in a half circle down and over the other groin.

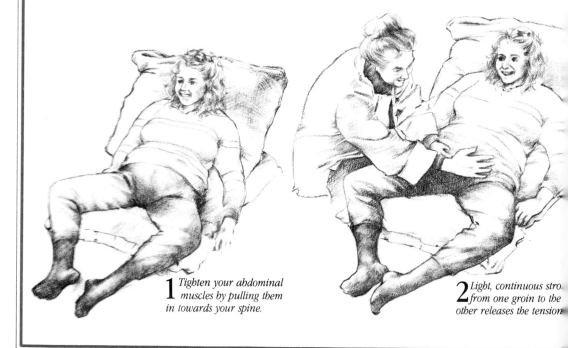

1 *Tighten your abdominal muscles by pulling them in towards your spine.*

2 *Light, continuous stro[ke] from one groin to the other releases the tension[.]*

The shoulders

Most people tighten their shoulders when under stress. Tight shoulders result in strained breathing and, because the tension usually involves the back of the neck too, can cause a headache. In labor, tension in the shoulders very soon results in heavy, panicky breathing which, in turn, leads you to hyperventilate. A side effect of this is a reduction in the amount of oxygen reaching the baby. If you know how to release your shoulders, you will not hyperventilate.

1 *Tense your shoulders and throw them back against the cushions.*

To feel exactly what happens with shoulder tension, press your shoulder blades back toward each other as if they were angel's wings and you could make them meet at the back. This is what a woman may do when she is finding it difficult to cope with strong contractions in the first stage of labor. She tenses her shoulders and presses them and her head back into the pillows. Notice how you feel when you do this. Is it affecting your breathing?

Now your partner rests one hand firmly over each shoulder, applying pressure with the heels of the palms at the front of your shoulders. You release immediately, flowing out toward the touch. Then the hands are slowly removed.

It is astonishing how often, when tension is building up in labor, that firm pressure on a woman's shoulders, or only the shoulder on the side nearest her helper, enables her to release.

2 *Firm pressure applied over one or both shoulders helps you release.*

The face

If a woman in labor is concentrating hard, or feels anxious about what her body is doing, the muscles around her eyes become tense and her brow furrows. Her jaw stiffens, her mouth gets tight, and it becomes difficult to release the vagina and perineum.

Frown as if you had a headache and were in a very bright light. Notice how you feel when you screw up your eyes and forehead. Using two fingers on each side of your head, your partner presses on the bone of the temples. Release as soon as you feel this touch. Then *very gradually* your partner reduces the pressure, as you visualize any residual tension flowing out and away.

The head

This exercise helps you to release the muscles of the scalp, which we often forget because they are under our hair. Shoot your eyebrows up toward the top of your head until your whole scalp feels tight. Your partner forms his or her hands into a cap, which is then rested against the top of your head. As soon as you feel the pressure, release. Let your eyes close slowly.

As your partner becomes aware of your tension easing, he or she slowly reduces the pressure. As this happens you can visualize any residual tension flowing up and out of your head. It is as if the hands are drawing out the tension from deep inside your head.

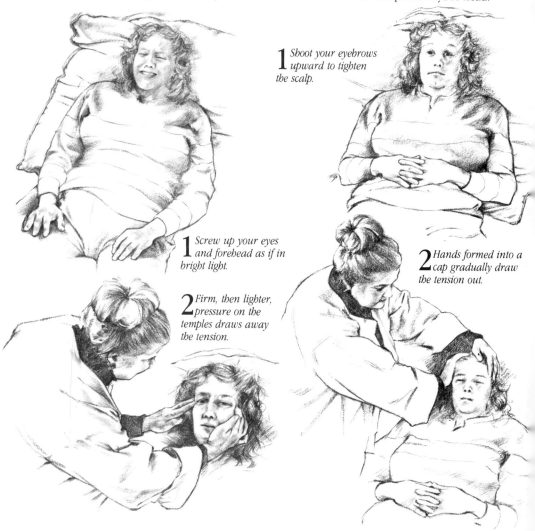

1 *Shoot your eyebrows upward to tighten the scalp.*

1 *Screw up your eyes and forehead as if in bright light.*

2 *Firm, then lighter, pressure on the temples draws away the tension.*

2 *Hands formed into a cap gradually draw the tension out.*

The arms

Tighten the arm nearest your partner.
Notice how it feels. Your partner watches
carefully, then places one hand firmly on
the front of your shoulder, with the other
over the inside of your upper arm, cradled
around the big muscle there, the biceps.
The hands are as if molded to your body.
As soon as you feel the warmth and
pressure of the touch, relax.

Then the hand on the inside arm moves
slowly and firmly, stroking right down to
your wrist. The other hand stays firm and
sure on your shoulder. As the hand moves,
focus on the feeling of any residual tension
flowing down your arm, out and away.

Movements like this, from the center of
the body toward the periphery, are helpful
because tension always flows from the
center, out and away. This slow, firm
stroking down the inside arm can feel
very good in labor. Try it at the start
of each contraction.

1 *Clench your fist to
tighten muscles all
down your arm.*

2 *The touch of hands on
your shoulder and
biceps eases the stiffness.*

3 *Slow, firm strokes down the
length of the arm help you
relax completely.*

The legs

Press your knees very firmly together. Notice how it feels. Your partner rests one hand on the outside of each leg, and you relax, letting your knees roll outward. The muscles released are those of your inside thighs—the adductors. When a woman feels her baby pressing down to be born she often tightens these muscles unknowingly. A vital part of opening up to let the baby be born is complete release of the adductors.

Easing cramps Sometimes in labor the inner thigh muscles get so tight that the woman's leg becomes stiff and her foot drawn up, with the result that she gets a painful cramp.

Stretch one leg out straight, so it feels stiff and taut, then flex your foot. To release the muscles, your partner places one hand on the *inside* of your thigh, molding the hand to the leg, then strokes slowly and firmly down to your ankle. You release to the warmth of the touch.

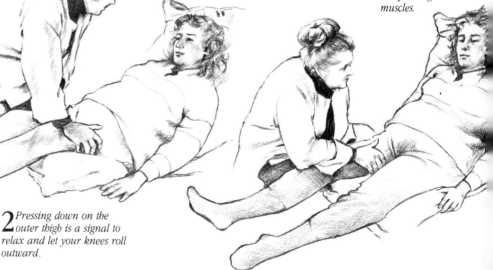

1 *Flex your foot to tighten your leg muscles.*

1 *Press your knees tightly together, contracting the inner thigh muscles.*

2 *Stroking down the len of the leg releases the muscles.*

2 *Pressing down on the outer thigh is a signal to relax and let your knees roll outward.*

Releasing tension Now see what happens when you press your knees out. Feel the tension as you do so. Then your partner rests both hands on the inside of your upper thighs, and you relax to the touch. With hands shaped to your inside thighs, your partner strokes slowly from the top of your legs down to your knees.

This massage is particularly useful as you reach the end of the first stage of labor, when contractions are coming about two minutes apart, and last a minute or more. At this time a woman often feels that her legs are cold. She may begin to shiver and shake, until her whole body is trembling.

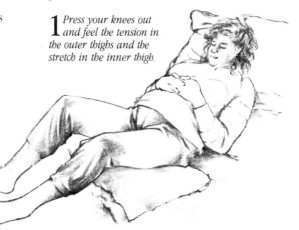

1 *Press your knees out and feel the tension in the outer thighs and the stretch in the inner thigh.*

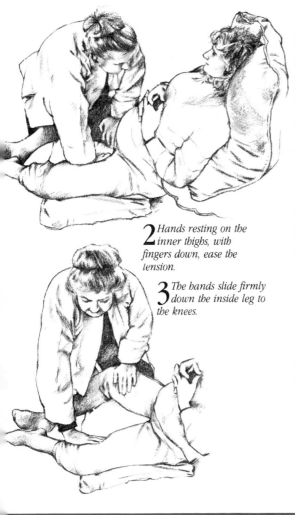

2 *Hands resting on the inner thighs, with fingers down, ease the tension.*

3 *The hands slide firmly down the inside leg to the knees.*

If this is your experience, you will find that massage of the inner thigh muscles warms your legs so that you feel they belong to you again and you can consciously release them. Your partner should use a very firm stroke as the hands slide down the inside of your thighs, and a gentle stroke coming up over the outside of the legs in a continuous flowing movement, helping tension flow out from the center of the body, down, and away. It is as if the hands are giving the message: "Open up, open up, the baby's coming out."

Releasing the pelvic floor muscles This type of massage also reminds you to release your pelvic floor muscles so that you can help the baby's head bulge forward in your vagina. Each downward movement of the hands has the effect of releasing the muscles through which the baby is coming to birth. To focus on this feeling, first contract your pelvic floor muscles as if they were an elevator going up to the second, third and then the fourth floor of a building. Pull them up and hold them. Then your partner rests both hands on your inside thighs, and you release the pelvic floor muscles down toward them, as if the elevator were going down to the basement. As the hands slide toward your knees, release still more, bulging your perineum forward.

The shoulders

For the next set of exercises, lie on your side, making yourself comfortable with pillows. Your back should be rounded, your head and shoulders well forward, and your underneath arm behind your back.

If a woman is lying on her side during childbirth and she becomes tense, she often adopts a fetal position. She curls up into a ball as if she were hugging pain to herself. Notice how you feel when you do this. Your shoulders will have tightened up so that they are near your ears. Your breathing will probably be affected too. Now your partner rests his or her fingers on your shoulders and applies firm pressure with the palms. You release, flowing out toward the touch.

Having your shoulders held in this way can be helpful if you tend to overbreathe during contractions. A thumb massage over your upper back and shoulders, or at either side of the spine, may also help.

The small of the back

Many women experience backache in labor, usually around the sacrum—the bone in the small of your back where the pelvis joins the spine. To find out exactly where this is, ask your partner to place his or her fingers over the large bones at the side of the pelvic cradle and then trace them around until the pelvis dips down at the back to meet your spine.

Imagine that you have a bad pain just there. Pull in the small of your back. You will find that you are sticking your bottom out and throwing your shoulders back. This is the typical picture of a woman with back pain in labor.

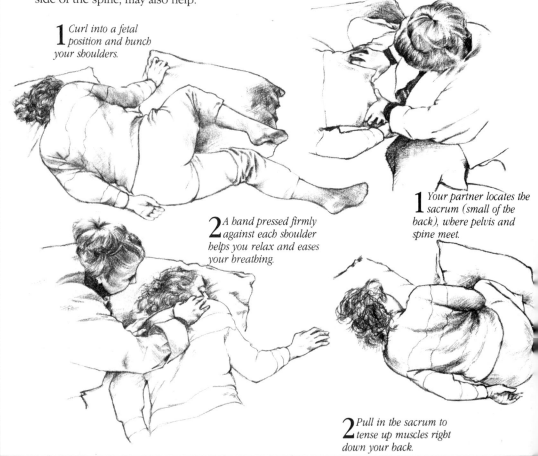

1 *Curl into a fetal position and hunch your shoulders.*

2 *A hand pressed firmly against each shoulder helps you relax and eases your breathing.*

1 *Your partner locates the sacrum (small of the back), where pelvis and spine meet.*

2 *Pull in the sacrum to tense up muscles right down your back.*

Applying pressure The tension that results from backache means that you suffer *more* pain from your own stiff muscles. To help you release, your partner now presses firmly and steadily over the sacrum, using the heel of the palm (not the fingers).

As soon as you feel the warmth and pressure, you relax, letting go and flowing out toward the hands. Muscles right down your back immediately soften and loosen.

3 *Firm, steady pressure over the sacrum loosens the muscles.*

4 *Deep massage around the sacrum may bring relief.*

Deep massage In childbirth, firm counterpressure like this may feel good, or you may prefer to be massaged. Massage is usually best done by moving the flesh—both skin and muscle—on the bone, rather than by merely creating friction. Your partner can use either a firm, circular motion with hands more or less stationary, or slide the hands across the top of one buttock to the top of the other and back again.

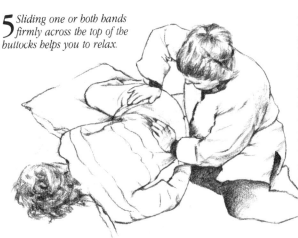

5 *Sliding one or both hands firmly across the top of the buttocks helps you to relax.*

Helpers and backache When a woman has backache in labor she may experience it for hours on end. The baby's head is pressing back against the sacrum and has to slide past it down into the birth canal. Helpers using counter-pressure or doing back massage often develop backache too, because they are relying on muscle strength in the arms rather than allowing their own body weight to flow down *through* the arms. Your helper may want to rest one hand on your hip, but should be careful not to exert pressure there, or lean on you, since that will cause you discomfort.

1 *Press your buttocks tightly together to tense up the muscles.*

2 *Slow but firm kneading of both buttocks eases the pain.*

The buttocks

Press your buttocks tightly together as if you have a piece of paper between them and somebody is trying to take it away from you. As you hold on to it, notice exactly how you feel. Your partner watches carefully. Now he or she rests one hand on each buttock, on the lower inside curve, and as you feel the warmth and pressure you release. Your partner will feel the tension slide away.

A woman in labor may tense her buttocks because the baby is pressing against her rectum and anus as it comes around the curve of the birth canal, and she feels as if it is coming out the wrong hole. She is often convinced that she wants to go to the toilet. The sensation experienced is preposterous and she automatically resists it by tightening up her muscles. When she tightens her buttocks she also tightens her pelvic floor muscles against the baby's head, almost as if shutting the door on it. Contracting these muscles can hold up the descent of the head and cause unnecessary pain.

Your partner can help you relax by firmly massaging your buttocks as if kneading bread dough. It is important to get down into the fat and muscle, very slowly kneading both buttocks at once. As soon as you feel the firm, reassuring touch, you relax.

The "tail" muscle

Think now of the muscles at the base of your spine, which form part of the pelvic floor. Imagine that you have a tail like a kangaroo. You can lift it off the ground and then drop it down.

Now kneel in front of a chair with your forearms on the seat, and lift your "kangaroo muscle" up. Your partner firmly rests a curved hand at the very bottom of your spine, just around the curve where your anus is. You release toward the touch.

1 *Firm pressure, or rhythmic "rocking" massage, at the very base of the spine relaxes the "tail" muscles.*

BREATHING FOR LABOR

Relaxation and breathing are so closely associated that it is important to explore them as part of a unity. You cannot really breathe correctly for labor unless your body is relaxed. As labor progresses you will spontaneously breathe more rapidly. If you breathe more quickly and at the same time heavily, you are bound to hyperventilate and flush carbon dioxide out of your bloodstream. This can make you feel very uncomfortable and, if severe enough, you will even pass out. The more you hyperventilate, the more you are likely to underbreathe— or even not breathe at all—*between* contractions. This is especially so if you have also had Demerol to relieve the pain. Though your body can cope with this, your baby needs you to go on breathing. Overbreathing, "forgetting" to breathe, and holding your breath are all harmful to your baby during childbirth.

In many cultures breathing in labor is deliberately regulated to help a woman work with the forces bringing her baby to birth. Among the Zulu, for example, breathing exercises are taught in pregnancy. A woman is supposed to go to the door of her hut each morning as the sun rises and take careful, controlled, full breaths through each nostril alternately.* She uses the same breathing in labor. In other cultures breathing is regulated by background sounds, including prayers, music, the beating of hands, or repeated phrases of encouragement, or by the swaying movement of attendants holding the mother.

Breathing for relaxation

Smooth, easy breathing rhythms can also help release tension and create a state of pleasurable relaxation. In labor this is particularly important because, since contractions come like the waves of the sea, there is a strong natural rhythm built in to the physiological activity. A woman can either resist this, trying to "switch off", escape from, or dominate it, or she can go with it and adjust her breathing to the compelling sweep of uterine power. She can only go with the rhythm if she can accept what is happening in her body and assent to it.

So the breathing taught for labor is nothing to do with "distraction techniques" and is certainly no magic method of eradicating sensation or guaranteeing that you do not feel pain. It is another way of getting in tune with your body and especially with your uterus.

Rest your hands over the lower curve of your abdomen. In late pregnancy you have a lovely melon shape there. Breathe as slowly as you comfortably can. As the breath enters your nostrils, allow them to dilate, notice the slight pause between the breath in and the breath out, and then breathe out through a soft, relaxed mouth as if you had on a new, glossy, and rather expensive lipstick. Enjoy that breath out. Notice what is happening to your abdomen. Feel it rising under your hands as you breathe in—a gentle swelling, like a wave building up. Then as you breathe out, the abdomen sinks back again and the wave

Practicing smooth, easy breathing helps you to relax and get in tune with your body for labor.

187

recedes. Be aware of the slight pressure under your hands as you breathe in, and feel the pressure withdrawing as you breathe out and the abdomen goes back to its former position.

Breathing down your back

You need someone to help you rehearse this. Try kneeling in front of a chair with your forearms and head resting on the seat and your knees well apart. Ask your helper to rest one hand firmly on each side of the base of your spine. Then breathe slowly right down your back, noticing the pressure against the hands as you inhale and how it gradually falls away as you exhale.

The greeting breath

When you are in labor, meet each contraction with your breathing, giving first of all a complete greeting breath. This is a deliberate, slow breath *out*. Imagine an early first-stage contraction lasting 45 to 60 seconds. Breathe slowly through the contraction, with the lower back spreading out and pressing slightly against the bed or floor as you breathe in, and the pressure being lifted as you breathe out.

The resting breath

As a contraction fades away, you give a long, slow, complete breath out through your mouth—a resting breath. This is important partly because it offers you complete relaxation at the end of a contraction so that you can rest and get refreshed before the next one, and partly because it signals to everyone in the room that a contraction is over. If the midwife or obstetrician wants to talk to you, or ask you to turn over, now is the time, between contractions—never during them.

In strong labor you may want to give several of these complete resting breaths once a contraction finishes. Do whatever feels good. If you always respond to the end of a powerful contraction by one or more resting breaths you can be sure that, however difficult contractions are, you are giving your baby oxygen by breathing fully.

Full chest breathing

You need a partner to help you practice this. Lie on your side with your back rounded, head and shoulders curved foward, legs well apart, and the upper leg drawn up and bent at the knee. Now lift your head as if stretching your spine all the way up the back so that you feel taller. Stretch your neck at the back, stretch all the way up your spine and then simply let it drop back into place; let your head settle comfortably on your shoulders. See that there is a good space between your legs. Then give a long breath out and relax completely. Allow your eyes to close if they feel heavy.

Think of your back. Your spine is not stiff like a lamppost. It is constructed with small vertebrae in a curving shape like a string of sausages. We often act as if our spinal columns were very stiff. Yet think of the way a cat moves and how movement ripples up and down

OPPOSITE

Preparing for labor need not be a solemn drill: you can make it a natural part of your daily life and involve your other child too.

the back. Now your partner rests one hand on each shoulder and massages with the flat of both hands from the top of your back right down to the bottom. The hands should be relaxed. Say if you would like the massage to be heavier or lighter, slower or quicker. Is it in exactly the right place? It should feel good. Relax toward the hands.

Then your partner rests the palms of both hands firmly above your waist on either side of the spine over the ribcage. They should be in a position that is comfortable for you and should not be pressing in on your waist (or where it once was!). Notice their warmth and strength. Breathe in through the nose and out through the mouth again so that the main level of breathing awareness is just where you feel the pressure and warmth of the hands, and listen to your breathing. Breathe down to where you feel the hands, expanding your ribcage, so that it is swelling out under the hands as you breathe in, and then it falls away from the pressure of the hands as you breathe out. Listen to it for a moment. Can your partner feel the pressure, building up as you breathe in and falling away as you breathe out? This is full chest breathing. It can be very useful, once labor starts, to meet the earliest contractions of the first stage of labor. You may be able to breathe like this all the way through your early contractions, concentrating on breathing into the area against which your partner is pressing the hands. When you are actually in labor you will not need the hands there because you will do it automatically and the contracting uterus itself will provide sufficient stimulus.

Upper chest breathing

As contractions strengthen, you may want to lift your breathing above them, as if over the crest of a wave. Contractions come like waves and you will find that you can cope with them more easily if you breathe more lightly and more quickly. At this phase of labor they may be coming every four or five minutes and lasting about a minute.

To practice breathing with these contractions, your partner should rest the palms of both hands on your upper back just below your shoulder blades. You breathe so that your main level of breathing activity and awareness is where you feel the pressure of the hands. You may find that you want to breathe more rapidly, perhaps through parted lips. You should be able to hear a crisp little sigh or "huff" with each breath out. Now if you rest your hand over your upper chest you will feel it rising and falling at the same time, rather like a seagull floating on a wave. In labor the wave of a contraction will be underneath and you will be breathing over the top of it. Remember to relax your shoulders; they are not doing any of the work.

If you can still breathe all down your back, do so. Only "lift" your breathing if you need to.

Butterfly breathing

As you go over the waves of contractions at the end of the first stage, just before the cervix is fully dilated and the uterus and vagina

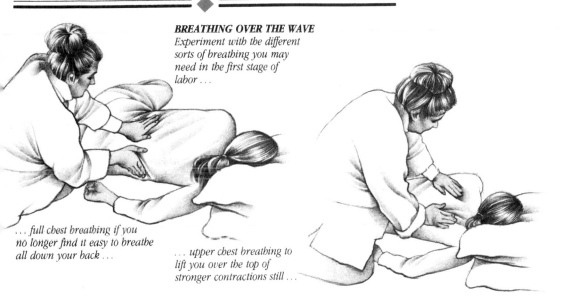

BREATHING OVER THE WAVE
Experiment with the different sorts of breathing you may need in the first stage of labor . . .

. . . full chest breathing if you no longer find it easy to breathe all down your back . . .

. . . upper chest breathing to lift you over the top of stronger contractions still . . .

become one birth canal, you may need to move up to the shallowest breathing of all—butterfly or mouth-centered breathing.

When the going is hard, women tend to raise their chins in the air, tense the muscles of the neck and jaw, and start to gasp and over-breathe. Instead, let your head drop forward onto your chest like a heavy flower on its stalk. Remembering to keep your shoulders loose, the back of your neck long, and your jaw released will help you to keep a steady rhythm and let your breathing "dance".

Butterfly breathing is the lightest, most rapid breathing you will want to use in labor. With all breathing you are bound to be using your diaphragm and lungs, but butterfly breathing is easier if you think of it as being centered in your mouth behind your cheeks and not in the throat. If you center your breathing in the throat, you will probably tense up your neck. Think of the space in your mouth, the space behind your warm, plumped-up cheeks. Either sit up in a chair or lie well propped up on the bed for this exercise. If you are lying flat, you can easily find yourself gasping and panting heavily when you are doing this type of breathing. So pile three or four pillows behind you, or try squatting, kneeling, all-fours, or standing positions.

Resting the plump pads of the tips of your fingers against your cheeks will help you to concentrate on this area. Part your lips in a slight smile like the Mona Lisa. Relax your mouth and you will probably find that you are salivating a little. Breathe lightly in and out through your parted lips. Start gently, then gradually double the rate of your breathing till it is like the ticking of a wristwatch.

Butterfly breathing may be quite difficult at first. You may feel that you are taking in or letting out too much air. Most people do to begin with, and find this the most contrived kind of breathing to learn. They think that they will never be able to manage it in labor, but then it

. . . butterfly breathing if you need it, to take you through to the end of the first stage.

comes quite naturally and they do not know how they could have coped without it. You may find that it helps to think in terms of a definite rhythm in which one beat is slightly accentuated: *one*, two, three, four; *one*, two, three, four; or *one*, two, three, four, five, six. If you do this, be careful not to expel a great deal of air on the accentuated breath or you will gasp in the following breath and start to hyperventilate. If you find it difficult to keep the rhythm, or find your throat getting tight, give a quick blow out through pursed lips and carry on with the light breathing immediately after.

After you have experimented with this breathing, try it once again, and this time notice especially if your shoulders or the back of your neck become tense. Drop your shoulders and relax. Under stress, it is tempting to breathe too heavily and sound as if you are a chugging piece of machinery. Try to keep your breathing as light as a whisper. When you rehearse, think of the sound of leaves in the forest floating to the ground, but bear in mind that in actual childbirth you will naturally make more noise than that.

You will want to use this sort of breathing only when you are coping with the strongest contractions, at the end of the first stage. When you reach this point, you may feel like a little ship in a storm at sea in the middle of huge waves and confusing cross currents. For most women this is the most difficult time of labor. Grantly Dick-Read used to call it "the pain period of labor". This does not mean that you may not feel pain at other times, but it is the time when you will need all your concentration and control.

Sheep's breathing

If we watch any mammal giving birth, a cat, for example, or a sheep, we notice that she does not take great breaths in and then "block" the birth canal by holding her breath. A sheep gives birth with rather light, quick breathing. Her breath is involuntarily held as she bears down and then she continues the light, accelerated breathing again.

During the second stage of labor, when the baby is traveling down the birth canal (see page 245), most women feel the urge to push during contractions. As a contraction builds up, you move from full to lighter, quicker breathing, your cheeks plumped up. Then the surge of desire to bear down comes and you hold your breath. As soon as you can breathe again you do so, then feel you have to bear down again—and so on until the desire fades, your breathing slows down, and then the contraction ends. You can practice this with only the slightest, most gentle push.

DIFFERENT POSITIONS FOR LABOR

Once you are fairly confident about your ability to relax and breathe rhythmically, explore some different positions which you may want to use in labor. There is no reason why you should have to be tucked up in bed all the time. There are definite disadvantages with the supine position (lying flat on your back) for your baby, since the bloodflow in the large veins in the lower part of your body may be obstructed by the heavy weight of your uterus and this can reduce the bloodflow through the placenta to and from the baby.

During the first stage of labor you will almost certainly feel happiest walking about or standing up. During contractions you will probably want to lean against a wall or your partner. If you have low backache, you can lean forward onto a heavy piece of furniture. Once labor is advanced, it will be easier if you already know the positions in which you are likely to feel most comfortable. Avoid getting stuck in one position; the essence of labor is *movement.* You can try sitting well up, firmly supported right up your spine; kneeling, leaning back over your heels or forward onto a pillow placed on a chair or bed or over the top of the bedhead; a knee-chest position with your knees placed either side of your body, rather like a frog; on all fours or squatting, with your back firmly supported. Some of these positions are illustrated on pages 198–199.

Your aim in all these positions is to give the baby as much room as possible in your pelvis by having your knees well apart and to allow the uterus to tilt forward onto your abdominal wall and away from your spine. In this position it assumes an egg shape, whereas when you are lying flat on your back it tends to be distorted from this natural shape. When you are upright you are also allowing gravity to help the baby down. In all these positions contract only those muscles you need to use to support yourself, and whenever possible use pillows, furniture, or another person to help you.

You can relieve low backache in labor, especially common when the baby is in an occipito-posterior position (see page 258), by getting into a position in which your abdomen can hang forward, tilting the baby away from your sacrum. It will also be convenient for back massage and counterpressure, and because the longitudinal axis of the uterus is then in line with the birth canal it may help the baby to rotate into the correct anterior position. If the baby is posterior, you will probably have bearing down sensations before you are fully dilated, and are more likely to be able to control the urge if you take pressure off your rectum.

Pressure on the umbilical cord interrupts the baby's blood flow through it. Resulting decelerations of the fetal heart which last after the end of the contractions may be noted if you are having continuous electronic monitoring (see page 303). This will lead your doctor to consider a forceps delivery for fetal distress. If you adopt a position in which your tummy is hanging forward, however, such as on all fours, both the baby and its cord will be tipped away from your spine and the pressure on the cord may be relieved.

Incidentally, it is a good idea to adopt an all fours position for delivery if the baby has large shoulders that get stuck (shoulder dystocia). It gives the assistant more room for maneuver, as the baby's head can be extended and drawn out and up toward your anus, so delivering the shoulder nearer your front, and the rest will then follow easily.

Sometimes contractions are inefficient from the start of labor and do not seem to pick up or, having been effective, become weak. In either case it is worth trying a position in which the uterus can most easily form a sphere. It may help to stand facing a wall, legs well apart and leaning forward with your hands resting against the wall.

PRACTICING FOR CONTRACTIONS AND PUSHING

The experience of labor is difficult to imagine before you have had a baby. Will contractions be unbearably painful or hardly noticeable? Some women think of the contractions as bigger and bigger hills they have to climb, each hill having its own peak, until they reach the mountain range at the end of the first stage.

The action of the uterus

When the uterus contracts, it is tightening up, just like any working muscle in the body. Make a very tight fist with one hand and raise your arm so that the big muscle on the inside of your upper arm, the biceps, tightens; then feel it with your other hand. You will notice that the biceps has become hard and is sticking out. If a man does the same thing, his biceps may stick out a good deal more than yours does, because his is probably a bigger muscle. The biceps gets hard

PRACTICING FOR CONTRACTIONS
By simulating contractions you learn to respond to painful stimuli with the use of breathing. It is best to practice this technique with your partner, who acts as your "uterus" by pinching a little flesh on your inside thigh between his fingers. You adjust your breathing rhythms according to the degree of pressure you feel. . . .

. . . and after a while it may be a good idea to change places. "Contractions"—like the real ones—can vary: some short, some long, some easy, some harder; some may even have double peaks. . . . For your partner it may be the first real inkling of what labor can be like.

as it contracts and it also protrudes. This is because the muscle fibers are shortened and thickened. The same thing happens, on a much larger scale, when the uterus contracts. Like your bulging biceps, the uterus bulges forward in your abdomen when you have a really strong and effective contraction. The strong contractions are the best of all for helping the baby to be born.

Place your hand just above your pubic hair line at the very bottom of the abdomen. The cervix lies under this area and it is here that you are likely to feel the strong, rhythmic pull as it opens, a pull that will feel tightest at the height of each contraction (see page 229).

You cannot do anything actively to help the baby down the birth canal until the cervix is wide open. A relaxed body and a mind at peace are the most important contributions you can make to the birth process at this stage. It is possible to train yourself to respond with neuromuscular release whenever you want to. Your breathing techniques can help your relaxation and your relaxation can help keep your breathing smooth and rhythmic.

Simulating contractions

Contractions are felt mainly as powerful pressure which comes whether or not you want it to, so when you are practicing for them work with a partner and allow him or her to simulate the contractions, deciding when they start, how strong they become and how long they last. Meet each contraction with a welcoming breath *out* and use the rhythmic breathing you have learned right through each one, with a long resting breath out at the end. Your partner sits beside you so that you have eye contact with each other. He (or she) pretends to be your uterus by taking hold of a piece of your flesh, the inner thigh, say, and squeezing it. He will find that grasping a small piece of flesh rather than a big area is more effective. He should be particularly careful if you have a varicose vein, lifting the flesh up off the leg instead of pressing down into the leg, and avoiding the area around the varicose vein. First he squeezes gently, and then tightens his grip to a strong pinch that lasts for about 15 seconds, after which he gradually releases his hold. The contraction should last about 45 seconds in all. This will help him to be aware of what you are feeling and how you react to stress of this kind, so that he can give you emotional support and encouragement.

In between these mock contractions, you can discuss with him how each one felt, and perhaps how he can improve his performance and you can improve yours. In labor this rest space between contractions should be used to prepare you for the next one: do not waste time discussing the contraction that has just ended.

It is a good idea to change places so that you become your partner's "uterus" and he can experience this firm gripping sensation and learn how to respond to it. This is important if he is going to be with you during labor and wants to be able to help you by breathing with you when and if contractions become difficult.

Practicing for stronger contractions

Switch roles again and imagine that labor is progressing, with longer and stronger contractions, each reaching its peak about halfway through. Remember, however, that contractions vary and that it is no good wishing for a "textbook labor" if your own labor proves to be different. Some contractions have their peaks about a third of the way through; some may even have two peaks. The important thing is that if you go with your uterus, you tune in with it rather like an orchestra responding to a conductor. The conductor in this case is the uterus. You have to be able, as it were, to "listen" to your uterus in order to react to it, and be in harmony with it. For these stronger contractions your partner grips the flesh of your thigh for a minute or a little longer.

When necessary during these longer contractions you respond by lifting your breathing above the contraction—breathing more shallowly and more quickly (see page 190). Relax your shoulders and toes; then, as the contraction becomes slightly less intense, allow your breathing to become slower and fuller.

Pushing

Pushing or bearing down is often described as an extraordinarily athletic activity, as if you could learn to do it the way you learn to do a gymnastic exercise. It should not be like this. It is, rather, a spontaneous welling up of energy which culminates in a triumphant push and an opening of the vagina.

However you are sitting now, rest your hands beneath the lower curve of your abdomen. Take a breath and hold it. Drop your chin forward on your chest and at the same time allow the bulge underneath your hands to press downwards and forward, so that *from inside* your abdomen you are pressing your hands out and moving them forward. You probably feel your perineum moving forward too. Allow the movement to carry right down through you until you feel the tissues of the vagina spreading out, and then rest. Did you get that feeling of something moving forward? When the baby is ready to be born, this movement helps its head to bulge farther down the birth canal. Though it is useful to learn how to do this beforehand, especially if you practice it without straining and useless effort, most women feel a spontaneous urge to do it anyway during labor (see page 245).

Before going on to practice this pushing movement, make sure that your bladder is empty. You can sit on a bed, or on the floor, with four or five firm pillows behind your back, knees flopped apart, and your heels drawn up near your buttocks. Or you can adopt any of the positions suggested on pages 198–199.

One of the best ways of rehearsing pushing is on the toilet since we also release pelvic floor muscles for defecation and so they are not put under strain. If you happen to be constipated, as many women are in late pregnancy (see page 121), this movement will help relieve the constipation and is an excellent exercise for encouraging spontaneous, easy bowel movements.

You will probably feel more comfortable in an upright position. This will be an advantage during labor as you will be more in control of what is happening, can open up easily for the baby to be born, and can see over the bulge to watch the birth if you want to. Gravity can help you. If you are lying flat, or almost flat, you are pushing the baby uphill because the uterus is almost at right angles to the vagina (see pages 246–247). In an almost upright position you can lean on your uterus and press the baby down.

After you have done this gentle pushing a few times, begin to work with your partner. To start with you might like to try sitting. Your partner sits near your head with a pillow over the forearm and supports your head and shoulders with it. This gives you a very wide base of support. With your helper's hands over your lower abdomen, you can both feel what is happening inside. Drop your head forward onto your chest, so that you do not strain with your throat muscles and produce a grunting sound. Take a breath. Lean forward and press from inside steadily out, slowly, gently; a little bit more; let it go; let the breath out and rest. While you are practicing, your partner's hand pressed firmly against your lower abdomen gives you something to press against and guide you. It is easier to bear down when your baby is actually in the birth canal waiting to be born because you have something to press against. Allow your pelvic floor muscles to bulge foward like a heavy sack of apples. When you have felt and noted the sensation this produces, lift your pelvic floor up again so that it is well toned and not sagging (see page 107). Think of it smiling.

Trying other positions

When you are confident that you have the feeling of pushing with complete release of your pelvic-floor muscles in this position, go on to explore other positions which may feel right when you are in labor. Experiment with every open position—on a mattress on the floor, on the bed, leaning over or against furniture, using cushions and other kinds of support, cradled by another human body—in which you can feel in touch with what is happening and free to let the energy of the uterus sweep through you to birth. An almost impossible posture in which to do this is, as you can imagine, lying flat on your back with your legs in the air in the standard lithotomy position, or with your knees scrunched up to your chest while you try to roll yourself into a ball—both standard positions for the second stage and delivery in contemporary hospitals.

During the eighties, however, there have been widespread changes in practice. Now in many hospitals in the United States, for example, women are encouraged to find any position, and make any movement, which is comfortable for them, and, if they wish, to give birth on a sheet or mattress on the floor.

With your partner's hand over your lower abdomen, you can both feel what is happening inside.

Practicing positions
for labor

*There is no reason to spend labor in bed. In fact, lying flat on
your back diminishes the oxygen supply to your baby and prevents
your uterus contracting efficiently. While you are pregnant, try out
different positions to find those which are
most comfortable for you.*

STANDING LUNGE
*A standing lunge position,
feet wide apart, is often
comfortable. You can lean
your forearms against the
wall and rest your head
on them.*

ON ALL FOURS
*Getting down on all fours is
one of the best positions for
relieving a low backache.*

SQUATTING
*When you are squatting,
your pelvis is wide open and
the baby's head is pressed
down. You may want to rest
your hands on the floor to
give yourself firm support. If
a full squat is uncomfortable,
use a low stool or a pile of
large books.*

KNEELING UP
*Kneeling up, legs apart with
your ankles turned out and
toes toward each other,
opens your pelvis and
releases tension in the back.*

SUPPORTED SQUAT
You may find it easier to squat with the help of a partner. Grasp each other's wrists and squat down together. Start with the weight on the balls of your feet and your heels raised; with practice, you may be able to get your feet flat on the floor.

KNEELING FORWARD
Kneeling with your legs spread wide, ankles out and toes turned in, gradually lean forward until your forearms are on the floor. This extends and relaxes back muscles and buttocks, and takes the baby's weight off your back.

HANGING ABDOMEN
Try kneeling on all fours, with your forearms on the floor, your knees spread wide and your abdomen hanging between them. In this position, you may like to rock backward and forward.

LYING DOWN
You can relax almost on all fours, but flopped forward onto a big floor cushion or bean bag.

Practicing positions for delivery

Try to explore different positions for delivery with the people who will be helping you at the birth, so that everyone has some idea of what to expect. Using a doll, a ball, even a grapefruit, as a substitute for the baby may be helpful.

SUPPORTED SQUATTING
You may find it more comfortable to squat. Again, you will need two helpers, who can support your knees when you are bearing down.

SUPPORTED KNEELING
Kneeling opens up the pelvis fully and aids the descent of the baby. You will feel most secure if you have the support of two helpers, one on each side of the bed or delivery table.

HALF KNEELING, HALF SQUATTING
This is the easiest position if you are delivering your own baby. It should give you greater stability than kneeling or squatting and allows you to guide the baby out.

LEANING FORWARD

This is especially good if the second stage of labor is fast, since it will slow you down a little. The midwife will guide your baby out, and then you can turn over and take her into your arms.

KNEE-CHEST POSITION

Kneeling down on all fours, with your head down and bottom up will slow down a very fast second stage. This will help you to feel more in control, as well as allow your vaginal tissues time to soften and stretch so that they are less likely to tear as the baby is born.

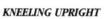

KNEELING UPRIGHT

Kneeling with your body upright speeds up a very slow second stage. The midwife can deliver your baby from behind and pass her through your legs, or you may be able to lift her out yourself.

Windows into
the uterus

Apart from the routine urine and blood pressure tests you will have every time you go to the doctor (see page 50), there are certain other investigations that may be done during pregnancy. Whether they are done at all, or how often they are done, will depend not only on there being some specific reason for them, but on the part of the country you are in and therefore on the sort of hospital or clinic you attend. Teaching hospitals have far more sophisticated equipment and are also engaged in research, so—for example—if you are in a large city you may have ultrasound two or three times during your pregnancy, whereas if you live in a small country town you may never have it at all.

ULTRASOUND

I found the scans at 16 and 30 weeks exciting because the images on the screen were explained to me.

Ultrasound (also referred to as a scan, or an ultrasound scan) works on the principle of bouncing very high frequency sound waves (far higher than the human ear can detect) off solid objects. It is a method which has been used for many years by fishermen to locate shoals of deep sea fish, and by navies to locate submarines in wartime. Echo sounders in yachts work in a similar way.

Uses of ultrasound

In pregnancy ultrasound is used to obtain a picture of the baby in the uterus. It is possible to see the tiny fetus kicking from the end of the second month, and after 28 weeks breathing movements can be observed. There are a number of reasons why scans are done:

To confirm pregnancy A scan can be used to confirm pregnancy very early on, before clinical tests are effective: it is capable of detecting changes in the uterus that cannot yet be revealed by physical examination. You can find out if you are having twins, for instance, when you are only eight weeks pregnant.

To establish the estimated date of delivery Scans are often routinely used in large hospitals, where you may expect to have them done at least two or three times during pregnancy. Your first scan will probably be done at about 12–16 weeks in order to establish the estimated delivery date. At this stage the age of the baby can be established to within 10 days (later in pregnancy it is more difficult to be precise because babies of the same age may grow at very different rates). You may then be scanned again in the middle and at the end of

◆

pregnancy, or even more frequently, at intervals of a few weeks. This is called serial assessment and does not mean that anything is wrong. Only when the scan is used in this way can the clues that it gives about the rate of fetal growth be taken seriously. In smaller hospitals you may never have a scan at all, unless there is a specific reason for it.

To detect certain handicaps Between 18 and 20 weeks, ultrasound can be used to detect certain abnormalities in the fetus, including spina bifida (see page 206), congenital heart defects, and gastrointestinal and kidney malformations.

To assess maturity in late pregnancy Late in pregnancy a scan is often used to indicate whether or not a baby is ready to be born. It cannot show whether the lungs are mature enough for breathing, but by measuring the size of the baby's head it can establish the approximate age of the baby and its stage of development.

To detect how the baby is lying If it is important to find out how your baby is lying in the uterus and a doctor cannot know for certain from manual examination, ultrasound can tell with accuracy. This knowledge may make all the difference to you if you want to have your baby at home, for instance.

If the baby is shown to be in a good position, you can proceed with confidence in your plans for a home birth. If the baby is seen to be lying awkwardly, you will accept that it might be more sensible to go to the hospital for the birth. Either way, you and your doctor can be guided by the information provided by the scan.

To assess the condition and position of the placenta When there is bleeding in late pregnancy ultrasound can be used to locate the position of the placenta. The danger is that the placenta might be

HAVING A SCAN
Because it involves such sophisticated equipment, an ultrasound scan may seem intimidating; if the picture on the screen is blurred and meaningless it may be disappointing; but if it is explained to you so that you can actually recognize your baby, it may be the most exciting moment of your pregnancy so far . . .

blocking the baby's way out of the uterus (a condition known as placenta previa, described on page 125). In fact a scan done in the first few months of pregnancy often gives the impression that the placenta is lying low on the wall of the uterus, but as the pregnancy progresses and the uterus enlarges the placenta usually proves to be in the right place after all. Occasionally bleeding in late pregnancy means that the roots of the placenta are becoming dislodged with prelabor contractions, indicating that the baby's lifeline would be cut if labor were allowed to proceed. A scan can show this clearly, and a cesarean section can be performed to save the baby. Used in this way, or as a preliminary to amniocentesis (see page 206), ultrasound has undoubted advantages.

AN ULTRASOUND PICTURE
Here is a photograph of a scan of a 14-week-old fetus. Unlike many other scan photographs, the image of this baby is easily distinguished. Often scans are meaningless to the untrained eye, partly because the baby is hidden behind other organs.

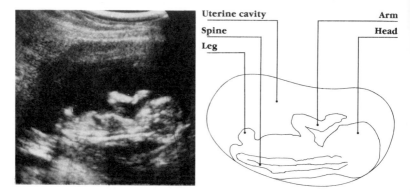

Uterine cavity   Arm
Spine   Head
Leg

How ultrasound works

You undress, put on a hospital gown, and lie on your back beside the scanner. Your abdomen is oiled and then a transducer is slowly passed over it in different directions. The transducer is a machine which picks up echoes from the different planes of your own organs and the developing baby's tissues, and which then translates the information into the form of a map on a screen like a television screen. A scan done in the first few months of pregnancy gains in clarity if your bladder is full and therefore clearly visible, so you will probably be asked to drink a lot of water first and not urinate for an hour or so before the scan. Do not expect to see an immediately recognizable picture of your baby, even in late pregnancy; if a doctor is present, ask to have the picture interpreted, because it may look more like a map of the moon than a baby, and you may find it difficult to make out the different parts of the baby.

The safety of ultrasound

As far as we know ultrasound is safe, certainly much safer than X-rays (see page 101), which provided the only method of finding out about the baby in the uterus before the scan was developed. On the other hand, high frequency sounds continued for a long time can cause damage to hearing in an adult. Questions have therefore been raised about possible effects on the baby's hearing since although the sound waves are bounced off the baby for only a short time, the baby may be vulnerable at certain stages of its development. Babies are not born deaf after having ultrasound, but no one yet knows if any of them will suffer delayed effects in later life.

Ultrasound does have other effects that are not yet fully understood. It causes heat to be generated in body tissues and tiny bubbles inside tissue may dance in reaction to the sound waves. Studies in animals show that powerful or prolonged doses of ultrasound can cause cell changes, and Doreen Liebeskind, a radiologist at Albert Einstein College of Medicine in New York City, has been able to produce permanent genetic changes in human white blood cells on the laboratory bench. This does not necessarily mean that diagnostic ultrasound at the level at which it is normally used in pregnancy is dangerous. But it does imply that we should be asking searching questions about possible long-term effects. It could be that ultrasound has some subtle deleterious effects on especially vulnerable babies in the first 12 weeks of pregnancy, during the time that the major organs of the body are being formed.

I feel I would have been given more information about the ultrasound scan beforehand. My husband waited for me outside and if I had known what a moving experience the scan would be I would have brought him in with me.

Some safety measures

It makes sense to expose pregnant women and the babies inside them to ultrasound only when a diagnosis is needed which cannot be made without ultrasound, and when that diagnosis would result in some change in the kind of care that is given. This rules out routine scanning at 16 weeks—now the accepted practice in many countries. It also rules out using ultrasound simply because parents would like to see a picture of the baby or to enable a woman to "bond" with the fetus. Many obstetricians are rather keen on this and believe that they can make a contribution toward ensuring that babies are well mothered by doing routine ultrasound scans. They do not realize that there are other—better and more intimate—ways of becoming aware of the baby (see pages 218–219).

When ultrasound is used, the length of time you are exposed to it should be limited, and when you are discussing what you can see on the screen, ask for the image to be frozen. Understandably, a woman is fascinated by seeing her baby's movements on the screen; in Denmark the scanner is linked to a video-recorder so that the examination can be replayed later, the woman can see her baby moving, and there can be full discussion about it without exposing the baby unnecessarily to ultrasound.

AFP SCREENING

Alphafetoprotein (AFP) is a substance produced in the early phases of pregnancy by the embryo's yolk sac and later on by the fetal liver. It is known that when the levels of AFP are abnormally high a large proportion of babies are found to be suffering from neural tube defects such as spina bifida (when part of the spinal cord is outside the baby's body) and anencephaly (the absence of a brain). The baby without a brain cannot live, but babies with spina bifida do sometimes live, although they are usually paralyzed below the waist and often develop hydrocephalus (water on the brain) as well.

Levels of AFP in a pregnant woman's blood double about every five weeks in the fourth, fifth, and sixth months of pregnancy, but earlier than this they are usually low. The best time to screen your blood for AFP is therefore in early pregnancy, before the 18th week. Results come through in two to three days.

If your dates are wrong and pregnancy is more advanced than you think, you may find that the AFP level seems suspiciously high. The proportion will also be high if you are expecting twins. In both these cases ultrasound will be used to tell you the real age of the baby and whether you are expecting more than one.

If the rate appears to be high for no obvious reason another blood test may be done to double-check; if the level of AFP is then found to be two or three times higher than the median level of a sample group, you will be offered amniocentesis (see below). But this means two or three out of every hundred women having amniocentesis, with the risk attached to it (one or two babies out of every hundred are miscarried). Some people say that the risk of amniocentesis is greater than the risk of bearing an affected baby if your AFP level is high. Although there are differences of opinion within the medical profession, AFP screening is now done as routine in the United States; the point at which you are offered amniocentesis will vary depending on the center where your blood is tested.

As with all medical intervention, solving the problem is a matter of a delicate balance between risks and there is no easy answer. If AFP testing shows that your level is high, discuss the matter with your doctor, taking your partner or a family member with you so that you can talk it over together afterward and make a shared decision about whether or not to have amniocentesis.

AMNIOCENTESIS

Amniocentesis is a procedure which has been developed to detect abnormalities of the central nervous system (spina bifida and anencephaly) and some other forms of mental handicap such as Down syndrome (mongolism). The sex of the baby can also be determined, so you can discover if any sex-linked disorders might have been inherited.

How amniocentesis works

Under a local anesthetic a hollow needle is inserted through your abdominal wall into the uterus, where about half an ounce (14 g) of the water in which the fetus is lying is sucked out. This fluid has been swallowed by the fetus and passed out of its body again either through its mouth or bladder; it is full of cells from the skin and other organs which, when analyzed, can provide valuable clues to the baby's condition. The fluid is then spun in a centrifuge to separate the cells from the liquid.

In the 1950s, when amniocentesis was first invented, mistakes were sometimes made and the needle penetrated placental tissues, causing occasional miscarriage. But now that ultrasound techniques have been developed, the position of the placenta can be accurately located beforehand and the risks of damage to the placenta have been very much reduced. There still remains a one or two per cent chance, however, that amniocentesis may cause miscarriage.

Because of this small but definite risk, there is no point in having amniocentesis unless there is a well above average chance of your baby being born abnormal. You must also have thought carefully about the implications of discovering that something is wrong with your baby and have decided that you would opt for termination. In some parts of the country, amniocentesis is offered to all women over 35, since the incidence of some of the disorders it is designed to detect rises sharply with age.

If an abnormality is revealed, counseling should be made immediately available to both parents. Since amniocentesis cannot be done until some time between the 14th and 16th weeks of pregnancy, when many women have already felt the first fluttering of fetal movement, the decision is often a distressing one to have to make and the termination is riskier than one performed earlier in pregnancy. The woman who is going through this experience needs generous emotional support from her partner and family.

CHORIONIC VILLUS SAMPLING

Chorionic villus sampling—CVS for short—entails taking a sample of tissue from the part of the outer membrane around the embryo that will later become the placenta, in order to diagnose whether or not a fetus will have a genetic handicap. One of the handicaps it cannot detect, however, is spina bifida. The great advantages of CVS over amniocentesis are that it can be done before 12 weeks—even as early as six weeks after conception—so that an abnormal fetus can be terminated much earlier; and that the test is done through the vagina rather than through the abdominal wall.

CVS is, however, still on trial and there are many questions to be answered before it becomes common practice. The trials are designed to discover whether CVS is sufficiently accurate for routine use, and whether there are risks which outweigh the benefits—such as a high incidence of infection and bleeding or spontaneous abortion (miscarriage) following CVS. We do not as yet know enough about amniocentesis and chorionic villus sampling to be able to say which is better.

***UMBILICAL VEIN
SAMPLING***
*A technique, performed
after the 18th week of
pregnancy, that enables a
sample of fetal blood to be
taken for testing. Guided by
ultrasound, a very fine
needle is passed through the
mother's abdominal wall
and into the blood vessels in
the umbilical cord. The
technique can also be
used to give blood
transfusions and
administer drugs.*

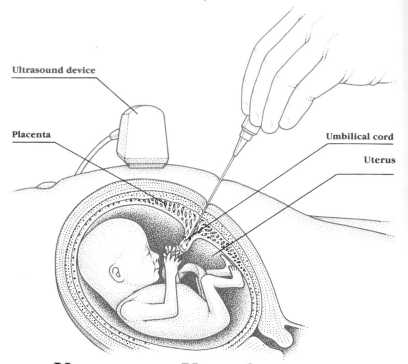

Ultrasound device

Placenta

Umbilical cord

Uterus

UMBILICAL VEIN SAMPLING

At the end of the seventies fetoscopy—photographing the baby with
a telescope introduced into the uterus—was the latest technique for
finding out what was happening to babies known to be at risk.
Unfortunately, the risk of miscarriage proved to be as high as 5–10
per cent. Fetoscopy has now been superseded by umbilical vein
sampling, hailed by Dr Stuart Weiner of the University of Penn-
sylvania as opening up "a whole new area of fetal medicine"*.

In umbilical vein sampling, a very fine needle is passed through the
mother's abdomen and uterus into the fetal vein in the umbilical cord
and blood is withdrawn so that it can be tested. Intrauterine blood
transfusions can also be given in this way, and drugs can be injected
directly into the baby. Because the fetal vein is frail in early
pregnancy, the technique cannot be performed until after 18 weeks.

Although still experimental, umbilical vein sampling is being used
in addition to amniocentesis and ultrasound; it is also used when
there is Rhesus disease (see page 103), in order to diagnose
hemophilia in a baby, and to check for metabolic disorders.

Dr Kytros Nicolaides, of King's College Hospital, London, estimates that when the method is used by experienced doctors, the risk
of losing a baby is only 1 per cent—the same as that for amniocentesis and chorionic villus sampling in that hospital. He emphasized to
me that "the greatest risk of any operative technique in pregnancy is
always the skill and experience of the operator."

The last few weeks

Your baby is almost ready to be born. The firm body is nestled in the cup of your pelvis, and the little arms and legs are plumper as the last layers of fat form to help the baby's temperature control system function efficiently after birth. Sometimes the baby gains as much as 8 oz (226 g) in a week at this stage of pregnancy.

Physical sensations

You may feel fewer big body movements but an insistent kicking underneath your ribs on one side or the other. If your abdominal wall is thin you may even be able to hold your baby's foot. There may be other strange movements, perhaps a sudden urgent knocking which continues intermittently for half an hour or more. This can be so pronounced that you may worry in case your baby is having something like an epileptic fit. But it is definitely not that. The baby may have hiccups, perhaps because it was gulping amniotic fluid; or it may have lost its thumb which it was contentedly sucking, and is "rooting" to find it again, with quick, darting movements of the head from side to side, just as after birth it will search for the nipple. The baby's head feels like a melon or coconut pressing through your bulging perineal tissues, making you sit down with care.

There may also be odd sensations in your vagina. Sometimes there is a sharp buzz like a mild electric shock or a tickle. The baby may be lifting and lowering its head against your pelvic floor muscles in another movement which it will do naturally after birth too, when put down on its front in an alert state. There are times when your baby is sleeping or drowsy and other very active times, often in the evenings.

I'm really enjoying this time and am looking forward to the birth.

Mixed emotions

Conflicting emotions are characteristic of these last weeks. You may be tired of being pregnant but on the other hand the state you are in now is a condition you know and understand, whereas in front of you there is an unknown challenge. So sometimes you want the baby out and long to get on with the labor. But at other times you feel safer as you are, and anxious about the future. Some women say that as the birthday draws nearer they feel irritated with the pregnancy and even with the baby. This produces an emotional state which makes them welcome the start of labor. Other women relish these last weeks.

You know how workmen whistle at you? Well, they always have at me, and I don't say I like it, but I'm used to them doing it. And now, of course, they don't.

Prenatal depression

It is very common for a woman to feel low and become depressed some time in the last six weeks of pregnancy. If you have been practicing carefully and preparing yourself for a natural birth you may experience a kind of stage fright and be convinced that you are going to forget everything when you are actually in labor. You may also be feeling physically tired and heavy with the weight of your burden.

Prenatal depression, though usually shortlived and spasmodic, is a fact of life for some women. It is made more severe by anemia (see page 128), so ask at the clinic what your hemoglobin level is at present and if necessary have extra iron. It is also partly a result of a need for more rest. You may feel very different if you lie down to rest in a darkened room in the middle of the day, have some early nights and adjust your activity to slower, gentler rhythms if possible.

If you find yourself becoming depressed at this stage of pregnancy have a talk with your childbirth educator who, probably a mother herself, will understand what you are feeling.

It feels as if the pregnancy is just going to carry on forever and ever, and it is never going to come out.

Diet in the last three weeks

As you come to within three weeks of the estimated delivery date you will probably find that you need small, frequent meals rather than several large ones each day. There seems to be no room for anything else. This is a time when you can build up reserves of energy for labor by adopting a diet similar to that used by marathon runners.

One California doctor works with long distance runners, in particular with cardiac patients who adopt running as part of their cure. He describes the typical nutrition of marathon runners as "a fresh, raw, high-fiber diet rich in linoleic acid and silicon."* Apparently they experience cravings for certain foods and also share a kind of folklore about what makes for vitality and endurance. Their diet is rich in high-fiber foods (roughage), and the active ingredient in all such foods is called silicon. It is also high in polyunsaturated fats, the most important of which is called linoleic acid, found in seeds, nuts, and whole grains. Linoleic acid, incidentally, is easily destroyed by exposure to oxygen, heat, and light. Marathon runners are mostly vegetarians, avoid greasy fried foods, believe that plenty of onions and garlic is good for them, and take large quantities of vitamin C.

As part of your build up to labor in the last two or three weeks you might like to plan a high energy diet on the same principles as these Californian runners. Start the day with some muesli mixture, including bran. You can eat this mixed with some raw fruit and yogurt— two other foods which the runners enjoy—and add some freshly chopped or ground nuts, seeds and grains.

Buy a new book on the preparation of salads at this late stage of pregnancy to stimulate your imagination. A handful of peanuts on a fresh vegetable salad will provide you with extra linoleic acid without giving you a high fat diet. A little finely chopped raw onion and garlic with seasoning added to cottage cheese adds something solid and particularly tasty to any salad. Have an occasional baked potato in its jacket, or sometimes wholewheat bread. Otherwise plan to eat mainly unprocessed foods with plenty of raw vegetables, citrus and other fruits of every kind, nuts and lots of yogurt. You will then be at peak form for the hard work of labor.

OPPOSITE

The last weeks of pregnancy are a time of conflicting feelings—uncertainty, impatience, and excitement.

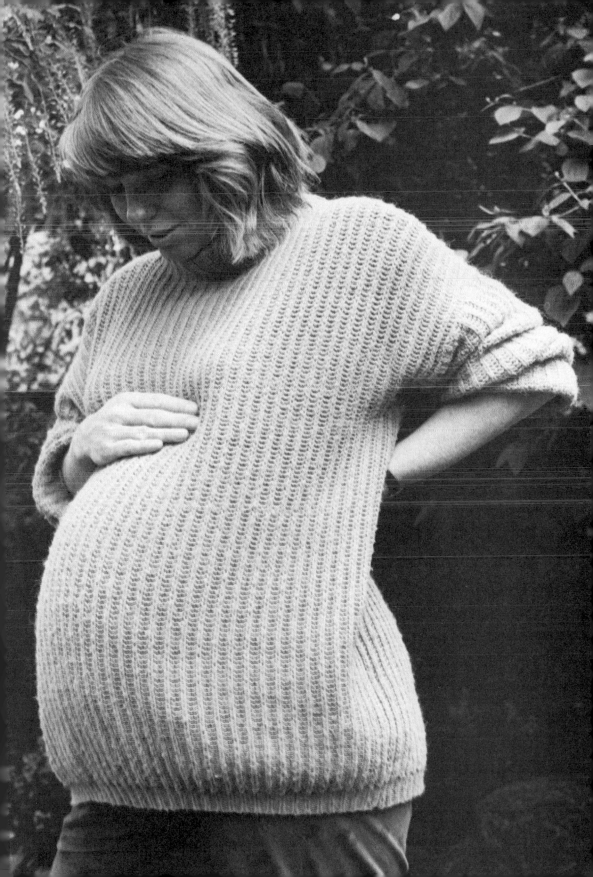

THINKING AHEAD TO LABOR

You will probably be thinking a great deal about labor at this time, wondering what it will be like. One of the things you can find out is the position your baby is in; remember to ask when you are being examined by the doctor. The ideal position for a straightforward labor (and by far the most common) is head down and anterior. But some babies present in different positions, as posterior or breech for example. Delivery may be less straightforward with the baby in these positions (see pages 257–264).

The baby who is presenting as a posterior

If your baby is lying head down with its back against your spine, limbs toward your front, it may be because you have a roomy pelvis so that it can still move around a lot. Women who think they are due but who really have another two weeks or so to go before delivery can have a baby who is still moving freely like this—sometimes posterior, sometimes anterior, sometimes lateral (ear forward). In this case

---

What do you need to pack?

Now is the time to be thinking about the things you want to have available during labor and afterward. Gather them together in a lightweight, easily carried container.

Comfort aids for labor

Thermos bottle for ice cubes, which are sometimes available in hospital.

Two small sponges to be dipped in iced water and used for sponging your face, wetting your lips, and sucking between contractions.

Chapstick or vaseline for dry lips.

Plant spray for moistening face with cold water.

Baby's hot water bottle or a picnic thermal pack to be heated up in water for use as a hot compress in the small of your back, between your legs, etc.

Talc, cornstarch or massage lotion to avoid skin friction when massaged.

Rolling pin to iron away backache (see page 261).

Hairbrush and ribbons or bands if your hair is long.

Books, cards, chess, Scrabble, crosswords, etc.

Honey to keep your strength up in early labor.

Fruit juice, herb teas.

Eau de cologne or toilet water.

Paper bag to breathe into in case you hyperventilate.

Beautiful object on which you can focus when necessary.

Nourishing snacks for your labor companion.

Camera.

Notebook to serve as labor log book.

Writing materials.

Phone numbers of relatives and friends.

Money for pay phones if in hospital.

Comfort aids for after the birth

Calendula and hypericum cream from a health food store or homeopathic pharmacy, for a sore perineum.

Bottle of witchhazel lotion with which you can soak the sanitary pad next to stitches.

Cotton nightgowns and robe.

Nursing bras.

Deodorant (you will perspire heavily in the few days after delivery).

Toilet bag and makeup.

Writing paper and envelopes.

Earplugs if in hospital ward.

---

pre-labor and early-labor contractions usually turn the baby into the anterior position without any intervention by the doctor.

If your baby seems to have settled in a posterior position, you may find that you can coax it to change during one of its waking periods by very firm hand pressure. The posterior baby is usually lying with its head on your right side. You want to shift it round and over toward the left. Treat the baby as if it were a sleeping cat which you were trying to scoop off the middle of a sofa and move over to the left side. Curve the side of your hand around the most solid section of its bulk and firmly, little by little, edge it over. Keep the fingers of your other hand over your navel. If you are successful the saucer shaped dip there (the space between the arms and legs of a posterior baby) will become—at least temporarily—a hard convex curve (the back of a baby in an anterior position). You will be able to detect the change as your navel will probably stick out. Talk to your baby as you move it. This is not simply a clinical exercise, but a bit of maternal persuasion.

Once the baby is stretching the uterus to its utmost it is a tight fit and you will probably not be able to move it. You will have to wait and see whether the first-stage contractions will do the work for you.

The baby who is presenting as a breech

Most babies tip head down—in the vertex or cephalic position—between the seventh and the eighth month. If your baby is still presenting buttocks first (breech) at around 36 weeks the doctor may decide to try and turn the baby—a procedure known as external version. This is a skilled maneuver and should always be done by a doctor—do not attempt it yourself.

I can't help thinking, what if the baby drops out? I might have it anywhere! I'm in a state of constant expectation, thinking, is this it, and then deciding, no it isn't.

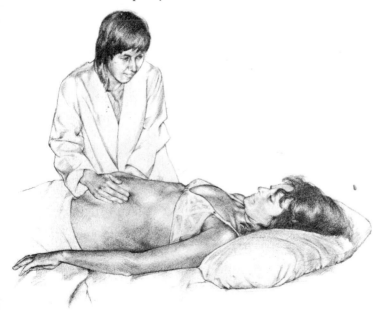

EXTERNAL VERSION
Your doctor may attempt this skilled maneuver if your baby has settled in a breech position. Sometimes the version is successful and a normal delivery can follow, but frequently the baby turns straight back into a breech position after the procedure is over. External version must always be done by a doctor; if done by an unskilled person there is a risk of the placenta separating from the uterine wall.

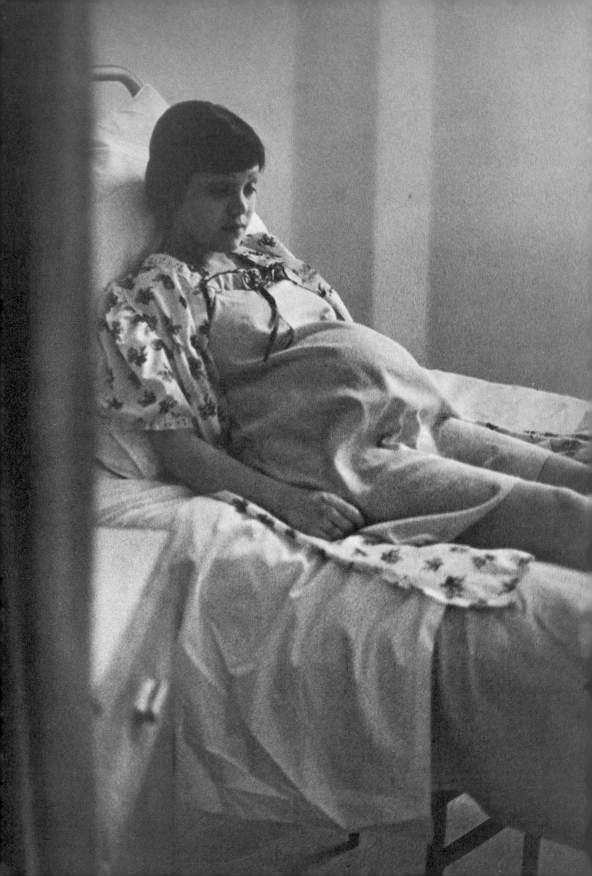

How external version is done You empty your bladder and then lie down on your back with your knees drawn up. The doctor will probably do an ultrasound scan to find exactly how the baby is lying and will listen to the baby's heartbeats before and after turning the baby. You may be asked to lie on a sloping examining table with your legs up and head down for about a quarter of an hour before the maneuver, so that the baby is encouraged to move clear of the pelvis. Spend this time relaxing deeply; use abdominal massage to help you release your tummy muscles and use your breathing to help you as well. Because the uterus often contracts when hands are pressing on it, and this makes it more difficult to turn the baby, the doctor may also use a muscle relaxant to lower the tone of the uterus.

When you feel the doctor's hands on your tummy, release and flow toward the touch. Give a long, slow breath *out* and let your lower tummy bulge out in a great wave as you do so.

Helping a breech to turn You can try to tip the baby up out of your pelvis yourself by adopting a position with your head down and your bottom in the air for 15 minutes three times a day (before meals). Some babies turn a somersault once clear of the pelvis—even after 37 weeks*. A knee-chest position, leaning over a firm bean bag on your front with your head on the floor and your hips as high as possible, or lying in the same position on a steeply sloping, cushion-padded ironing board propped between the bed and the wall or a solid piece of furniture, offer a range of options—none of them, it must be admitted, very comfortable in advanced pregnancy! But if you are able to turn your baby, it may make the difference between a vaginal and a cesarean birth.

Taking up this position for 15 minutes 3 times a day may encourage your breech baby to turn.

If the version is successful and the baby turns, walk around for an hour or two so that there is the best chance of fixing the baby head-down. Some babies turn straight back into the breech position. Seven times out of ten, however, external version at 37 to 39 weeks is successful*. But if the baby tips back again into a breech position you will have to accept that she prefers it; discuss with your doctor the sort of delivery you will have (see page 261).

BEING "OVERDUE"

Concern about the best things to eat, the position of the baby, and whether labor will be straightforward can be preoccupying in the last few weeks. If you actually go *past* the estimated date of delivery you may really begin to worry; you are now consigned to the category of the woman who is "overdue."

The estimated delivery date

The date that you are given at the beginning of pregnancy for your baby's birth (EDD or EDC) is only a statistical mean. Studies show that only 5 per cent of babies arrive on that day. If you look at the 95

OPPOSITE
It is natural to feel despondent if the hospital is concerned because you are "overdue," but the majority of babies arrive after the predicted date.

babies out of 100 who do not put in an appearance on the "correct" date you find that three out of ten babies come before the EDD and seven out of ten come *after* it. This is partly because women's menstrual cycles are of different lengths, and ovulation—and hence conception—may occur at different times within it. But by the time you reach the end of your pregnancy you may not be able to prevent yourself from fixing on the expected delivery date as your goal. If it comes and goes and nothing happens, you may become very depressed. Each day that passes seems like a week, and each week more like a month. Unless you plan for activity and recreation during this time your morale will drop to rock bottom.

If you find that you are getting despondent, remind yourself that, though very few babies are born on the day predicted for their birth, nine out of ten do put in an appearance within ten days of the expected date. There is nothing abnormal about a baby who is nine days "late". Many women, however, are made to feel "under sentence of induction" if they go as much as a week past their expected date. Some obstetricians routinely induce labor when the woman reaches the tenth day following the estimated date, and this is done without further investigation. If your pregnancy is normal and you are in good health, being ten days "late" is a very poor reason for induction.

Whether induction (which is described on page 297) is really necessary or not depends entirely on the baby's wellbeing at the end of pregnancy. The baby's wellbeing, in turn, depends on the condition of the placenta.

> ═ ❝ ═
> *The doctor says he wants to induce me on my due date because my blood pressure is up. I do want to have a natural birth but the time is coming nearer and nearer. It's hanging over me like a date set for execution.*
> ═ ❞ ═

The aging placenta

At the end of pregnancy the placenta looks like a piece of raw liver about the size of a dinner plate and the thickness of your little finger. Like every other human organ, it has a youth and an old age. An elderly placenta works less well. If labor does not start at the right time (which may be anywhere between two weeks before and two weeks after the estimated date of delivery—and very occasionally later still) the placenta may fail to support the baby in the uterus. The baby is then deprived of nourishment. This is why obstetricians are concerned if a pregnancy is prolonged much past the date worked out for the birth. Even so, a baby who is thought to be overdue may prove at birth not to be postmature at all. There are various ways in which the condition of the placenta can be assessed. Some are tests which doctors do to you; probably the most reliable method is one which you can do for yourself (see page 218).

Urinary estriol tests

One way of finding out whether your placenta is functioning well is to measure the output of estriol in your urine or blood. (Estriol is a form of the hormone estrogen, important for the baby's growth.) The level of estriol produced by the placenta rises throughout pregnancy; just before labor starts, it drops. The level also drops if you have high blood pressure or toxemia (see page 126), as it will if you have bleeding in late pregnancy, kidney disease, or diabetes. A lower level than normal suggests that the placenta may not be doing a good job of nourishing the baby and excreting its waste products. If doctors are considering whether to induce labor, they may therefore perform this test.

But the proportion of estriol in urine can vary by as much as 30 per cent with different readings; there are day-to-day variations, even when everything is normal. You therefore cannot rely on one or two tests alone. There should be a series of readings of all the urine over a period of 24 hours, or weekly blood tests. If you are admitted to the hospital with toxemia, regular tests may be performed. If they indicate that the placenta is not functioning well your obstetrician will suggest induction of labor. But the estriol level is only a clue to the condition of the placenta, and it should not be acted on alone. When levels of estriol output are compared with the information provided by ultrasound to assess the baby's growth, there is often a discrepancy, so obstetricians tend to use the two types of test together to try to find out what is happening.

If there is no urgent need for induction (and your doctor will certainly make it clear if there is), you may first want to monitor fetal activity as an additional check on how the baby is faring (see page 218). There is some evidence that observations you can make yourself are more likely to give an accurate picture of the baby's condition than medical tests.

Antepartum cardiotocography

This test uses an electronic fetal monitor (see page 303) to see if the baby's heartbeat shows the usual variations. If the heart rate is satisfactory, there is no need to induce labor or to do the more complicated oxytocin challenge test (below).

Oxytocin challenge test

This test is sometimes called a "stress test" to distinguish it from fetal movement recording (see below), which is a "nonstress test". It is occasionally used when a baby is thought to be overdue to see if it would be better off born.

How the test is done The uterus is made to contract with oxytocin dripped straight into your vein; the reactions of the fetal heart are then observed. The heart rate will probably react to each contraction by slowing down. As long as it returns to normal as soon as the contraction ends, the baby is not considered to be under any particular stress and induction is therefore unnecessary.

On the other hand, if contractions affect the baby's heart rate so much that it slows down and remains slow for a time between contractions as well, then this is considered to be evidence of fetal distress. In these circumstances labor may be induced immediately:

larger amounts of oxytocin will be introduced into your veins to stimulate contractions, and the delivery will be very carefully monitored throughout; alternatively the doctor may decide that the safest option is to perform a cesarean section.

Fetal movement recording

Just when I think there's never going to be a movement there's a terrific leap and then the baby's wriggling all over the shop. Keeping a kick chart has made me much more aware of the baby's waking and sleeping times.

One of the most accurate ways of knowing if a baby is doing well while still inside the uterus in late pregnancy is something you can do for yourself. This is to note the baby's movements. In the last weeks of pregnancy, until it engages, the baby usually wriggles, dips and turns, bangs and kicks, and moves like a porpoise from side to side in great sweeps of activity which you can actually see through your clothing. Once it has engaged it often moves less because it is a rather tight fit. Even so, a vigorous baby moves even after it has gone down into the pelvis, though the movements then tend to be just the knocks from knees and feet. You feel as if you have a rolling coconut in your groin or just behind your pubis (the head turning), and later the strange buzzing sensation of the engaged head bouncing against the pelvic floor muscles (see page 209).

You may not normally be aware of most of these movements while you are busy but as soon as you sit down to rest, or lie down hoping to sleep, you cannot help noticing them. They are a good sign that your baby is healthy. Studies of fetal activity show that every baby has its own individual pattern of waking and sleeping inside the uterus, and by late pregnancy you will have probably noticed what your baby's pattern is. But sometimes you may be awake and expect a kick; if nothing happens it can be disconcerting. In fact, the baby is probably fast asleep; if you have had an alcoholic drink or taken sleeping pills, your baby will probably be affected by them too.

Often it is when you go to bed that you both notice your child's vigorous movements ... regular movements are a sign that all is well ...

Mothers do vary a great deal in the extent that they observe fetal movements. Sometimes this awareness is related to the amount of amniotic fluid, since the water cushions movements. If you are preoccupied and concentrating hard on something else you may also be less aware of fetal activity. If you are still working outside the home, or busy inside it, there may be too much going on to notice fetal movements. But each woman's experience of the movements is fairly consistent if her baby is thriving in the uterus, bearing in mind that the nature of movements changes after the baby has engaged, as described above.

If for any reason it is thought that your baby may be "at risk" (usually because you have not put on weight for two or more weeks, your tummy has not got bigger during this time, or because you are "overdue" in relation to your EDD), you can use your own knowledge about your baby's movements to keep a check on its wellbeing inside you. It is a satisfying feeling to know that monitoring your baby's activity is more likely to be an accurate gauge of how the baby is than a series of complicated tests done by other people. Researchers compared what they called a "daily fetal movement" chart, drawn up by women, with a placental function test designed to measure the total excretion of estriol in the urine over a period of 24 hours (see page 216).* When the amounts of estriol in the urine were low but the mother said that she was aware of a normal number of fetal movements, every single baby was born alive. Unfortunately when the estriol levels were normal but the mother noticed that her baby was hardly making any movements in the uterus at all, three out of ten babies died.

Suppose that you have gone past your dates, and the obstetrician is beginning to suggest taking you into the hospital for observation and to talk about possible induction; you can then start to keep a systematic fetal movement chart. If your baby is not being adequately nourished in the uterus and your placenta is failing in its function, fetal movements will diminish over a period of three or four days and some time after that they will stop altogether. If you leave it this late, birth will probably be by cesarean section in order to ensure a speedy delivery and to care for the baby. But if you monitor the gradual decrease in movements, and tell the doctor as soon as you observe this happening, you will probably be induced, but be able to deliver the baby normally and a cesarean won't be necessary.

When to take action

If you have observed no movement at all over a period of 12 hours and your baby does not wake up at night, go to the hospital or to your own doctor and ask if you can have the fetal heart checked. If you are in the hospital fetal activity can be checked immediately with ultrasound. A transducer is placed on your tummy near the baby's heart. You tell the doctor or midwife as soon as you feel movement.

It has been discovered that there is an effective minimum number of movements which can tell you that the baby is all right; ten movements, of any kind, in a 12-hour period indicate that all is well. If you notice fewer than ten movements in that time your baby may *still* be fine, since 2·5 per cent of daily counts made by women who have healthy babies fall below that, but the indications are that the baby would be better off born in the majority of cases.

The "Count to Ten" chart

The "Count to Ten" chart* is a way in which the mother records fetal activity in half-hour blocks of time on squared paper. It is very boring to have to observe your baby's movements all day and much easier simply to note down the first ten movements in a 12-hour period and stop when you have recorded them. The way in which the chart is often used in a hospital is to tell the mother to start recording fetal movements at 9 am and go on until ten are recorded. She is told to black in the square corresponding to the time at which she has felt the tenth movement.

If you are going to do this as a record for yourself use squared paper and indicate the days of the week along the top. Put the hours of the day down the lefthand side, beginning with the time at which you have decided to start recording. It is probably better to start late in the afternoon (but it should be at the same time each day), and record during the evening. This seems the sensible half of the day because you are more likely to have a stretch of time when you are sitting down, reading, listening to music, chatting, or watching television, and from experience this is known to be a time when fetal movements are often felt. If you start at 4 pm and go to bed at 10 pm or later you then have a clear six-hour period for noting movements.

On your chart you fill in the block in which the fifth movement occurs. A baby who is not very active will take a longer time to get to the fifth movement. If you do not feel any movements by the time you lie down to sleep at night call the doctor first thing in the morning, say that your baby is hardly moving at all, and ask if he will check the fetal heart and activity. (You will probably find that as soon as you settle down to sleep the baby starts moving. If this happens, record the time; but if it is not yet the fifth movement of the day do not shade in the square.)

The point about this method of assessing the baby's welfare is that it is something active you can do for yourself. From both your and the baby's point of view it is completely noninvasive, as well as being incredibly simple.

FETAL MOVEMENT
RECORDING
This way of assessing your baby's wellbeing is especially useful if you are apparently "overdue". Starting at the same point each day, mark the square against the time when you feel your baby's 5th movement. If you do not feel any movements by the end of a 6-hour period contact your doctor without delay. And if you feel fewer than 5 movements it is also advisable to call the doctor.

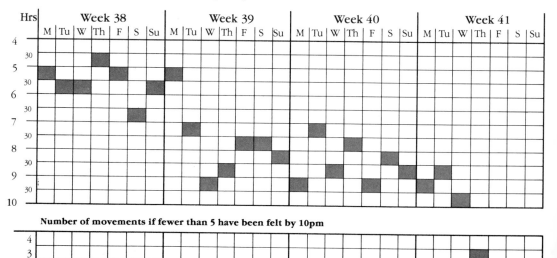

The experience of birth

Moments of birth

The cervix is fully dilated to 10 cm and the midwife feels the position of the baby's head as it moves down the birth canal. The mother is now free to go with the great sweeps of energy that accompany the overpowering urge to bear down and is caught up in an act that requires intense concentration. Her partner gives himself fully to helping her cope with each contraction.

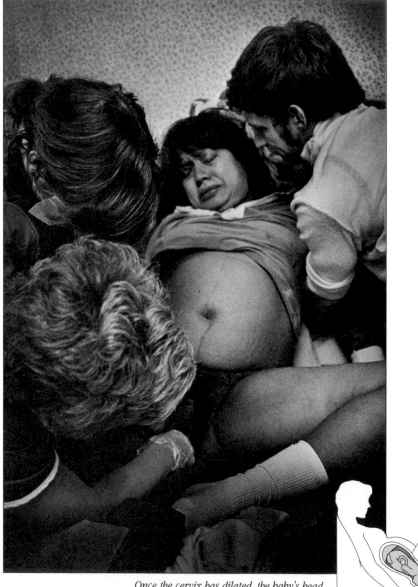

Once the cervix has dilated, the baby's head moves down through the pelvis.

The appearance of the head

The baby's head has slipped under the mother's pubic bone and emerges. Because it has rotated in the birth canal, it is now facing downward. The midwife feels to make sure that the cord is not around the baby's neck.

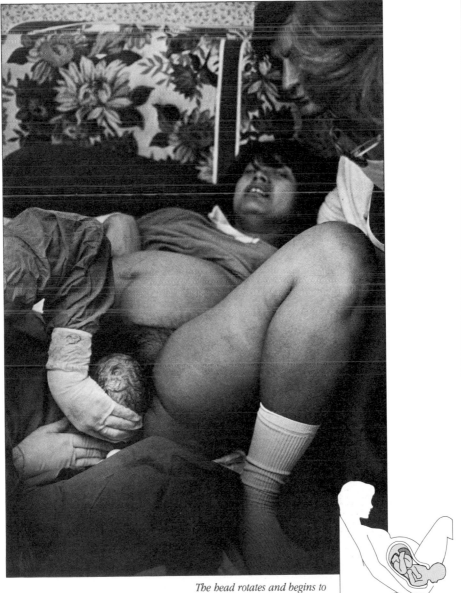

The head rotates and begins to emerge from the birth canal.

Rotation of the head

The baby's head starts to rotate again, so that it is once more in line with the shoulders. Now that she has pushed the head out, the mother is relaxed and happy, and sits up to catch the first glimpse of her child.

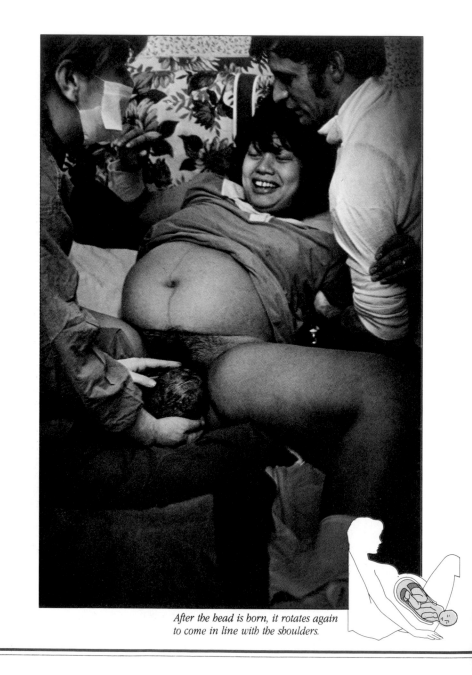

After the head is born, it rotates again to come in line with the shoulders.

Birth of the body

The baby's body follows, helped out by the midwife. He is already breathing. The hair is damp and the skin still crinkled up like a rose petal before it has opened. The parents look on in wonder.

The shoulders slide out, one after the other, followed by the rest of the body.

Becoming a family

*The long-awaited moment. Joy and a celebration as the mother
holds her child in her arms for the first time. Still attached to the
placenta by the umbilical cord, he lies safe and warm against her
tummy after his journey to life.*

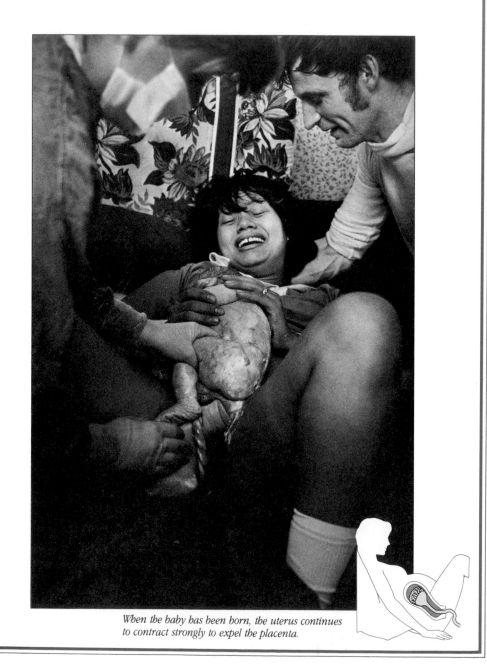

When the baby has been born, the uterus continues
to contract strongly to expel the placenta.

What happens in labor

There are three stages of labor. During the first the cervix is being drawn up into the main body of the uterus and dilating; in the second the baby is pressed down through the birth canal and this stage culminates in delivery; during the third the placenta and membranes are sloughed off the lining of the uterus and expelled.

Having said this, it is important to add that for many women labor is an overwhelming and dramatic experience and you certainly are not sitting around thinking in terms of neat stages. There is no fanfare of trumpets to tell you when the first stage is really under way or when the second stage has started. Some women have a clear physiological message, such as the breaking of the waters or sudden strong, regular contractions, leaving them in no doubt that labor has started and that this is unmistakably *it*, and when they reach the end of the first stage they know with equal certainty that they are now in the second stage and *have* to push. For a great many women, however, the different stages of labor shade over into each other. The experience is rarely as tidy and compartmentalized as books on labor seem to suggest, and the third stage may even pass completely unnoticed as you hold your newborn baby in your arms and marvel at it.

Buildup to labor

Labor starts with the gradual softening and ripening of the cervix at the base of the uterus. This can take days and days or can happen overnight, especially if you have had a baby before. Once the cervix is soft and stretchy the uterine contractions—which are occurring anyway in late pregnancy—tend to draw it up bit by bit, so that it gradually changes from being a long canal hanging down in your vagina to being a dip in the bottom of the uterus, the tissues having been pulled up into the lower segment of the uterus.

You are not considered to be in labor when all this is happening. Your labor has not started in medical terms until you are having regular contractions which are effectively dilating (widening) the cervix; it is work that has to be done before it is possible for the cervix to open up. Usually this means you are at least 3 cm dilated (see page 244) before you are considered to be in labor. In fact many women already have a partially dilated cervix by the time they realize that they are having contractions.

It is obviously more pleasant for you if your body is working for you while you are carrying on with your work and shopping and eating and sleeping and seeing your friends. You cannot possibly be tensing up and fighting your body when you are busy doing all these things and leaving your uterus to work undisturbed and unremarked on. So carry on normal living for as long as is comfortable.

First signs of labor

Three things can indicate that labor has started or is about to start: a show appears, the waters break, or contractions begin.

A show appears This is the bloodstained mucous discharge that you have when the cervix is beginning to stretch. Until the start of labor this mucus has acted as a gelatinous plug in the cervix, sealing off the uterus. Its appearance is a good sign that there is some definite activity round the cervix. But it can come out two or three weeks before you actually go into labor and contractions are established, or it may appear when your labor is so far advanced that you do not notice it. So, although you can take it as an encouraging sign, do not rush off to the hospital. Go on with your everyday activities or, if it is night, have a hot milk drink and go back to sleep.

The bag of waters breaks When the membranes surrounding the baby have been pressed down like a wedge in front of its presenting part (usually the head) and pressure has built up, the bag pops. It may do this suddenly with a rush of water or, and this is more likely, with a slow trickle. In fact, you may not be quite sure whether the bag of waters has burst or you are wetting your pants. If you are not sure, forget it (if you can) and carry on as usual, unless you are still several weeks away from your EDD, in which case you should call the doctor at once. If it is more than three weeks before your baby is due it is important for you to be in a place where special care is ready for the baby at delivery.

You will probably have been told to call the hospital or your doctor or midwife if the waters break and you lose a lot of water at once. This is because, if labor is slow, taking 24 hours or more from the rupture of the membranes, there is a chance of your baby becoming infected. Also, if the baby's head does not fit properly into the cervix, there is a chance that the waters might sweep the cord down through the cervix, which in turn might mean the blockage of the oxygen supply to the baby. If, therefore, you do not know how your baby is presenting before you go into labor, you should be prepared to go to the hospital immediately after the waters break, in case the baby is breech or its head is high. Today obstetricians usually decide to stimulate the uterus into activity once the waters have gone. If you are sure of the presentation, give nature a chance and allow yourself three or four hours of gentle everyday activity before leaving for the hospital. Contractions will usually start during this time.

There is no need to worry about having a "dry" labor, with the baby traveling down an unlubricated birth canal, as there is no such thing. Your amniotic fluid is completely reformed every three hours. Actually a "wet" labor is more likely and can be uncomfortable, since a continual leaking throughout labor is cold and unpleasant. If you are leaking, wear a sanitary pad and change it frequently.

Contractions start They usually feel like a tight elastic belt slung under your bump and round into the lower part of the small of your back, being drawn tighter, gripping for 15 to 20 seconds, and then being released. This sensation occurs again after ten minutes, or even sooner. These might be the Braxton Hicks "rehearsal" contractions, which some women experience as quite painful at times in the last three weeks or so of pregnancy. These then tend to be called "false" labor. All this means is that you thought you were in labor, with good reason, but were not.

If you want to be fairly sure about being in labor, time your contractions over a period of 30 minutes or an hour, make a note of the interval between the start of one and the start of the next, and also note down the length of each contraction. The contractions need to come closer and closer together and to last longer (40 seconds or more) before you can be confident that labor is being established.

During contractions the muscle fibers at the top of the uterus tighten, pressing in and down on the center and producing an upward pull on the cervix. When the baby's head is pressed down by

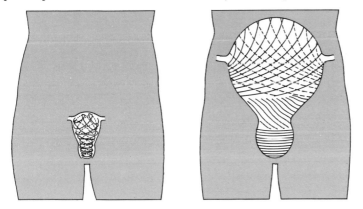

MUSCLE BUNDLES
The uterus is composed of spiral muscle bundles which in early pregnancy start to unfold into an open-latticework formation at the top of the uterus. If you think of the uterus as a clock, the muscle bundles are spaced out most between 9 and 3— that is, over the fundus of the uterus. By the end of the pregnancy these bundles of muscle have unfolded much more and are stretched lengthways.

a contraction, the muscles and fibrous tissues of the cervix are drawn apart. In a straightforward labor most of the physical sensations caused by contractions come from this area in and around the cervix, apart from a hardening and swelling felt at the top of the uterus.

Once the contractions are going well, they have a regular rhythm, a wavelike shape, and last longer and longer, while the interval between them is reduced. One woman said she felt her contractions like heat from an oven. First the oven door opened a little and then more till she was in the full blast of heat. Then it closed again.

The first stage of labor

Although we do not know for certain what starts labor off, one theory is that when the tissue in the baby's adrenal gland is mature it produces cortisone. This triggers off a remarkable process. It changes the balance between the amount of estrogen and progesterone produced by the placenta, the estrogen level dropping

Using gravity to help your labor

If you stay more or less upright in early labor, and continue to move around, the downward force of gravity will help push the baby out. Your contractions will be more effective, too, and should prove less painful than if you were lying down.

SQUATTING
If you find squatting comfortable, crouch down between your partner's legs and lean back against him, using his knees for support; then you can rock or rotate your pelvis.

SUPPORTED LUNGE
With firm support from your partner and one foot raised on a chair, stool or low table, you can move into a supported lunge.

PELVIC ROCKING
Try rocking your pelvis backward and forward or making slow, circling movements as if you were belly dancing.

BENDING FORWARD
You can lean over a bed or window sill and rock your pelvis while your partner applies counterpressure to the small of your back.

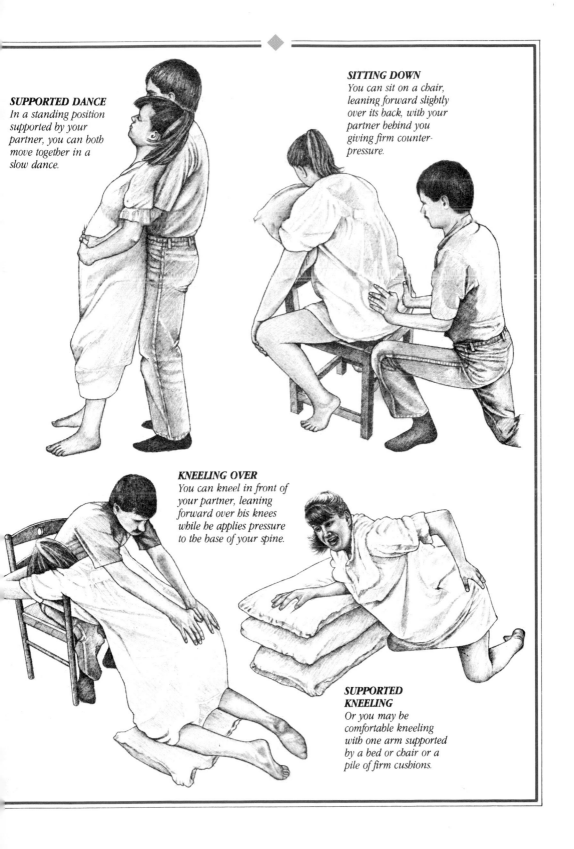

SUPPORTED DANCE
In a standing position supported by your partner, you can both move together in a slow dance.

SITTING DOWN
You can sit on a chair, leaning forward slightly over its back, with your partner behind you giving firm counter-pressure.

KNEELING OVER
You can kneel in front of your partner, leaning forward over his knees while he applies pressure to the base of your spine.

SUPPORTED KNEELING
Or you may be comfortable kneeling with one arm supported by a bed or chair or a pile of firm cushions.

and the progesterone level going up, and this in turn initiates the production of prostaglandins. The prostaglandins act on the uterus to make the contractions you have been having in late pregnancy bigger and closer together. So the contractions of early labor may feel like Braxton Hicks contractions, but heftier and more regular.

These more efficient contractions press the baby's presenting part down to the base of the lower segment of the uterus and against the cervix. This then becomes progressively more stretched and thinned out as the muscle fibers are pulled up into the upper segment. The effacement and stretching of the cervix next trigger the production of oxytocin from the posterior pituitary gland, and this stimulates the uterus into a steady rhythm of contractions. Labor is under way!

Moving around in labor

Going to bed early in the first stage of labor and becoming more or less immobile can slow down labor or interfere with it starting effectively because the presenting part may not be pressed down against your cervix. When you are upright, moving around, you have gravity to help you; everything is being pressed down.

In this position the uterus is contracting against the force of gravity.

It was not till the end of the eighteenth century in Europe that women began to lie down to give birth. Before that time they had walked around during much of labor and used labor stools or sat up in bed or on a chair. Birth stools were designed like horseshoes, with the open part at the front, were low on the ground so that the woman squatted, and sometimes provided support for her lower back as well as handgrips. As a result she was in a physiologically excellent position.

Mauriceau, then the obstetrician to the French court, introduced the lying down position and it soon caught on because people sought to imitate the manners of the court. When forceps were introduced (see page 306), obstetricians found that they were easier to use on a woman who was lying flat. Still later, the lithotomy position, in which the patient lies on her back with her legs fixed to raised stirrups and which was first devised for surgery on gall stones, was introduced. This highly artificial posture is often terribly uncomfortable for the woman, pressing her uterus against the big blood vessels in the lower part of the body. This interferes with her circulation, causing hypotension (low blood pressure), and also with the production of urine; it can cause fetal distress.

Research on the effect of different positions in the first stage of labor* has shown that most women prefer to be up and about, not lying in bed, and that contractions are stronger and labor shorter with the woman in an upright position. The uterus is working nearly twice as efficiently to dilate the cervix.

So, between contractions keep walking around. Try full pelvic rocking and circling movements as if you were belly dancing. If dilatation is taking a long time, also try soaking in a warm bath or squatting on a low stool under the shower.

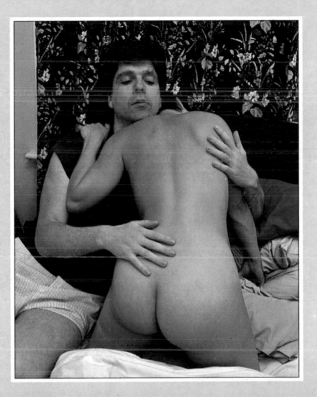

The first stage of labor

The first stage of labor is by far the longest, and it helps to be upright and moving around. A woman needs a loving partner or someone else she trusts to hold and encourage her and to share the experience with her.

Kneeling forward or lying in warm water eases the pain of strong contractions.

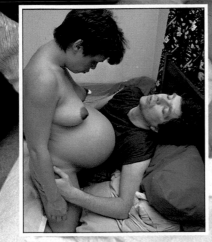

A firm back massage—your partner breathing with you—gives comfort and reassurance.

A long labor is very tiring. Rest is needed too. Bean bags and pillows are piled up so that the woman can relax in a semi-upright position.

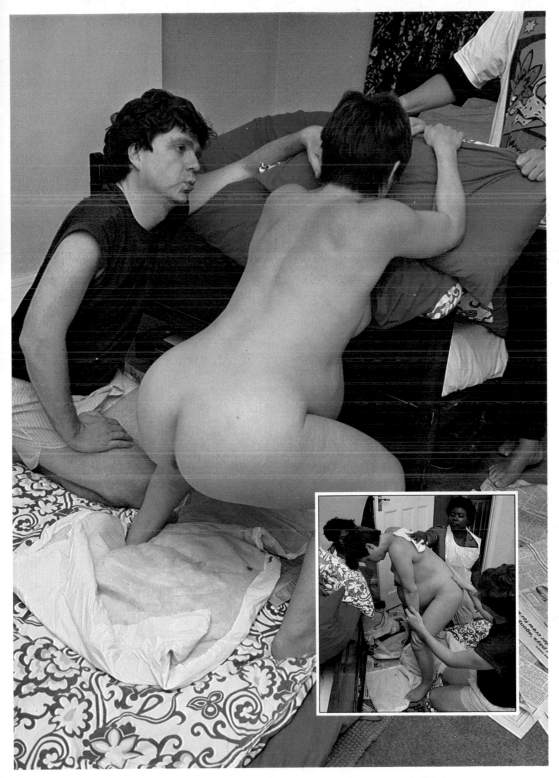

Open positions, legs well apart, help the progress of labor.

In the late first stage huge waves swell and rush through the woman's body. Her helpers are like anchors in a stormy sea.

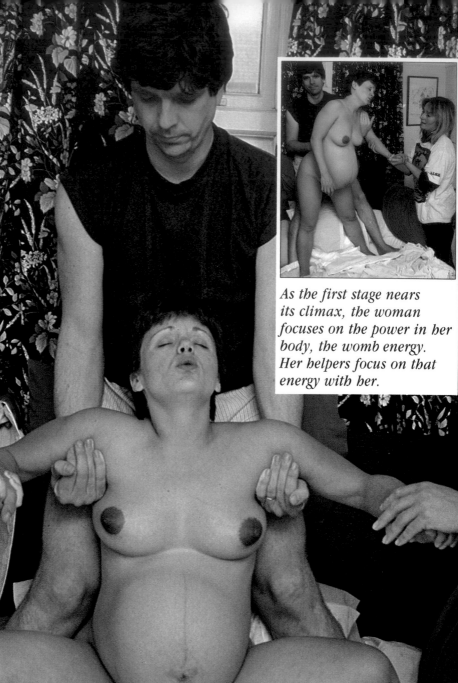

As the first stage nears its climax, the woman focuses on the power in her body, the womb energy. Her helpers focus on that energy with her.

When to go to the hospital

Unless you feel strongly that you need to be in the hospital during this time, or your doctor has advised that there is a special reason why you should come in as soon as there are any signs of labor starting, it is best to stay at home and carry on as usual. This is partly because of the psychological effect of going to the hospital, being admitted and prepared and getting into bed. If you have only just begun labor, all this can stop it entirely. There are many women who have gone to the hospital with regular contractions that are still more than five minutes apart and who have then gone out of labor and have either had to wait around with their morale dropping steadily or have had an intravenous oxytocin drip inserted in an arm vein to stimulate the uterus into action.

Knowing that your contractions will be coming one every two minutes and will last about one minute or longer just before the baby is born may give you some perspective on your labor when it is just starting. Having contractions every five minutes can be tiring and some women experience this for 12 hours or more (usually when the baby is in a slightly awkward position, facing the mother's front instead of her back, see page 257), but the baby cannot possibly be born when contractions are coming this far apart, so if you are happier at home, stay there. Keep a careful record of what is happening, time the contractions now and again, and be ready to go to the hospital as soon as the membranes rupture or contractions come more often than every five minutes.

Of course you must bear in mind the distance from your home to the hospital and the difficulty of getting there. If you are going in your own car, it is as well to have done a trial run beforehand at the rush hour to see how long it can take and to be sure that you know the way, even in deep snow, hail, or fog, and also any short cuts that may be convenient. Your partner should drive steadily, but not fast, and certainly not braking suddenly at corners or at lights. Decide early what you will need to make the journey comfortable and whether you would prefer to be in the front or back seat. If you are calling an ambulance, find out well in advance how to do this and, if you are relying on getting to the hospital by taxi, have a list of numbers pinned up by the telephone in case one is not immediately available.

Admission procedures

When you arrive at the hospital, a nurse will take you to a little room where you will be "prepped" (prepared) for labor. She will ask you questions about how labor started, if the waters have broken, and if so when, how often contractions are coming, and so on. She will do some of the things you are already familiar with, such as requesting a urine sample, checking your blood pressure, feeling the position of the baby through your abdominal wall, and listening to the fetal heart. She or a staff doctor will feel through your vagina and into your cervix, to tell if you have started dilating. If you are already partially dilated, the waters may be broken (see page 291). This is done routinely in many hospitals at 3–4 cm dilatation, and sometimes before this phase has been reached. If you want your membranes to remain intact until they rupture spontaneously, say so before your internal examination.

It used to be hospital practice to shave a woman's perineum, and in some hospitals every perineum was required to be as bald as a hard-boiled egg. Still today some attendants like the hair surrounding the vagina to be clipped short. Women have spoken out strongly against the unnecessary, uncomfortable, and degrading practice of perineal shaving; research has shown that it is useless in avoiding infection and, however carefully done, always results in some injury to the skin.

Some hospitals still give an enema to empty the lower bowel, but there is no point unless a woman is very constipated. In the hours before labor starts, most women have loose motions. In this way the lower bowel is cleared naturally.

After you have been examined you will be asked to don a hospital gown; it is usually done up at the back, but if you hope to have your baby at the breast immediately following delivery you will find it easier to wear the gown with the opening at the front. In a few hospitals now you can choose to wear your own clothes. Select something made of cotton rather than a synthetic fabric, as hospitals are often over-heated. Whatever you wear should be loose, so that you can move freely. An external or internal fetal monitor may be attached to assess your baby's heart rate and response to contractions as well as the strength of the uterine contractions.

In some hospitals your partner may be asked to wait outside while you are prepped, but today many nurses take it for granted that a couple want to stay together. It can seem a very long time to be separated and if your partner has been helping you cope with contractions up till now, it is good to go on having the same kind of support. It also gives the midwife or nurse a chance to talk with the father, which means that she is meeting you not as an isolated patient but in your relationship with your man. If you have chosen to have someone other than the father with you, they should be able to stay, too. Labor is not a good time in which to have people coming and going. You will be able to relax knowing that you are with someone who understands you and is giving continuous emotional support.

A doctor may come into the room, too, to assess progress or to discuss your case. If you have any questions, take this opportunity to ask them. If you are planning a natural birth, want to walk around in labor, or have any other wishes, remind the doctor or midwife of these and ask if they have been or can be noted on your chart.

Make a note of the length of contractions and any other physical signs so that this information is available when you phone the midwife.

Countdown for birth at home

If you are having your baby at home, plan ahead, and make sure that any major chores do not pile up. When you think you are in labor, start to prepare for the birth. Put a plastic sheet (a shower curtain also works well) on the bed and if the bed is not already at right angles to the wall move it to this position. Put out the things that the midwife has asked you to have ready on a small table or better still a cart, arranged on a freshly washed towel or pillow slip and cover them with another piece of cloth. Arrange the lighting so that the midwife can direct some light onto your perineum for delivery and so that the other lights can be dimmed or turned out when required. Put the baby's clothes out and a change of clothes for yourself. Boil some water: this will be used mostly for tea, but is also useful for washing your perineum after delivery.

Then turn your mind to what you are going to eat and drink for the next three days and also what you may want to offer visitors. You will have been wise to have stocked up your cupboard and freezer well in advance. If you put anything in the oven at this stage, take a timer with you when you go to the bedroom and pin a reminder in a prominent place, or your labor may be accompanied by the smell of burning.

Call the midwife, if possible before she goes out on her rounds, to let her know that you may be needing her later, and pin all important phone numbers by the phone. The midwife will probably call to check how you are doing and will leave you telephone numbers of where she can be contacted throughout the day.

Transition

Toward the end of the first stage, when you are between 8 and 10 cm dilated, you are in transition.

For most women the very end of the first stage is stormy and challenging. Contractions follow each other relentlessly with hardly a pause between, and they tend to become arhythmic, with sharp peaks and sometimes with more than one to each contraction. The buildup of energy with each may be so sudden and tumultuous that there is no time for slow breathing and you must adapt straight away and breathe much more lightly and quickly if you are to soar over the top of the peaks with your breathing. The very length of the contractions may demand every bit of concentration and determination you are able to summon, and you will need strong emotional support and unfailing encouragement. Your partner's attention must not waver for a minute and he should repeatedly communicate to you his confidence in you and his love.

Every time a big contraction came part of me said "No, no" and I answered mentally "Yes, yes."

At the same time other physiological signs may occur which can be unsettling, until you remember that they are indications of progress and that if you are aware of three or more of them, then you are likely to be 8 cm dilated and hence in transition. Feeling hot then cold, then hot again, your cheeks flushed and your eyes shining bright, suggests that you are in transition. So does a fit of hiccups or belching, or you may even feel nauseous and actually vomit. Perhaps your legs feel icy cold and begin to shake uncontrollably. One of the surest signs is feeling that you have a large grapefruit pressing against your anus or that you want to empty your bowels. You might have a catch in your throat that stops your easy rhythmic breathing or you involuntarily hold your breath or start to grunt. You may suddenly feel that it is all too much hard work and that you cannot go on and would like to go home and forget about having a baby. Or you may become irritable with everyone and hypercritical of the help your partner is giving.

Not all women experience these signs, but a sufficient proportion do to make it a good idea for your partner to memorize them, so that at the right moment he can say: "I think you are in transition." You may have forgotten you are having a baby by this time and are simply concentrating on the work of handling each contraction. You are also very likely to feel that you are not making any progress at all and have lost all sense of time. Since in transition you may get an urge to push before you are fully dilated, you may be told to continue breathing and not to hold your breath until you absolutely must.

Pushing powerfully and for a long time against an incompletely dilated cervix can make it puffy and swollen so that the opening actually closes rather than opens wider. This is why you may be asked not to push until you cannot avoid pushing. This is wise advice, because then you can be quite certain that your body is really ready to push and you will also enjoy the surrender to the great sweeps of energy that come with the contractions in a way you cannot if you are just pushing because someone has told you to do so.

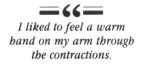

I liked to feel a warm hand on my arm through the contractions.

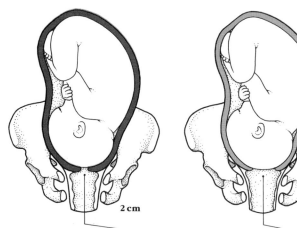

2 cm   6 cm   10 cm

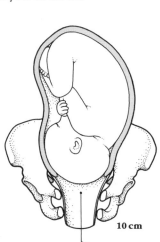

DILATATION

The cervix has to be 10 cm dilated (widened) before the uterus can press the baby out. The time taken to reach full dilatation (shown right, life-size) varies enormously: some women are 3 cm dilated before they realize they are in labor, others take hours to reach 5 cm.

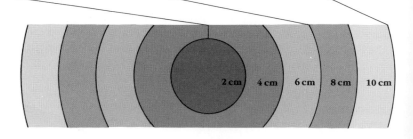

2 cm   4 cm   6 cm   8 cm   10 cm

Transition may be very brief—just a few contractions—or it may last an hour or more. It is likely to last longer if the baby is in an occipito-posterior position (see page 257). The cervix has to dilate to 10 cm before the baby can be pressed down through the opening. At full dilatation (10 cm or the width of the palm of a large man's hand including the thumb joint) the cervix is open enough for the baby's head, its largest part, to ease through. There are spaces between the baby's skullbones, the fontanelles, which can close up as the baby slides down the birth canal, so shaping its head to make the journey much less arduous, even for a 9 lb (4 kg) baby. This is why, especially in first labors, the baby's head is molded, sometimes into a rather peculiar shape; this gradually disappears in the first week or so after the birth (see page 331). As soon as the cervix has dilated to 10 cm, the second stage of labor starts.

The second stage of labor

The second stage of labor is the most exciting. During the first stage the cervix has thinned out and opened. At the end of the first stage the cervix is open to 10 cm, making the uterus and vagina one birth canal. Then follows a wonderful time when you can begin to push. The second stage of labor is often described as if it were sheer, grinding, hard work, but you will *want* to do it. You will probably have an overpowering urge to bear down and press the baby through the birth canal. This is passionate, intense, thrilling, and often completely irresistible, and for some women it is the nearest thing to overwhelming sexual excitement. Pushing is not something you decide to do with a rational part of your mind, but a force that sweeps through your body and culminates in the delivery of your baby.

I felt wonderful sensations of involuntary pushing. The midwife examined me and I heard the blessed words, "There's no cervix left."

There are a few women who do not feel much of an urge to bear down. Sometimes women who have had other babies do not experience a strong pushing urge. The whole process may be gentler; the mother seems not to need to do much bearing down because that baby is going to be born very easily anyway.

There are three to five urges to bear down with each second-stage contraction, though sometimes we talk about these contractions as if they were all push. Frantic pushing results in your becoming desperate, straining to press the baby just that little bit farther. This is not necessary, because surges of desire to bear down come with each contraction, and it is important to go with each as it comes; allow yourself to hold your breath, bear down, and open up with the surge, which usually lasts five or six seconds, no longer. Only you can know when these surges are there. Some people think it is a good idea for a woman to hold her breath for as long as she possibly can in the second stage and only then is she really working hard. However, research suggests that prolonged breath-holding is not only exhausting for the mother, but can also be dangerous for the baby because it reduces the oxygen content of the blood. So trust your spontaneous feelings and do what comes naturally.

Your baby's head appears

When the top of your baby's head can be seen for the first time, it looks like a wrinkled walnut in the vagina, not like a baby at all. Your partner will probably see this before you can, and will be able to tell you the color of the baby's hair. With the first baby the second stage make take one or two hours. With the second or subsequent baby it may take only ten minutes.

Then there comes a time when the widest part of the baby's head is just at the birth opening and does not go back in between contractions. You feel stretched to your utmost. At this moment of "crowning" it is important not to go on pushing, even though you feel very much like it, otherwise you might tear the perineal tissue. The doctor or midwife may perform an episiotomy if they think you might tear (see page 294). If you want to avoid having one, just before the head crowns start to *breathe* the baby out instead of pushing it out (see page 192), and in this way it may slip forward. The midwife or obstetrician checks to see that the cord is free of the neck and may insert a mucous catheter in the baby's mouth and suck any mucus out. A rubber bulb like the top of a turkey baster may also be used.

The baby's head slips under your pubic bone and extends, the chin being automatically lifted off its chest. As the head emerges, damp and sticky with mucus, it is often a violet or purple color. This is nothing to worry about: the child has not yet taken that first great gasp of air that will oxygenate the blood.

The journey through the pelvis

About 80 per cent of women have good, well-rounded pelvises for childbirth. Problems may be encountered if your pelvis is narrow: an android pelvis, for instance, is shaped like a triangle at the brim, which is hard for the baby to negotiate. Even when the pelvic shape is not ideal, the uterus works to press the baby into a neat package which, given time, can often make the journey without difficulty. Basically the baby consists of two balls which move against each other. The ball with the largest diameter is the baby's head. The other ball is the baby's trunk with the limbs well tucked in. The action of a uterus that is contracting well results in the baby being molded into the right shape for the journey down the birth canal.

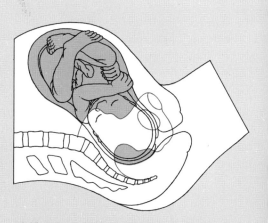

1 *The vagina is almost at right angles to the uterus. So the baby has to negotiate an angle similar to that of the foot putting on a high boot. But there are several bones that may stick out and hold up the baby's progress. The sacrum is the big bone in the spine which forms, together with the pubic bone at the front and the hip girdle at the sides, the pelvic brim. Once the baby's head has traveled below the pelvic brim, it is in the pelvic cavity.*

Normal female pelvis

Android pelvis

The baby may be covered in vernix, a cold-creamlike substance which coats the baby's skin in the uterus and makes it look as if it has been spread with cottage cheese. The head has been molded by its journey down the birth canal, so it may be an odd, pointed, or bumpy asymmetrical shape, and the forehead may recede and the baby be almost chinless. The nose is often flattened like a prizefighter's and there are little red marks between the eyes and on the eyelids.

At delivery, the baby's head is facing downward but the shoulders are still turned sideways inside you. Once the head is free, it turns to come in line with the shoulders. You may need another push for the shoulders. The doctor or midwife may press the baby's head down so that the shoulder nearer your front slides out first, then the head is lifted up so that the lower shoulder slides out next. Then the whole body slithers out and your baby is born!

There is often a great gush of water, and the baby may be already breathing and crying, its limbs lashing and its face puckered up with what looks like rage. The lower end of the body seems very small in comparison with the head end, apart from the genitals which often look extraordinarily large. All this is normal. If the baby is not yet breathing, attendants suck out the respiratory tract, and hold the child's head downward, and, if necessary, they may give oxygen. If you are well propped up, you will be able to reach your baby, provided he or she is lying over your thigh or has been delivered up on to your tummy, and you may want to reach down straight away and take your daughter or son in your arms.

I felt the baby's head pop around and she was born. And she was a girl! All the time I had been desperate for a son but I didn't mind. I held her and she just lay there and liked it.

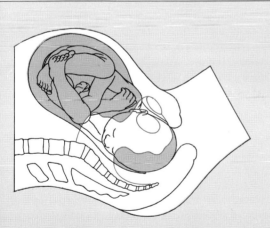

2 *Once the baby has negotiated the pelvic brim, it moves on to the pelvic outlet, bordered by the coccyx (the tiny bone at the base of the spine) at the back, the bottom of the pubic bone at the front, and the ischial spines, which are the two projecting crests on the side walls of the pelvis. The coccyx slips out of the way as the head comes through.*

3 *Usually the downward pressure from above that is provided by good contractions will ease the baby's head down so that as it comes through the steepest curve at the beginning of the vagina the muscles at the back of the neck extend. In effect this means that the baby is facing downward just before and as it is delivered.*

The third stage of labor

Though you may not feel the contractions, your uterus continues to contract after the birth of the baby. This makes the placenta separate from its lining, since the placenta cannot contract. As the uterus squeezes down into a firm, hard ball the placental mass is automatically peeled off. This process has been compared to stretching a piece of rubber on which a postage stamp has been stuck; when the rubber moves, the stamp becomes detached. The sinuses in which the placental blood vessels were rooted are closed by the tight squeezing of the uterus, and these contractions prevent excessive bleeding from the uterine wall.

When the placenta has detached itself, the midwife or doctor may pull on the cord (see page 296). Take a breath, hold it, and bear down at the same time to help this process. You can ask that instead of having cord traction, you can push again and do it by yourself.

There is a squelchy, slippery feeling as the placenta slides out. The person who delivered you examines the placenta carefully to see that every part is there. Pieces of placenta left inside could cause unnecessary bleeding, pain, and infection in the postpartum period. Though the placenta looks like a large piece of raw liver, it was the tree of life for your baby. You may be interested to examine it yourself and see the difference between the rough side, which was against the wall of the uterus, and the smooth side, which lay toward the baby like a soft, velvety cushion, and to note the network of blood vessels that provided your baby with its life support system.

The nurse will help you on with a couple of sanitary pads, as there will be some bleeding now and for several days, resembling the height of a heavy period. The length of time during which there is a bloodstained vaginal discharge (lochia) varies greatly between women. Some new mothers bleed for just a few days after the birth, others for as long as five or six weeks.

Being together

In many hospitals the staff tidy up at this point. They wipe and weigh the baby, examine you to see if you need stitches, give you a wash, change your gown, shorten the baby's cord and reclamp it. But practice is changing fast and many now give the parents the opportunity for a quiet time with their baby immediately following the birth, only doing the basic essentials and leaving the couple for an hour or so to get to know their baby. Being together should always come first. Tidying up can be done later. It is far less important. If you need stitching, it is usually possible to have the baby with you throughout this procedure. Suturing (the technical term for stitching) is done under local anesthetic and usually takes a long time, sometimes as long as an hour, since careful embroidery has to be done and the underlying layers of muscle must be correctly aligned. So keep your baby in your arms or near enough to touch.

Birth under water

*Babies can be born in water—either in a
special pool or in the bath. In warm water,
contractions are less painful, it is easier to
relax, and the tissues of the perineum are
soft and supple.*

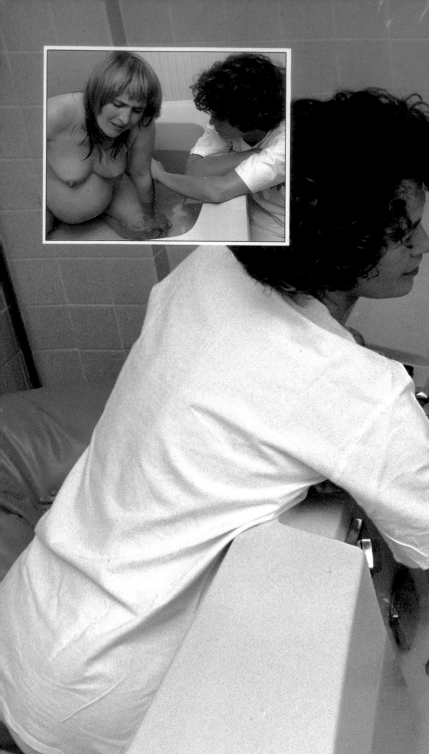

The mother kneels and her midwife can feel the baby's head just inside the vagina. As the midwife monitors the fetal heartbeat, one child watches, eager, quiet, and intent.

The baby's head slides out under water.
The mother reaches down to feel it.
While blood is still pulsating through the
cord, the baby gets oxygen under water
and does not need to breathe.

With a supporting hand from the midwife, the mother lifts her baby out of her body and up into her arms. The baby is pink, vigorous, and wanting to suckle, so she puts her to the breast and helps her latch on. She gets out of the water to deliver the placenta.

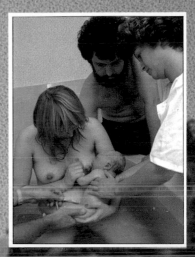

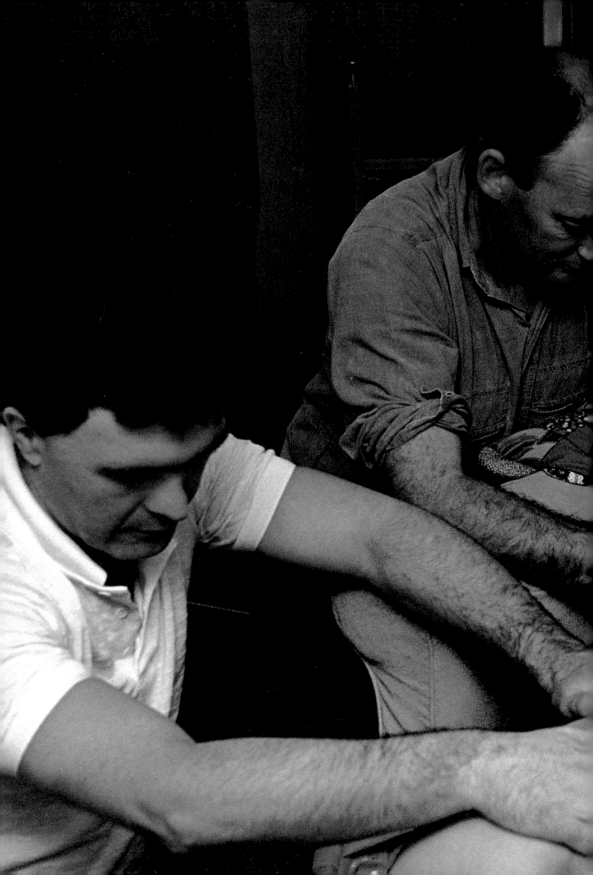

Birth on all fours

When a woman feels most comfortable kneeling on all fours, the baby may be born from behind. The warmth of her helpers' touch helps to release tension. As the baby's head slips out, the doctor cradles it in his hands.

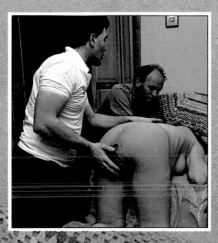

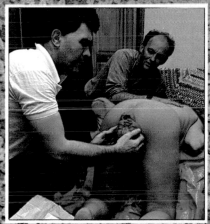

The doctor catches the baby as she tumbles out. He passes the warm, slippery bundle through to the mother, who sits back and holds her close, triumphant and overjoyed at the new life in her arms.

Different kinds
of labor

However much people may advise you not to have any preconceptions about your labor, just to be ready for whatever comes, it is difficult not to have some, because it is almost impossible to prepare yourself to cope with a situation that you have not imagined in advance. So it is useful to think ahead to the major variations on the theme of childbirth which you might confront. However, it is still vital to keep in the forefront of your mind the normal, rhythmic and harmonious pattern of a straightforward labor. Otherwise all the medical technicalities may seem bewildering, and you may interpret each uncomfortable physical sign as an indication that something has gone wrong.

This chapter looks at some different types of labor, all of which can throw you unless you understand what is happening.

Labor with a posterior baby

When the hard back of the baby's head presses against your sacrum or slightly to one side of it, the baby is said to be in an occipito-posterior position. Most women have some backache in labor, but women with posterior babies may have it all the time, so much so that the labor can be described as a "back labor". Few women with posterior babies do not have backache, which can be the most tiring and stressful thing about a labor—especially if, as is often the case when the baby is posterior, it continues *between* contractions as well as during them.

Another characteristic of labor with a posterior baby is that it starts very slowly, often over a period of several days, and contractions are usually experienced as one big one followed by a feeble one. Plan for morale-boosting activity during a long first stage. Don't go into the hospital too soon. A walk in the park or the country is probably better. Eat and keep up your strength in early labor and have plenty of fluids, remembering to empty your bladder regularly. Your partner also needs stamina in a back labor, to keep you going by giving you his total attention during difficult contractions.

The baby will probably rotate at the very end of the first stage or on the onset of the second and things will be plain sailing from then on. About 5 per cent of posteriors do not rotate and then the hard work has to be continued in the second stage and you may need obstetric help (see page 306) to deliver the baby. But the chances are that the baby will swivel around by herself and then be able to complete her journey down your birth canal with ease.

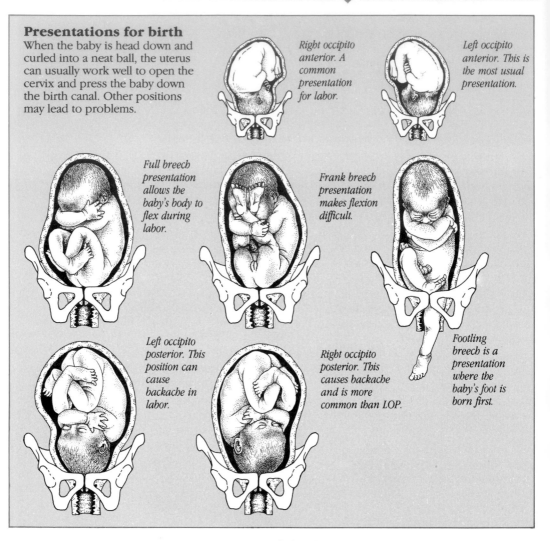

Presentations for birth

When the baby is head down and curled into a neat ball, the uterus can usually work well to open the cervix and press the baby down the birth canal. Other positions may lead to problems.

Right occipito anterior. A common presentation for labor.

Left occipito anterior. This is the most usual presentation.

Full breech presentation allows the baby's body to flex during labor.

Frank breech presentation makes flexion difficult.

Left occipito posterior. This position can cause backache in labor.

Right occipito posterior. This causes backache and is more common than LOP.

Footling breech is a presentation where the baby's foot is born first.

Ways of dealing with a back labor

You may find that some of the things described on the following pages are helpful in the first stage of back labor.

Heat A hot water bottle wrapped in a towel, or a hot compress (in the form of a face-cloth or small towel wrung out in really hot water) may bring relief, applied to where you feel most pain. A hot shower with the water pulsing on the back also helps.

Changes of position Keep upright and moving around for as long as possible. In this way you tip the baby down to press through the pelvis and birth canal instead of right into the small of your back. Crouching, leaning forward, kneeling, squatting, getting onto all fours, and lying on your side with your back well rounded, your head and shoulders curved forward and a good space between your legs, may all be positions in which pain is eased. They may also encourage the rotation of the baby's head.

Pressure Ask your partner to provide firm pressure, either right over the place where your pelvis joins your spine or to the left or right of this if the pain is more to the side. He should use the heel of the palm of one hand, with the other resting over it, and press his body weight down through his arm. Or you may prefer the feel of knuckles. It is sometimes comfortable to sit on your own knuckles, one hand under each buttock, so that firm pressure is applied there as your own weight is put on them.

Stimulus on pressure points may help you to handle the pain more effectively. One place where deep pressure of a thumb or finger may feel good is on your bottom, level with the top of the slit between your buttocks and a little more than the width of your palm out toward the leg on each side. Experiment to find the spot: it feels tender, but pressure on it is satisfying. If you are in a position in which you are tilted forward, your partner can apply pressure to the spot on both of your buttocks at once. If you are on your side he will be able to reach only one, but even this may help. These areas are called "pain prevention points" in one system of psychoprophylaxis.

Chinese pressure points Your partner can exert pressure on parts of the body far away from where you are feeling pain, but where a really strong stimulus can offer almost miraculous relief. Known as *shiatsu* or acupressure, this can be particularly effective in childbirth when used on the feet. One pressure point is just below the center of the ball of the foot. Another is between the fleshy pads under the big toe and next toe. Your partner holds one foot firmly, exerting very strong pressure with a finger or thumb on the chosen spot, and providing light counterpressure with the rest of the hand over the top of the foot.

There are many acupressure points on the buttocks, too. Kneel forward over the seat of a chair or lie threequarters over on your side so that your partner can "map" the places on your buttocks where it feels good to have strong, steady pressure. Try, for example, pressing up just under the curve of the buttocks, and beneath the bony pelvis at either side of the buttocks. Another place where pressure can be very effective is on the inside wrist, between the tendons. Care should be taken to press only with the fleshy pad of a finger or thumb—not with the nails.

It is surprising how strong the pressure from finger and thumb can be on the right spot, and in all these places continuous pressure will produce a tingling, buzzing sensation. Acupressure can provide effective pain relief during powerful contractions, whether they are felt on your front or back, and wherever the pain is centered.

FOOTWORK
Applying pressure to certain parts of the feet can relieve pain from contractions. One spot is just below the center of the ball of the foot; another is between the fleshy pads under the big toe and the next one.

Relieving a back labor

Pressure above and to either side of your buttocks can greatly relieve a tender and aching back . . .

By pressing his pelvis against your lower back, your partner can make you more comfortable while having a rest himself.

He can apply firm pressure to your sacrum by leaning over you and allowing his full weight to pass down through his arm . . .

Or he can roll a rolling pin wrapped in a towel slowly and evenly over your lower back.

Massage Massage may feel better than pressure, or can feel good alternated with pressure. The massage that suits most women best is firm, slow, and steady, moving the flesh and muscle on the bone. You can use powder, cornstarch, or massage oil to avoid skin irritation, and your helper should have some cream to rub into his hands if he has to apply massage for a long time.

Another effective way of giving massage is to use a rolling pin. Knot a face towel or hot compress towel around it to get more grip.

If you are in the kind of environment where you can really do as you please, your partner can sit on the bed with his pelvis against your lower spine and lean back against you. This provides welcome rest for someone who after several hours of working to relieve backache may develop back pain himself!

Labor with a breech baby

Labor with a breech sometimes starts with the waters leaking. This is because the baby's bottom does not fit the opening cervix as well as the oval of the crown of the head, and so part of the bag of waters becomes wedged between the baby's bottom and your cervix. It is important that you call the doctor if this happens to you and the baby is not yet engaged. The risk is that the cord might slide down as well and be caught between the baby and the cervix, so that the oxygen supply to the baby is cut off.

If the waters do not break early in labor, stand up and keep walking around through the first stage, until they break spontaneously. There is a strong case to be made for not doing an amniotomy (see page 291), since if a breech baby is left in its bag of waters there can be no pressure on the cord.

After the waters have gone, the best positions are on all fours or on your side. You may have backache and if so your partner could exert pressure with the knuckles over the small of your back.

The second stage of a breech labor

You may be moved to an operating room before the second stage starts, in case you should need an emergency cesarean section. Sometimes your partner is shown to the waiting room at this time. If you want to stay together make this clear.

Many doctors prefer to deliver breech babies with the woman in the lithotomy position (see page 232), since they feel that they have most control over the birth this way. But you will probably be more comfortable sitting, with your partner giving you a firm base with his shoulders and arm behind you, or sitting on the bed behind you, or you may prefer to squat or be on all fours.

It is usually best to let the second stage proceed with no voluntary exertion on your part until the body is born and the head is about to slip out, so that the baby's body is born on contraction waves only. (It may be easiest to do this if you are on all fours.) Concentrate on total release: breathe, rather than push, the baby out.

Breech birth

Breech babies can be born vaginally as long as the pelvic outlet is wide enough for the head to pass through it.

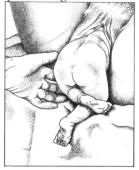

1 *The buttocks are usually delivered first, followed by the legs.*

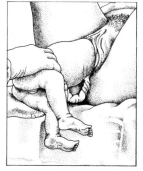

2 *The baby turns so that the shoulders can emerge as easily as possible.*

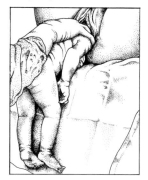

3 *The baby's own weight draws the head down and its legs are then lifted to deliver the head.*

If the baby has both feet up by its head the doctor may slip a gloved hand in to draw down a leg and turn the baby into a footling (see page 258). Relax and breathe as this is done. Once the foot is down the baby can then take the curve of the birth canal more smoothly, as its legs are no longer splinting its spine. If you are not having an epidural (see below), an injection of local anesthetic is given in your perineum if an episiotomy is to be done (see page 294), before the baby's head is delivered. It takes one or two minutes to be effective.

Most obstetricians do a large episiotomy with a breech so that the head can be delivered unimpeded, and some do two cuts, one each side of the perineum (a bilateral episiotomy). But if you give birth with breathing instead of pushing, your tissues may fan out well and an episiotomy may not be essential. Since there is unlikely to be an opportunity for discussion at the time, when things will be happening fast, talk about this earlier on in your labor (between contractions). Otherwise the doctor will probably do an episiotomy.

Once the episiotomy is done, the doctor can deliver the head, using hands or forceps to cradle it. You will be asked to push for the head and will probably find that you need to bear down only once.

Sometimes women can help to deliver their own breech babies by leaning forward and lifting the baby's legs up, while the doctor or midwife controls the delivery of the head and supports a shoulder. I first saw this done by mistake when a very helpful midwife told a first-time mother to put her hands down and touch her baby while its head was still inside her. The mother was so excited that she held the baby's legs, lifted them, and as she did so the head slipped out without an episiotomy.

Epidural anesthesia (see page 286) is often used for breech deliveries and indeed has largely replaced general anesthesia. It means that you only feel a pulling sensation, and that even if delivery is complicated you are awake and aware and can hold your baby as soon as it is breathing well. An increased number of obstetricians routinely do cesarean sections (see page 308) for all first-baby breeches. Discuss this with your obstetrician. Even if a cesarean section is the safest option for your baby, there is no need to be unconscious if you do not want to be.

Some doctors prefer to do routine cesarean sections for all breech babies, and explain their practice by saying that vaginal delivery lowers a baby's IQ. In fact, it is doubtful whether there are any long term benefits for the baby of cesarean section over vaginal birth. Carefully controlled follow-up studies of the health and behavior of $2\frac{1}{2}$- and $8\frac{1}{2}$-year-olds who were born bottom-first have revealed that the mode of delivery makes no difference at all*.

When thinking ahead to the kind of birth you will have for your breech baby, it is important to remember that the pelvis is not a rigid, confined space. During pregnancy the joints relax, bones move more freely on each other, and the pelvis actually expands to make more room for the baby. Moreover, both the width and the size of the

Breech birth in the squatting position

Taking up a squatting position, with your partner supporting you from behind, is a good way to give birth to a breech baby. It allows the pelvis to open up completely and makes the best use of the force of gravity.

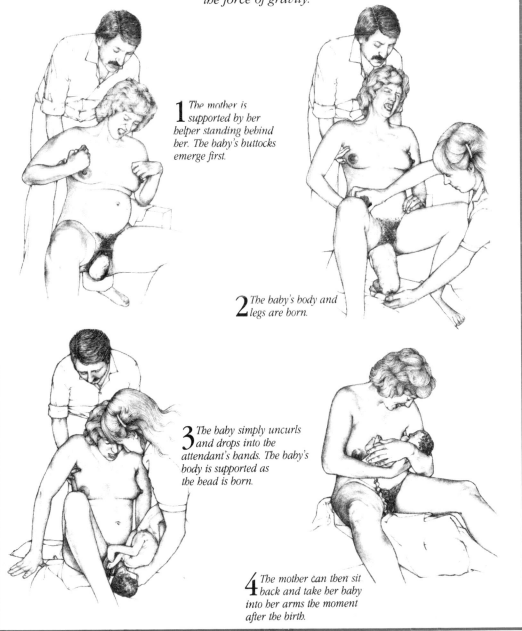

1 *The mother is supported by her helper standing behind her. The baby's buttocks emerge first.*

2 *The baby's body and legs are born.*

3 *The baby simply uncurls and drops into the attendant's hands. The baby's body is supported as the head is born.*

4 *The mother can then sit back and take her baby into her arms the moment after the birth.*

opening from front to back are increased in 28 per cent of women when they switch from lying down to a squatting position*.

In Dr Michel Odent's practice most women with breech babies have vaginal births. He likes the woman to be upright: "Our only intervention will be to insist on the supported squatting position for delivery, since it is the most mechanically efficient. It ... is the best way to minimize the delay between the delivery of the baby's umbilicus and the baby's head. ... We would never risk a breech delivery with the mother in a dorsal or semi-seated position*." If the first stage of labor goes well without any intervention, a woman has every chance of a vaginal birth. But if first stage contractions are inefficient and yet painful, and dilatation does not progress, a cesarean section is decided on.

Short sharp labor

She came so quickly there was no time to get to the delivery room. All was calm and peaceful. A mother in the next bed slept right through.

It is wrong to assume, as do some obstetric textbooks, that a short labor is bad for the baby. In many apparently short labors the cervix is dilating gently (see page 227) over a period of days before you realize you are in labor. And some short labors can be delightful. But however easy it might be physically, a violent precipitate labor is emotionally demanding and may leave you feeling drained and shocked.

If, from start to finish, your labor lasts less than an hour or two, you may need a great deal of active help from your partner, as well as his emotional support: in effect it is like starting straight in at the very end of the first stage. Your partner needs to concentrate with you and to maintain eye contact and breathe with you. Remember that breathing has to be light to avoid hyperventilation. Your partner may hyperventilate if everything is happening quickly and he becomes anxious or excited. So remind each other to keep the breathing butterfly-light over contraction peaks.

When you feel the baby pressing like a grapefruit against your anus it may be easiest to avoid pushing if you turn on your side, with your knees drawn up. But whatever position you choose, push only when you have to and then for as short a time as you can. Open your mouth, drop your jaw, and relax your lips. Then continue breathing in and out through a relaxed mouth and concentrate on releasing all the tissues around your vagina as they fan out and open wide.

If the baby is coming very fast in the second stage you will probably need to blow as well as breathe quickly to stop yourself from pushing. If you feel as if you really must push, blow as if you were extinguishing a candle flame to reduce the intensity of the push (see page 192). You will not stop the push altogether, because the expulsive power of the uterus is there whatever you do, but you can limit it to a certain extent.

Some women feel after a labor of this kind that they want the baby inside them again; they wish that they could go back to the beginning, because everything happened so fast that they cannot make sense of it. Some even feel "cheated". If this is so with you, talk through each event of labor with your partner, fitting the pieces together, and relive the birth in your thoughts until you can see its shape.

Long-drawn-out labor

A lengthy labor can be psychologically taxing as well as physically exhausting. You need constant confident emotional support from someone who loves you and does not leave you. Yet unfortunately a prolonged labor tends to make a man anxious about what is happening, unsure of his role, and often feeling that he ought to leave it all to the professionals.

A long-drawn-out labor can seem prolonged for two reasons: you may be unable to differentiate clearly between the lead-in to labor proper—sometimes called the "latent" phase—and active labor; and active labor itself may then be prolonged because contractions are faint and infrequent, or because they are not achieving dilatation of the cervix. In these cases, psychological support, accurate inform-ation and an opportunity to rest are vitally important. Even if contractions seem ineffective and dilatation is slow until you reach 4 cm, everything may seem to coordinate suddenly so that from then on labor goes like a bomb. Over 90 per cent of women having a lengthy latent phase go on to have a normal labor and delivery if given the chance*. So don't immediately assume that if labor takes several days to start it is going to be like that right through. Have relaxing hot baths, sleep or rest in different beds if possible so that you have a change of scene and automatically take up different positions. There may be a couch, an easy chair, or even a rug to lie on as a change from your usual bed. Do not go into the hospital until you think you would feel happier there. Even if you have a long first stage the second may be completely normal.

The progress of your labor is assessed in terms of the rate of dilatation of the cervix (see page 244). Provided the baby is all right and its heart tones are regular, *slow dilatation at the onset of labor does not harm the baby*, however tiring you find it. Slow dilatation in the early phase is not the same as complete lack of progress over several hours once active labor has started (that is after about 3 cm); then the baby may be exposed to special risk and the heart rate may slow down. Do remember that it is difficult for people to be accurate about dilatation: you may be examined by someone who says you are 5 cm dilated, but an hour later someone else says you are only 4 cm or perhaps 5 cm dilated, when by then the first person examining you would have reckoned you to be $5\frac{1}{2}$ cm dilated.

A squatting, crouching or kneeling position during contractions often helps.

Ways of dealing with a long labor

In a hospital it is often difficult to walk about and alternate periods of rest with sessions of activity. But if you can do this, it is the best natural way of helping a uterus which is contracting ineffectually to start working far more efficiently.

Be sure that you are taking enough fluids, as you can forget to drink and become dehydrated. You may be given an intravenous "cocktail" of dextrose solution to keep up your strength and ensure that you do not become dried out. If this is the case, get into an upright position beforehand so that you are not then stuck lying down with a drip in your arm. If you have to stay in bed, take up positions in which the long axis of the uterus is in line with the birth canal. You can do this by kneeling or squatting, and it is one of the most effective non-invasive actions you can take. You can do this *before* taking drugs for pain relief (see page 284), having an epidural (see page 286), or accepting hormone acceleration of labor (see page 301).

Sometimes fear or anxiety seems to prevent a uterus from functioning well. If physical difficulties have been ruled out, work together with your partner on facing up to any worries that may be on your mind. Together create an atmosphere which is psychologically positive, concentrating on the reality of the baby who is coming to birth and on the visual image of the cervix opening up. In parts of New Guinea when labor is long drawn out the woman is urged to confess any hidden anger she may feel because it is thought that labor will proceed smoothly and easily once she has got rid of the negative feelings she is bottling up.

Throughout labor I was conscious that I could only go with the contractions. It was like a marathon.

Dysfunctional labor

One thing that may hold up labor is incoordinate uterine action. Unfortunately it is possible to have massive contractions and yet for the upper segment of the uterus not to be able to draw up and pull open the lower section. It is as if one part of the uterus is working against another part. The result is dysfunctional labor and failure to progress. With this kind of labor, floating or crouching in a deep bath, with lights dimmed, might help; if there is still no progress, an epidural and augmentation of labor with an oxytocin intravenous drip set up may be the answer. If you choose an epidural, you will have time for a rest and then, if you wish, the anesthetic can be allowed to wear off so that you can push the baby out yourself.

Giving support
in labor

It is now accepted in most hospitals that there is a place for fathers in the birth room and that many couples want to be together for the birth. There is still some way to go before many hospitals are as welcoming to a woman partner. Any woman should be able to choose exactly whom she wants with her for this important experience in her life. If the baby's father cannot be with his partner, or if the woman feels he is not the right person to help her, she may want to have a woman friend or relation with her instead. In many cultures it is not acceptable for the husband to be present. In the past, women in childbirth have always been supported by other women. And a woman should not be deprived of personal support because she does not want her partner with her, or because religious or cultural tradition prohibits it.

Research has shown that the presence of a birth partner reduces the need for painrelieving drugs, shortens labor, makes it an easier and happier experience for the woman giving birth, and results in fewer babies needing intensive care*.

Whoever is going to support a woman in childbirth, it is important to learn in advance exactly how to help most effectively. Childbirth education classes can be very useful in teaching how to give emotional and physical support, in exploring emotional aspects of birth, and in understanding the stresses felt by a birth partner. Although this chapter is addressed mainly to fathers, it is also meant to give guidance to anyone helping at the birth.

The father at the birth

The man who knows what he can do to help is in a much better position than the one who is merely invited in to the labor room, but who has no idea of what is going on. He has every opportunity to be an informed and knowledgeable participant. It is not just a question of holding his partner's hand, although this can be a way of giving emotional support, but of being able to judge where and when she needs guidance and encouragement with relaxation.

He has also learned how to breathe "over" the contractions so that he can breathe with his partner at times when she needs extra support. He knows how to rub her back and do gentle, light massage over her lower abdomen when the uterus is opening up, and how to apply firm pressure to her shoulders, arms and legs.

It can, however, be one thing to learn how to give support in the friendly atmosphere of a small childbirth class where couples are

We didn't plan on him being there for the birth. But the doctor took it for granted that he would come into the room, so he did. And he was pleased as Punch! He was grinning from ear to ear afterward and he told everyone that he had been at the birth. His family thought it was disgusting.

working together, with much discussion interspersed with laughter, and quite another to put that learning to use in a large, impersonal, hospital. Confronted in labor with masked figures in white or green whom he has never met before, whose names he does not know, in a strange clinical environment, he can feel out of place, in spite of consent by the hospital to his presence at the birth.

This is why it is a good idea for him, as well as for his partner, to have seen round the hospital and especially the labor room before the birth. Women sometimes say that it was when they were approached with some unfamiliar piece of equipment in birth that they began to tense up, and that if they had known what it looked like and how it worked they would have found it much easier to stay relaxed. And men who have been giving good support to their partners before apparatus of this kind is used sometimes give up, as they feel that the machinery is controlling the labor.

This is understandable, because when a drip stand or monitoring equipment is brought to the bed it is difficult for the man to get close to his partner, and because a monitoring belt which fits round her abdomen may make it impossible for him to massage that area. In most hospitals, too, once the labor is monitored and speeded up, a nurse stays with the patient all the time, so the intimacy that the couple had in earlier labor is lost. This can lead to them feeling that experts and machinery have taken over.

THE KIND OF SUPPORT YOU CAN GIVE

It is not a question of just being there for her sake, but for your own. You don't know what you're missing if you're not at the birth. It was the most tremendous experience of my life!

The first and most important thing for a companion helping a woman during the long first stage of labor is to be relaxed. This is difficult in an exciting situation, but any tension or anxiety is immediately communicated to the mother. If labor is different from what you expected, awareness of what is happening can worry you more than the woman, who is enveloped in the force sweeping through her body and who may actually shut out all irrelevant stimuli. You, however, may be made anxious by the doctor's tone of voice, the nurse's remark to a colleague, or by the (quite normal) appearance of bloodstained mucus during a contraction. Ask for information, because if you are in doubt about anything, it is better to find out *early* rather than late. In many hospitals you will not be given full information unless you ask. Speak slowly and quietly. Move slowly and deliberately. Touch your partner without haste, resting a relaxed hand on her body and, when you lift your hand away, do so slowly. If you are massaging her, stroke very slowly.

Distractions in the labor room

When helping her to achieve focused concentration on what is happening in her body during contractions, never break that concentration by chatting to anyone else, watching a machine, or allowing

◆

yourself to be distracted by what is going on around you. As well as causing the woman in labor to tense up, modern equipment often fascinates her companion, who may become so involved with watching the monitor, for example, that the pregnant woman takes second place and feels that emotional support has been withdrawn. You should not forget that, however sophisticated the machinery, it is in fact the woman who is having the baby. Once labor is well under way, your attention should be on her, and encouragement by word, touch, or look should be given with every single contraction.

On the hospital's side too an induced or speeded-up and monitored labor becomes an interesting clinical exercise. Midwives, doctors, and students may come in to watch. Teaching may go on at the bedside. Discussions about the equipment sometimes take place while the woman is busy with a contraction and would appreciate silence so that she can concentrate better. Although you cannot insist that everyone is quiet during contractions, you can indicate politely by your own silence and attention to the woman in labor that you are not available for conversation, and by doing this can help her to enter a "circle of solitude" with you, and the baby coming to birth.

Occasionally machines break down and engineers arrive. This can be very distracting for the woman in labor, and may even be alarming. Fortunately she is not dependent on the monitor or other pieces of equipment to have her baby. Give her your full and undivided attention. Be on the same level, at the head of the bed, not towering over her. Use eye contact to give her emotional support. If she is coping well, she may like to close her eyes and handle contractions without looking at anybody, but if the going gets hard, suggest that she open her eyes and that you go through it together. This is likely to be of special help at the end of the first stage of labor, when her cervix is anything from 6 cm to fully dilated.

Positive support during contractions

Everything you say should be positive. Avoid saying "You're not relaxed here" or "Your shoulders are tightening." Instead say something such as "Your feet are beautifully relaxed. Do the same with your hands" or give her positive instructions such as "Pull your shoulders down and now let them go." When she is doing well, tell her so: "Good. Good. Beautiful. You're doing really well." This helps most as contractions reach their peak. It can be useful to hold her shoulder firmly during big contractions, and if she has practiced relaxation techniques that help her flow out toward your touch (see page 173), these will help her keep her shoulders loose and so avoid hyperventilating. Between contractions talk together about where she likes to be stroked or held.

She may find it helps her to work with her contraction if you describe to her what is happening as the uterus goes into action: "You are opening up wider and wider. Your cervix is being pulled up and open and the baby's head is pressing right down." Ruth Wilf, an

Hold her firmly but gently and give her encouragement with each contraction . . .

experienced American midwife, suggests that if the woman seems out of touch with her body the support person should quietly discuss with her, between contractions, any negative thoughts she may be having. This gives you something to work on during the next contraction. Create an image for the next one—the baby pressing down, the cervix opening up—and use your hands to suggest gradual opening. After the next contraction ask, "How was that compared to the last one?" The woman may be able to suggest other things you can do to help her focus her concentration.

Understanding the labor's progress

As well as needing to be told what progress she is making, she also needs information about what is being done by her birth attendants. Being in labor can be very disorienting. Chloe Fisher, Nursing Officer for Community Midwifery in Oxford, England, who has the art of helping women get in touch with their bodies in labor, says that fear of the unknown is the main reason why women panic in labor and that a request for painrelieving drugs is usually one for reassurance about what is happening. A woman may be distressed because she does not realize the progress her labor is making. She loses all sense of time and each contraction may be so enveloping that she cannot see the pattern of her labor. So be clear about progress and if you can, prepare her also for what is about to happen. For instance, if the waters have not broken by the time contractions are coming every two minutes, you can be fairly sure that they will break soon. If she is about to have an amniotomy (see page 291), prepare her for the renewed strength of contractions after it and discuss with her how she might change her breathing to cope with them. In the second stage remind her that the hot, throbbing, tingling feeling is a sign that the baby is just about to be born and will soon be in her arms.

Know when to be quiet. This depends very much on your empathy with her. Talk when it helps, but keep quiet when you can give other forms of support. Facial expression, gesture, touch, and massage are important. One of the best ways of helping is to rest a hand on her shoulder with the other hand at her wrist as she goes through the contraction. If she has backache, she will welcome firm pressure or massage over the sacrum, or slightly to one side of it (see page 260).

How to help with breathing

Breathe with her through difficult contractions. Do not wait until she is tense to start the breathing. Begin with a relaxed breath out together. Keep closely in rhythm with her own breathing at the beginning of the contraction so that there is a partnership. Do not impose a radically different level or rate of breathing on her or it will become a fight between her breathing and yours. If she starts to drag through the contraction with heavy gasping breaths, this is the time to differentiate your breathing from hers.

When appropriate, move your hand in a light butterfly-wing movement to stress the lightness of breathing necessary when the uterus is at its tightest.

Help her enjoy complete relaxation between contractions. This is especially important in stressful labors, as otherwise the woman carries her tension from one contraction to the next and it is cumulative. When she is relaxed, you can talk together about how to meet the next contraction. Avoid complicated anatomical and physiological terms. When you speak about the uterus or cervix, remember it is "your" uterus and "your" cervix, just as it is also "your" or "our" baby. Words used during contractions should be simple, rhythmic, and repetitive.

Coping with pain

Labor companions are often unsure whether or not they should mention the word "pain". For some it is taboo. It is imperative to acknowledge pain when it exists and not pretend that it is not there. To do so is to deny a woman the validity of her own experience and to say in effect: "You aren't feeling what you think you are feeling, and if you are, there must be something wrong with you or with your labor." If she tells you it hurts, agree and say, "I understand" or "Yes, I realize that." It might be the moment to add, "Your uterus is working very hard" or "The baby is pressing right down" and also to help her see the pattern of her labor. If she is more than 6 or 7 cm dilated, you will know that she is at the most difficult part of labor. Show her with your hand how far she is dilated. Help her change position, freshen her up with a face wash, brush her hair, use massage. Give her your total, undivided attention. Emotional support of this kind can take the place of drugs for pain relief.

The most undermining thing you can do to a woman in labor is to encourage her to feel sorry for herself. The woman who is told, "Oh, my dear, I can't bear to see you in such pain," or words to that effect, is being deprived of emotional support. Even the expression on a helper's face can give that message, sometimes more clearly than words. We would not think much of someone who leaned over the side of a liner and called to the person in the water, "It looks terrible down there. The waves are so huge and, poor thing, you look as if you are drowning. Do you want an injection?" Yet this is the equivalent of the sympathy and the offer of "something to take away the pain" that some attendants offer to a woman in labor. The woman who has prepared herself for labor often wants help to cope with the mountainous waves rather than the offer of a drunken stupor or sensation-free childbirth. If she wants drugs for pain relief, this should be her own decision. If she does ask for Demerol or an epidural, she should do so freely, not because she has been persuaded or coerced by someone else.

Staying together

If you feel queasy or that you must have a break, just tell your partner you will be back in a moment and stroll out. Although you may be asked to go out when the doctor comes in or when examinations are done, this is not necessary. It seems that fathers are sometimes asked to go out because doctors and nurses are embarrassed to do things to the woman in front of her partner. But women often feel they especially need support when they are being examined or when drugs for pain relief are offered, and for you to go out then can be the worst time. This is one point in labor when the woman, who is at the focus of all the care provided, can herself speak up and state her preferences. She could say, "I'd very much like my husband to stay, please. Don't send him away. I really need him," or "I don't think I'll

Sometimes it can help her just to know that you are there . . .

be relaxed if he goes out." If the doctor and nurse are doubtful, she could add, "He's learned about what happens and understands it pretty well. He's being a wonderful support!" You have no legal right to insist on being present so, if the doctor is adamant, you must go out, but you can ask if you may come back in at the earliest possible moment and can linger outside, making your message clear. Problems of this kind may not arise, and in labor reports couples often say how helpful and friendly everyone was, but it is wise to have a contingency plan in case everything is not straightforward. It should not be forgotten whose labor it is: the hospital staff and any machines should be there to assist, not take over.

Start and stop labor

Some labors seem to come to a full stop for a time and a woman may be stuck at 4 cm dilatation or more for several hours. This is a sign for a change of activity and if possible a change of scene. Lying flat on one's back is not a good position for labor, from either the woman's or the baby's point of view. You can see that she does not slip down in the bed. Remember that when she is lying on her left side or is upright the blood flows more freely through the placenta to the baby than it does when she is lying flat on her back.

It is not a good idea for the woman to lie still for long periods and you can suggest that she may like to roll over onto the other side occasionally or to sit well up. If she is sitting up, supported by four or five pillows, there is not the same problem of decreased blood flow to the baby. It is also fine if she wants to squat, kneel, sit upright, stand, or adopt any of the many positions which women often spontaneously choose in labor (see page 198). But these are obviously limited if drips and machinery are in use.

If no machinery is being used when labor comes to a stop, encourage her to get up and move around. If she is already walking around, suggest a bath or a shower, perhaps a back massage, and then rest in bed with hot water bottles wherever she aches. Jamaican folk midwives give the woman a good douse down and then wrap her in hot towels and offer a drink of hot thyme or mixed-spice tea when labor fails to progress. Perhaps we could learn something from this.

A full bladder can cause unnecessary pain. It used to be thought that it could also hold up labor but there is no evidence that this is the case. For her own comfort, remind the woman to empty her bladder every hour and a half, or more frequently if she seems to need that. If progress is slow, help her to feel that her natural pace is the right pace. Each labor is different and having a baby is not a competition to see who can do it fastest or who can most nearly conform to a norm. Especially when labor is long drawn out, affirm your confidence in her own body rhythms.

Between 8 and 10 cm dilatation the woman may feel lost and tossed in the sweep and turmoil of contractions following on each other almost without a break. Keep eye contact and breathe with her through each contraction. Letting her know that you trust her own natural rhythms is nowhere more important than at this point, when many women are made to feel that it is a race to the finishing line. Her legs may feel very cold and begin to shake, and you can help her by firmly massaging the inside of her thighs.

The lull

There is often an apparent pause in labor of 20 minutes or more when the woman's cervix is just about fully dilated. She may have no urge to push, and may feel no contractions, yet her attendants are alert for the start of the second stage. They expect action but nothing seems to be happening. They may worry that the uterus is not going to do its job of pushing the baby out, and some may try to get the woman to push even though she does not feel like it, so that she quickly gets exhausted.

If the woman feels rushed and that there are anxious eyes upon her at this point, she becomes tense and anxious herself. Reassure her that there is all the time in the world. This is a normal part of the unfolding birth process—the "rest and be thankful" phase when the baby's head is still not deep in the pelvis. She does not need to do any straining for the head to drop lower. This almost always occurs naturally if she is able to rest and refresh herself.

So help her stand up, perhaps take a shower, offer her a sponge down and put some fresh music on the tape recorder. She may want to walk around, gently rocking and circling her pelvis, perhaps enjoying slow belly dance movements. You can stand cradling her body against yours as she does so, holding her shoulders, elbows or wrists, and move *with* her. After half an hour or so—occasionally an hour or more—contractions pick up, and with renewed energy and excitement the woman enters the expulsive stage of labor. She has had a welcome interval before the drama of the second stage.

Support for the second stage

When the woman begins to push the baby out, she can be in any position which feels comfortable to her: held firmly in your arms, or cradled by your body, or with something solid to grasp or over which she can lean. She needs to be free to round her back, roll her shoulders forward, and rest her chin on her chest during contractions. You can help by providing physical support if she wants it and, perhaps, by reminding her to keep her head forward at the height of each pushing urge (without making any attempt to force it forward). From time to time give her a wrung-out cloth or ice cubes to suck.

Do not mention the word "push". Say "open up" instead. Straining only wastes energy and results in uncoordinated expulsive efforts. If you suggest she does not push at all unless she feels she has to, she will push in the right way at the right time.

Avoid clockwatching, too. It can be as disastrous to have one eye on the clock all the time in the second stage of labor as it would be if

OPPOSITE
Yours to share—the birth not only of a new human being but of a new family.

274

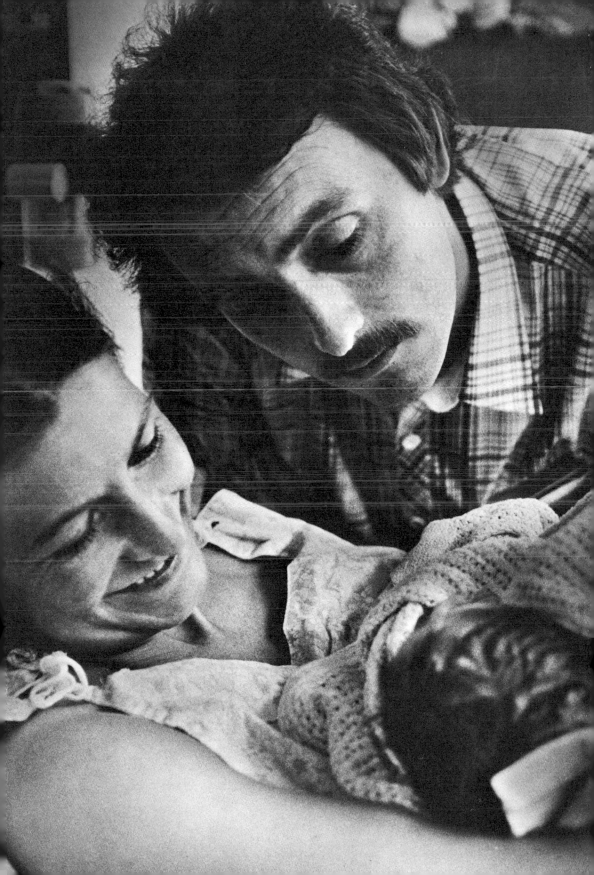

you were watching the clock while trying to make love. The woman needs to feel secure in a world without time or standards of performance, simply able to be herself and experience the intensity of what her body is telling her to do. If the pushing urge is strong and difficult to control, and it looks as if everything is happening too fast, help her lie on her side or get down on all fours, as this may lessen the impulse. Encourage her to put her hands down and feel even before any part of the baby's head is oozing through the vagina, then use a mirror for her to see the top of the head as it crowns. If you see that the crown is moving forward, but she is still holding her breath, say quietly "*Breathe*". She should immediately breathe out and go on breathing in and out with a dropped jaw.

Sharing in the birth

Many women are anxious that they might be too small. Reassure her that there is room, and her own feelings of openness and flexibility will help to make room. The power of suggestion is so great that each word and phrase used can affect her ability to work with her body.

When you are with a woman in childbirth, you share with her a journey into the unknown. The helper is like the lookout on a yacht sailing at night, watching for the coastline and helping to steer her through. She needs your constant presence and to be left alone is the most frightening thing of all. Giving support in labor needs vigilance, skill, patience, an understanding of that particular woman—her rhythms, her responses to stress—an awareness of what she is thinking and how she is feeling at each moment, and your complete commitment to this task. Sometimes it demands endurance and courage. It can be hard, exhausting work. But yours, too, is the excitement, the deep satisfaction, and joy when a child is born.

Wonder, astonishment at the reality of this new person, and overwhelming tenderness are some of the feelings a new father may experience.

SURPRISE DELIVERY

If you are with a woman in labor who is giving birth before a midwife arrives or before you can get to the hospital, the most important thing is for you to stay calm and give her quiet, confident support. Drop your shoulders and relax! Tell her she is doing well. Hold her in your arms and help her feel secure.

Making her comfortable

If the room is cold, heat it. The baby will need a warm environment after birth. If you can, place a pile of newspapers or a plastic sheet or tablecloth under the mother. She may like to sit or kneel on a firm cushion or bean bag. Cover whatever she is on with a sheet if there is one available. Find some big towels, a blanket or something else warm to wrap the baby in. Offer her sips of water if her mouth is dry.

Put pillows or some sort of support behind her back, shoulders and head to allow her to sit up comfortably unless she prefers some other position: her own feelings about this are likely to be right. If traces of feces appear at her anus, wipe with cotton or toilet paper down and away from the vagina. Boil some water and leave it to cool. It can then be poured between the mother's legs after delivery to clean her up. Wash your hands and scrub your nails thoroughly.

If she is already pushing, remind her to "open up" and not to hold her breath or push at all unless she feels she needs to. Just before the head crowns, tell her to pant, so that from then on she breathes the baby out instead of pushing it out. She can push gently between contractions if delivery is slow.

If there is a loop of cord around the baby's neck as its head slides out, hook a finger around it and lift it over the head. *Do not pull the baby or the cord*, as this may detach the placenta from the wall of the uterus before it has stopped being the baby's life support. If a membrane is over the baby's face, lift it off. When the head is born, allow it to hang by its own weight and this will tend to draw forward the shoulder nearer the mother's front. Either you or she can catch the baby. Lift it up on to the mother's upper thigh or tummy, head slightly down so that any mucus can drain.

After the delivery

Cover the mother and baby with a coat or blanket, or better still a quilt, which is light and warm. Put a bowl between the mother's legs ready to receive the placenta as soon as she feels more contractions. There is no need to cut the cord immediately. Enjoy the peace after delivery as you together admire the baby and wait for the placenta. Make her comfortable. She may be shivery and appreciate a hot water bottle. She might like a cup of tea and may even be ravenously hungry. When the baby is ready to suck put it to the breast and see that the nipple is well back in the mouth. Telephone for a midwife or doctor.

If this surprise delivery happens in a car, away from any help or home comforts, there is no need to do anything about the placenta or cord. However, if you have a plastic bag or some newspaper, you can wrap the placenta in it and try to keep it above the level of the baby.

If you are at home and are not able to get a midwife, boil up shoe laces or soft string for tying the cord, and scissors for cutting it. If the placenta does not come after about 20 minutes, get the mother to kneel and give some long, slow blows out. It should slip out then. (Do not pull on the cord.) Put a bowl under her buttocks and pour warm boiled water between her legs. She can keep her uterus contracting and reduce bleeding from the placental site by massaging it firmly.

Tie the cord about 4 in (10 cm) from the baby and again about 6 in (15 cm) and cut with sterilized scissors or a new razor blade between the ties. Check that there is no bleeding from the cord stump. If there is, do another tie nearer the baby.

The greatest heat loss from a newborn baby is from its head, so cover the back of the head. Keep mother and baby cuddled together. When birth comes by surprise it is unlikely that anything will go wrong. This is just nature at its most efficient.

The help a woman needs in childbirth is usually very simple and straightforward. The most important element in it is to stay calm, confident, and emotionally supportive.

Dealing with pain

"I've got a very low pain threshold. I can't stand going to the dentist, so I can't *think* what labor is going to be like!"

"The idea of the pain really worries me. I've never really experienced severe pain, and I can't imagine what it's like to be in pain for hours and hours and hours."

"What is labor pain like? I mean is it like breaking your arm or a bad headache or menstrual cramps or indigestion—or what? If I knew more what it was going to be like I could face it better."

These three statements express what many women who are pregnant for the first time feel, but perhaps do not acknowledge or put into words: fear that pain is going to be overpowering, a sense that they have never experienced pain that tested their inner resources, and ignorance of the kind of pain that is likely to be felt.

Putting pain in its context

People often think that pain is just a matter of a "high" or "low" threshold. There are very few women who think that they have a high threshold and can bear pain as well as other women. In fact, the idea of simple thresholds like walls, with some of us possessing high walls and others low ones, is a myth.

It is now known that in human beings the pain sensation threshold is exactly the same*. In one study in the United States, members of Italian, Jewish, Irish, and Old American ethnic groups were all given electric shocks ranging from mild to fairly strong, and every single person said pain occurred at exactly the same point. Yet obviously people do not *react* to pain in the same way and there are times when a pain which you once bore easily becomes too much to take and you cannot stand it any more. Toothache that you can cope with when you are busy and preoccupied can be absolutely shattering when you go to bed, lie down, and try to sleep. So you cannot judge the degree of pain by how an individual reacts.

People may see a pain-producing stimulus as a test of their power to *endure* pain, and so may not be ready to admit to being hurt. In the Sudan, for instance, a young man who cannot bear pain loses social esteem and is unlikely to find a girl to marry him. As in many cultures, the ability to bear pain stoically is part of a code of values.

In every society there are cultural stress points, situations which are seen as threatening and thus predispose people to feel pain. When we know what makes people anxious in a particular society, we can begin to understand these stress points. In many societies some painful stimuli are linked with pleasure. Take lovemaking for example: slightly painful stimulation may be deliberately sought because it is sexually exciting.

The context within which pain occurs is important. As an experiment*, electric shocks were given to test people first when they were feeling relaxed and cheerful, and then when they had been made anxious. The electric shocks were felt as much less painful when the subjects were feeling cheerful. In another study*, as many as 35 per cent of a doctor's patients experienced marked pain relief when given a placebo, an inactive substance which they believed was a painkiller. It has also been found that the degree of pain tolerated bears a direct relation to the rate of increase in pain, rather than to the level of pain reached*. A person experiencing a pain stimulus that gets worse rapidly feels it more than someone experiencing just as strong a stimulus that takes longer to reach the same point.

This may have particular relevance to very rapid labor, especially an induced labor (see page 297), when the pace is more than a woman can cope with. We sometimes talk about labor as if a long labor were difficult and a short one easy. But speed alone can give no indication at all of how a woman experiences her labor.

Pain perception always involves not only a recording of the stimulus by the brain, but judgment as to its importance, its precise significance, and its place in the scheme of things—the meaning of the total situation in which the stimulus occurs. Labor pain, like all other pain, is a function of the whole person, and we can go even farther than that and say that the experience of pain in labor is profoundly influenced by the values of the society in which the woman grew up.

So labor pain is partly a product of personal and social values about the meaning of childbirth. The way we eat, sleep, empty our bowels, make love, have babies, and die makes these experiences more than simple biological acts. They all express ideas, for the most part shared, about good and evil, beauty and ugliness, the pure and the polluting, what is considered to be healthy and what diseased, and what is normal and what abnormal.

Pain relief in other cultures

There are two myths about the ways in which women in the Third World give birth. One maintains that labor is always horrific and dangerous, but that women do not cry out because of strong taboos against showing that they are in pain. The other suggests that the women all have completely painless births, and just squat down in the fields and have their babies before getting back to work again. The truth is probably in between. In many Third World countries healthy women have straightforward labors. Other, malnourished women suffer a great deal.

Most cultures have methods of relieving pain in childbirth, so there is obvious recognition that it exists. But the ways in which pain is relieved and labor made more comfortable are radically different in the technological Western countries. We can give complete relief of pain and remove all sensation from the waist down with regional anesthesia. This is what an epidural does (see page 286). We have other forms of pain relief which partially remove pain or which eradicate the memory of it. We rely on pharmacological substances to do this for us. Herbal medicines are used in the Third World and some of them have narcotic or moodchanging properties, just like modern drugs, though it is much more difficult to prepare the right dose when you are using plants. There are also other kinds of help which are much favored in these countries and which used to be employed in the West but tend to be ignored in hospitals today. They include religious and magic rites, different kinds of counter-stimulation, massage, hot and cold compresses, changes in position, and emotional support from others sharing the experience with the woman in labor. These supporters hold her, stroke her, rock her back and forth, and live through the birth *with* her rather than do things *to* her as a patient.

Much of what is done by birth attendants in other cultures is meant to provide simple, practical help based on the handed-down experiences of generations of women. It is also intended to have a psychosomatic effect, helping the baby to be born by influencing the mind of the woman in labor. This practical and psychosomatic help in labor may be forgotten or not understood in our modern hospitals. Yet there are advantages in being able to cope without drugs if possible, because all powerful drugs have side effects and they all go through the mother's bloodstream to her baby.

Imagining your labor in advance

In preparing for birth it is a good idea to work out how you might like to be helped to be more comfortable and also how you can use your mind to help your body through relaxation, focused concentration and ideas and mental images that produce a pattern and harmony between what is going on inside your uterus and the way you think about it. You may find that this is difficult to conceptualize before you have your first baby.

Trying to master your body or running away from the sensations you are experiencing can actually produce pain, because you are bound to become tense and then chemical messages are sent instantaneously into your bloodstream which affect your whole metabolism. This causes changes in blood pressure and heart rate, breathing, sweating and skin, digestion and defecation, and muscle tone. Psychosomatic factors can even change the action of the uterus itself in ways we do not yet fully understand. A woman who is very anxious may have a long labor because her uterus does not work efficiently or stops contracting altogether.

What labor feels like

In a normal labor any pain experienced is quite different from the pain of breaking a leg, for example, or being injured. The physical feelings produced by a strongly contracting uterus are powerful and challenging. They are likely to involve a combination of sensations, a very tight squeeze, a pulling open of tissues and the firm downward pressure of the solid ball of the baby's head through a passage which is being slowly stretched wide.

In films you sometimes see a pregnant woman suddenly double up, her hands clasped over the top of her abdomen. The director is telling viewers that labor has started. But it *never* happens like this in reality. Instead there is likely to be a sensation of being gripped by tightening muscles low down in your abdomen or in the small of your back. All the sensations are at hip level. Nor is the feeling a sudden one. It has a wavelike shape, building up to a crest and then subsiding and disappearing until the next contraction. There is always a rest period between each. As contractions get stronger, longer and closer together the tightening may extend right round your body, so that it feels more like a circle of thick, wide elastic across your pelvis which is being steadily drawn in, held firm, and then slowly released again. Or you may be conscious of expansion during contractions and be most aware of the top of the uterus spreading and rising, tilting forward in your abdomen, while the great muscle squeezes its lower part open and presses the baby down.

As your contractions reach their peak, you may feel as if a wide band of elastic is being stretched tightly round your body.

"Pain with a purpose"

The feelings that this produces may be painful, but it is pain with a purpose and different from the pain of injury. Contractions are not painful in themselves, and in fact the uterus contracts strongly and rhythmically at intervals in the second half of pregnancy usually without causing any pain. It is the peak of the contraction, when the muscle is working hardest and is making most progress, that is most likely to be perceived as painful, and this may last as long as 30 seconds or as little as 15 seconds.

The idea of a pain that is *qualitatively* different from other kinds of pain is difficult to accept for anyone who has not experienced it. Yet sheer physical effort, like that involved in running a race or climbing a mountain, produces just that kind of "functional" pain, the ache of muscles that are working very hard. If the athlete thought only of pain instead of about winning the race, she would give up. If the mountaineer thought that her aching muscles were the sign of some dreadful physical injury instead of the natural result of working them so hard, she would forget all about her goal and lose the feeling of triumph when she reached the summit.

Pain in labor is the byproduct of the body's creative activity. Contractions are *not* pains. They are tightenings which may be painful, especially when they are being most effective. There is an art in approaching each new contraction, thinking "Splendid! Here's another one!" and later, as you approach the end of the first stage, when they are their strongest, "Oh, this is a really good one!"

When you are in the thick of labor, your whole self is involved. It is almost impossible to think about other things or to hold a part of yourself back in any way. The intensity of labor can be frightening, especially for the unprepared woman who does not know what to expect, or for one who wants to keep it all at the level of a learned skill, doing her exercises in much the same way as she might carry out a three-point turn in a driving test. This is why preparation merely for handling contractions is never enough. You also need to prepare yourself mentally and emotionally for the overwhelming nature of the sensations and feelings of labor.

Hypnosis

Some women find that hypnosis is an effective method of relieving pain in labor, and it has the great advantage over chemical anesthetics in that it does not reduce the baby's oxygen intake. In fact, about a quarter of women who have had hypnosis in childbirth say that they experienced no pain, but results do vary and most women who have hypnosis need chemical pain relief as well.

The common belief that hypnosis involves some kind of magic trickery and that you can be made to do anything the hypnotist wishes is very wide of the mark. Hypnosis is simply a state of increased suggestibility and you can prepare yourself with a good practitioner so that you can, if you wish, use *auto*-hypnosis.

People who are able to go into a deep trance are completely immune to pain while in the trance and can have a forceps delivery or be stitched up after an episiotomy without a local anesthetic. It has been calculated that two out of every hundred women can go into such a deep trance that they could even have a cesarean section without feeling any pain*.

If you agree to have hypnosis in childbirth you are usually trained in progressive relaxation to remove anxiety, and taught to think positively about childbirth. If you want to do autohypnosis, the hypnotist will suggest that you can put yourself to sleep and wake up when you wish. After the birth the doctor will suggest that you will in future be hypnotized only by a medical person for a therapeutic purpose, so that you need not be afraid of being put into a trance by anyone using hypnosis for their own purposes or for fun.

It may be that all good childbirth classes teach an element of autohypnosis. Childbirth educators do not usually like to admit this. Yet in many ways thinking ahead to labor constructively, when one is deeply relaxed, is using the power of suggestion. Whether or not you decide to try hypnosis, you can use autosuggestion and fantasies about labor and the baby in a creative way to prepare yourself for childbirth, knowing that this is the safest analgesia of all.

Acupuncture

Acupuncture is another way of reducing pain in childbirth. There are basically three kinds: the traditional Chinese method involving the use of needles in the limbs, and two European methods—one in which needles are inserted in the ear, and another providing transcutaneous electronic nerve stimulation (TENS) with pads attached to the woman's back or sometimes other places. The great benefit of TENS is that the woman can move around as she wishes and herself controls the timing and degree of stimulation. In Beijing nowadays acupuncture is used in preference to epidural anesthesia for 98 per cent of cesarean sections*. It is sometimes combined with small quantities of drugs.

The advantages of acupuncture are that it is noninvasive, easily administered by someone trained in the method, instantly reversible, and babies are in better condition at birth than after Demerol has been given. Some studies show that acupuncture shortens the first stage of labor for women having their first baby. Women say that they feel more in control of labor and delivery than when they have drugs for pain relief*.

TENS is increasingly available in hospitals in the USA. If you want acupuncture you will have to locate a hospital that permits this and you will usually have to make your own arrangements for your acupuncturist to be with you during childbirth.

Using water

You probably already know how soaking in a hot bath can relieve pain, whether you have experienced backache, aching muscles from strenuous exercise or menstrual pain. And many women have discovered that it can be comforting in labor. Lying in warm water increases venous pressure so that veins can return blood to the heart more efficiently. It enhances cardiac action and slows the pulse rate. Total relaxation in the warmth and comfort of a bath may help the uterus contract more effectively. But it does more than this. Water both counteracts the force of gravity and any pressure a woman feels against her back and buttocks, and also reduces pressure felt from inside the body, so there is a further painrelieving effect*.

Sometimes pain is so much reduced and dilatation proceeds so fast as a woman surrenders herself to the water that a baby slips out while she is still enjoying the bath. This is quite safe, since the baby only takes a breath when lifted clear of the water, and for a few minutes after delivery blood is still pulsating through the cord, thus providing the baby with oxygen. After the baby has slipped out of your body, the midwife will rest a finger on the cord so that she can feel the blood pulsating through it. You may like to do this too.

Dr Igor Charkovsky in the USSR has the woman give birth in a deep transparent tank, and the baby is born under water. He does this, however, not so much for the mother's sake as in order to produce what he has claimed are superintelligent babies. He believes that since the fetus has been floating in the amniotic fluid for nine months, if the baby is born into an ordinary atmosphere, the brain suddenly becomes much heavier, and this causes brain cells to die.

In a water birth, the baby should never be left in the water, but should be lifted into the mother's arms. You know yourself how cold you can feel after getting out of a bath. The baby quickly becomes chilled too, so she should be dried at once and then wrapped with you in big bath sheets so you do not get cold.

Some birth centers are now installing deep pools in which women can float in labor. There are other portable pools on the market which can be used for home births, including plastic pond liners (which can be bought from garden centers and placed inside a timber frame), or you can buy specially constructed waterbirth tanks which are thermostatically controlled.

It is probably unwise to decide in advance on giving birth in water. A woman for whom floating in water feels blissful late in the first stage of labor is very likely to want to get out of the water once the second stage starts. She should do whatever feels right at the time.

DRUGS FOR PAIN RELIEF IN LABOR

There is a variety of painrelieving drugs available, and different drugs suit different women. It is important to understand what can be used and how each type works so that you can make your own informed decision as to whether you want the help of a drug, and if so which particular kind. Whether or not you have drugs in childbirth—and how much you have—is up to you. As one obstetric anesthesiologist has stated: "The only arbiter of pain is—or should be—the patient . . . a stereotyped prescription cannot cope with individual variations in response to pain."*

All drugs for pain relief in labor, whether given by injection or inhaled, pass through the mother's bloodstream to the baby. They all affect the baby—some more than others. None of them actually does the baby any good. When you are considering whether or not to accept drugs in labor, bear in mind also that some forms of anesthesia and analgesia can interfere with your first meeting with the baby and subsequent bonding.

Tranquilizers and analgesics

Tranquilizers are used to relax you if you are anxious and tense and also to lower your blood pressure. Given intramuscularly, tranquilizers take effect in 15 minutes; taken by mouth they are effective in 30 minutes. If taken during labor, tranquilizers tend to make the baby limp and floppy at birth, and probably also slow to suck. They interfere with the newborn's temperature control, too.

They are sometimes used in combination with analgesics, Demerol for example (see below), to increase their effectiveness, though some obstetricians are critical of this practice.

Demerol The drug most widely used for analgesia (taking the edge off pain) in labor is a narcotic, Demerol. It is usually given by intramuscular injection in doses of 50 to 150 mg. It takes effect in 15 minutes and lasts for two to four hours. Some women like it and say it helped them cope with difficult contractions by making them feel relaxed and slightly drunk. Others hate the effects of Demerol and call it "stupefying", and say they were woozy and out of control.

A fairly common side-effect of Demerol is nausea. One or two women out of every ten vomit when they are given Demerol. It is sometimes combined with an antihistamine to prevent sickness, but this tends to make you even sleepier.

Large amounts of Demerol are present in the baby if this is injected within five hours before delivery, and especially in the three-hour period before delivery. When it is given intravenously the concentration of Demerol in the baby's cord blood is only slightly below that in the mother's bloodstream. Demerol can cause breathing difficulties in the newborn, who may then need to be given oxygen. If a baby is born with respiratory depression after its mother has had Demerol, it is given an antidepressant.

With the Demerol I felt the pain but was so dizzy that I couldn't do anything about it.

Other narcoticlike drugs which are approved by the Food and Drug Administration for use in labor are nalbuphine (Nubain) and butorphanol (Stadol). Vistaril and Talwin are used in conjunction with one of the above medications to counteract some of their side effects such as nausea, vomiting, and dizziness. Stadol is 40 times more powerful than Demerol. Phenergan is a drug that is given with Demerol (Mepergan) so that less Demerol is necessary and it combats the nausea. But it impairs blood clotting in the baby so that bleeding in the tissues may occur.

Gas anesthetics Inhalant anesthetics such as nitrous oxide (laughing gas) and halothane are offered for the actual delivery. This leads women to believe that the birth of the baby entails excruciating pain. It is a shame to have gone all the way through labor only to be "put out" for the most rewarding part, the culmination of nine months' waiting. Not only does the mother miss her baby's first cry but she may remain too sleepy and disoriented to be with her baby and breastfeed right after the birth.

Other possible side effects include respiratory depression, hemorrhage, irregular heart rate, nausea, and vomiting. Babies born under a heavy dose of anesthesia may have difficulty breathing and adjusting to life outside the uterus.

"Twilight sleep" A combination of a tranquilizer, an analgesic, and an amnesiac is known as "twilight sleep". Many women have described it as "twilight nightmare" because of its side effects. The usual amnesiac scopolamine (also known as "scope" or "the bomb") can cause total disorientation which may not end when the labor ends, thus its nightmarish quality. It is supposed to make women forget their labor but, in fact, most women report hazy memories of having felt like an animal howling in pain.

Local anesthetics

Local anesthetics can also cross the placenta but they are least likely to affect the baby when they are injected into the area around the vagina and the perineum. This is done before an episiotomy (see page 294) and before a forceps delivery (see page 306) if other anesthesia has not been given.

When local anesthetics are used to bathe nerves that cover a large area of the body, they are called *regional* anesthetics.

Paracervical block is a series of injections of local anesthetic around the cervix. It affects the baby immediately and in three out of ten babies the heartbeat becomes slower (a condition known as bradycardia)*. Some babies have died as a result. Paracervical block is rarely used in the US for this reason.

Spinal anesthesia is given by injection into the cerebrospinal fluid in the lower back. Its effect is to numb the woman from waist to knees. It takes about five minutes to work. If you have a spinal you have to lie flat for around eight hours after delivery to avoid a postspinal headache and should be careful not to lift your head quickly. Spinals are considered dangerous because blood pressure drops and hence the oxygen supply to the baby is reduced, progress slows down, and a forceps delivery is usually necessary. However, they give good pain relief.

Pudendal block is an injection numbing the nerves in the perineum given at full dilatation, often before an episiotomy.

Epidural anesthesia is injected into the space between part of the spinal cord and the dura, the outer membrane around the spinal

I felt very woozy and out of control. I didn't really know what I was doing after I had it. I couldn't concentrate on my breathing or remember what I had learned in classes. And I was just overwhelmed by the pain, but helpless to do anything about it. Never again.

HAVING AN EPIDURAL
It is important to make your back as convex as possible when you are being given an epidural so that the vertebrae are spread out. This makes it easier for the anesthesiologist to insert the needle between the bones. You must, of course, stay completely still while this is being done.

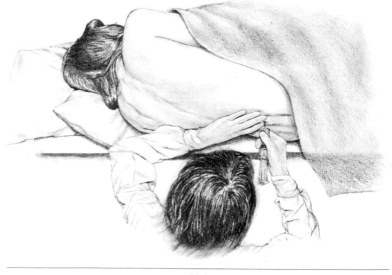

cord. Additional injections can be given through a fine plastic tube which is left in place after the first injection. This is preferable to another injection, as an epidural takes about half an hour to set up. An epidural may be given with you sitting up and curled forward or lying on your left side curled up into a ball.

An epidural can provide complete relief from pain and can even be used as an anesthetic for a cesarean section. It removes sensation from the waist down, either completely or partially, while allowing you to remain conscious. For a painful, prolonged labor it seems the perfect answer. Many women have said how marvelous the epidural was, but it should be your own choice—no one should be put under pressure to have one. Some hospitals give epidurals to all first-time mothers, unless there is no time to give one.

Epidurals do not always work. It may be difficult to inject into the right place or the anesthetic may take on one side only, so that you get the odd feeling of contractions occurring in half your body.

The anesthetic used is similar to that used by dentists, and you feel it like liquid ice numbing your tummy, bottom, and legs. Even though it only anesthetizes part of you, it must be given by a skilled anesthesiologist and under sterile conditions. If by mistake the needle punctures the dura you get a complete spinal: you are more heavily anesthetized and may have a bad headache which can last a week or more after the birth.

An epidural lowers blood pressure, sometimes drastically, so that other drugs may have to be given to raise your blood pressure again. Because of this, an epidural is sometimes given to a woman whose blood pressure is high, even though she may not be having a painful labor. In one study 39 per cent of women having epidurals experienced hypotension, though it did not last longer than one hour. The proportion went up to 47 per cent when women were also receiving an oxytocin intravenous drip (see page 298)*. When your blood pressure suddenly drops, you feel sick and faint and may vomit. This sudden lowering of blood pressure affects the baby too, since the oxygen-bearing blood supply is pumping more weakly and slowly through the placenta.

Having an epidural may mean that a whole train of other procedures is started which you did not bargain for. Because you have no feeling in your bladder, it will need to be emptied by catheter. Because you may not feel any urge to push, the obstetrician may rotate the fetal head with forceps or manually*.

Since there is an increased chance of having a forceps delivery once an epidural has been given, you may want to let the anesthetic wear off as you reach the very end of the first stage and to refuse more. On the other hand, if you have not felt first-stage contractions at all and have to cope with the long hefty ones near full dilatation, the experience can be an overpowering one.

Research into women who have had epidurals reveals that they are sharply divided in their opinions about them. In one study many

Nearly every mom in this hospital has an epidural; anyway they wire you up to things and do so many things to you that I thought, well, at least I won't feel all that. I mean, they might have forgotten that I could feel if everyone else couldn't.

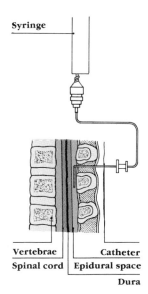

Syringe

Vertebrae		Catheter
Spinal cord		Epidural space
		Dura

If you have an epidural a needle containing a catheter is inserted between the vertebrae into the epidural space and then withdrawn; the catheter is left in place in case a supplement is needed.

women were very happy with their epidurals and said things like "It was a miracle!" and "It was pure magic." But 18 per cent of women regretted having the epidural and said, in effect, "Never again!"*

Women praise epidurals when: it was their own decision, and theirs alone, to have one; they felt among friends; the epidural provided effective pain relief; there was minimal other intervention; and the mother managed to push the baby out herself. Women are highly critical of epidurals when: they felt that they were not able to make a free choice about having one; they did not feel that they were in an emotionally supportive environment; the epidural was not effective; delivery was by forceps; and there were side effects—they felt sick and giddy, suffered headache, or had long term problems such as pain or numbness which they attributed to the epidural.

An epidural anesthetic passes into the baby within ten minutes and studies are still being carried out on the possible effects of an epidural on the baby*. Some studies suggest that the baby becomes nervous and jittery while others show that it is very drowsy after delivery,* but this may vary according to what drug is used.

If you decide to have an epidural, bear in mind that some of the difficulty you might have in coping with the baby in the week or so after the birth may be connected with the anesthetic, not because you are incompetent. You will soon be over this period and interaction between you and the baby will rapidly become easier.

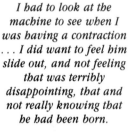

I had to look at the machine to see when I was having a contraction . . . I did want to feel him slide out, and not feeling that was terribly disappointing, that and not really knowing that he had been born.

Caudal A caudal is like an epidural, except that it is injected into the epidural space around the sacrum and blocks only that area rather than the larger area blocked by an epidural. A greater dose of anesthetic is necessary, and a caudal is usually given for a short term pain relief to a woman having a very difficult second stage.

The future of drugs in childbirth

Hospitals should provide an environment and the kind of personal care in which each woman is free to accept or reject painrelieving drugs as and when she wishes. Whatever drugs are given to you in labor, your consent should always be obtained beforehand.

Fear, anxiety, loneliness, and feeling you are part of a factory for producing babies all increase the experience of pain. Understanding what is happening inside you and what is being done to help you and your baby, knowing what you can do to help yourself, feeling you are among friends and having someone you love with you all make pain much more easily bearable.

Modern obstetric anesthesia, used only when necessary, is fairly safe for the baby, but one consultant anesthesiologist warns that "numerous questions about the effects of drugs given to the mother on mother-baby interaction and future child development require an answer"* and stresses that long term studies should be carried out to assess exactly what risks are being taken. For the present this still remains a largely unexplored field of research.

Toward the medical control of birth

You have the right to decide what happens to your body before, during, and after childbirth. You are not bound, either in law or out of politeness, to agree to procedures and investigations to which you object. If things are done without your consent, it is a form of assault. Your consent is implied when you are forewarned about some kind of obstetric intervention and concur by remaining silent.

You are also entitled to be given full information about anything that is being done to you and your baby, can reasonably expect to be able to ask questions about it and to be given honest answers. If you do not ask questions, professionals may take it for granted that you do not want to know any more, and even that to offer further information might make you uncomfortable.

Your right to choose

In all medical procedures it is a question of carefully balancing the relative risks of a policy of intervention on the one hand and a policy of "wait and see" on the other. To be able to make an informed choice you may value the counsel of skilled professionals, but ultimately *you* make the decision. This applies both to *where* you have your baby and *how* you have your baby. If you want natural childbirth, go all out to get it. Plan for it, prepare yourself for it, and do everything you can to create the right setting for it to take place. But also be flexible so that if something in your physical condition or that of your baby indicates that modern technology can be used with advantage you do not miss out on its undoubted benefits even if this means that the birth is less "natural."

A woman having a baby has responsibilities as well as rights. One of the most important of these is the responsibility to give the baby the best possible start in life. Some obstetricians believe that whenever a machine or a procedure is available which permits greater medical control of childbirth it ought to be used. An equally valid view is that one should be selective in the use of technology, employing it where necessary, but bearing in mind that birth is also a psychological experience which affects the relationship between mother, father, and baby—perhaps for a long time after.

The best environment for birth

The highest quality childbirth and the best welcome into life for the baby must include emotional as well as medical aspects of birth. If you accept medical help, it does not automatically follow that you give up concern about the psychological dimensions of the experience. Technology need not, and should not be permitted to, ruin a woman's personal experience of childbirth.

When machines are used *in place of* warm and friendly human relations they seem to take over. But when they take second place to emotional support and encouragement and you feel free to reach your own decisions about how much aid to accept, they can be a useful adjunct to good care, especially when the risk to a baby is considered to be higher than usual.

Many couples can bear witness to ways in which sophisticated modern apparatus made them feel more secure in childbirth and was used to help rather than hinder. But for this to happen the environment provided for birth has to be a very special one and all those coming into contact with the expectant parents need to be able to give of themselves and not only their technical skills. For it is only in such a setting that there can be trust, honesty, and self confidence.

The growing use of technology

Obstetricians are discovering new ways of controlling a process which 30 years ago was left to nature. Many now say "Why stand by watching and intervene only when something goes wrong?" and believe that instead labor should be regulated from start to finish. To do this effectively they need to be able to monitor exactly what is going on in the uterus and what is happening to the fetus at every second and to intervene at any point to ensure that cervical dilatation, the strength of contractions, and the biochemical state of mother and fetus conform to a predetermined form. This is called *active management of labor**.

Many inventions are appearing on the market which obstetricians, quick to seize an opportunity to reduce the perinatal mortality rate, want to buy for their units. Some women hate this intrusion of machinery into what they feel should be a natural process and question its benefits for the labor and the baby. Others find security in knowing that labor is controlled by the obstetrician with all his machinery; they like knowing exactly when the birthday will be and are relieved to know that labor will not last longer than 12 hours at the most. In some hospitals the love affair with technology is gradually giving way to a new concern about the quality of human relations. But there is no standard recipe that will suit all women. The vital element is *personal* care.

COMMON PROCEDURES IN LABOR

When you arrive in the hospital, you may be given an amniotomy, linked to a fetal monitor, and hooked up to an intravenous drip. During the second stage, an episiotomy may be performed to hasten delivery. Some women experience many kinds of intervention during the course of their labors and unless you specifically tell the obstetrician or midwife that you do not want your labor controlled in this way there is a chance that you will have at least one of them.

Artificial rupture of the membranes

Artificial rupture of the membranes (ARM for short) or amniotomy has come to be accepted as a normal routine in most hospitals and is often performed as part of the "prepping" done after you are admitted. The membranes surrounding the fetus are punctured with a small tool like a crochet hook through the open cervix. Routine amniotomy is now open to question, however. When the membranes are allowed to rupture spontaneously, they tend to do so toward the end of the first stage of labor*. In 12 per cent of women the membranes remain intact right through to delivery. Some membranes rupture spontaneously when the midwife or doctor touches them during a vaginal examination.

Since there are no nerve endings in the membranes their rupture is not painful. All you feel is a gush of warm liquid. Be prepared for contractions to increase in intensity after this has happened. ARM can speed up labor by 30–45 minutes if the membranes have not ruptured spontaneously by the end of the first stage, since the baby's head is pressing harder against the cervix once the cushion of fluid has gone, and this produces a rush of oxytocin in your system which triggers off strong contractions.

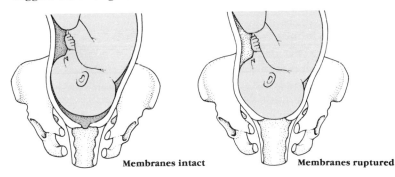

Membranes intact   **Membranes ruptured**

RUPTURE OF THE MEMBRANES
Spontaneous rupture of the membranes usually indicates that the cervix is starting to open. The baby's head then presses right against the cervix and contractions are intensified. This may also happen after artificial rupture of the membranes.

Reasons for amniotomy

Besides being a part of induction, rupturing the membranes also allows the obstetrician to assess the state of the amniotic fluid. When a fetus is in distress it passes meconium, the first contents of the bowels, into the water, which is easily seen in the fluid released. Many obstetricians believe that amniotomy is important to assess the condition of the baby. Once it has been done, it is possible to insert an electrode in the baby's scalp, so that its heartbeat can be recorded throughout labor (see page 303).

Some obstetricians prefer to use an *amnioscope* to examine the amniotic fluid while keeping the membrane intact. A coneshaped instrument is introduced through the vagina and cervix with a fiber optic light inside it. This technique is less invasive than ARM.

The risks of routine amniotomy

Pressure on the cord Intact membranes protect the baby's head. The amniotic fluid equalizes pressure on the head and amniotomy takes away the cushion of water in which the fetus lies, so exposing its head to the direct effect of contractions. Rupture of the membranes also gives rise to the possibility of pressure on the cord, which may hinder the flow of blood through it. It is not rare for a baby to have the cord round its neck, and without the cushion provided by the amniotic fluid, such babies are particularly vulnerable to pressure on the cord. It has also been suggested that once the amniotic fluid has gone, the fetal surface of the placenta is compressed, which may reduce the flow of blood to and from the baby*.

Pelvic infection Amniotomy introduces the possibility of pelvic infection*. Since infection is more likely if labor continues for more than 24 hours after amniotomy, operative delivery may be necessary if the baby has not been delivered naturally by that time.

Sometimes, when the membranes are ruptured before labor is going strong, contractions later become weak or stop altogether, and it turns out that the woman was in "false" labor. Because of the risk of ascending infection if labor takes a long time following rupture of the membranes, it is often decided to stimulate the uterus with an oxytocin intravenous drip.

Deceleration of the baby's heartbeat Some studies have demonstrated that after amniotomy there are more early decelerations in the baby's heartbeat. These early decelerations come at the start of a contraction and the heart is back to normal by the end of the contraction. The slowing down is slight, by less than 40 beats a minute. Many obstetricians consider this innocuous and quite normal*. Because babies born after amniotomy have been demonstrated to be in good condition, with high Apgar scores (see page 328), some doctors have concluded that the procedure does not subject the fetus to any special stress during labor.

Head molding Other obstetricians are concerned about head molding and disalignment of the cranial bones, which may be increased after amniotomy. There is some disagreement about this but, in any case, the molding of the baby's head gradually disappears during the first week or two of life.

So amniotomy raises many questions which have not yet been adequately answered. It is a subject that you may want to discuss with your obstetrician. You have a right to be fully informed. You can, if you wish, request that amniotomy be done not as a routine but only if the baby is showing signs of distress.

The partogram (labor record chart)

The partogram consists of a series of graphs used in hospital to record the main obstetric events of labor against a time scale of 24 hours. It is particularly useful for isolating problem labors, for instance when the baby is posterior and the mother is getting worn out. In the course of a normal labor it is also a clear record of progress made so far for any new staff that may come on duty. But sometimes the routine use of the partogram can lead to a slow labor being accelerated even when the woman is not tired and the baby is not under stress.

ES 9/53

Last Name **NEWELL**   First Name **VIVIENNE**

PARITY **0+0**

Age **24**   Date **6·4·80**

L.M.P. **8·25·79**

E.D.D. **6·1·80**

Duration of Labor **12 HRS**

Duration of Ruptured Membranes **8 HRS** / before admission

Fetal heart rate *Charted in beats per minute, with 120–160 beats considered normal. (Any deceleration is shown as an arrow down to the lowest level.) The condition of the amniotic fluid (liquor) is also recorded. C means "clear", M "meconium-stained", and B "blood-stained".*

Contractions *Frequency, strength (by shading) and length of contractions in seconds are shown here.*

Cervical dilatation *The degree of cervical dilatation is noted every 3 or 4 hours and a dilatation curve is drawn. If there is a 2-hour delay compared with the statistical norm, the obstetrician usually stimulates the labor with an oxytocin drip. The descent of the head through the pelvis is also indicated.*

Drugs *Any drugs given are noted, as well as general remarks. After delivery the Apgar score is recorded (see page 328).*

Blood pressure *The mother's blood pressure and pulse are recorded about every 20 minutes. The upper level is the systolic pressure, the lower one the diastolic pressure (see page 48).*

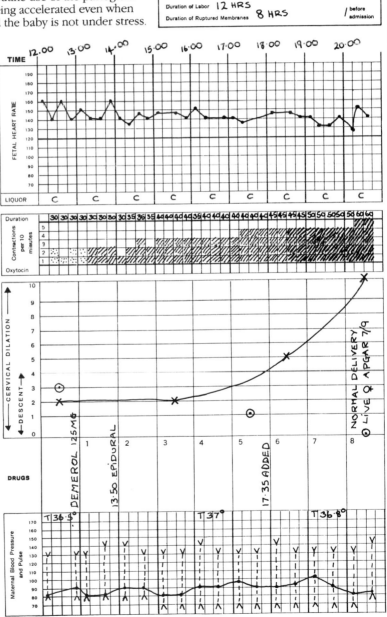

The intravenous drip

In almost all hospitals, an intravenous drip (IV) is set up for every woman in labor. A fine catheter (hollow tube) is introduced into a vein in your arm or hand and fixed with adhesive tape so that fluids can be infused straight into your bloodstream. The argument for setting up an IV is that once a vein is open, emergency action can be taken rapidly and your strength can be kept up without your needing to eat or, sometimes, even drink anything. This means that if a cesarean section is necessary (see page 308) and a general anesthetic is used, your stomach is likely to be almost empty already and therefore there is not a great deal of risk that you will regurgitate or inhale its contents.

Dextrose, a glucose solution, may be given through an IV to act as a "pick-me-up" in labor. Since it bypasses the stomach you do not have to digest it. Dextrose is useful if labor is long and tiring and you are becoming dehydrated, or if lactic acid builds up in the course of a difficult labor, causing acetone to appear in the urine—an indication that your body is short of glucose.

If you have an IV set up, it is especially important to remember to empty your bladder regularly: every hour is not too frequent. You will be accumulating fluid and should urinate frequently to stop urine building up in your bladder.

Once an IV is set up, other substances can be introduced by the same route. This may be done without your consenting to or even being aware of the administration of drugs. If you have an intravenous infusion and the bag or bottle is changed, ask what it is. Your partner will be able to get close enough to read the label. Oxytocin is introduced by this means. The label will probably read "pitocin." You can find more information about this in the section on induced labor on page 297.

You need not consent to an intravenous drip unless you are confident that there are good reasons for it. It is yet another way in which women are sometimes made needlessly uncomfortable in labor. The IV can be very useful when needed, but used routinely it merely makes it difficult for you to move. In most hospitals where intravenous drips are used as a matter of course it is taken for granted that the woman in labor stays in bed.

Episiotomy

An episiotomy is a surgical cut made to enlarge the birth opening. It is done with scissors, under local anesthetic, just before the baby is born. It can be midline (down from the bottom of the vagina toward the anus) or mediolateral (sloping out to the side, away from the anus, or down and then out again in the shape of a hockey stick). Occasionally, an episiotomy is made on each side of the vagina, for example when a breech baby with a large head is being born. This kind of incision is known as a bilateral episiotomy.

Since the incision is made through both skin and muscles, careful repair of the wound must be done afterward. The local anesthetic given before the episiotomy was performed is usually enough for the repair. If not, more can be given. It takes a few minutes to take effect, and the doctor or midwife should wait until the area is fully anesthetized before stitching the wound. The suturing is done with a curved needle and it may take as long as an hour to sew up a mediolateral episiotomy or one which has been extended by tearing. Stitching a midline episiotomy is usually quicker because there is a natural dividing-line between muscles in the midline, which makes the repair simpler to carry out.

The stitches can be left in as they are the kind which dissolve. But have a look at the area in a mirror every couple of days to check that they have disappeared, since sometimes they do not drop out and become embedded in tissue. You may feel as if you are sitting on thorns. When this happens the stitches should be snipped out by a midwife or doctor on or before the tenth day after the birth.

Reasons for episiotomy

Some obstetricians believe that all first time mothers should have an episiotomy to relieve strain on their tissues and to get the baby delivered quickly. When there are signs of fetal distress, an episiotomy can speed delivery and make birth easier for the baby. You may be told that it is a good idea to have an episiotomy because "a straight, clean cut is better than a nasty, jagged tear" which is more difficult for the obstetrician to sew up. Sometimes episiotomy is done in an attempt to prevent damage to tissues inside the vagina when there is evidence of "buttonhole" tearing (that is, a series of very tiny lacerations deep inside the perineum).

The practice of routine episiotomy is still favored by many North American obstetricians and those on the European continent, but is declining in British hospitals. In the seventies, almost 100 per cent of women had episiotomies in some hospitals in Britain. Now the proportion is generally below 40 per cent. As soon as a research project investigating episiotomy was begun in any hospital—that is,

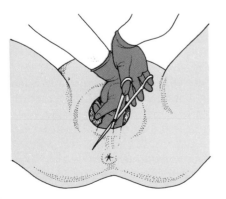

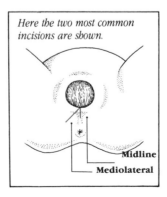

Here the two most common incisions are shown.

Midline

Mediolateral

HAVING AN EPISIOTOMY
An episiotomy is done as the baby's head crowns and between contractions. The local anesthetic, combined with the numbing effect of the baby's head pressing against the perineum, means that the cut is rarely felt.

as soon as questions were asked about its necessity—the rate dropped by about a third, even before any results were obtained.

Problems with episiotomy

A trial conducted in Dublin revealed that women with an intact perineum or only a superficial tear experience less pain after childbirth than those who have an episiotomy. The pain after an episiotomy is about the same as that from a second-degree tear (one that affects the underlying muscle). Women are more likely to have severe tears into the anus when they have had an episiotomy than if they have not had one*. Another trial, in England, showed that there is no advantage in episiotomy over a first- or second-degree tear*.

Many women say they feel terribly uncomfortable when making love for several months after having an episiotomy, and they tend to resume intercourse later than women who have had a tear.

There are other problems with episiotomy which should be borne in mind: if done too early—before the perineum has thinned out—it can cause unnecessary bleeding; sometimes the cut is much larger than a tear would have been; and quite often the stitches get infected and antibiotics are necessary*.

With skilled guidance at delivery and a gentle birth (see pages 313–324), more and more women are now having no injury to the perineum—and this makes an enormous difference to how they feel in the days and weeks after the baby is born.

Managing the third stage

A now widely accepted method of controlling the third stage of labor, the expulsion of the placenta, is to give an intramuscular injection of oxytocin after the delivery of the shoulder nearest your front (the anterior shoulder). The placenta then usually separates from the lining of the uterus with the next contraction and is expelled within five minutes of the birth.

However, if the placenta does *not* separate completely after the injection, it can be trapped by the powerfully contracting uterus. So attendants clamp and cut the cord as soon as the baby is born and then press a hand on the top of the uterus, pulling on the cord at the same time in order to get the placenta out.

If the placenta is left to separate naturally, it may take half an hour. Clamping of the cord immediately at delivery may make a retained placenta more likely. If the cord is not clamped until after it has stopped pulsating there is much less chance of a retained placenta and postpartum hemorrhage. This may be because when the cord is clamped blood cannot flow out of it, so encouraging the now defunct placenta to be peeled away from the uterine wall. Instead the placenta stays firm and full.

If the third stage is allowed to proceed naturally, your first physical contact with your baby produces a rush of emotion that is accompanied by the release of oxytocin. This *natural* oxytocin keeps the uterus firm and causes further contractions. Once the placenta has separated the doctor or midwife gently places one flat hand over your lower tummy, just above the pubic bone, and you push against the hand, so delivering the placenta and membranes. It is often a help to have a hand to push against like this. The alternative is to squat over a bowl or pail and to deliver the placenta with gravity to help.

CONTROLLED CORD TRACTION
After the birth of your baby, your uterus continues to contract strongly to expel the placenta. You may be asked to push the placenta out, once it has peeled off the wall of the uterus, by pushing against the doctor's or midwife's hand placed against your lower abdomen, while he or she gently pulls on the cord with the other hand.

There is no reason for a cord to be clamped before the placenta has been delivered except for convenience, although occasionally the cord is so short that it is impossible for the mother to hold her baby unless it is cut first, or it is twisted in a succession of loops around the baby's neck at delivery and so is cut to enable the baby to slide out. In fact, if a woman is Rhesus negative and her baby is Rhesus positive (see page 103) there is a strong case for delayed cord clamping. If the cord is clamped before it has stopped pulsating, when there is still blood flowing through it, the chance of a flow of Rhesus positive blood back into the mother's circulation increases.

INDUCED LABOR

Induction is the medical way of starting off labor, and keeping it going. When labor begins naturally, the uterus becomes sensitive to hormones present in your bloodstream at the end of pregnancy. When labor is induced the doctor tries to obtain a similar result by flooding your system with hormones, until they reach a level much higher than that which occurs naturally. This can be done by introducing synthetic hormones into your bloodstream, through a continuous intravenous drip, or by inserting prostaglandin pessaries into your vagina. Both these methods are usually combined with artificial rupture of the membranes.

Induction procedures

At present a great deal of research into these methods is taking place in hospitals. Remember that you have the right to receive full details of what is going to be done and why, *before* being admitted to hospital for induction, and you can choose to accept or refuse it once you know the facts.

Stripping the membranes Some doctors strip the membranes to stimulate labor. This is done by pushing the membranes away from the cervix by hand, while leaving them intact. This is a rather uncomfortable procedure, but may start things off.

Artificial rupture of the membranes (see page 291) will be performed as the only means of induction if you are near your dates. Most obstetricians believe that, once the membranes are ruptured, the baby ought to be born within 24 hours, because there is some risk of infection if labor is long drawn out. So you need to be aware that if your labor is started by ARM, but is slow to get going, it may then have to be accelerated with hormones.

Prostaglandin suppositories One way of inducing labor commonly employed in Britain is to use suppositories of prostaglandin gel which are introduced into the cervix. If the gel is inserted during the evening, labor may have started by the following morning. In fact, it may be unnecessary to have amniotomy and an oxytocin drip as well, and prostaglandin gel has the great advantage of allowing you freedom to move about in labor.

Oxytocin drip If induction involves being connected to an oxytocin (pitocin) drip, ask that the IV be placed in the arm or hand you use least. If the connecting tube is short, you cannot easily move your arm or change position without dislodging it, but there is no need for it to be short, and you can ask for it to be securely fixed so that you can still change position. Many women have discovered that when they are in labor they get a backache simply from lying in one position for too long, quite apart from the backache that is often a result of contractions. A glucose solution is often passed through the IV first. The IV can be turned down or even stopped once 5 cm dilatation of the cervix has been reached. It is usually kept in until after the end of the third stage, since it can control bleeding from the uterus by keeping it contracting hard.

Why induction may help

Induction is an invaluable obstetric technique when a baby must be born without delay. Many doctors believe that between 15 and 25 per cent of women and their babies benefit from either induction or acceleration of labor. Some believe that these figures are too high, while others again that 60 per cent or more of labors ought to be induced. If you have symptoms of preeclampsia (see page 126), including high blood pressure, albumin in the urine, sudden excessive weight gain, and edema (puffiness resulting from fluid retention), this is a good reason for induction, since the baby may not continue to be well nourished inside your uterus if the pregnancy is allowed to go on. If you have had a previous forceps delivery because a baby was a tight fit, inducing the next baby before it is at term may allow you to give birth more easily.

Induction before the EDD

Some babies stop growing because the placenta, through which they receive nourishment and oxygen, is not working well at the end of the pregnancy, even before there is any question of being "overdue", and even though the mother may be feeling fit and healthy. Such babies may do better outside the uterus.

Induction after the EDD

Between 10 and 12 per cent of women go two weeks or more "overdue" (known as "post-dates"), but in only 1 per cent of these babies is there any evidence of post-maturity. What has often happened is that the date of the start of pregnancy has been miscalculated. In only 3 per cent of women is pregnancy unusually long.

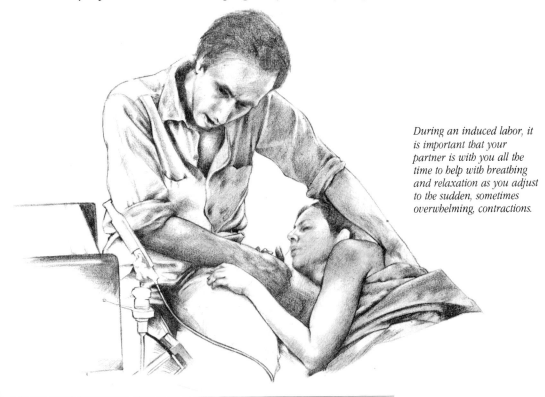

During an induced labor, it is important that your partner is with you all the time to help with breathing and relaxation as you adjust to the sudden, sometimes overwhelming, contractions.

If you are 42 weeks pregnant there is a chance of the placenta not functioning so well because it is aging. However, *premature babies are most at risk*, so the obstetrician needs to be sure that the baby really is overdue before inducing it. Some doctors make it a rule to induce if you are more than a week overdue, others like all their patients to deliver at about term and bring you into the hospital if you are a few days past your dates. Tests can be done to find out whether the placenta is working efficiently and therefore whether induction is really necessary (see page 216).

The length of induced labors

Although you may have a rapid labor with induction, this cannot be guaranteed. Some obstetricians prefer labors not to last longer than ten, eight, or even five hours and deliver with forceps or by cesarean section if labor is longer than they believe it should be. When a policy of routine induction is introduced in a hospital, there is a big increase in the number of cesarean sections performed. Since there is so much variation in obstetric policy, it may be a good idea when discussing the possibility of induction with the doctor to ask what his or her practice is. Depending on whether or not you want a short, sharp labor, this may affect your decision about whether to agree to induction if it is not urgently necessary for your baby's sake.

Possible problems

Induction is a form of intervention which, while extremely useful when really necessary, is not without risks, and in coming to a decision the relative risks of leaving the baby inside your uterus and inducing labor have to be assessed.

Unripe cervix It has been stated that "the major factor governing the success of induction is the state of the cervix."* When the cervix feels soft—like your lips when you hold your mouth slack—then it is ripe and ready for labor. Unfortunately, induction is often done before the cervix is ripe, and in consequence the uterus may not respond to the hormones. If the membranes have been ruptured, then the only way to get the baby born is by cesarean section.

Powerful contractions If the uterus is triggered to work harder, labor is more violent than it would be if it started naturally. In an induced labor there are often two "peaks" to each contraction, and each may last one minute or longer. Women who have had babies before, and whose previous labors were not induced, say that contractions start more powerfully and that there is not much leadup to each contraction, but instead a sudden "explosion". There may be only a short interval between them; just time to let out one relaxing breath and then you are into the next one! You may find you need to go straight into the breathing techniques you will have learned for about half dilatation (see page 190).

Interrupted blood flow Extremely powerful contractions are likely to interfere with the blood flow through the uterus and so cause fetal distress. In one study it was discovered that fetal distress was significantly more common in women having oxytocin, that the babies were more likely to have low Apgar scores (see page 328), and that far more babies went to the nursery to have special care*.

So it is important to have expert assistance if you are being induced and essential for the baby's heart to be continuously monitored. If you experience a contraction that lasts longer than 90 seconds, let the obstetrician know immediately. Even with a small dose of oxytocin some women have a prolonged contraction in which the uterus clamps down on itself—and on the baby. There is no test by which the sensitivity of your uterus to oxytocin can be known beforehand, so it is best to start with a small dose and gradually build up till good contractions result. The aim should be to simulate normal labor.

Measuring contractions

During an induced labor a pump may be used to monitor the pressure of uterine contractions and stop the flow of oxytocin when the uterus is contracting too hard. Another machine automatically adjusts the flow according to the amount of pressure in the uterus which is measured by a small intra-uterine pressure catheter so that the woman does not have to be strapped into a tight belt to record the contractions. Both these pieces of equipment solve the problem of the too strong, harsh labor which often results from doctors infiltrating more oxytocin into a woman's bloodstream than her particular uterus needs.

Accelerated labor

Labor is said to have been accelerated (or augmented) when it has already started and then, for some reason, has been speeded up by the use of an oxytocin drip. If a drip is used *before* the cervix has started to dilate progressively, even though you have felt contractions and have had a "false labor" or many Braxton Hicks contractions, you are being induced, not accelerated.

Labor may be accelerated when there is uterine inertia or incoordination, that is, when the uterus is not working effectively (see page 266). Some of the most difficult labors are long ones, and if you are becoming tired out with back pain for example, acceleration may help you cope, because it stimulates uterine action.

If it looks as if labor ought to be induced or accelerated, there are breathing skills you can use to deal with the challenge (see page 190). You need not give up, feeling that the doctors have taken over.

Induction with epidural anesthesia

In some hospitals you may be offered a "package deal" of induction combined with epidural anesthesia. (For more about epidurals see page 286.) Women who accept the package deal offered know that labor will take place on a certain day and that complete pain relief will be available. This new style of childbirth is attractive to many obstetricians and to many women too.

As with any intravenous drip, if you are receiving a large quantity of fluid, it is important that you should remember to empty your bladder regularly. If you cannot urinate (and you usually cannot if you have had an epidural) the nurse will insert a catheter and draw off the urine for you. A full bladder makes contractions painful by acting as a barrier between the baby's head and the base that forms the front of your pelvic arch.

Elective induction

Elective induction, also called induction for convenience, is induction that has no medical benefit.

Some doctors believe that most women should be induced. Some think it is the only way in which *all* labors can be efficiently managed. They say it is important for women to be in labor when staff are on duty, that hospital organization is easier when it is known how many women will be in labor each day, and that it is better if women are not in labor at night.

There will always be those women who go into labor spontaneously at inconvenient times, but the earlier they are induced the less this is likely to happen. So some obstetricians believe that induction any time after 38 or 39 weeks is right for most women. The logical development of this approach to obstetrics is that spontaneous labors will be considered "emergencies" and the "normal" labors will all be induced.

The US Food and Drug Administration has, after considering the research, withdrawn approval for the use of oxytocin for the elective induction of labor, asserting that it can expose both mother and baby to unnecessary danger.

Coping with induction

While there are basic questions that women need to ask about induction and acceleration of labor in terms of our whole style of childbirth in the West, these may not seem very relevant if your doctor advises you that your labor should be induced. It may come as a shock. You may even feel that all your careful preparation for the birth of your baby is pointless now.

Many women have enjoyed induced labors and coped with them well. But unfortunately many whose labors were induced say that they did not have any choice and that they were given inadequate information. Yet the British Department of Health and Social Security has stated: "A mother should have learned about induction at antenatal classes and if later it appears that induction would be the safer course of action for her, she should have every opportunity of discussing it with professional advisers. Knowing what is likely to be involved, she can make a fully informed decision about it."*

The important thing is to ask questions. Do not wait and hope that the obstetrician will explain things to you. Discuss it all fully, learn about what happens, and share in the decision-making rather than feeling it is all being decided for you. When you have the facts and your obstetrician's advice, take time to weigh it up and choose what seems to be the best way, always leaving your mind open to new evidence which may later point to a different course of action. It is your baby and your body and the experts are there to help you.

ELECTRONIC FETAL MONITORING

The electronic fetal monitor is used to track the fetal heartbeat and to record the pressure of the uterus during contractions. Either a transducer is placed over your abdomen near the baby's heart (external monitoring), or an electrode is inserted through the open cervix and clipped to the baby's scalp (internal monitoring). A printout, which is usually in the form of a continuous graph on a long spool of tape rather like ticker tape, shows the baby's heart rate in relation to the work done by the uterus. The monitor is a compact box which can amplify the baby's heartbeat so that it becomes clearly audible. It incorporates a flashing light which also registers the baby's heart, but this can be turned off. If anything goes wrong the monitor sounds an alarm, though this often indicates something wrong with the machine rather than with the baby.

The external monitor

An external monitor has two straps which are attached to your abdomen. One strap holds the tochodynamometer (a pressure gauge to record contractions), the other holds an ultrasound transducer which registers the baby's heartbeats.

The internal monitor

The internal monitor, which is more accurate, is inserted through your vagina and cervix and fixed to the skin of the baby's head. It is

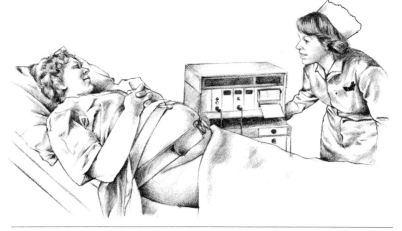

ELECTRONIC FETAL MONITOR
The monitor is usually near the bed and you can see when the next contraction is starting even before you feel it, and can get ready to meet it with your breathing. On the right of the monitor is a printout which shows the fetal heartbeat on the left and contractions on the right.

connected to a catheter leading to the machine and another catheter is inserted into the uterus to record electronically the pressure of contractions, or you may wear a single strap around your abdomen to hold the tochodynamometer. An internal monitor cannot be used until the membranes have ruptured spontaneously or have been ruptured artificially, and until the cervix is dilated at least 2 cm.

Advantages of monitoring

The monitor is particularly useful in high risk pregnancies and when labor is induced or augmented with an oxytocin drip, since the length, power, and frequency of the contractions produced by the drip must be carefully watched and their effect on the baby observed lest they prove too stressful for it. Until recently induction was often done "blind", and enormous, turbulent contractions were produced which sometimes cut off the fetal blood supply. This is much less likely nowadays since, by monitoring all these artificially aided births, it has been discovered that small amounts of oxytocin are effective.

Another undoubted advantage of monitoring is that the monitor indicates when the next contraction is beginning, so that, however drowsy you are feeling during labor, you can breathe out and relax, and get ready to breathe over it.

Problems of monitoring

Many women say that the abdominal strapping for the external monitor is very uncomfortable. Some even say that the pressure of the transducer on their tummies was the most painful thing about labor. Sometimes the internal electrode slips off the baby's head or, if an external monitor is being used, the baby moves and its heartbeat is lost. Some new external monitors have transducers which track the position of the baby's heart so that they do not lose it in this way.

As with an intravenous drip, having an external monitor means that you must remain more or less in one position lest the transducer slips off. As we have seen, this immobility means discomfort for you (page 294) and possibly problems for the baby. So monitoring may actually sometimes produce the failing fetal heart rate which it then records. If you are being monitored, turn on your side before the monitor is put on, although you may find that even this position becomes uncomfortable after a while.

Some women in labor are wired up to the monitor only to find that nothing is being recorded at all because the machine is not operating. It is very irritating to be immobilized and connected to a machine when it cannot possibly be doing anything to help. Yet staff sometimes appear shocked at a woman's request for the transducer to be detached so that she can move about and get on with her labor unhindered. If this happens to you, you are entirely justified in being insistent that the monitor is disconnected. But when the monitor is working well some women find it reassuring to know that every heartbeat of the baby is being recorded.

Telemetry

Monitoring by telemetry (radio waves) is an advance on the older method and allows you to be up and about in labor unattached to wires but continuously monitored at the same time. The equipment is less cumbersome and the machinery can be placed at some distance from you. Telemetry is not yet widely available in the US; in the UK most women prefer it, labors seem to go faster, and babies do better. Because you are able to be upright, you may feel less pain, and the uterus can work more efficiently.

But even monitoring by telemetry is usually invasive, since an electrode is clipped onto the baby's scalp, though a method of sticking the monitor on with epoxy resin is now available. Any invasive technique (one which entails entering your body) introduces added risk of infection. This is a risk worth taking when there is reason to suspect the baby is encountering difficulties, but *not*, many people would think, when everything seems to be straightforward.

A scalp electrode probably causes the baby some pain. (It is uncomfortable to prick your finger on one.) It remains on the baby's head till after delivery, when it should be removed gently and deftly, not merely pulled. In 85 per cent of newborn babies a rash appears at the site of the electrode and in 20 per cent a small abscess develops*. Sometimes the child is left with a permanent bald patch.

Interpreting the data

Although it is estimated that the fetal monitor enables an obstetrician to save one life for every 1000 babies monitored, the interpretation of data is of first importance. The machine by itself can do nothing to make childbirth safer. It is only too easy to interpret normal variations in the fetal heart as pathological, sometimes because of the design of the machine, or to miss out on clinical signs that something is wrong because the monitor indicates that everything is normal. Obstetricians and midwives experienced in auscultating the fetal heart and assessing clinical conditions have a skill which is being neglected today as more and more confidence is put in electronic machines.

Half of all babies show some irregularities of heartbeat during labor. Usually this is of no significance. We don't know how they manage it, but babies actually sleep during labor. They change from rapid eye movement (REM) or dreaming sleep to deep, quiet sleep for a period of up to 40 minutes, and then back again. As the sleep state varies, so the heart rate changes; in deep sleep, the heartbeat stays steady, and the printout of the heart rate tends to be flat. Until the deep sleep was understood, this kind of trace made doctors anxious; but it has now been discovered that the baby only has to be roused a little for the heartbeat to pick up. One way of doing this is to touch the top of the baby's head. Mothers have their own ways of achieving the same result—changing position, for example, or even talking to the baby—and this may reassure the doctors.

The baby's heart rate is usually between 120 and 160 beats per minute. A quicker rate than this is termed tachycardia, and a slower rate, bradycardia. Incomplete understanding of the normal range of variation in the fetal heart rate during and between contractions leads to a great deal of intervention. In Spain and West Germany, for example, when abnormal fetal heart patterns are recorded, obstetricians stop the uterus contracting by introducing drugs into the mother's bloodstream. In all countries, electronic fetal monitoring has led to more forceps deliveries and cesarean sections being performed, and the introduction of a monitor in any hospital is associated with a sharp increase in the rate of operative deliveries—though this often drops after a while.

Testing the baby's blood

Some obstetricians believe that the baby's blood should be tested to check the findings when the monitor suggests fetal distress since, if the baby is in difficulties, this always shows up in the blood chemistry. This extra test might cut down the number of unnecessary cesarean deliveries. One kind of electrode both records the baby's heart rate and tests its blood.

It has usually been accepted that if a blood test reveals high levels of lactic acid, which builds up if the baby is short of oxygen in the second stage of labor, the baby's brain will be damaged. But it is now known that, if it does become short of oxygen, a healthy baby can switch to another kind of metabolism which allows it to draw on energy reserves built up over the previous weeks; in this way the baby can survive on less oxygen with no ill effects. Indeed, babies whose blood is acid at birth often have high Apgar scores (see page 328). And neurological studies on four-year-olds whose blood was acid at birth due to oxygen shortage show that this had no harmful effects.*

HELPING THE BABY OUT

In most hospitals nowadays about one woman in every four or five is delivered by forceps, though the rate is higher in some hospitals.

Forceps delivery

Forceps look like metal salad servers and dovetail into each other so that they cannot press too far in on the baby's head. If the woman has not already had an epidural an injection to numb the birth outlet is given first. The curved blades are inserted one at a time and cradled around the baby's head, one at each temple. Forceps are of different shapes for different situations: most bring the baby down the birth canal, though some are simply used to lift the baby out. If the baby's head is occipito transverse or occipito posterior (see page 257), the obstetrician may first turn the head manually or may use curved Kiellands forceps for the delivery to rotate the head from the transverse or posterior to the anterior.

Vacuum extraction

Sometimes a vacuum extractor is used instead of forceps. This works like a miniature vacuum cleaner to suck the baby out. A vacuum cup is attached to the baby's head. It may take between 10 and 20 minutes to be applied. During this time if you want to push, push. Once the cup is on, it helps if you can bear down, so that the baby is pressed down from above as well as being pulled down the birth canal by the suction applied from below.

Reasons for forceps delivery

Forceps or vacuum extraction is used when delivery needs to be hastened because your blood pressure has risen dramatically, for example, or because there are signs of fetal distress, or when the baby is in an unusual position, making its journey through the pelvic outlet more difficult. The obstetrician has to use clinical judgment to decide whether your baby will pop out like a cork from a bottle given a firm, long pull or whether it is so firmly wedged that it might harm both the baby and you to deliver vaginally. Sometimes after forceps have failed a cesarean section is performed (see page 308).

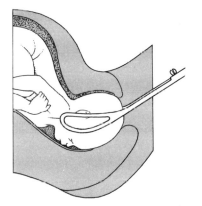
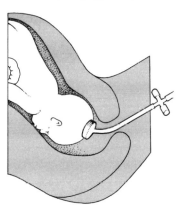

HELP WITH DELIVERY
These forceps (far left) are the kind used simply for lifting the baby's head out of the birth canal. Vacuum extraction (left) can sometimes avoid a difficult forceps delivery, and the suction cup may be attached to the baby before it has started to descend the birth canal.

Forceps may also be used if you have had an epidural (see page 286), as you may feel too numb to work with contractions.

A forceps delivery is frequently advised if you are having a prolonged second stage. Different obstetricians have different ideas of what a prolonged second stage is. Some would say that it is any second stage of longer than half an hour in which there are no signs of progress. Many set a definite time limit on the second stage and instruct nurses to call them when it looks as if this stage is extending. Some believe that this is rather doctrinaire and that the important thing is to observe whether or not the baby is coming down the birth canal progressively, while checking its condition carefully and regularly.

Some women seem to be able to cope with long second stages without tiring, whereas others quickly become exhausted. If you have already had a long labor and then a slow second stage it is difficult to retain enthusiasm and, unless given a great deal of encouragement, you might hope that someone would just come and take the baby out of your body one way or another.

Sometimes a woman may be given encouragement to push or is persuaded to hold her breath too long, when she does not feel any spontaneous urge to bear down. This is because the nurse knows that the delivery will be by forceps unless the baby is born within the time decreed by the obstetrician, so she tries to avoid the intervention by getting the mother to push more strenuously in the hope that this will help the baby to be born before the deadline comes.

Avoiding a forceps delivery

If you have been struggling to push the baby out and it is suggested that forceps may be necessary either because the second stage is taking too long, you are becoming too tired, or the fetal heart rate is slow, explore the effect of *not pushing*. You may find that you do not need to push at all for several contractions—a welcome rest for both you and the baby—and then there is an unmistakable and irresistible pushing sensation which is much more effective than pushing just because you are following instructions. It is a good idea to stand, squat, or kneel so that gravity can help the baby out.

CESAREAN SECTION

The doctor gave me an internal exam and said, "It's not dilating any more—I'll have to do a C-section on you." And I remember saying, "Oh no, I don't want to have a C-section!" I was so emotionally involved in this whole process that it was like robbery.

If the obstetrician tells you that you need to give birth by cesarean section, this means that you will be anesthetized and your baby will then be delivered abdominally rather than vaginally.

The most common reason for cesarean section is cephalopelvic disproportion, when the baby's head is too large to pass through the pelvis. Some obstetricians prefer to deliver abdominally all breech babies, or all breech babies of first-time mothers, because they believe it is safer for the baby. But size of the baby in relation to the maternal pelvis and the way the baby is lying are factors which should also be taken into account. If fetal distress is picked up by an electronic monitor and the obstetrician becomes anxious about the state of the baby, he or she may decide to do an emergency cesarean section. Abdominal delivery may also be performed for twins, or when amniocentesis has revealed that a baby is damaged, for very low-birthweight babies and on women suffering from diseases such as diabetes, renal disease, and chronic hypertension.

The rise in cesarean births

Cesarean rates vary but, in Britain, they make up between 10 and 15 per cent of all births. In some cities in Latin America, 85 per cent of babies are delivered abdominally, whereas in the Netherlands the overall rate is less than 10 per cent. The rate is much higher in the United States and is increasing rapidly—in some hospitals it is 50 per cent or more. But there has not been a corresponding rise in the fetal survival rate. And cesarean section imposes on women extra risk, unnecessary pain, and, often, post-operative infection.

Where in the past the obstetrician would have corrected a baby's bad position by external version through the mother's abdominal wall (see page 215), the tendency now is to deliver by section rather than attempting to turn the baby first. As a result many doctors nowadays no longer know *how* to perform external version.

More and more women are now included in the category of "high risk". The age at which a woman is considered obstetrically high risk went down from 40 to 35, then to 30, and now in some hospitals anyone over 27 is included in this category. If you are over 27 and it seems likely that there may be problems with your labor, you may find that you are advised to deliver by cesarean section.

It is also the practice to do *repeat* cesarean sections even when the conditions which resulted in the first section are not present: "Once a cesarean, always a cesarean". Some US doctors argue that the uterine scar might break open during a subsequent labor, but British obstetricians normally allow the labor to proceed naturally but are ready to do a cesarean if necessary. One professor of obstetrics says that problems of scar separation are "much less than the one per cent that is often quoted" and that even if the scar is pulled open by strong contractions "careful monitoring of the fetus and mother usually means that any harm to either is rare"*. Vaginal birth after cesarean (VBAC) is urged whenever possible by the American College of Obstetricians and Gynecologists.

Planned cesarean section

The decision to perform a cesarean section is often made days or weeks in advance. A section will usually be planned if it is known that the baby is in a difficult position to be delivered vaginally, or if there is evidence of cephalopelvic disproportion—although you can be certain that there is genuine CPD only when you are actually in labor. The baby must be delivered abdominally if the placenta is lying at the bottom of the uterus in front of the baby's presenting part (placenta previa). Surgery is either arranged for the 39th week or in some cases you are allowed to go into labor naturally, knowing that a cesarean section will be performed.

Unplanned (just-in-case) cesarean section

During a long labor in which there is little progress, the obstetrician may make the decision to perform a cesarean section for no other reason than that dilatation is slow.

Emergency cesarean section

Some reasons for a planned cesarean section (such as cephalo-pelvic disproportion) may also apply to an emergency section, when they have not been obvious until labor. An emergency section may

I felt no pain. I looked at trees through the operating room window. I could feel the skin incision like a finger being run over my abdomen. When the uterus was cut open it felt rather as if somebody was rummaging in a chest of drawers.

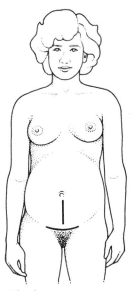

The classic cesarean incision is vertical. Though it is still used in emergencies, the horizontal incision is now more common, mainly for cosmetic reasons.

also be decided on during a long labor in which the baby is in obvious difficulties and is short of oxygen; if the placenta is failing to service the baby sufficiently or is becoming detached from the lining of the uterus—causing the mother to hemorrhage; or if there is a prolapsed umbilical cord.

Anesthesia for cesarean section

Cesarean section has traditionally been performed with the patient under general anesthetic, but epidural anesthesia (see page 286) is becoming more common for this operation. Though general anesthesia has to be used when a very quick decision is made to do a section, those women who have had epidural anesthesia usually like being awake and aware of what is going on and being ready to welcome the baby as soon as it is lifted out.

General anesthesia If general anesthesia is used, you are given as small a dose as possible for the baby's sake, and you may be unconscious for only a few minutes. All the preparation for the operation is done while you are awake and you are often given pure oxygen to breathe in during this time. It should be possible to arrange for the baby who is in good condition to be held by the father while you are unconscious.

Epidural anesthesia You are given the epidural after being taken to the operating room—the dosage is larger for this surgery than it would be if an epidural were being given just for pain relief. An anesthesiologist checks carefully to see that the anesthesia is sufficient for the operation and is ready with general anesthesia should the epidural not take effectively. There is no postoperative nausea and vomiting as there often is with general anesthesia. An epidural is also safer for you because you cannot inhale your stomach contents, and safer for the baby, who does not receive a knock-out dose of anesthesia. Another advantage is that you can hold your baby and put her to the breast immediately after the operation.

Horizontal or vertical incision

Incisions for cesarean section are either horizontal or vertical. The classical incision is vertical but is rarely done now unless there is no time to spare. The main advantages of the horizontal incision are that it is done low down near the line of the pubic hair, in the area which would be covered by a bikini, and that a horizontal scar is less likely to break down than a vertical scar.

What happens during a cesarean section

Before you have a cesarean section a nurse will shave off your pubic hair and slip a catheter into your bladder so that it is kept empty. In the operating room sterile drapes are put around your tummy and if you are going to be awake a screen is erected at about waist level so

They told us it was a girl so I thought she'd been born and asked if she was all right. "Have a look" they said and pushed the screen down to show us her spindly little legs sticking out from my body. A few seconds later out came her head and I felt wonderful. I don't think I've ever enjoyed anything so much in my life.

that you do not see the surgery. Your tummy is washed in antiseptic solution. If there is anything you want to know, ask.

You will be given an epidural or general anesthetic. When your whole tummy is numb or you have become unconscious, a small cut is made through the lower abdominal wall below your navel to reveal the lower uterine segment. Packs of surgical gauze are pressed in to keep other organs out of the way. A horizontal slit is made through the muscle and the bag of waters bulges through it. The obstetrician pops the bag and sucks out the amniotic fluid—if you have had an epidural, you may hear the glug-glug-swoosh sound—and uses one blade of the forceps or a hand under the baby's presenting part to ease it out of the small opening, at the same time pressing with one hand on the upper part of the uterus so that the baby is pressed down through the incision.

If you have had an epidural, it may be possible for you to watch the birth at this stage. Ask the doctor to put the screen down for a few moments. You will see your baby emerging and, from your horizontal position, will not see anything gruesome. In fact you will have eyes only for your baby and will not think about the surgery that has been done. The baby is lifted out, suctioned with a mucous catheter, and once it is breathing well can be handed to you or your partner. The whole birth process from the beginning of surgery need take only about four minutes.

As the baby is being delivered you may be given an injection of oxytocin to make the placenta peel away from the wall of the uterus. It will then be lifted out through the abdominal opening that has been made. The obstetrician stitches the cut in the uterus, layer by layer, with absorbable sutures. Suction instruments are used to draw out blood and amniotic fluid, and then the obstetrician repairs the abdominal wall. This takes much longer than the birth—up to an hour—and entails repairing the skin with non-absorbable sutures, steritapes, staples, or metal clips which have to be removed later.

Having your partner with you

Not all couples want to be together during surgery. You may worry that perhaps it will be too much for your partner to cope with, or he may expect to find the experience so distressing that he feels he will be unable to give you any support. Those couples who do want to be together do so because they feel that the birth of a baby, by whatever route, is something they want to share, that it should be family-centered, and that, if the mother is not able to cuddle the newborn baby, the father should be there to do so.

If you do want to be together and your cesarean is planned, try getting to know your obstetrician well in advance. Once you have built up a relationship, ask if your partner can be with you at the birth. If the answer is no, ask politely for the doctor's reasons. If it is not normal practice at that hospital, you may convince the doctor that you are both concerned enough to want to be the first couple to

It was Joanna, our childbirth educator, who convinced us not just to accept the word of a doctor who said "No, husbands cannot be present at a cesarean birth."

experience a cesarean birth together there. There is always a first time. If your partner is present, he sits up by your head supporting you emotionally; there is no necessity for him to watch the operation, since the screen restricts his view.

After the delivery

After the operation, say you want to hold your baby if he or she is not already beside you. An intravenous drip is left in for some hours so that you can be given plenty of fluids straight into your bloodstream if necessary. If you had general anesthesia, you may feel sick and weak for the first day or so. As soon as you feel you can move about in bed a little, do so. Even wiggling your toes and rotating your ankles is good and prevents pooling of blood in your legs.

Whatever anesthesia you have had, the chances are that the nurses will help you get up later the same day. Though it hurts, moving around is important to avoid thrombosis. To move off the bed, work your way to the side of it, pressing your buttocks together, and taking some of the weight of your body on your hands. As you get up you may have a lot of bleeding from the vagina. This also happens after a vaginal delivery and is simply the blood that has pooled in your pelvic region while you were lying still. Stroll around the room to encourage good circulation and use the slow, complete breathing you learned in childbirth classes.

If you feel you need drugs for pain relief, ask for them. Though you probably want to be awake to enjoy your baby you cannot do this if you are in severe discomfort. The more your partner can be with you, even while you doze, the more you can relax, feeling that the baby is being looked after by someone who loves her.

Dressings will probably be removed three or four days later. Because the obstetrician has had to cut through muscle, your tummy will look very big and soggy. Once the dressings are off you will be able to have a bath. The stitches inside your body dissolve naturally, but the external stitches will be removed toward the end of the first week. Do not worry about them bursting open—with every layer stitched separately there is little chance of any such damage.

After general anesthesia fluid collects in the lungs and has to be coughed up. A nurse will teach you how to do this so that it causes least discomfort. The breathing techniques you learned in pregnancy can help you too.

It is natural to feel a flood of conflicting emotions after cesarean birth. Some women say that they are grateful to have the baby, but at the same time they feel "cheated."

A cesarean birth is a surgical operation and you need time to recover from it as from any abdominal surgery. For the first six weeks after the birth you should avoid any heavy lifting. If it is possible to arrange for extra help at home, especially if you already have a toddler who expects to be lifted, it is an enormous benefit to have someone else to do the more strenuous work.

After a cesarean birth it helps your circulation if you can get moving soon.

Gentle birth

At birth eyes open for the first time on a new world. Your baby's life outside your body begins. Yet your baby already has nine months' experience of life inside the uterus. The ancient Chinese dated life from conception rather than from delivery and perhaps this corresponds more nearly to reality. The baby started off as the chance collision of a ripe egg and a sperm. Forces which have their origin far back in creation poured energy into the cells, nourishing and multiplying them to make an embryo budding on a stalk and drawing sustenance from your uterus. Gradually as the days passed a fully formed being developed, albeit in miniature, and there was already at the third month a fetus whose main task was one of growth and maturation. As week followed week its senses became sharper so that it was increasingly aware of its surroundings, responding to your movements, and to bright light, loud sounds and music. This long-drawn-out period of preparation culminates in the dramatic journey into the brilliance and bustle of our own world.

What Is It Like To Be Born?

Birth is an intense experience not only for you: for the baby, too, it is the climax of a time of growing and waiting. The new human being is caught up in a rush of powerful uterine activity, which squeezes it out from the confines of the tight muscle enveloping it and the cradle of bone in which it has been rocked, into a separate existence.

Traveling from the depths of the uterus, under the arch of bone and out through the soft, opening folds of the vagina, the baby passes through a barrage of different kinds of sensory stimulation. It is the original magical mystery tour and must be more astonishing and full of surprises than any mystery tunnel traveled through in search of excitement in a fairground.

The baby's experience of labor

Pressure builds up over the crown of the baby's head where it is directed through the dilating cervix, which is pulled up over its head like a turtleneck sweater. Pressure is also directed over the baby's buttocks as the uterus contracts down on them and propels the baby forward. So the baby is fixed between the uterus gripping its bottom and the cervix being progressively drawn over its head. This pressure causes the baby to roll into a ball, head tucked in and knees bent up, arms folded over its chest. The upper part of the head, not yet hard bone all over, is molded so that the brow is pressed backward.

As the baby is forced downward the crown of the head also confronts resistance from the pelvic floor muscles, which are springy

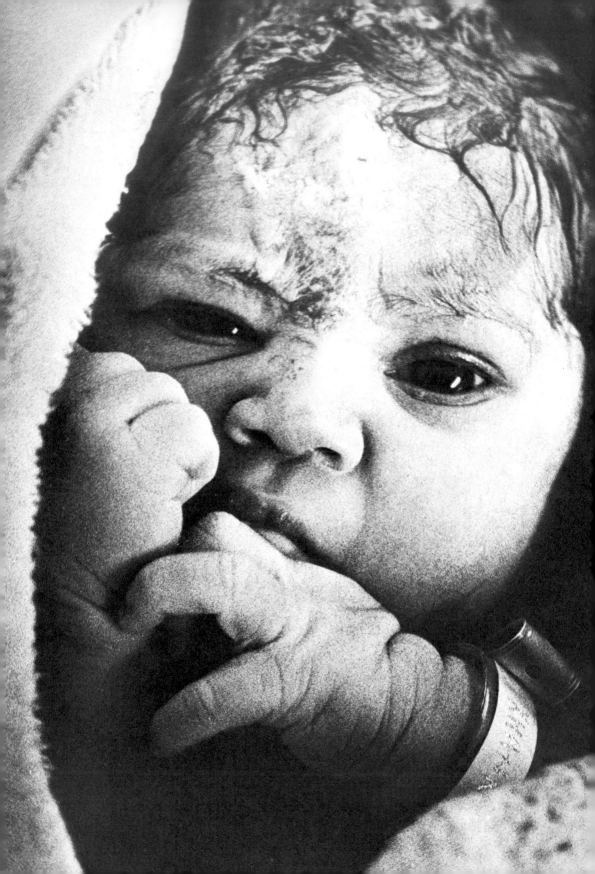

and firm and which are also little by little eased over its head. The passage is narrow but yielding and the baby's whole body is massaged vigorously with each contraction as it gradually descends.

Beneath the stretched abdominal skin and the thinned translucent wall of the uterus itself the baby in the last weeks of pregnancy has been aware of glowing light whenever bright sun or artificial light shone on your body. It must be rather like firelight or the light cast by a red-shaded lamp. When the journey to birth begins the baby is pressed deeper into the cavity of the pelvis, under arches of bone and a canopy of thick supportive ligaments and muscles. Perhaps it is a sensation rather like traveling through a long, dark avenue of overhanging trees.

The baby is not just a hunk of flesh or a life-sized doll. It is a human being fully equipped to feel pain and pleasure, a *person* coming to birth. The baby cannot remember or anticipate in the same way that we can, but it nevertheless feels keenly and is a fully sentient being. The uterus holds and presses tightly in on the child not yet born, with steadily escalating power. By the end of the first stage of labor it is embracing the baby tightly for one or two minutes at a time. Each hug begins gently and grows tighter and tighter till at the height of the contractions the baby is being gripped fast for 20 to 30 seconds. Then the wave of pressure recedes again and the baby floats once more in its inner sea: it is in labor along with you.

Newborn reflexes in labor

In some obstetric textbooks the baby is described simply as "a passenger", and purely in mechanical terms, as two ovoids, the head and the trunk, the long axes of which are at right angles to each other and which can take the curve of the pelvic axis independently. While this is accurate as a description of the mechanics of fetal descent, it leaves out any mention of what the baby might be doing during this process and how the reflexes with which it is born are probably also functioning during labor.

The baby changes its position in response to the power unleashed in your body, and does this not only because of mechanical forces which act on it but probably also because it is making active movements. It is working *with* you toward birth, your partner in the struggle, not just a passenger, and can do this because of inbuilt reflexes (see page 329). A newborn baby turns his head in the direction of a touch, moves his head up and down against a firm surface, curls his toes down when pressure is applied to the ball of the foot, lifts his foot up and puts it down at a higher level when pressure is applied over the top of the foot, and makes forward stepping movements when tilted forward with his feet against a firm surface. Two of these actions probably operate to help the baby onward in its journey. One is the reflex to move its head up and down against firm resistance, which means that it actually wriggles its way forward through the cervix and the fanned-out tissues of the vagina

OPPOSITE
Still damp from birth, the gently delivered baby is alert to learn about the world . . .

with much the same action that we make when putting on a new sweater with a rather tight neck. The other is the stepping movement when the resistance is offered to the feet, so that in effect the baby pushes away from the solid wall of the uterus as it tightens around it.

The impact of the outside world

In the second stage the head has to take nearly a right-angled bend. The pressure builds up until it swivels the neck around so that the baby is facing downward ready to slide out. You can imagine that this provides a very sharp stimulus to the baby, a message which says unmistakably "Things are changing. Wake up! It's all systems go!" At last the crown of the head oozes through the vagina and remains there. Perhaps you reach down with eager hands to stroke the damp, warm top of your baby's head. This is the first greeting.

The head slips out and suddenly the baby encounters space and air. The shoulders and chest slide forward, followed by the whole body. There is a gasp and air rushes into the lungs, inflating them for the first time. The damp inner surfaces of the lungs, previously clinging together like wet plastic bags, open up with the first cry with which the baby meets life.

Air, space, the baby's own limbs moving in an unfamiliar medium, weight, strange sounds, glaring lights, cold hands picking the baby up, turning it over—all at once a myriad of new sensations assail the newborn. Not only must lungs fill with air and start to function rhythmically, but the circulation must find new pathways.

Labor as a stimulus

In his book *Birth Without Violence**, Dr Frederick Leboyer calls the mother "a monster" because of the pain he believes she cannot help but inflict on the baby as it passes through the throes of birth. But the process of being born can also be seen to involve stimulation and awakening for which the baby is ready and which prepares it for life. Looked at from this point of view, muscles hold and embrace the baby, triggering powerful sensations, then soften again in a rhythmic pattern. The space between contractions is like the trough between two waves. Inevitably the next wave comes and again the muscles tighten firmly around the child.

Though labor is undoubtedly traumatic for some babies, others look extraordinarily peaceful and contented after delivery. It may feel to you as if you are swimming in a stormy sea when you reach the end of the first stage of labor. You may be anxious that these massive squeezings of the great muscle of the uterus are causing your baby suffering. Yet in spite of the relentless onslaught of contractions as full dilatation approaches, the baby who is pressed through the cervix and down the birth canal in this way responds more vigorously to life than most babies do who are merely lifted out through an abdominal incision. The 9 in (23 cm) journey squeezes out fluid and mucus from its nose and mouth so that the baby born vaginally has less mucus in its respiratory tract than one delivered by cesarean section and is better prepared for the great new activity of breathing.

Welcoming your baby

Have you thought about how you want to welcome your baby into the world? Frederick Leboyer believes that just as our attention has now been drawn to the mother's experience of birth, so we must focus on the baby's needs and learn how to reduce its suffering. For him this is not just a matter of safe or speedy delivery, a question of making sure that the baby has enough oxygen or is not traumatized by delivery, but one of greeting the baby with consideration and gentleness.

Most babies cry at the shock of birth and this first cry ensures that a rush of air enters the lungs. But if they *go on* crying Leboyer asserts that there is something wrong. The crying of abandonment and distress is quite different from the healthy crying of the newborn. Yet people often take persistent crying for granted and even smile indulgently and say, "She's got a fine pair of lungs!" The newborn baby continues to scream because of insensitivity to her needs and the lack of a sufficiently caring environment. If the setting for birth is changed and, above all, if the attitudes of those assisting are different, so that the baby is treated with respect, Leboyer says, the child will become quiet, will open her eyes, will reach out with her hands, and start to discover herself. But if this is to happen the birth room must be calm and hushed, the lights dimmed and those handling the baby must do so slowly, carefully, and lovingly. This is *gentle birth*.

CREATING A CARING ENVIRONMENT

Gentle birth need not start only as the baby is born. In the way that labor is conducted and in the whole atmosphere of the birth room an environment of peace and serenity can be created. Though Dr Leboyer is concerned with what is done to the baby *after delivery*, a mother and baby are so close and in such a subtle and yet intense relationship that everything done to you during labor must affect the way in which you are able to respond to your newborn baby. If you are treated as if your body is merely the container from which a baby is removed, or as an irresponsible child who has to be given orders, you will find it very difficult to be in harmony with the forces which are bringing the baby to birth, with your own body in its work of creation and also with the baby. The caring environment for the newborn starts with a caring environment for you, a respect for your rhythms, patience to wait and watch and loving support.

I lifted her out and up on to my tummy and held and stroked her. It suddenly burst on me that this incredible little creature had come out of my body—and I was bathed in love for her.

Dimming the lights

It is irritating for you to labor under bright lights, just as it is for the baby to confront brilliant fluorescent light at delivery. For a gentle birth all unnecessary lighting is switched off so that the room is softly illuminated, with a clear light only on the perineum. Instead of lying flat on your back or with your legs suspended in lithotomy stirrups you need to be in a position you find comfortable and in which you can be an active birthgiver. Many women like to be sitting up, crouching, or kneeling so that they can catch the first glimpse of the baby's head and can put their fingers down to touch it even before it has started to emerge through the vagina. We have already seen (on page 232) that an upright position has many advantages for the mother in terms of mechanical function. If you are well raised you are also in a splendid position for greeting your baby.

When the head crowns some women put their hands down to caress the top of the baby's head. It feels warm and firm and as it eases forward you touch more and more warm, damp, silk hair. This first contact between mother and child is beyond excitement; it is a moment of awe and for some women it approaches spiritual ecstasy.

Then the head slides out and turns to align with the shoulders still inside and you can see your baby's profile; with a rush the shoulders and whole body are born. As the baby slips out and starts to breathe the lights can be dimmed further so that the baby can take its time to open its eyes in the half-light. Many years ago Maria Montessori, the educationalist, stressed that babies are assaulted by bright light. She said that they should be able to begin the gradual exploration of the world with their senses in a soft glow and shadows, similar to the uterine environment they have just left. Yet in the past we have subjected newborns to harsh hospital lights and have acted as if they were unable to see or hear.

Reducing the noise level

In nonviolent birth there is no unnecessary conversation and those attendants who speak do so in hushed voices. Leboyer believes that the mother should be quiet too and that excited voices can startle the baby. He thinks that there is too much emphasis nowadays on the father's presence in childbirth and that fathers sometimes get too emotional. Couples who value sharing birth together would not agree with him. I feel myself and know many women who also feel that it would not have been possible to go through labor and birth without the child's father there.

In fact couples often do cry out with astonishment and wonder when they see their baby leap into life and this is a spontaneous outpouring of emotion, an integral part of childbirth with joy, which *in itself* is a life-enhancing experience for both parents. We don't work out carefully exactly what we are going to do when we are caught up in other sorts of peak experience; we don't weigh up the different factors and come up with a calculation. To do so would be to diminish the experience. Life is exultant and we are borne along with it. Birth is that kind of climactic process. It is an act of love, the continuation and culmination of the passion which started the development of that baby.

OPPOSITE

Hold your baby close, against the warmth of your skin, and share with her the first moments of life.

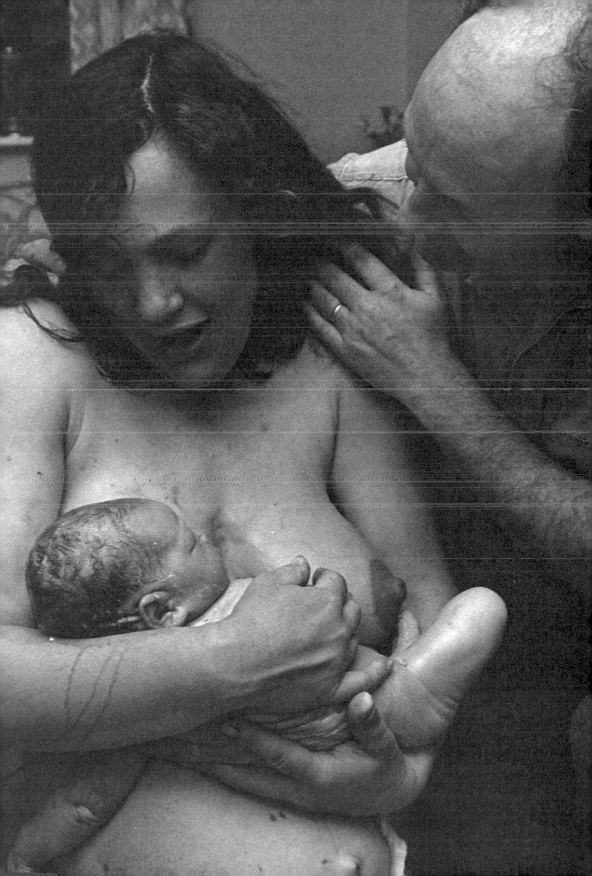

Physical contact

It is because birth is a peak experience that arms reach out to take and hold the baby and draw it close. It is not just that this small, wrinkled, vulnerable baby is yours and that therefore you decide to take it in your arms (though unfortunately this is just how it is for some women in a loveless, uncaring environment); if the right atmosphere exists you are totally enveloped in a rush of intense feeling. This does not mean that the baby is neglected in an orgy of self-indulgent emotion, as Dr Leboyer believes. The baby is drawn into the warm circle of love between the parents and becomes part of it. This is what it is for not only a baby to be born but also a *family*.

In nonviolent birth the baby is handled gently and slowly without haste. There are no rough, quick movements. He or she is delivered up onto your tummy or over your thigh. If you ask beforehand it is often possible to do this yourself and the midwife or doctor will remind you to reach out and draw the baby onto your body.

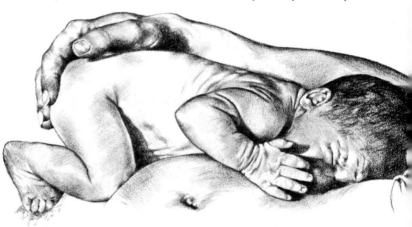

The baby can be delivered straight onto your tummy for its first moments of life; there it is in direct contact with your warm skin and can also still hear the familiar, reassuring sound of your heart beating.

Frederick Leboyer believes that the baby should be lovingly and gently massaged until he or she stops crying and becomes calm. Only then does he think the baby is ready to go to the mother's arms. In his own obstetric practice he used to do this massaging. But many women think that this is yet one more way in which professionals, however caring, attempt to take over childbirth and to intrude on the mother's natural role. Wherever gentle birth is done today it is usually the mother who holds and caresses her baby. You do not have to learn how to massage your newborn. The way you explore and stroke it is spontaneous and right. But this is only possible if the baby is naked and in skin contact with you. Babies are often bundled up in wrappings in case they lose heat. It is true that new babies quickly become chilled unless they are in a warm atmosphere and are held close. Research now taking place shows that the baby, even the low-birthweight baby, keeps warmer when in flesh to flesh contact with his mother and nestling against her breast than the baby who is wrapped up and put in a bassinet. So ask a helper to slip your gown down over your shoulders or to take it right off before delivery.

A blanket can easily be thrown over you and your baby or a heater can be placed over both. Mothers often feel chilled and shaky after delivery and appreciate the warmth themselves.

If your baby is handed to you bundled up in a cloth, unwrap the covers and cuddle it close. Do not be afraid to talk to your baby. He or she will respond to the sound of your voice and will be especially sensitive to the higher-pitched tone of a woman's voice*. The baby is also getting to know your unique scent and by the time she is a few days old will already prefer a cloth which has been against your body to one which has been close to another new mother's body.

Delaying the clamping of the cord

Frederick Leboyer believes it is important to wait to clamp the cord until it has stopped pulsating. Midwives always used to wait, but nowadays the whole birth is so often rushed that the cord is sometimes clamped and cut immediately while blood is still flowing. Even though this blood is not particularly well oxygenated—because the placenta begins to peel off the wall of the uterus as soon as delivery takes place—it is blood which really belongs to the baby Unless there are reasons for clamping (such as a Rhesus negative mother who has already produced antibodies against her Rhesus positive baby—see page 103) it seems a good idea to wait a few minutes for the cord to become flaccid, when the baby has no further use for it. There is no reason why the cord has to be cut at all until after the placenta is delivered; it is separated only for convenience.

You can rest your fingers on the cord and feel the blood throbbing through it and wait for the moment when it stops completely. Cutting the cord between two clamps is a very simple procedure and something which a father may enjoy doing. If you would like to do this, ask in advance.

Some obstetricians are concerned that blood could drain back into the placenta and the baby even become short of blood if it is placed above the placenta with the cord still unclamped. This is not a good reason for early clamping or for refusing to place the baby against your body. The baby can be rested over your thigh, where it will be below the placenta and you can easily see and touch it if you are well propped up. Mucus usually drains out naturally and there is no need to use a mucous extractor, though the baby should be carefully observed and an extractor used if the airways are blocked.

Waiting for the rooting reflex

Your baby may emerge from your body already wanting to suck. But many babies are not quite ready and need time to feel secure before they reach out to find the nipple. The rooting reflex (see page 329) is a sure sign that the baby is ready to be put to the breast. Wait until the baby shows interest rather than stuff your breast into her mouth.

It was a forceps delivery. But the doctor took the forceps off after the head was born and said "Come on, deliver the rest of your baby yourself!" I reached down and lifted him up. And they dimmed the lights and he lay making sucking noises on my tummy.

Leboyer believes that mothers often try to nurse before the baby is ready and that then even nursing can be another assault on the newborn. Many women today are anxious to nurse immediately after delivery and perhaps their anxiety to do this in an alien environment, and one which they may even feel is hostile, makes them rush things. Be patient if you can. Let the baby rest against your bare breast and in his own time he will start to explore with mouth, hands, and eyes. This time is precious for you and your baby. It cannot be speeded up without interfering with spontaneous, natural rhythms. After a while the baby will probably begin to lick your nipple and then will seek it and, with a little help as you lift your breast into its searching mouth, will latch on and begin to suck.

The Leboyer bath

An important part of the Leboyer style of birth is the warm bath in which the baby is supported shortly after delivery and in Leboyer's film illustrating gentle birth, the bath is given even before the mother holds her baby. Leboyer believes that the baby needs time to feel safe again in the medium which it has just left in the uterus—water—and that suspended in a bath the baby becomes peaceful and sometimes positively beatific, discovers itself and starts to open its eyes and explore the world around. It is true that some babies seem to enjoy the bath very much, but only if it is done slowly and calmly and if the water is deep enough for the baby to float. The ideal way of giving a bath is to use a deep container with a thermal lining (such as a picnic ice chest) and to have an air heater over the bath.

You may find that the hospital where you are having your baby does not allow a bath because of the risk of hypothermia (chilling). Unfortunately cold air ventilation ducts have been incorporated into the design of many modern maternity units and the baby in water or exposed to this air is likely to get chilled. Many hospital pediatricians are concerned that the baby can lose a great deal of body heat while wet or in a bath, through evaporation, and say that if a bath is given at all it should be done speedily, which defeats its purpose. You obviously cannot add hot water to a bath when the baby is in it and you know yourself how shivery you feel when you get out of a hot bath into a relatively cold atmosphere. It is much harder for a newborn baby, who cannot shiver yet and whose largest area of heat loss is her big head, to keep warm.

The baby can maintain heat by using its brown fat to create warmth, just like a bear or any cold-adapted hibernating animal, although a low-birthweight baby does not have enough brown fat to do this. Muscular activity and crying also help the baby keep warm, and a baby in a cool room will hyperventilate, though one with respiratory depression cannot do this. Another way in which heat loss is reduced is that blood vessels near the surface of the skin tighten up, so increasing tissue insulation, rather like double-glazing over the surface. But babies who have received some drugs from

A bath in warm water can be very comforting for the newborn baby.

OPPOSITE

Slowly, carefully, lovingly . . . sensitive handling is what your newborn needs most after the turbulent journey from womb to world . . .

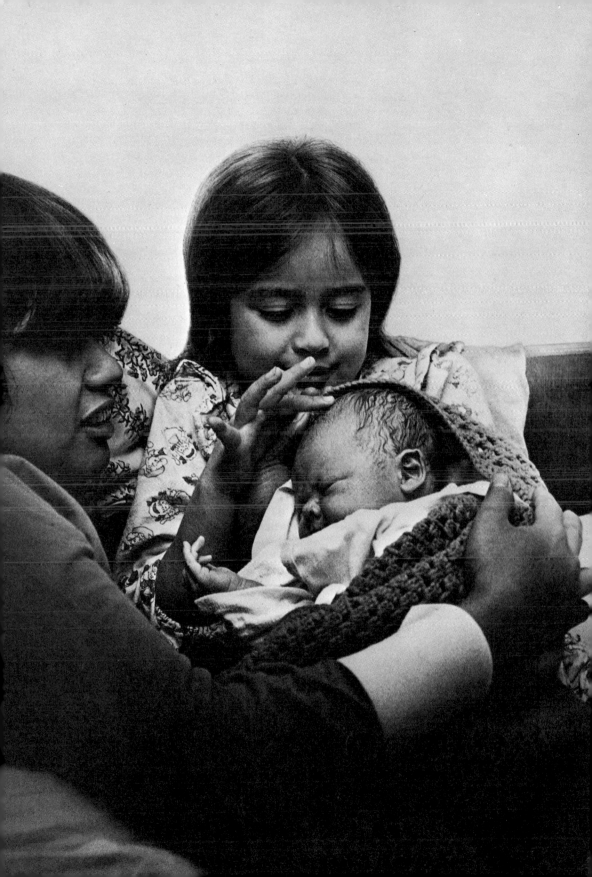

their mothers' bloodstreams, including Demerol and Valium, are not only sedated but unable to prevent heat loss efficiently. So if you want the Leboyer bath to be given, bear in mind that you should not have had Demerol or Valium in the last five hours, that your baby should be full term, weigh more than $5\frac{1}{2}$ lb (2500 g) and should not have had breathing difficulties at delivery.

Parents are sometimes very doubtful about the advantages of the bath, preferring to be in skin contact with their baby and to let him or her suck at the breast indefinitely instead. If a baby is happy lying against his mother and ready to go to the breast after a little while it seems purely ritualistic to insist on putting him in a bath because of preconceived ideas about how babies *ought* to behave.

Dr Michel Odent* uses the bath in a different way. The baby goes first to the mother's arms and sucks if he is rooting; only then is he immersed in a bath, and instead of the doctor bathing the baby the father takes over this responsibility, but close enough to the mother so that she can see and touch too. It can be moving to watch a father doing this first service for his newborn child and to see them both looking for the first time into each other's eyes.

A midwife described what happened in one case when a father bathed his baby in this way: "The baby, who had been resting quietly with its mother, gradually opening its eyes, now seemed to wake to its surroundings and gaze serenely around. It is this serenity which is so remarkable and such a joy to watch. The baby's body was totally immersed in the water, which kept it warm, and gave it total relaxation. After five to ten minutes a midwife took over and gently lifted the baby on to the warmed towel below the overhead heater. Not one cry while all this was going on, and all handling was done with an awareness that the baby had never been handled before and that its skin was acutely sensitive. There were no sudden jerks, movements, or pulling while the baby was being dressed. I now realize that the crying which so often accompanies these tasks is the result of sheer fright."*

Sometimes both parents give the bath together and in some home births the mother bathes with her baby in a well heated bathroom.

After the delivery

Gentle birth does not finish with the minutes after delivery. It is part of a continuum, a flow of interaction between you and your baby beginning in pregnancy and going on into the weeks following childbirth. It is not just a question of how the delivery is conducted or even whether you are able to hold your baby right away. It is a matter of creating an environment in which throughout the 24 hours you have free access to your baby, feel it is yours and can act spontaneously. You need to know that everyone around you understands what you are feeling, and to be confident of emotional support as you learn to be parents and start to discover more about this unique being who has come into the world.

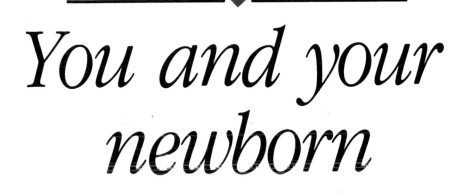

You and your newborn

The first hours of life

The hours immediately following birth are for many women some of the most intense they experience in their lives. A peak experience like that of giving birth does not suddenly end after you have had half an hour holding the baby or terminate conveniently when the lights are turned out. After such a dramatic and exciting time it is not surprising that some women are unable to sleep for a while, and that many remain in a party spirit for hours or even days after.

Unfortunately many hospitals treat the time after birth as a time when, once clean and tidy, you should be quietly resting; if you are too excited to sleep you may be offered sleeping pills or tranquilizers. Most hospitals do not make provision for the continuity of passionate feeling which ensures that motherhood becomes part of you as a person and is not just something which you are trying to learn. These overpowering emotions impel you through the interim period between the time when you feel you know nothing about your baby and are meeting her as a stranger, and the moment when you realize you know *everything* about her and have become centered in this tiny new existence as much as you are in yourself.

I felt I could have got up and danced the rest of the night.

Your first meeting with your newborn

You look down at this new little person, feel the weight of the body as he or she begins to relax after the struggle to birth. The head is the biggest part, the hair silken and perhaps still wet and curled in damp fronds or streaked back as if after a swim. Ears are tiny and carved like convoluted shells and the fingernails too are like the little pink shells you picked up from the sand when you were a child. If the baby is still crying the mouth looks huge, a most efficient organ capable of reaching out and grasping on to the breast for its essential nourishment. And the cry itself, a high-pitched, almost animal wail (though when the baby is sleepier it is more of a lamblike bleat), is well adapted to summon immediate attention, to drive you to find out what is wrong and how you can answer the baby's needs, and to be intensely anxious until you have stilled the crying. It is a biological mechanism of vital importance for survival.

As you hold the baby, the hands start to scan the air, encountering space, meeting the face, perhaps brushing against your body or hand. The fingers move and undulate like sea anemones, starting on the important task of finding out about this new world.

If lights have been dimmed the baby will open wide eyes and look straight at you some time during this process of unfolding. It has been discovered that newborn babies find the human face the most attractive thing to look at, far more so than woolly bunnies or painted ducks, and the moving, speaking human face is best of all.

Testing the newborn

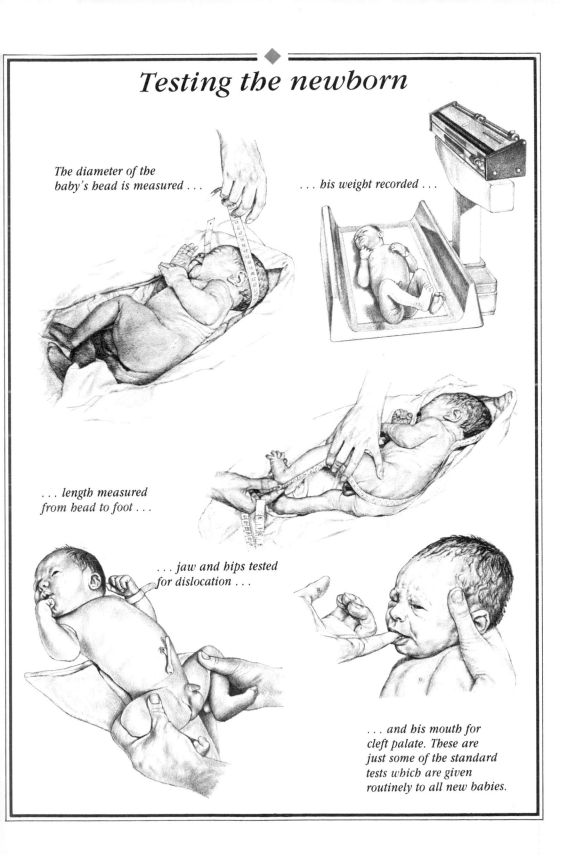

The diameter of the baby's head is measured . . .

. . . his weight recorded . . .

. . . length measured from head to foot . . .

. . . jaw and hips tested for dislocation . . .

. . . and his mouth for cleft palate. These are just some of the standard tests which are given routinely to all new babies.

The experience of bonding

The environment into which the baby is born and the attitude of all those handling the baby are important not only for the baby's sake but for yours too, and for the relationship between you. It is far more difficult for a mother to feel her baby belongs to her and she to it—to *bond*—if she does not have time immediately following birth to begin to get to know her baby*. An important element in this is naked skin contact. The baby should not be wrapped up and turned into a solid little package which you are allowed to hold but not to explore. It should be delivered onto your body and you should be able to put the baby to the breast as soon as it is ready to suck.

Marshall Klaus and John Kennel*, working at a hospital in Cleveland, recommended that mothers should be able to hold their babies naked on the delivery bed and have undisturbed time to get to know them, and should then be encouraged to look after them themselves, with help available if they need it. They should have their babies with them and be responsible for them for at least five hours a day and be given ample emotional support from hospital staff.

Still in many hospitals the hours after birth are considered to be time in which you and your baby are medically processed, during which you must pass tests of fitness before being pronounced not "at risk" and discharged into society.

What tests are carried out?

As soon as the baby is born the midwife or doctor assesses the baby's condition and rates it according to something known as the Apgar scale. This is done by simple observation of the baby's breathing, skin color, muscle tone, and general vitality. The highest number of marks is ten and most babies get seven or over. Once you have had a cuddle a further check is made on the baby. Many women say they like this checkup being done close beside them so that they can see what is happening and can discuss anything that they find worrying with the pediatrician. If the baby stays by your side and never leaves you this will happen as a matter of course.

The Apgar scale

Immediately after birth your baby is tested on five basic points; it is tested again when it is about five minutes old. Even babies who get low marks the first time usually score nine or ten when they are tested the second time.

What is tested	Points given		
	0	1	2
Heart rate	Absent	Below 100 beats per minute	100 beats per minute or more
Breathing	Absent	Slow or irregular	Regular
Skin color	Blue	Body pink, extremities blue	Pink all over
Muscle tone	Limp	Some movements	Active movements
Reflex response	Absent	Grimace only	Cry

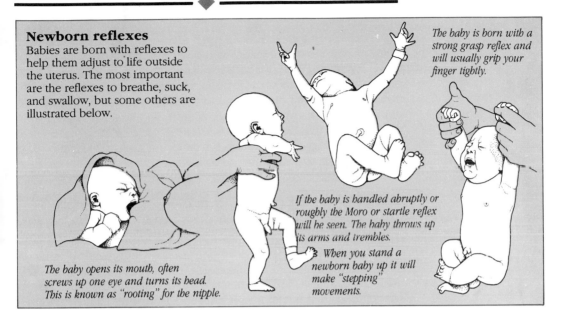

Newborn reflexes

Babies are born with reflexes to help them adjust to life outside the uterus. The most important are the reflexes to breathe, suck, and swallow, but some others are illustrated below.

The baby is born with a strong grasp reflex and will usually grip your finger tightly.

If the baby is handled abruptly or roughly the Moro or startle reflex will be seen. The baby throws up its arms and trembles.

The baby opens its mouth, often screws up one eye and turns its head. This is known as "rooting" for the nipple.

When you stand a newborn baby up it will make "stepping" movements.

The baby's weight and length are recorded. The depth of breathing is noted, whether or not his or her extremities are still blue, whether he or she responds vigorously to stimuli and seems strong and healthy. Certain specific things are looked for, too. These include the head size, a check that the genitals are normal and—in a boy—whether both testes are descending. If the baby has not already passed meconium the anus is checked to ensure that it is formed normally. And the baby's heart is listened to (auscultated). The upper part of the mouth is examined to ensure that the palate is complete, and the legs are gently bent up and circled outward to make sure that there is no dislocation of the hips. Gentle feeling of the baby's tummy will disclose whether the liver and spleen are the right size and feeling around the top of the baby's head reveals the state of the skull bones. In many states it is law that prophylactic eye treatment must be introduced into the baby's eyes to prevent blindness from gonorrheal infection. This may be a silver nitrate solution or an antibiotic solution or ointment. The baby may also get an injection or oral dose of Vitamin K.

Relating to your baby

Unfortunately sometimes the adjustment of mother and baby to each other is treated as of secondary importance to this process of medical screening. As a result many new mothers lack confidence in handling and relating to their babies. Much of what is called "postnatal depression" probably results from a mother's inability to relate to her baby; it feels to her as if the baby belongs not to her, but to the hospital. It can be even more difficult for a man to feel that his baby belongs to him than it is for a woman. In one Stockholm maternity hospital men were shown how to handle, change, bathe, and weigh their babies and were helped to understand the emotional and physical stresses of pregnancy and birth of their partners. This was done on two separate occasions while the women were in the postpartum ward. It was discovered that these fathers became more involved in baby care later on and it seemed that they were more understanding than another group of fathers who had not been given the chance to become involved with their babies in this way.

Research shows that *both* parents need an unhurried and peaceful time with their baby in the hour following delivery.

HOW YOUR BABY MAY LOOK

Your new baby may have a low, sloping forehead, a receding chin, hair in sideburns (low on the brow, in the nape of the neck, and sometimes down the back as well), an odd, bumpy-shaped head which has been molded like a ripe grapefruit in its passage down the birth canal, a squashed boxer's nose, and blotchy skin. Yet to most new parents their baby looks beautiful! You respond in a protective, caring way to the wonder of this new human being who has come out of the inner depths of your body, having been pressed and kneaded and squeezed out of the uterus and down the vagina to the outside world and into your waiting arms.

Even if you are unaware of feeling anything remarkable at the time, you will probably look back at those moments as being special, as you piece together the fragments of the birth experience and place it in its setting of life lived. This kind of reflection and thinking back is especially important after a difficult labor and probably comes spontaneously to most women if they allow themselves time and do not try to forget about what happened to them.

How the baby has had to adjust

Enormous changes occur as the baby adjusts to the challenges of an extrauterine existence. One of the most dramatic things that happens, though unseen, is the change from fetal to newborn circulation, with the blood flowing along different pathways. When the baby is inside you all the blood flows in and out through the umbilical cord and bypasses the lungs which do not need to function (see page 66). And since the placenta is doing much of the work that will later be performed by the baby's liver and kidneys, little blood needs to be carried to these organs in the intrauterine state.

At birth the first great gasp of air causes pressure changes in the whole circulatory system so that blood enters the lungs, liver and kidneys. The increased pressure in these organs brings about the collapse of the umbilical blood vessels and of the bypasses around lungs, liver and kidneys. Once these pressure changes have taken place the system goes on working for a lifetime and the blood vessels which are no longer used waste away.

Why your baby may look strange

Many things you notice about your baby may worry you. It helps to understand the wide range of the normal and to realize that the baby may look very different once it has uncrumpled after a few days.

Lanugo The dark hair which may be over large parts of the newborn's body, especially if it is premature, is called lanugo and drops out over the next week or so. The hair on the head is often a different shade from that which will grow in a few weeks' time as the original hair gradually disappears. One of my babies was born with almost black hair and in a few months was a flaxen blond.

Vernix The creamy substance which may be on the baby's skin, sometimes covering it thickly, is vernix. It is produced by skin cells as they drop off into the amniotic fluid and forms a protective coating. Vernix is gradually absorbed, so it is not necessary to wipe it off, except on the head, where it tends to stick to the hair, and in the folds and creases under the arms, in the neck and the groin.

Caput Some babies are born with a peculiar bump like a large blister on their heads, often just off center. This is where the head was pressing down through the inadequately dilated cervix before the second stage of labor; the swelling does not affect the baby's brain, and will gradually go. The bump is known as a caput.

Some babies are born without any covering of vernix; others are still quite thickly coated with it.

Molding Usually the brow is sloped back and rather low in the newborn baby, but some babies have high, domed heads like figures in an Egyptian hieroglyph. This is the result of molding of the head of a baby who was posterior.

A baby who was presenting by the face is usually very swollen, bruised and puffy but, again, this gradually goes.

Mongolian spots Some babies have patches of slate blue skin on their tummies or backs. These are called "Mongolian spots", are nothing to do with mental handicap or Down syndrome, and are completely harmless. They occur most often in families of Asian and Mediterranean origin.

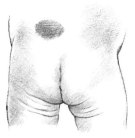

Mongolian blue spots look like bruises and gradually fade with time.

Sexual characteristics A newborn baby's genitals can look very large, especially if the baby is premature. Sometimes there is milk in the breasts of both girl and boy babies (called "witches' milk"). It is harmless and disappears without treatment. It is a result of withdrawal of estrogen received from the mother's bloodstream and the action of prolactin released by the baby's pituitary. Some baby girls even have a kind of period—pseudo-menstruation—as the result of the withdrawal of maternal estrogen. Again, it is nothing to worry about, and stops within a few days.

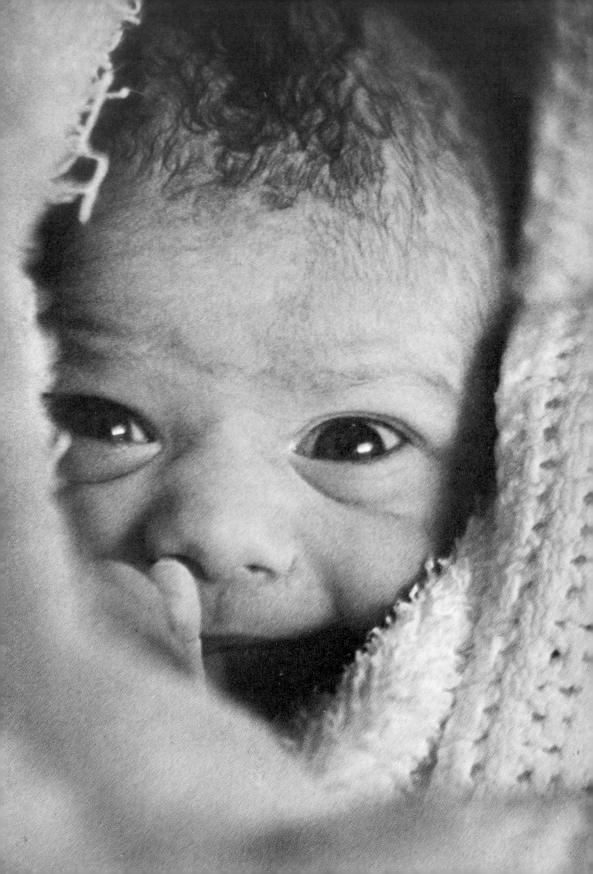

Bonding as a gradual process

Some of the reactions that you have to your newborn baby are instinctive. You respond to the sight of the baby's plumpness, the rounded head, the large forehead, the smell of the skin, the bright gaze of her eyes which look as if they say "So that is who you are!", to the baby's cry, her exploring hands and mouth, and to her vigorous movement, and the extraordinary compactness of her neat little body. But even instinctive behavior needs the right setting if it is to be released and unfold into appropriate nurturing. Then you can go on to learn from the baby how to respond to her signals.

Bonding is often talked about as if it were instant glue which sticks a mother and baby together the minute after delivery, and some women who do not spend the time after the birth with their babies worry that they have failed a test in motherhood and are anxious that this will have lasting effects. In fact bonding is a gradually unfolding process which only *starts* then and develops during each hour you and your baby are together. During all this time you are learning about each other and further physical changes in you are triggered off by stimuli provided by the baby. The most obvious of these is the milk ejection reflex (let down response), which is stimulated by the baby's crying and searching for the nipple, the touch of his mouth against the breast, and his sucking.

One aspect of hospital care which Klaus and Kennel stress is the way in which doctors and nurses can support the family—not just the mother, father, and baby, but also other children. Older brothers and sisters should be able to have close contact with the baby too and be made welcome in the hospital. In practice, some hospitals are restrictive about sibling visiting.*

The importance of the time after birth

Wherever you are having a baby, and even if you are "high risk" and need obstetric help, provision should be made for a quiet, intimate time together after birth during which you can begin to feel that you belong to each other. It can be done in a big teaching hospital just as it can in a small unit and *it is part of the job of the hospital to create that environment for each mother, each father, and each baby.* Discuss it with your doctor. It is only when doctors, nurses, and midwives know what women want that they will be sufficiently tuned in to offer the loving environment which is every baby's birthright.

The minutes, hours, and days after birth are a time for emotional "work" which may be no less significant in the lives of the newborn baby and of both parents than the sheer physical work of labor. The hospital should provide an environment which supports these unfolding emotional processes. New mothers and fathers do not need to be shown how to develop a relationship with their babies. They do need, however, to feel that they are among friends, to be handed the baby at birth, and to be left in peace and privacy together.

OPPOSITE
Cocooned in the cradle of your arms . . . the most comforting security in the first hours of life . . .

The baby who needs special care

About 6 per cent of all babies weigh $5\frac{1}{2}$ lb (2500 g) or less (the internationally agreed definition of a low-birthweight baby). Such babies can be divided into two categories—preterm and small for dates—and they will probably require special care.

Half or more of low-birthweight babies are born too soon—preterm or premature babies. There seems to be no obvious reason why such babies should be expelled from the uterus so early, and research is still being carried out into the causes of preterm delivery.

Small for dates babies are born at the right time but have not flourished in the uterus in the last months of pregnancy for a variety of reasons. Sometimes this happens because of malnutrition in the mother, her smoking, high blood pressure or preeclampsia, because the placenta has not been working well (placental insufficiency), or because she was carrying twins or more. These undernourished babies often have difficulty during labor, are short of oxygen, and have problems with breathing after delivery. They may suffer from hypoglycemia (low blood sugar, see opposite) and have convulsions. A few small for dates babies, however, are small right through pregnancy for genetic, chromosomal, or other reasons.

I spent long hours in the nursery just watching my baby or cuddling him through the incubator portholes. Sometimes I cried a little.

The baby with poor temperature control

Low-birthweight babies may have problems during labor too and are also more likely to have poor temperature control, because there is very little fat under the skin. They may be jaundiced, difficult to feed, and susceptible to infection. Their skin is usually red because the blood vessels are visible through the thin layer of fat. Such babies are kept warm in a nursery which is warmer than the wards and are cared for in incubators. A thermostat may be strapped to a baby's tummy so that the temperature can be regulated according to his or her needs. Sometimes a baby is placed under a plastic heat shield and wears a hat. Tiny babies who are kept warm grow faster*.

The baby with breathing difficulties

Premature and low-birthweight babies may have interrupted breathing (apnea) in the early days. This is why a very tiny baby is nursed on a special mattress which sets off an alarm if breathing stops. All that is usually needed to start the baby's breathing is a little stimulation of the baby by touch.

One in every ten premature babies has insufficient surfactant in its lungs. Surfactant reduces the surface tension in the lungs, allowing them to expand and stopping them deflating entirely with each breath out; it normally develops before the baby is ready to be born.

A baby usually inflates its lungs with the first breath after delivery and they pop open like parachutes. With the first breath out, half the air is retained, so that breathing after this is much easier. The baby who has not enough surfactant has to work hard to breathe and may become exhausted in the struggle to get enough air. It breathes very quickly, its chest collapses with each breath out, and it looks blue and grunts as it breathes. This condition is called respiratory distress or hyaline membrane disease. It is obviously important in these cases to give the baby oxygen and to help its breathing.

Other babies who may suffer from respiratory distress are those born to diabetic mothers (even though they are large babies), those who have not had sufficient oxygen during labor, those delivered by cesarean section (see page 308), and babies who develop pneumonia as a result of infection.

If the pediatrician decides to give the baby oxygen, a small catheter is inserted through the cord stump into an artery so that blood samples can be taken about every three hours to test the amount of oxygen in the baby's blood.

Oxygen can be given with continuous positive pressure so that the baby's lungs are kept open. A tiny catheter is inserted through the baby's nostrils, or a face mask or headbox is used. Another method is to apply negative pressure around the baby's chest so that he or she does not have to work hard to breathe. The baby is put into a machine that looks like a miniature iron lung with a neck seal, so that all you can see is the head. Sometimes a mechanical ventilator is used, which takes over all the work of breathing for the baby.

The baby with low blood sugar

A baby may have low blood sugar (hypoglycemia) if it has a low birthweight or is premature and also if its mother is diabetic or if the delivery was difficult. The hypoglycemic baby may have breathing difficulties and be jittery or lie limp and apathetic.

Treatment involves making sure that the baby is getting ample nourishment, so the pediatrician may decide to set up an intravenous glucose drip. It is because of the risk of hypoglycemia that a very tiny baby may be given additional feedings, even though there are no obvious symptoms of low blood sugar.

Neonatal jaundice

If your baby looks beautifully suntanned as if just back from a cruise in the Bahamas, he or she has jaundice. A newborn baby has a surplus of red blood cells which are broken down after birth. During this process a yellowish substance called bilirubin is produced, which has to be excreted by the baby's liver. Sometimes the liver is unable to cope rapidly enough with the large amount of bilirubin and it builds up in the blood, giving the skin a yellowish tinge.

It was difficult to believe he was mine, fighting for life in the incubator, red like a boiled lobster, and pathetic little arms and legs and bulging eyes like a frog. I didn't feel anything except pity.

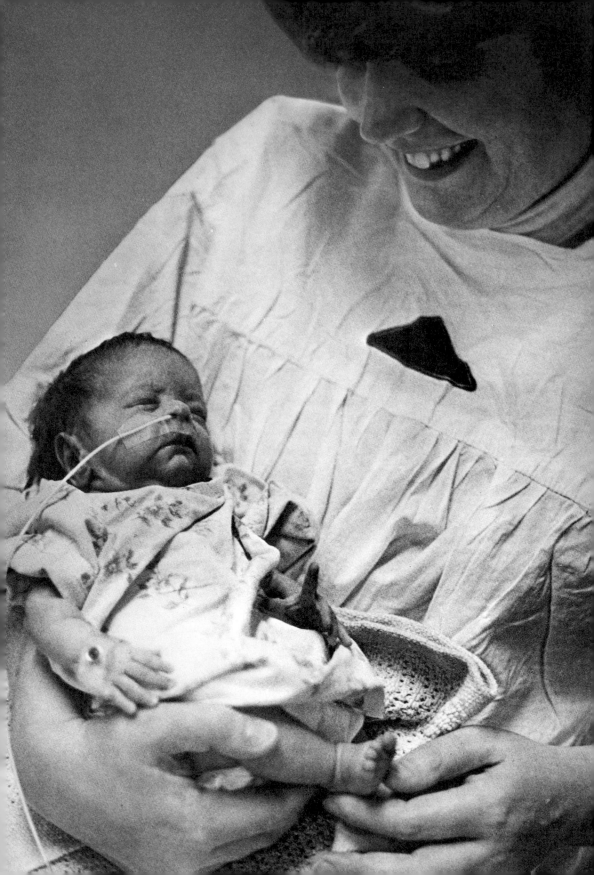

Physiological jaundice About half of all babies develop jaundice. It is usually harmless and is then called physiological jaundice. Jaundice is most likely to develop after the second day of life and to disappear after a week. In premature babies jaundice tends to be most marked on about the fifth or sixth day of life and to go on longer—often for ten days or more.

A jaundiced baby needs sunlight and frequent feeding. If you have the chance, put your baby beside a window and, if it is warm enough, uncover the baby so that light can reach its limbs and trunk.

Jaundiced babies tend to get very sleepy and do not readily wake. Yet they should have plenty of fluids to cope with the bilirubin, so need to be roused for feedings—perhaps every two hours.

If the bilirubin level is high, the pediatrician may decide to use phototherapy on a baby to bring the level down. This light treatment produces a photochemical breakdown of bilirubin into substances which are then passed out in the urine. The baby is blindfolded so that the light cannot possibly harm its eyesight. This can be distressing for a mother who feels out of touch with her baby when she cannot make eye contact with it. When you lift your baby away from the light for its feeding, take off the eye covering.

Hemolytic jaundice Pediatricians always watch the jaundiced baby carefully because, although neonatal jaundice is a common and not very serious complaint, the baby may be jaundiced as a result of a blood group incompatibility between the mother and baby. This is called hemolytic jaundice and can damage the baby's nervous system and brain cells. Sometimes too the jaundice is associated with infection, with a metabolic condition such as low blood sugar, or even with the administration of drugs to the mother in pregnancy.

Feeding the baby in special care

It has been shown that very small babies do best if they are fed soon after delivery,* so a low-birthweight baby may be given a milk feeding within two hours of birth. The best food is its own mother's breast milk, but this will take a few days to be produced in quantity. The baby can, however, be put to the breast if strong enough to suck, to derive benefit from the protein and antibodies in the colostrum that is already there (see page 350). Supplements of Vitamins D and K are often given, and if phosphate in the baby's bloodstream falls, supplementary phosphates, too.

A baby who cannot suck is usually fed through a small, soft catheter, a nasogastric tube, which is passed through a nostril down into the stomach. Feedings should be small and frequent—about every half hour—or a slow continuous drip is often best for a sick baby. If your baby is being fed in this way it is usually possible for you to help with the feedings once you can express your own breast milk. If you have any difficulties, contact one of the breastfeeding organizations which are listed on page 383.

OPPOSITE
Even if your baby has to spend some time after birth in special care, she still needs your loving presence.

Relating to the baby in special care

Your baby may look lost and lonely if she has to be cared for in an incubator. You will feel she belongs to you if you talk to her and touch her reassuringly through the portholes.

I looked at her lying there with tubes and adhesive tape everywhere and I felt a wave of longing to grab her and pull out all the equipment and take her away with me.

It is distressing for parents to see their baby in intensive care, attached to tubes and wires, isolated in an incubator. They may feel as if the baby is just another interesting specimen. Very low-birthweight babies look so fragile and weird that it can be difficult to see them as real people: your baby may look to you like an odd, misshapen doll or a little animal and not your child at all. On the other hand you may feel passionately that the baby belongs to you and want to grab it away from all the machines and other contraptions so as to hold it close. The obvious skills of those working with sophisticated technology can make parents feel clumsy and awkward so that they lack confidence to handle their baby. Yet it is important to do this. *All* babies need touching and talking to and, if they are well enough to be taken in your arms, they like being cuddled. If your baby is in an incubator, you can stroke her through the portholes. Tender, loving care may be just as important for the health of your baby as modern medical technology.

Many hospitals now have rooms where mothers of babies in special care can stay to be close to them, help look after them, and breastfeed them. It is better for both mother and baby and makes it easier to build close links between them if the mother stays in the special care unit rather than merely visiting. When a woman can start to look after her baby herself, she begins to feel that her baby belongs to her. One intensive care unit has rooms where babies are cared for by their mothers, with a glass wall at the side of the baby's cubicle so that nurses can keep a constant eye on the babies. A nurse in this unit said: "One thing the nurses must not do is to take away responsibility for the baby. We always try to make a mother feel it is her baby, even when it is very small and sick."

Losing a baby

Many women know what it is like to have an interrupted pregnancy, although the distress caused by even an early miscarriage is often underestimated. Stillbirth, on the other hand, is now rare. But still today, for a small number of women, the birth is also a death.

Women who make the painful decision to have an abortion, because of fetal handicap, or for any other reason, may grieve deeply, too. This is so even though they know they have made the best possible choice in the circumstances and have behaved sensibly. Abortion should never be dismissed as simply getting rid of an unwanted pregnancy. Yet it is still largely a taboo subject, and women often have to go through the experience alone, without help, deprived of the emotional support they need, and socially isolated.

It might seem easier for people to sympathize with a woman whose baby dies at birth. Yet often they do not know how to help and they withdraw from her grief in embarrassment. After all the happy expectations and preparations the woman has made, she goes through a labor which culminates in the delivery of a stillborn baby, or a frail or handicapped baby who dies a week or so after birth. Her arms are empty and she is left alone. The more we reduce perinatal mortality, the more isolated is the woman whose baby dies.

MISCARRIAGE

A miscarriage usually comes as a shock, yet one in every five pregnancies probably ends in miscarriage or "spontaneous abortion". In three out of four cases this occurs before the tenth week and sometimes even before the woman realizes she is pregnant.

Threatened miscarriage

In the first three months of pregnancy, you may notice a heavy feeling around your pelvis and in the pit of your tummy and have periodlike twinges and aches.

Sometimes you may have bleeding that is really a suppressed period. This happens when there is insufficient pregnancy hormone to stop your period, even though it will be scanty. Such bleeding is not a miscarriage and the blood comes from the endometrium, not from the placenta or the baby. Sometimes this too occurs at the time when each period would have been due, and right through the early months of pregnancy each would-be period is marked by slight bleeding. Your doctor may advise you to have injections of progesterone to stop this bleeding.

If you have any bleeding or pinkish staining of mucus from your vagina, probably the best treatment is rest in bed. The blood that you see is not the baby's blood but yours, and comes from the maternal side of the placenta where it is not adhering to the uterus, or from around the cervix. Lying down increases the blood flow to your uterus and, if the placenta is not firmly rooted, gives it a chance to attach itself more firmly to the lining of the uterus.

Inevitable abortion

An "inevitable abortion" is a miscarriage which occurs because the baby is no longer alive and, whatever you do, the bleeding is bound to continue. If the fetal heart cannot be detected by ultrasound (see page 202), the abortion is inevitable and you might just as well be up and about and let it run its course. If ultrasound picks up the baby's heartbeat, there is only a 10 per cent chance that you will miscarry, even though you may go on bleeding for a while.

Possible causes of early miscarriage

The cause of early miscarriage is often not known. Fortunately defective embryos with abnormalities that would not allow them to survive after birth are usually miscarried, and a large proportion of miscarriages are probably the natural way of getting rid of imperfect babies. Sometimes there has been no development beyond the very early stages of segmentation and what is termed a blighted ovum is passed. It is estimated that one in six miscarriages results from fertilized eggs that do not develop properly.

Don't believe it when they say it doesn't matter if you lose a baby early in pregnancy. This was my baby and I wanted her, not just any baby, but that special baby.

After it had been noted that more women than usual miscarry in early pregnancy during flu epidemics it was discovered that a high fever can result in miscarriage. There is more about this on page 102. Sometimes the presence of uterine fibroids (common in older mothers) or an oddly formed uterus means that there is not enough space for the pregnancy to develop.

Late miscarriage

Miscarriage after the 12th week of pregnancy is about three times as rare as early miscarriage. Miscarriages are more likely to occur as you grow older (over 35), if you have had difficulty in conceiving (if it has taken more than six months), and if you have had two or more previous miscarriages. If you have had only one miscarriage before, there is no obvious reason why the next pregnancy should not be straightforward. After three miscarriages there is a 50/50 chance of miscarrying again, so talk to your doctor *before* you become pregnant and plan extra rest from the first days after possible conception.

"Incompetent" cervix Late miscarriage is often the result of a weak or "incompetent" cervix which starts to dilate long before it should. The bag of waters is wedged between the baby and the cervix and ruptures as the cervix starts to dilate, so the first sign may be the breaking of the waters. This type of miscarriage is particularly likely if a woman has already repeatedly miscarried in mid-pregnancy. An incompetent cervix may be the result of a previous abortion, if it was done after the 12th week, or a previous difficult labor. There is more information about an incompetent cervix on page 105.

Placental insufficiency Miscarriage after the 20th week may mean that the placenta has failed to function in servicing the baby. (After 28 weeks the loss of the baby is termed a stillbirth.) If there is evidence of poor placental function and inadequate growth of the baby in the uterus, bedrest will allow a better flow of blood through the placenta to the baby. One of the ways in which you can affect the efficiency of the placenta is by making sure that you have a good diet during pregnancy. If you have had a miscarriage, it is a good idea to start a high-standard diet before you become pregnant again (see page 86). If you have had a series of miscarriages, keep any large blood clots from the latest one (a vacuum-sealed jar is suitable) for the doctor to see and perhaps have tested in a laboratory.

Guilt about a miscarriage

Every woman who has had a miscarriage wonders if anything she did or failed to do caused it. A miscarriage can happen at any time so that most women will be able to think of some event that might have triggered it off. You had a row with someone in the office, your mother-in-law came to stay, you slipped in the street, had just had intercourse, or were overtired from a party the night before. But, whatever your guilty suspicions, none of these things has been shown to cause miscarriage. However, it can be difficult to convince yourself that you are in no way responsible.

Grieving for the lost baby

Talk with your partner about your feelings. Even if you have not yet felt fetal movements, the loss of your baby is sometimes emotionally shattering. If you have had miscarriage after miscarriage or are slow to conceive, you may experience every single period as the loss of a baby and grieve as a result. This grieving is necessary for you to be able to look forward to the future with confidence in yourself as a "real woman". Suppressed grief always causes trouble later.

Your partner, however, may not have accepted the reality of the pregnancy by the time you miscarry and so it can be difficult for him to understand why you need to mourn, but it will help you if he can give time to listen. Or you may find you can talk more easily with another woman who has been through a miscarriage herself.

After it is all over, the longing to start another pregnancy can interfere with relaxed and spontaneous sex. And the more anxious you are to conceive the more tense you become and the less likely to get pregnant. If you feel that you are getting anxious and that this is spoiling your sexual relationship, try having a vacation from each other and coming together again at the time when you expect to be ovulating (see pages 56 and 367).

STILLBIRTH

"I'm so sorry. Your baby has died." Almost every expectant mother has thought at some time that someone might say these words to her. For some women it is a nagging fear which haunts them and threatens to punish them for negative feelings they have about the baby and becoming a mother or for daring to expect too much of the birth and the baby. Sometimes, not as often as in the past, but nevertheless in about 10 out of every 1000 births, it really happens and the baby dies before, during, or shortly after birth.

The experience of loss

In spite of everything that anyone can do you are suddenly confronted with the experience of loss. This is a loss not only of the baby, but of all the hopes and expectations of yourselves as parents and the new images of the self that have been built up through pregnancy.

Nothing can take away the suffering that comes as a result of stillbirth. This is so even when the care given to you is loving and sympathetic, though such emotional support can help you gradually deal with the experience and eventually come to terms with it. Unfortunately some members of hospital staff cannot cope with their own feelings of guilt and distress when a baby dies, and you may be left alone in your room, avoided as much as possible by nurses and doctors who do not want to "upset" you by referring to what has happened. When they do talk to you, they may urge you to put it behind you, say that you will forget what happened when you have another baby, or tell you to think of your partner. The more such advice is given the longer the experience may take to live through.

The task of grieving is a personal and intimate one. It consists of slowly and painfully—and sometimes you may feel that you will never succeed—integrating the experience into the total pattern of your life and finding a place for it in which it has meaning. Once you have done this you will be able to stand back from it a little and will no longer be overwhelmed by it. This process cannot be hurried and, if an attempt is made to force the pace, grieving will be delayed and you may be overpowered by grief at a later stage of your life.

Stillbirth in Third World societies

A hundred years ago everyone expected a certain proportion of babies to die. You bore ten and reared six if you were lucky. In many Third World countries even today babies are not named or publicly spoken of for the first few weeks because the chances are that they will not survive. It has been suggested that the mothers themselves are able to remain slightly emotionally detached from a new baby whose life may be transitory*.

In these societies death is incorporated into the web of life and there are supportive rituals to deal with it, whereas we are ill-prepared in Western society for facing death. We each struggle to find

> ❝
> *We were left alone together and we sat and held her. She was perfectly formed. We wept together. It was a very important time for us.*
> ❞

our own way and often feel that we are the only people who have ever faced such emotional upheavals. Death is a shocking intrusion into the normality of existence.

Facing up to the loss

If professional helpers know that something is going wrong with your birth, you have a right to expect them to give you information, discuss the difficulties openly and honestly, and stand by you as you try to cope emotionally with what is happening. Women who have been through this ordeal say that it helped to realize that they were being told the truth and to be fully involved rather than shielded from the event by the mystique of medical practice.

If your baby dies while still inside the uterus, you know that you are carrying a dead baby. It is as if your uterus, a place of life, has become a grave. The obstetrician may advise that it is safer to wait to go into labor naturally, which often happens within a couple of weeks, but may offer you induction if you wish. Many women feel an urgent need to "get it over with"; others that they want to spend the last remaining days possible with the baby inside them.

When something so distressing happens, there is no easy "solution", no one course of action that can wipe out the anguish. Sometimes a man asks what he can say or do to help his partner and to make the suffering less, or other family members or friends want to help but do not know what to do. People are so different in their responses to loss that the most helpers can do is to make themselves available, to reach out, and be ready to receive whatever the bereaved person wants to tell them, without holding back for fear of intruding or feeling embarrassment at her grief. The most valuable thing they can offer is a *waiting silence*, without tension or unnecessary words, so that the sufferer's pain can flow into them.

I wish I'd asked to see him. It all happened so fast. Now I long to have seen him and held him. But it's too late.

Mourning for the baby

This may sound simple, but in fact it can be very difficult, because grieving is not just a matter of tears and sadness, but also numb shock and guilt and anger, all of which are felt at different phases of the experience. It is not easy to acknowledge destructive guilt, and perhaps even harder to cope with anger which may involve hostility against people, including doctors and nurses, who tried to help.

For you the time immediately following the death of a baby may be one of frozen half-awareness of what has happened and it is often not till three weeks or so afterward that you begin to live through these other phases of grieving.

It is sometimes difficult for a mother to mourn her stillborn baby because she never really knew this person over whom she is grieving. It can be still more difficult if you have not *seen* the dead baby and realized that your bulging tummy held a living creature that has since died. This is why some pediatricians think it is a good idea for a mother to touch her stillborn child and encourage her to do so.

The baby's burial

You and your partner may wish to discuss together arrangements for the baby's burial. Some women do not wish to know where the baby is buried, but others do. It is up to you to learn as much or as little as you wish to know. Some women feel afterwards that perhaps the baby was a figment of their imagination and never existed at all. It was removed from them like a tooth which was causing trouble and extracted. You may think of your baby's body being handled with indifference and lie wondering what "they" did with it.

The effect on your relationships

Being depressed affects all our relationships with other people, including those we love and need most. Though the death of a baby may draw you and your partner closer together, it introduces stresses into the relationship which may be too severe for you to cope with. You may both need help from other people. Your partner has to grieve too and yet may feel that it is "unmanly" for him to show weakness and that he must be strong to support you. The result may be that he simulates a matter-of-fact acceptance of the inevitable and leaves you feeling isolated because he does not understand.

If the baby lived for a time and went to the special care nursery, your partner probably had a chance to go there and see and touch the baby while you may have stayed in the ward. So you rely on his descriptions and the details he can give you to be able to build up a complete picture. Yet a man who is himself depressed and grieving may find it difficult to talk about such things without showing his own distress and may resist it, so giving you the impression that he is holding back on vital information.

Losing a baby almost invariably causes a deterioration in the couple's sexual relationship too. It is difficult to feel sexually excited when you are depressed. And even as time goes on, when you are beginning to "function" again, feelings of pleasure can be followed by a rush of grief. When you start to enjoy life again, even when you start to feel sexually aroused, you may both feel at times that you are betraying your dead child*. So both of you need to give understanding to each other.

If you have lost your baby and want to be in touch with others who have gone through this experience, contact the Compassionate Friends or one of the organizations listed on page 383.

THE NEXT PREGNANCY

If you are pregnant following an abortion or if you have lost a previous baby as a result of miscarriage or stillbirth, or if your baby died after birth, the previous experience tends to cast its shadow forward. Strangely, this tends to happen even if you really did not want that particular pregnancy to continue.

A woman who has lost a baby through accident, who has had miscarriages, for example, or a crib death, may feel angry that the emotions of one who has had an abortion should be discussed in the same context as her own ordeal and even that the woman who got rid of a baby deserves whatever happens to her. Yet the experience of loss may be equally haunting and the sense of guilt even greater.

We tend to compare and contrast the progress of the present pregnancy with past pregnancies. If a previous pregnancy had an unhappy outcome, it colors our view of the whole experience and it is natural to become acutely conscious of risks and dangers. We do not always realize that this is what we are doing, since a common way of trying to deal with fear and anxiety about repeating a distressing experience is to attempt to shut out thoughts of it, to protect ourselves from the painful experience of yet another failure.

A woman who feels guilty about aborting a previous baby or who feels somehow responsible for a miscarriage may transfer this guilt to the present pregnancy and be anxious that she is going to have a terrible labor, bear an abnormal baby, or lose the baby as a kind of retribution or punishment. It is not a rational or even necessarily a conscious thinking through of the risks, but a kind of primitive expectation that automatic punishment comes from the gods.

If you try to forget what happened or to put it to the back of your mind, you will be unprepared for the emotions that may assail you in situations of stress, when you have a vaginal examination or when you go into the hospital. And when labor starts you may find that you cannot help thinking back to the loss of the other baby.

You may tell yourself to be sensible and not to dwell on negative thoughts. Though understandable, this is rarely successful. You are right to acknowledge your feelings and also justified in getting those who care for you to take them seriously. But do not leave this till the end of pregnancy and certainly not until you go into labor. Try to find the kind of preparation for birth and parenthood that includes frank and open acceptance of any previous unhappy experience.

In a pregnancy following the loss of the baby women often experience painful, disturbing dreams about bearing a damaged child or losing the baby and feel that in some awful way this is their own fault. The dreams may be clearly about birth and babies or may be heavily disguised. The baby is often represented in such dreams as a doll or small animal or one's own tooth or limb, and death as the irretrievable loss of anything that is treasured.

You may feel that you are carrying a baby of the same sex as the previous one or even that you are pregnant with the child you lost before. That is one way of trying to cope with the painful experience. In fact, some people even say, "Have another baby and you'll forget about it." But of course you cannot really substitute one baby for another or replace a lost baby by getting pregnant again. It is vital for both you and the baby you are bearing that you work through to an acknowledgment that this baby is its own unique self.

The joy of another pregnancy may be suffused with grief at the loss of your previous baby.

The first ten days

It is recognized that a woman who bears a child who is handicapped or ill, or who has a baby who dies, needs to pass through a period of grieving. It is less well understood that for *any* woman the time immediately after birth is experienced as a loss which she needs to grieve over, however perfect the baby. As a new mother you are on the threshold of a new beginning which entails the death of some aspects of your self and, with the birth of a first baby, the relinquishing of the self as child and as adolescent.

EMOTIONS AFTER DELIVERY
Unexpected emotions

Many women need time to part with the fantasy baby which they carried inside them before they can come to terms with the real baby who has been born. The real baby is often astonishingly different from the one they imagined they were bearing. The death of a fantasy which has been cherished can be a painful process. It is especially threatening if the baby is premature and needs to have special care, or if it suffers from any form of handicap. But even a healthy, mature baby may be so unlike what you expected that you cannot come to terms with its reality or with the fact that it turns you into a mother with different responsibilities from those you had before, who is emotionally committed to that baby for every minute of every day.

Changes in mood

All the intense feelings you have during the hours and days after giving birth have a biological survival value for the baby. Without them you would be just a caretaker. Sometimes your emotions are mind-moving and if you had not just had a baby would rightly be thought pathological. But during the first week after birth they are perfectly normal and experienced by many more women than ever openly admit to them.

It is not just a matter of depression. In fact you may feel you are on a permanent high. But it is likely that at some time during the first five days after the birth you will experience an abrupt drop in mood and a sudden feeling of depression. Your stitches are uncomfortable, the hospital routine is intolerable, you start to worry about the baby or whether you will be a good mother, or you simply feel flat because the party is over and it is now "the morning after the night before." Then again you may experience violent mood swings and feel you are on an emotional roller-coaster in the days immediately after the birth. You are probably more likely to feel like this if you usually have pronounced mood swings anyway. Our society often has a very

OPPOSITE

A mother "teases" her newborn with the nipple . . . soon her baby will be enjoying one of the great pleasures of the early months of life . . .

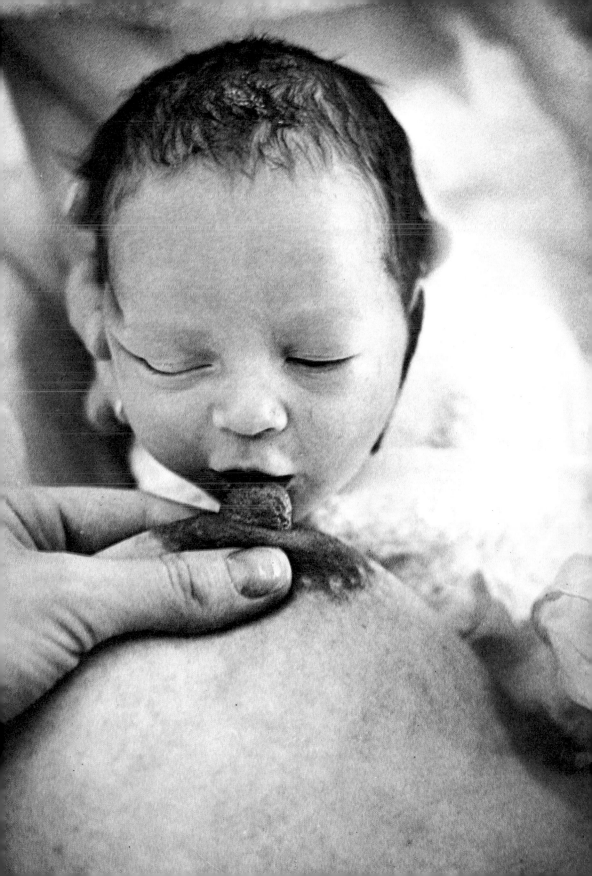

romanticized stereotype of the new mother in a frothy pink negligée, a cherubic baby in her arms. The violent mood swings of the post-partum period can come as a shock because they are so different from the way you think you *ought* to feel.

Needing to behave spontaneously

You do not become a different person once you have had a baby: it is just that all the colors of your personality may become more vivid. This is why you may want to cry and then a short while later laugh helplessly at something which is not really very funny. And this is why indignation you may feel about something or someone in the hospital—and above all longing for your baby if he or she is in a nursery—seems to have a physical impact, knotting your stomach, drying your throat, burning you up.

> *The hospital was so busy and there was so little opportunity to sleep that I came out exhausted.*

Some women who have their babies in the hospital are emotionally unstable until they get home. For them an institutional setting for the postpartum experience is unsettling and confusing. They seem to have a great need to be *in their own place*. There is nothing abnormal about you if you feel like this. The important thing is to acknowledge the kind of person you are and for your partner to accept it too and make arrangements decisively and as speedily as possible.

If all seems to be well with you and the baby, the best thing is to arrange to leave the hospital as soon as possible. Ask to see the pediatrician and let him or her know how you feel. A visiting nurse will visit you at home if you wish.

The complexity of your emotions

Your partner may be experiencing violent emotions himself at this time; he too may be torn between laughter and tears after the delivery. Our society tends to stress that men ought to be strong and

Being in a hospital ward where the atmosphere is friendly means that you can discuss your baby and any worries that you might have with other mothers.

offer wide shoulders for the new mother to lean on, but in fact some men are so deeply touched by the experience of birth that they undergo much the same emotional turmoil as the new mother. A new father may suffer acutely on leaving the hospital, because he is surrendering you and his baby to the care of strangers. In spite of the rejoicing and excitement, there may be a strange undercurrent of grief. The intimate bond linking him to the woman who has borne his child is cut by an enforced separation. When he returns to the hospital it is to come as a visitor.

The awful thing was having to go away and leave them both in the hospital 1½ hours after the birth. The separation then was very hard to bear and I felt quite sick.

YOUR CHANGED BODY

After you have had a baby you encounter your body in a dramatically changed state. Whereas before you enjoyed your smooth body heavy with fruit, the curve of your abdomen like an enormous melon still awaiting the harvest of birth, you may feel after delivery astonishingly alone, bereft, and empty. If you are in the hospital without people you love near you, in the care of people who treat you as just another "mom" or worse still as an involuting uterus, a sutured perineum, and a couple of lactating breasts, you need time to come to terms with your changed body and to rediscover yourself as a person.

For many women the euphoria of having given birth and of having produced a real baby, which comes as a delightful surprise at first, gives way to this confrontation with the body. Changes in the breasts associated with breastfeeding can be an ordeal for some women. Many set their sights at the birth, seeing labor and delivery as the challenge, and are ill prepared for the new challenges that follow immediately after. One mother who felt a revulsion at her much changed body exclaimed: "But it was all supposed to be *over!*" Once the baby had arrived she wanted her self back again.

Weight loss

Immediately following delivery you probably feel beautifully slim and lightweight. You have lost the combined weight of the baby, the placenta, the amniotic fluid and membranes. It is only when you first put your hand down on your tummy that you become aware of the folds of skin, like a soft and soggy cream puff. When you first catch sight of yourself naked in a full-length mirror you may be horrified at the amount of weight you have put on: the thickened waist, the heavy thighs and (if you are breastfeeding) the ballooning breasts—which you and your partner may enjoy if you were small and flat before, but which can be too much of a good thing if you were top-heavy anyway.

Water loss During the week after childbirth most women sweat out the excess fluid they no longer need, and any puffiness you may have noticed in your legs and ankles will disappear; so will the plumped-out facial features and the fluid which might have been retained in your fingers, making them fatter than usual.

Restoring muscle tone If you use your abdominal muscles your tummy will flatten after a few weeks, but you cannot achieve this if you go without exercise. Some exercises suitable for the early post-partum period are illustrated on pages 352–353. Brisk walking is good for abdominal muscles: if the weather is suitable put the baby in a carrier against your body and walk, in the country if possible.

At first your pelvic floor muscles may feel as if they are sagging like a heavy hammock, but their tone will be gradually restored over the next three months and if you use them regularly, without straining them, rehabilitation will be complete.

BREASTS AND BREASTFEEDING

The sooner you put your baby to the breast the sooner its gut will be lined with colostrum, a substance which forms a protective "paint" and a barrier to invading bacteria. Colostrum also provides the baby with antibodies to diseases to which you yourself are resistant. Ready in your breasts at the end of pregnancy, it is the earliest form of milk, rich in protein, and an ideal first concentrated food for your baby.

The milk ejection reflex

When your baby sucks the action stimulates an area in your brain (the hypothalamus), which in turn stimulates the pituitary gland at the base of your brain to release oxytocin into your bloodstream. Oxytocin flows into the blood vessels in your breasts and causes specific cells around the milk glands deep inside your breasts to contract. This has the effect of squeezing the milk out through the tiny holes in your nipples.

You will probably feel the warm, tingling glow of the milk ejection reflex immediately preceding the flow of milk. This occurs as the oxytocin-carrying blood rushes into the breasts and you feel them getting warmer. Infrared photographs of lactating breasts show that they really do grow hotter in response to the baby's cry.

A baby needs to suck at the breast, not just the nipple.

The first feedings Notice what happens when you put the baby to the breast. She should have the nipple deep in her mouth and as much of the areola as will make a good mouthful. Cuddle the baby close and wait. Drop your shoulders: if they feel really stiff *pull* them down and then let them go. It may take a few minutes for the sensation to come and then suddenly it is there: deep inside both breasts, not just the one the baby is sucking, there is a prickling, buzzing feeling as if champagne is flowing through your veins and at the same time a wave of heat flowing towards your nipples. And then you see the baby's jaws beginning to work, and the strong steady movement of the bone at the top of the baby's jawbone, just by her ear, as she begins to swallow as well as suck. The milk ejection reflex can happen when you just think about feeding the baby or if you hear her cry. If she is not in your arms you can press the palm of a hand firmly against your breast and the milk flow—which will be a slow but steady dripping from the nipple—will come to a stop.

The difference between sucking and feeding

Having milk in your breasts is just the beginning. Obviously the important thing is to *release* it so that it flows into your baby. For nutritional purposes it is not enough to have a baby sucking at your breasts, though he will enjoy this anyway. He needs to *swallow* and until this happens is not feeding. Hospitals are more relaxed than they used to be about the time babies spend at the breast, but if you are in one where feeding time is still restricted, you should count this time from the moment the baby is actually feeding, not from when he is just sucking.

Even before the reflex occurs the baby gets some milk, because it collects in the ducts just behind the nipple. This is called "foremilk" and is rich in protein. It usually keeps the baby happy until the rush of milk comes with the reflex. But if you give a baby foremilk only, because he is not sucking for long enough to stimulate the reflex, your milk supply will dwindle or never build up.

If you feel embarrassed or selfconscious or experience strong emotions of anxiety, fear, or anger, the milk ejection reflex will probably be slower in coming and sometimes does not occur at all. This is why the setting for breastfeeding in the first days after birth is so important and why emotional support from someone who understands how you feel is helpful. Even though you may think you have emptied a breast, a fresh reflex can occur when you put the baby back to it again. A breast is not like a pitcher of milk, but has a constant supply provided the baby gives the right stimulus.

I had an image of glowing with motherly calm, but breastfeeding isn't a bit like that: it's so sexy, I can't believe it!

Little and often

If you are concerned about the amount of milk the baby is taking, bear in mind that the frequency of feedings is more important than their length. Though some babies, especially in the first four to six weeks of life, enjoy sucking more or less continuously at certain times of the day, the main nutritional content of the milk has been obtained during the first five to seven minutes. This is why many short feedings, the baby dropping off to sleep in between, is for many mothers and babies the perfect style of feeding in these first weeks. You may be able to unplug the baby's mouth gently from your nipple by depressing the breast with a finger or by slipping a finger just inside the baby's mouth to break the vacuum—but don't, whatever you do, just pull the nipple out.

Babies who like sucking for comfort

Some babies always wake up and fuss when you do take them off the breast. These are usually babies who have such a strong need to suck in the first six weeks or so that they never drop off the nipple for long. Then it makes sense to consider providing the baby with a pacifier for

Postnatal exercises

Many of the exercises recommended during pregnancy are also good for getting your figure back after delivery. It is important to remember, though, that postnatal exercises should be progressive. Do only the gentlest exercises for the first day or two then move on to the more strenuous ones shown here. Never do an exercise that hurts you.

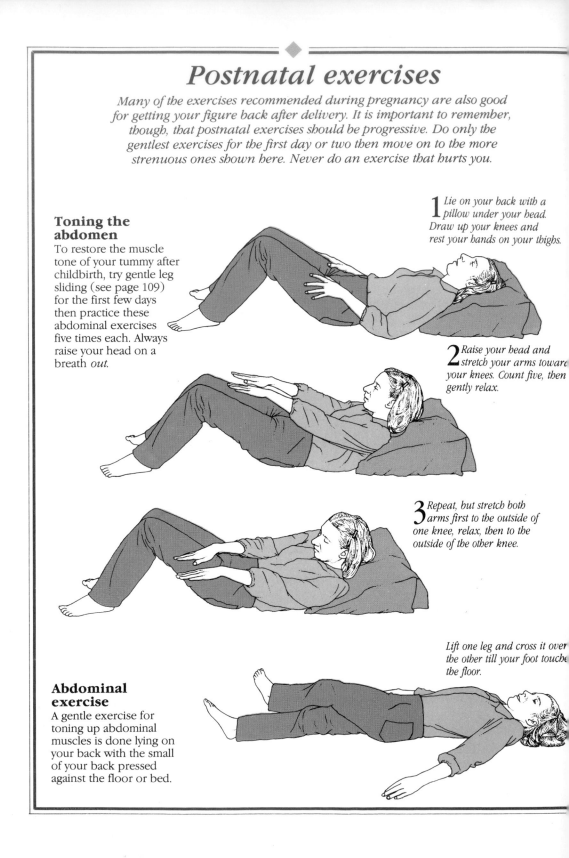

Toning the abdomen

To restore the muscle tone of your tummy after childbirth, try gentle leg sliding (see page 109) for the first few days then practice these abdominal exercises five times each. Always raise your head on a breath *out*.

1 *Lie on your back with a pillow under your head. Draw up your knees and rest your hands on your thighs.*

2 *Raise your head and stretch your arms toward your knees. Count five, then gently relax.*

3 *Repeat, but stretch both arms first to the outside of one knee, relax, then to the outside of the other knee.*

Lift one leg and cross it over the other till your foot touches the floor.

Abdominal exercise

A gentle exercise for toning up abdominal muscles is done lying on your back with the small of your back pressed against the floor or bed.

Lying comfortably

If you have had stitches, lying on your front may be the most comfortable position for you. Pillows placed under your hips help your pelvic organs to return to their usual position and allow you to practice pelvic floor exercises and pelvic tilting. A pillow under your head and shoulders will take pressure off your breasts.

Put two pillows under your hips not your abdomen, so that your back is not hollowed and the abdominal wall is relaxed.

Repairing the rectus muscle

If your rectus muscle has separated, this exercise, done from about three days after delivery, can help.

Lie on your back, knees bent and hands crossed over your tummy. As you breathe out, raise your head slowly, pulling in your tummy and holding the rectus muscle together. Do this exercise a few times twice a day.

Roll your right shoulder slowly backward around and around in a complete circle ten times. Then do the same with your left shoulder.

Encouraging the milk flow

Many women find that their milk flow slows down when they are resting. The first sign is usually a red patch of inflammation, often in the outer part of the breast where your arm has been pressing against it. If your breasts are not too tender, the answer is vigorous arm movement.

Grip your wrists with your hands and hold your arms in a square in front of you with your elbows well up. Push the skin of your wrists toward your elbows, gripping firmly. Do this ten times.

alternative sucking satisfaction, and with some additional help in dropping off to sleep, such as rocking, regular rhythmic sound or the old-fashioned lullaby.

You may feel very "drained" when nursing is long drawn out: if you are tired and the baby is constantly demanding to be fed, it is easy to think that you cannot be providing enough milk. Though this is sometimes the case, many babies want to go on feeding nonstop because they like it so much, not because they are starving. So after about ten minutes' sucking it is sensible to put the baby down or hand him or her over to a friend or your partner for a cuddle. Relax a bit; offer some more breast milk at whichever side feels most generously supplied; then have another break, and so on.

Each baby's feeding pattern is different

Breastfed babies do not suck continuously through a feeding. They enjoy bursts of sucking, stop for a while, then start again. This is normal. If you think about meals you enjoy you will realize that you do not chomp away nonstop either. Nor do you want an equal quantity of food at each meal. Babies are the same.

Think of each feeding as divided into different courses. Some will be seven- or eight-course banquets, but others will be only two courses. You will gradually be able to work out when the baby likes the banquets, and then you may be able to cater for them by arranging your day to fit in with this pattern. Somehow anticipating and preparing for feeding sessions of this kind makes them much easier to cope with and you are less likely to feel exhausted by them.

Is breast milk enough?

You may wonder if and when your baby needs any food other than your breast milk, especially if you secretly feel that your baby is not having enough milk from you.

Water Many hospitals still give water to babies. If the room temperature in the hospital is high this may be a good idea, but it is usually not necessary when you go home. The baby needs milk, not water. If your baby is producing six or more wet diapers in the course of 24 hours and is having no other fluid, and if the urine is pale amber or colorless, this is an indication that she is having enough milk from you. You will probably find that *you* are thirstier than usual. Drink as much as you like, though there is no point in having more than you want, since it will not produce more milk.

Supplementary bottles If you are concerned that your baby is not having enough milk and you start to give supplementary bottle feedings, the amount of milk you are producing will diminish, since it is demand that stimulates supply.

Using a bottle for supplementary feeding or to replace nursing (supplementary bottle feeding) in the first two months of life can

> **" **
> *The first 6 weeks I felt I was doing nothing but feeding her. I was partly proud, partly outraged at not being able to get on with my ordinary life.*
> **" **

mean that the baby grows accustomed to the type of sucking action which is used at the bottle. The large bottle nipple can provide a sort of super-stimulus to which the baby responds more readily than to your nipple. And if the nipple has a large hole in it so that the milk comes quickly she may soon come to prefer bottle to breast.

Solid foods When you introduce solid foods be prepared for your milk supply to be automatically reduced. This is one reason why the early introduction of solid foods is counterproductive. It replaces food the baby needs, human milk, with food which she does not need until she is about six months old. A baby's appetite cannot possibly cope with human milk *plus* all the other foods which are on the market. Manufacturers of so-called "baby foods" are often responsible for breastfeeding difficulties which start at three to four months, a common time for mothers to discover that they are failing to produce enough milk.

Test weighing Weighing the baby before and after a feeding (test weighing) is a method of finding exactly how much breast milk he or she has taken. It is pointless unless done over 24 hours, since the baby takes different quantities at different times; even then it tends to increase your anxiety and make you feel inadequate. A much better guide to a baby's wellbeing is feeling good muscle tone and noticing if she is alert and responsive.

More frequent breastfeeding When you want to increase the quantity of milk you are making, put the baby to the breast more often. If the baby has not gained weight, or has lost weight, nurse him every time he stirs over a 24-hour period. If the baby is very sleepy rouse him after every two and a half hours if you can, except at night. Unwrap him, talk to him, and "woo" him with the breast. I call this my "Twenty-Four Hour Peak Production Plan". It works in the first weeks after birth and is also useful at about six weeks.

Breastfeeding difficulties

Engorged breasts Many new mothers find that they are engorged on the third or fourth day after delivery, when the milk really floods in. The longer you go between feedings the more likely you are to be painfully engorged. A cold compress, such as a cloth with some ice inside, resting against your breast, will ease the pain of engorgement, and with the baby's frequent sucking will help you through this difficult transitional phase. The hospital will have a breast pump that you can use if it is important to draw off some milk and if you find it difficult to express by hand, but draw off only enough for comfort.

Sore nipples Nipple soreness, especially when the baby is a vigorous sucker, is common in the first few weeks and does not mean that you will fail at breastfeeding. Studies show that those mothers who go on to enjoy breastfeeding include many women who have had initial trouble with sores and cracks, and that the only difference between these and others who give up is that they persevere. Go topless whenever you can; avoid using soap on your nipples or using breast pads against them, and let them dry off after nursing, exposed to warm air (it is best not to use a towel).

Cracked nipples Sometimes a crack appears at the point where the nipple joins the areola. This is almost invariably because the baby has not fixed well on the surrounding tissue and obtained a really good mouthful. If a baby drags on the nipple stem and does not draw the nipple into the back of the mouth, not only will you have problems with sores and cracks but also the baby will not be able to take enough milk after the first spurts at the beginning of a feeding.

A soft, flexible nipple shield made of rubber with a wide brim like a Mexican sombrero can sometimes help to relieve soreness caused by cracks and make nursing tolerable until the nipple has time to heal. Avoid using plastic-lined breast pads, since if there is any leaking your nipples will be sitting in the damp.

Breast tenderness If you develop a red area on a breast, nursing more often can help. Ensure that the baby is well latched on. Exercise your arms to increase the circulation to your breasts (see page 353). If an infection develops and you run a temperature at the same time as having a red area, cold compresses and oral antibiotics prescribed by the doctor will quickly treat it. Continue nursing the baby, as this makes it far less likely that you will develop an abscess.

Excitable babies Some babies nurse with great bluster and excitement, spluttering and coughing and really making a meal out of it. In the first weeks they suddenly draw back as they start to choke, pulling on the nipple at the same time. Or they may let go for a second and then grab on again, but because they have jerked their heads back they now have only the nipple stem in their mouths so that they are dragging on the place where the stem joins the areola. These babies need a calm environment in which to nurse. Talk to yours soothingly

EXPRESSING YOUR MILK
If you need to use a breast pump because your breasts are engorged or because your baby cannot take milk from the breast, it is a good idea to use one that converts into a bottle.

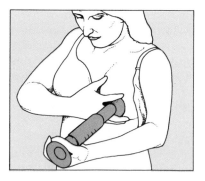
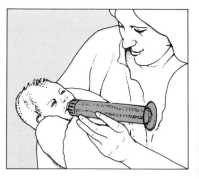

and reassuringly, and reposition her firmly and securely. If your milk comes with a sudden rush after the ejection reflex has occurred, see if a little boiled water or mint tea, which can be given by spoon or in a bottle, encourages her to relax at the breast. If your milk streams out fast you may need to express a little before each feeding.

Sore abdomen After a cesarean section breastfeeding may be difficult because you find it almost impossible to settle with the baby in a position where she is not pressing on the wound. Try placing a pillow on the wound and lie on your side, or sit up and pop the baby's legs under the arm on the same side as the breast you are using.

Giving breast milk in a bottle

When you desperately need sleep and your partner wants to give some feedings, it can be a good idea to express some breast milk after each feeding, and store it in the refrigerator (perfectly safe up to 24 hours). Use a sterile plastic container. If you want to keep your milk longer than 24 hours, freeze it. Express after each feeding, either immediately or about 30 minutes later. If you find that milk shoots out of one breast when you put the baby to the other you can collect this milk too. If you are not good at expressing by hand buy a small breast pump. Never boil breastmilk. Frozen milk should be warmed gradually by running the container under warm water.

BOTTLEFEEDING

If you decide to bottlefeed or want to give occasional bottles for convenience, the formula you choose for your baby should be as much like your own milk as possible. No manufacturer has yet been able to invent anything but a product which *approximates* to human milk, because your milk adapts to your baby's individual needs. Substitute milks are a great improvement on unmodified cow's milk, however, and those which are "humanized" have the proportions of fats, sugars, and trace elements changed so that they are more like the real thing. Discuss with your doctor, midwife, or nurse the choices available. Most babies thrive on formula. But you do need to be scrupulously hygienic in preparing it.

Hold your baby close, cradled in your arm, when giving a bottle.

Preparing bottles

If you are using bottles it is vital that your kitchen and all utensils are clean and that you sterilize both bottles and nipples carefully, by boiling them in a pan for 15–20 minutes and following the instructions on the can of formula. You can make up enough feedings for 24 hours, put caps on the bottles, and store them in the refrigerator. It is then easy to feed your baby whenever he or she shows signs of hunger, just as you would if you were breastfeeding.

Never leave warm formula about for more than a few minutes as bacteria will multiply. After the feeding, always throw away any leftover milk, clean out the bottle immediately, and sterilize it. Keep nipples in sterilized covered containers. When you go out do not take warm milk with you. Take it cold, straight from the refrigerator, and reheat it in a pan of hot water or an electric bottle warmer. It is tempting to tuck the bottle under the bassinet covers to keep it snug and ready immediately the baby wants it. But if you do this you are running the risk of feeding your baby milk which is harboring bacteria capable of causing gastrointestinal illness.

Though it seems pleasanter for a baby to have warm milk, this is not strictly necessary; if the baby is impatient for a feeding and you are in a hurry it is quite all right to give her a cold bottle.

Powdered formula must be thoroughly mixed. Some brands dissolve more easily than others. Even the tiniest lumps can block the hole in the nipple and, if your baby splutters or vomits, can be inhaled and cause trouble with breathing. When you are making up dried milk, measure it very carefully and never put in an extra scoop to make it richer, as this overloads the baby with minerals which his system can only absorb with difficulty.

The baby who is fed on formula may go longer between feedings since the milk takes longer to digest. If you were worried about whether your baby was having enough breast milk it can be very reassuring to know how much he or she has had from the bottle. But avoid trying to make the baby finish the bottle just because it is there. In hot weather give drinks of water too and introduce sips of fruit juice, since the bottlefed baby will need extra Vitamin C. But formulas do contain some extra vitamins, so do not give vitamin supplements unless advised to do so by your doctor, and then take care that you do not exceed the prescribed dose.

My baby's doing very well on the bottle! My husband shares looking after him, enjoys giving the feedings. All the gushing about breastfeeding from women who were willing to go on for years really put me off!

Feeding for pleasure

When bottlefeeding, remember to hold the baby close, cheek against your breast, just as if you were breastfeeding. Though it may produce a less comfortable cushion for the baby's head, a man can do this too. The baby may sometimes like to lie nestled against your partner's bare skin, and fathers who give a feeding in the middle of the night like this say how much they enjoy it.

Never prop a baby up to feed on its own in a crib, however rushed you are. It can be dangerous, and it means that the baby misses out on one of the most important experiences of early life.

SLEEP AND CRYING

After being awake and alert, eyes wide open, for an hour or so after birth, the baby often sinks into a deep sleep for about 24 hours, waking only to suck and then dropping off to sleep again while still at the breast. It is a period often followed by another lasting about 24 hours, in which the baby may be sucking almost continuously. This is a normal pattern. It is the frequent sucking which stimulates your milk supply. Some babies suck in short bursts, get drowsy, then suck again. Others will sleep for two to three hours between more prolonged sucking sessions. Some babies start a pattern of evening fussing when they are one or two weeks old which may continue for as long as three months. Though tiring and perhaps worrying for you, this is also completely normal.

Sleep patterns of newborn babies

When your baby is asleep you will sometimes notice that the eyelids flicker and the eyeballs are moving behind them. This is rapid eye movement (REM) sleep similar to that which adults have the dreaming time. It has been discovered that REM sleep is essential for mental wellbeing and if people are not to become exhausted*. These little eye movements also stimulate the flow of blood to the brain. Even if the baby seems to be stirring and is making little jerking movements or fussing noises, this is not a time to wake her. This kind of sleep is probably just as important for babies as it is for adults.

The meaning of your baby's cry

Another innate biological mechanism is your baby's cry on waking, which alerts you to care for her. The baby may also cry whenever you undress her and seem to hate being without clothes. This is nerve-racking for the new mother and father, especially if you are about to bathe her. But remember that the baby was held firmly inside your uterus, hugged by its tightly enclosing walls. If your baby startles and cries when you change a diaper or when you start taking off her clothes, keep your movements slow and firm. With one hand hold the baby's arms over its chest, as they would have been folded inside the uterus at the end of pregnancy, and speak soothingly.

You will soon discover that the baby has different cries to express different needs. But in the first weeks the cry nearly always means *hunger* and the right thing to do is to let the baby suck. A wet or dirty diaper does not really matter to the baby.

PRACTICAL CARE

There is a great gap between studying something in a book and doing it in practice. Experiment and see what works for you.

Bathing your baby

It does not matter how you bathe your baby, for example, so long as he is head-above-water, keeps warm, and has a chance to enjoy it. Many babies hate being undressed and abhor being bathed in the first weeks of life, and make you feel you must be a tyrant for ever doing either of these things to them. And because they cry you are convinced that you must be utterly incompetent and hopeless as a mother. The single most important thing to remember is to talk to your baby while dressing, undressing, and bathing him.

Content, asleep and oblivious of the world, your baby may well be dreaming . . .

If you do not want a very hot bath yourself, you can take the baby with you into your own bath. This provides the baby with a personal swimming pool. Start by placing him facing you on your knee and have a conversation. Then you will discover that you can work out little games together and the baby will find out what fun it is to splash. Have ready the biggest bath towel you can find and make the patting dry fun too, so that the whole process is enjoyable.

Diapers

You will not be able to manage without diapers. The choice is between disposable and washable diapers. Disposables come with a plastic backing. They come in different sizes, shapes, and absorbencies. Their obvious advantage is that they eliminate washing. Washable diapers are cheaper than disposable ones, as well as being highly absorbent. Bear in mind that babies often dirty their diapers before, during, and after a feeding, and that many like to suck every two or three hours at first. You will have to decide how often you are prepared to change your baby! You may find you need as many as 24 washable diapers to see you through the 24 hours, and possibly more if you do not have an efficient clothes drier. Alternatively, there may be a diaper service available in your area.

Changing diapers Diaper changing can be done any way you like. At first take it gently and give yourself time and privacy so that you can work out your own style of doing it. A firm surface helps. Have everything you need close at hand before you start, including a diaper pail into which you drop the dirty diaper, a dampened facecloth or some wipes, baby powder, and A & D ointment for diaper rash.

Clothing

You don't need a layette! Though it can be fun to collect together tiny clothes for your baby, it is not really necessary, and since he or she will quickly grow out of these first- and even second-size garments there is little point in spending much money on them.

Your older child will not feel left out if you involve her in looking after the new baby . . .

Newborn babies lose heat very rapidly, so need to be kept warm and cozy. You can do this in any way you like, but several fine layers are usually warmer than one thick one. When you can, choose things which do not have to be pulled over the baby's head, as most babies hate narrow neck holes. In very cold weather the baby's head ought to be covered outdoors.

Avoid strings and ribbons near the baby's mouth and hands, and large-holed lacy knitted jackets and shawls in which the baby will catch little fingers and toes. You are bound to be given bootees and mittens; these are wriggled off, lost, and get dirty and probably germ-ridden. Stretchy one-piece suits are better for keeping feet covered, and babies should be able to get at their hands and explore with them when they are awake.

A baby carrier is not strictly clothing but is important for your mobility. The most useful item of clothing is something for you, not the baby. It is a big wraparound overcoat, cape or other voluminous top garment. Then you can tuck the baby in a baby carrier against your body underneath your cloak with just her face peeping out, and you know that your own body heat is providing warmth and that the outer garment is holding the warmth in around the baby. The baby carrier you use to begin with should be one of those where the baby is held in front of you and the head is supported.

The challenge of new parenthood

Though most women look forward to the time when they will have their baby at home, taking an important part in family life, the first days at home alone with a new baby can be ones of worry and even panic. You may suddenly feel like a stranger in your own home as you try to understand and cope with the needs of this demanding new person. You will soon learn to interpret the different cries of your baby, however, and you may want to take advantage of your local available visiting nurse service.

Visiting nurse service

Your doctor may arrange for a visiting nurse to come to your home after you leave the hospital. She will assist you with the aspects of baby care that you are unsure of. If your baby was premature or sickly, she will teach you any special procedures you need to know. The visiting nurse is concerned with the physical and emotional wellbeing of every member of the family, not only with the baby.

Postnatal checkup

Your postnatal checkup will be arranged for between five and seven weeks after the birth, and is an important way of ensuring that you have complete physical rehabilitation after childbirth. The obstetrician will give you an internal examination to see if your pelvic floor muscles are well toned and the uterus and bladder correctly positioned, and will check on the state of any scar tissue. If sexual intercourse is difficult and uncomfortable or if you are feeling depressed and unhappy, tell the doctor at this visit. If you are dissatisfied with any aspect of care you have received or seek further explanation of things that have happened to you in labor, take the opportunity to discuss these things with the doctor.

My lovely nurse helped get my baby "fixed" on the breast and showed him what he was missing!

SEX AFTER CHILDBIRTH

For many women the full flood of passion is slow to return after childbirth. So much has happened in your body that you may need time to find yourself again and get in touch with your feelings. If labor was unpleasant or delivery traumatic you need time, too, to *like* yourself again and to trust your body.

If you have had stitches you may feel at first as if you will never want to make love again. If you are one of the minority of women who do not have stitches you may not be able to wait to make love. So there is a great difference in attitude, depending very much on the state of your perineum. The initial healing of the episiotomy wound (and it is a wound) often takes two weeks or longer and even then you may be very conscious of scar tissue at the lower end of your vagina.

Rediscovering each other's body

Make sure first of all that your partner knows which areas are likely to feel sore and help him discover what feels good and where. Do not attempt to have intercourse at first and certainly do not try to *prove* anything to yourselves. Choose a quiet time when you need not be rushed, perhaps after a feeding when you know the baby is most likely to settle and sleep soundly. Use a lubricant jelly, squeeze a little on your partner's fingers and, taking his hands in yours, guide him, showing him where you like to be touched. Many couples need two or three exploratory sessions like this before they feel sufficiently confident and passionate to have complete intercourse. If you rush it, you may have unexpected discomfort and will then tense up in anticipation of pain next time, and because your pelvic floor muscles have contracted will experience more pain.

When you feel you are ready for intercourse, adopt a position in which your partner's weight is not going to drag on the lower part of your vagina or, if you are breastfeeding, is not on your breasts. For example, if you lie or sit with your legs over the side of a low bed, feet on the floor, your partner is able to penetrate you gently without pressing against or pulling on any tender areas. You will probably feel extraordinarily full up. Release your *throat* and this will help the release of muscles around your vagina. Do not aim for simultaneous orgasm. It is usually much more comfortable and pleasurable for you in the weeks immediately after having a baby if your partner comes to orgasm first and then stays still inside until you have an orgasm too.

Adjusting to your changed body

You will learn a lot about each other and sometimes sex will be funny, sometimes tender, occasionally passionate. Even if you do not feel that you are making a wild success of your sex life in the first few months, lovemaking helps you and your baby by releasing oxytocin into your bloodstream which helps the uterus contract so that it returns to its previous size and shape and encourages the flow of breast milk. When you do have orgasm, milk may actually shoot out from your nipples.

You will probably find that your shape has changed after a first baby. The labia, like the outside petals of a flower, are softer and fleshier, and away from the site of the episiotomy you may find the entrance to the vagina also more yielding. If your uterus is still involuting, you will feel after-contractions following lovemaking. This is a good sign. If they are uncomfortable, use a hot water bottle against your lower tummy or back.

OPPOSITE

As you gain confidence, caring for your baby becomes an exciting opportunity for you to learn more about each other.

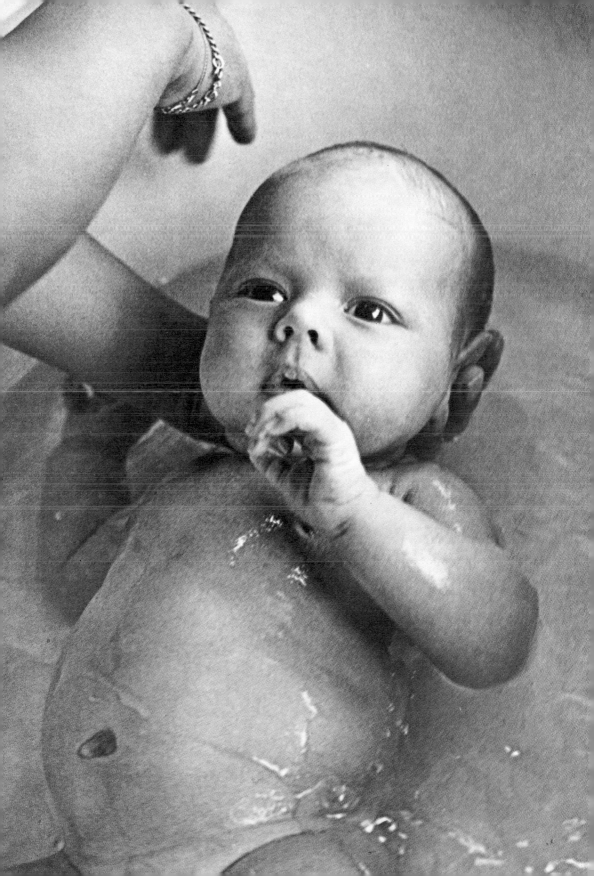

Even if you thoroughly enjoyed lovemaking, you may feel slightly sore afterward, once the sexual intensity has faded. Again, this is normal. A cold witchhazel compress may feel soothing.

Painful intercourse

For some women intercourse after childbirth is acutely painful and no amount of trying to relax does away with the pain. This is called "dyspareunia". It can occur when stitches have been inserted too tightly and the surrounding flesh has become puffy and swollen (edematous) and perhaps is infected. Ask your doctor or midwife to look at the sore area as soon as possible. Sometimes it is just a question of nicking a few stitches, sometimes a matter of taking antibiotics. If you have pain up near your cervix, it may be that the transverse cervical ligaments have been torn and it takes time for them to repair themselves. Make sure that your doctor knows that you are having this sort of pain.

Many women worry that they have become "frigid" after childbirth. Often a lack of interest in sex is caused by tiredness. Try to rest with your feet up and if possible sleep at some time during the day when your baby sleeps. Even the most active baby sleeps sometimes, and it is a question of discovering your baby's pattern and taking advantage of it. This is more difficult if you have a toddler too, but many toddlers enjoy a cuddle in bed or on the sofa.

Although you may not feel like making love for some time after childbirth, it is sensible to have explored sensations and had intercourse *before* your postnatal checkup. Most women with new babies are so busy that it is not easy to fit in another appointment to discuss sexual difficulties and they hope that if they take no notice the problems will disappear. Make a note of where and when you feel pain and let the doctor know that you are experiencing dyspareunia and that you want help.

Sex after childbirth takes you on a new journey with your partner. It involves discovery, change, in some ways for many women a fresh awareness of the depth and drama of their sexual feelings, and for both of you a new closeness and tenderness as parents of the baby who has been born of your love.

CONTRACEPTION AFTER CHILDBIRTH

There is no easy answer to contraception and what pleases one couple is completely unsuitable for another. Many couples now consider the matter in advance so that they can have intercourse safely whenever they feel ready. You may find that a combination of methods works best for you but, whatever kind you select, study carefully the correct method of use and never deviate from the routine. It is not worth being worried about another pregnancy when you are only just beginning to enjoy the results of the last!*

Breastfeeding

If you are breastfeeding, your periods may not come back till you wean the baby or start introducing her to some form of solid food. Ovulation, and hence the possibility of conception, can occur a couple of weeks or so *before* you have this first period. Breastfeeding tends to reduce fertility but is not an effective contraceptive unless you are suckling the baby intermittently right through the 24 hours and are giving her no other food or fluid at all.

Coitus interruptus

Hoping that your partner will withdraw before ejaculation, and deposit semen outside your vagina, is not a reliable method either, though it is very common throughout the world. In spite of working well for some couples, it demands great control on the man's part and may lead to dissatisfaction for you both. Sperm can flow from the penis *before* ejaculation and if you have intercourse again within a short time, live sperm may already be present in your partner's urethra and be introduced into your vagina before ejaculation. Sperm do not have to be deposited right inside your vagina for you to become pregnant, and even a drop or two of semen leaking against the labia may contain a million sperm or more.

Natural family planning

Natural methods of birth control entail identifying the period of ovulation, the phase of the menstrual cycle at which you are most fertile, and then abstaining from intercourse during that time. It is impossible to calculate the time of ovulation accurately using a calendar alone. The traditional rhythm method, the only method of birth control officially approved by the Roman Catholic Church, relies on keeping a record of the menstrual cycle and daily monitoring of basal body temperature, using a special thermometer. More effective is the symptothermal method which combines charting your temperature with observing changes in the cervical mucus. There are drawbacks, however: in the first year or so after childbirth a woman may not have a regular menstrual cycle, and it can be difficult to work out the significance of the changes she observes; natural methods require instruction from someone who is really skilled in using them, and a commitment from both partners.

Ovulation prediction There are kits on the market that can tell you if and when you are ovulating, though they are expensive. They work in a way similar to chemical pregnancy tests (see page 27), and signal, by a color change, the presence of luteinizing hormone in your urine, which increases a couple of days before ovulation. You start testing the urine several days after the beginning of a period and go on testing, at the same time each day, noting exactly when the equipment records a surge in luteinizing hormone. You should not empty your bladder for four hours beforehand. Two to three days after you have observed a color change you are at your most fertile.

The condom

The condom (rubber) is the most widely used of the barrier methods and, employed carefully, is effective. It has no harmful side effects. The one big disadvantage after childbirth is that your vagina may not be well lubricated and may be tender following episiotomy. Unless you use a lubricant cream the latex rubber sticks and drags, interfering with pleasure and reducing confidence. So have some artificial lubrication ready, but avoid vaseline, as this rots rubber. Do not use old condoms; their shelf life is about two years.

The diaphragm

If you used a diaphragm before you became pregnant you will probably need a larger size after you have had a baby, and it must be fitted by a doctor or midwife, who cannot do it accurately until about six weeks after childbirth. The diaphragm should be left in place for at least six hours after intercourse; do not, however, leave it for longer than eight hours if you have had any kind of bladder infection during pregnancy or following the birth, since pressure of the rubber rim on your bladder can sometimes cause irritation and exacerbate an infection. Use one teaspoonful of spermicidal cream on the diaphragm; never use vaseline. It is probably best not to dust with powder as some manufacturers advise, since some kinds of powder contain carcinogenic substances. The diaphragm does not affect breastfeeding and the spermicidal cream or jelly cannot harm the unborn baby if you should conceive accidentally. The success rate ranges from four pregnancies for every 100 years of use to as high as 29, but the efficiency of the diaphragm depends very much on the motivation and care of the user.

Sometimes ligaments running across the cervix are slack after childbirth and the diaphragm cannot be wedged snugly up under the pubic bone but slips out of position, especially when you bear down.

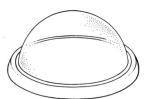

The diaphragm is more effective when used with a spermicide.

The cervical cap

This is a rigid, thimble-shaped rubber dome which fits by suction right over the cervix itself and has to be placed in position very carefully by you. It can remain in place the whole month, from period to period. It is about as safe as the diaphragm. It is not easy to find but some women's health groups import them from England.

The sponge

This is a soft round sponge of polyurethane foam, looking rather like a doughnut, which is impregnated with spermicide. It is inserted deep into the vagina and over the cervix. Each sponge is used only once. It must be left in position for at least six hours after intercourse. Its reliability is still in question.

Spermicides

Foaming spermicides are more effective than creams or gels because they effervesce into every crevice. However, you may find that this characteristic in itself interferes with your pleasure in intercourse. Spermicides in the form of foaming tablets or suppositories are not so reliable, because women often do not place them sufficiently high up in the vagina.

If you notice any vaginal irritation with a particular brand, try changing to another. Some spermicides come in pre-filled applicators; others have to be measured out into an applicator. One problem is that you are supposed to lie on your back so that the spermicide does not drip out before intercourse, and this may not be your position of choice.

Spermicides are safest used in combination with a diaphragm, cap, or condom. The pregnancy rate is anything between five and 30 pregnancies for each 100 years of use.

The intrauterine device

It is usually easier for an intrauterine device (IUD) to be inserted into your uterus and retained without excessive cramping once you have had a baby. So it may be that the IUD will suit you. The failure rate is between one and five pregnancies for every 100 years of use, depending on the skill of the doctor who inserts it. Copper IUDs need to be replaced every few years and after each insertion you may feel faint and sick. You should not have intercourse for the first few days, and may notice some bleeding after intercourse during the first month or so. Plastic IUDs can be left in longer; some need to be changed only every seven years.

Many problems associated with IUDs are related to the way in which they are inserted, so the longer you can go without changing an IUD, the safer it will be.

Pelvic infection is common with an IUD and is more likely when there is a string attached to it, since infection ascends from the vagina up through the cervix. Infection should be treated with antibiotics, all of which pass through into your milk, though the only obvious effect on the baby may be that his or her stools become loose. In some ways the thread is reassuring: occasionally an IUD is expelled or buries itself in the uterine lining and many women like to have some means of knowing whether their IUD is still there.

Rarely an IUD actually perforates the uterus, and this is more likely to happen if it is inserted within a short time after delivery when the uterine wall is thin and soft. An IUD with a rounded rather than a spiky edge is less apt to do this.

There is also an IUD which releases 20 micrograms of levenorgestrel, the hormone used in the progestogen pill. It is an effective contraceptive and has fewer side effects than many other kinds of IUD that are commonly available.

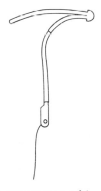

The copper 7 is one of the types of IUD most commonly prescribed.

Oral contraceptives

Though the pill is the most reliable method of contraception so far invented, there are certain conditions, some of which are not evident until pregnancy, that indicate that you should not choose the pill as your postnatal contraceptive. If you have high blood pressure which continues after the birth or if it has been discovered during pregnancy that you have diabetes, you should *probably* not go on the pill. If you are suffering from severe postnatal depression, it may be wiser to avoid the pill. If you developed varicose veins during pregnancy, you should watch for any pain in your legs which could be a sign of a blood clot. If you have had a blood clot in a vein (thrombophlebitis), you should *not* take the pill.

Progestogen changes the bacterial flora of the vagina and some women develop thrush for the first time when taking the minipill (see below). If you have already had thrush this may not be the contraceptive you should choose.

The pill also needs reassessment as you get older. If you are over 35, the risk of a cardiovascular disorder is increased significantly. If you smoke heavily as well, you should not be taking the pill, as you are running grave risks with your health.

The combined estrogen-progestogen pill, almost 100 per cent effective in preventing pregnancy, is definitely *out* if you are breastfeeding. It affects your metabolism and therefore indirectly the baby. It may alter both the quantity and the quality of milk and there may possibly be long-term effects on the child.

The progestogen-only pill Many women who breastfeed are prescribed the progestogen-only pill, the "minipill". Since it contains no estrogen, it probably does not prevent ovulation but works by thickening the cervical mucus, making it difficult for sperm to travel beyond the cervix, and by preventing the normal cyclical changes in the endometrium (the lining of the uterus) which allow a fertilized egg to implant. It is a less effective contraceptive than the combined pill, but has fewer side effects. The failure rate ranges from one to four pregnancies for every 100 years of use. It has to be taken every day without a break and must be taken at about the same time each day to be effective.

Many women say that though their milk supply was diminished for a few days after they started taking the minipill, feeding on demand, more or less continuously, for a day or two brought the supply back to normal. On the other hand, we do not really know what effects these powerful synthetic hormones may have on the baby.

The morning-after pill A series of high strength contraceptive pills is taken within three days of unprotected intercourse. Two pills should be taken as soon as possible after intercourse, and another two 12 hours later. This morning-after pill is useful in an emergency but, because of the strength of the hormones taken, it is not a wise form of contraception and often makes a woman feel nauseated.

GAINING CONFIDENCE AS PARENTS

Many women in our society have no experience of babies and some have never had a newborn baby in their arms before. They are anxious that they will not know when the baby is hungry, that they will drop or drown it in the bath, that they will never be able to stop it crying or that the baby who is not crying has stopped breathing. New mothers are often too ashamed to talk about such feelings and may even repress recognition of them. Talk with other mothers and you will find that you are not alone with such anxieties. Talk about good feelings too—when the baby falls asleep and lies in your arms in perfect contentment, the soft, downy head resting against your skin, when he opens his eyes wide and gazes at you with excited attention, or when you watch her satisfied sucking at your breast.

You are not just a caretaker of the baby but a partner in a unique and evolving relationship. You learn more about each other every day, synchronizing with each other as dancers do. You respond to facial expression, eye movement, muscle tension—even breathing—quite spontaneously. When you act like this *you are invariably doing the right thing*. When you are selfconscious you miss steps in the dance and confidence drains away.

The developing relationship between a mother and her baby is a process that needs time to unfold and blossom, patterned, just as a hyacinth bulb or a crocus is patterned, by the laws of its own inner energy. Yet this is only part of the dance. The baby's father too has his own special kind of interaction with his child as well as with you. When a man is fully involved with his baby, enjoying her, responding to her needs, and getting to know her as intimately as you do, the pattern becomes even more intricate and exciting.

Twins can give you twice the pleasure if you take time to enjoy them...

Sharing in parenthood

Parenthood is a shared task. In the past fathers missed out on the baby's early months and were supposed to be interested in their children only when they started to play games and talk. Babies have astonishingly strong personalities and are different from each other even in the early weeks. It is worth getting to know the person who is your child from the outset. The man who turns his back on this opportunity to share in the relationship with the newborn baby may be denying a whole aspect of himself.

Being a parent is not just an endless series of repetitive tasks or a heavy responsibility, though all parents see it like that at times. It is a journey of discovery—discovery of the baby's personality, of who you are, who your partner is, and who you are *becoming* together.

Pregnancy week by week

This is a week-by-week guide to what may be happening to you and your baby throughout pregnancy. As different women's pregnancies develop at different rates, do not expect to be at exactly the same stage for the week described. Read the information for the two weeks either side, too.

Since pregnancy is dated medically from the first day of your last period, the record begins with what is termed the third week of a 40-week pregnancy, the week of conception.

WEEK 3

You have ovulated and an egg is traveling along one of the two fallopian tubes toward your uterus. During intercourse one of the millions of sperm your partner has ejaculated has fertilized the egg while still in the fallopian tube.

Your baby is a cluster of cells which multiply rapidly as they continue the journey along the fallopian tube.

WEEK 4

You have probably not noticed anything different, though some women have a strange, metallic taste in their mouths.

The fertilized egg has arrived in your uterus and, after floating in the uterine cavity for about three days, has embedded itself in the uterine lining. It is nourished from blood vessels in the lining of the uterus, and the placenta begins to form around it.

WEEK 5

You are beginning to think that you may be pregnant. Your period is late, but you can't be sure, because you may feel as though it is about to start at any time. Your breasts are slightly enlarged and tender and you may find you need to urinate more often than usual.

The embryo is about $\frac{1}{10}$ in (2 mm) long and would be visible to the naked eye by now. Its spine is beginning to form and the brain has two lobes.

WEEK 6

You may be feeling sick first thing in the morning or when you are cooking a meal. Your vagina will have become a bluish or violet color. From the 6th day after your period was due it should be possible to find out by a urine test whether or not you are pregnant. Your uterus is now the size of a plum.

The baby has developed a head and trunk, and a rudimentary brain has formed. Tiny limb buds are beginning to appear. By the end of this week its circulation is beginning to function. The jaw and mouth are developing and 10 dental buds are growing in each jaw.

WEEK 7

You may sometimes feel dizzy or faint when you stand for a long time. Your breasts are noticeably larger; small nodules (Montgomery's tubercles) may appear on the areolae at about this time, while your nipples may become more prominent. By this date the doctor should be able to confirm your pregnancy by a vaginal examination.

The limb buds have developed rapidly and now look like tiny arms and legs. At the end of these limbs are small indentations which will later become fingers and toes. The spinal cord and brain are now almost complete and the head is assuming a human shape. The baby is now about $\frac{1}{2}$ in (1·3 cm) long.

WEEK 8

You may find that you have "gone off" certain foods. Many pregnant women can no longer drink alcohol, even if they previously enjoyed it, and a dislike of cigarettes or tobacco smoke is common. Your hair may seem less manageable than usual. You may also have a slight vaginal discharge. This is quite normal as long as it is not irritating or painful.

The baby now has all its main internal organs though they are not yet fully developed. The eyes and ears are growing, and the face is beginning to take on a human shape. The baby is just under an inch (2·5 cm) long.

WEEK 9

You may notice changes in your skin because of the pregnancy hormones in your system. Any wrinkles you have may be less obvious. Your gums may be softening, again because of these hormones, and you need to be especially careful about dental hygiene now and through the rest of the pregnancy. The thyroid gland in your neck may be more prominent.

The baby's limbs are developing very rapidly, and fingers and toes are beginning to be defined on the hands and feet. The baby is moving about gently to exercise its muscles, although you cannot feel these movements. At this point the baby weighs only about as much as a grape.

WEEK 10

Your uterus has expanded to the size of an orange, but is still hidden away within your pelvis. You should be wearing a bra with good support by now. If you buy a bra that fits your breasts but is adjustable to allow for later chest expansion, you may not need to get another size during the rest of your pregnancy.

The placenta, to which the baby is attached, begins to produce progesterone in a process which is completed by the end of the 14th week, when the progesterone produced is sufficient for the placenta to take over the function of the corpus luteum. The baby's ankles and wrists are formed, and fingers and toes are clearly visible. The baby has grown to about $1\frac{3}{4}$ in (4·5 cm) long.

WEEK 11

If you have been nauseous during the last weeks, the sickness should gradually lessen from now onward. The amount of blood circulating through your body has started to increase, and will go on increasing until about the 30th week. You should be thinking about arranging childbirth education classes, as they often tend to get booked up early.

Your baby's testicles or ovaries have formed, as have all of its major organs. Since these organs will not develop much further, but will merely continue to grow during its time in the uterus, the baby is relatively safe from the risk of developing congenital abnormalities after the end of this week.

WEEK 12

You will probably attend your first prenatal visit this week. You will have a complete medical examination and the doctor will be able to feel the uterus by external examination, as it has risen above your pelvis. Arrangements are made for you to have appointments once a month until you are 32 weeks pregnant. The first visit is the time to ask about anything bothering you.

The baby's head is becoming more rounded and it has eyelids. Its muscles are developing and it is moving about inside the uterus much more. It is now about $2\frac{1}{2}$ in (6·5 cm) long but still weighs only $\frac{1}{2}$ oz (18 g).

WEEK 13

If you have had early-morning sickness this will probably have gone completely by the end of this week. From now on your uterus will be enlarging at a regular and noticeable rate.

The baby is now completely formed. From now on its time in the uterus will be spent growing and maturing until it is able to survive independently of its mother.

WEEK *14*

You will be feeling less tired than you were at the beginning of your pregnancy and will probably feel quite fit and active. You may notice a dark line (the linea nigra) down the center of your abdomen. This will probably start to fade after the baby is born. Your nipples and the area around them are also starting to darken. Your uterus is the size of a large grapefruit.

The baby now has eyebrows and a small amount of hair has appeared on its head. Its heart can be heard by ultrasonic scan. The baby drinks some of the amniotic fluid and can urinate. It is now receiving all of its nourishment from the placenta and measures about 3¾ in (8–9 cm).

WEEK *15*

Your clothes will be getting too tight for you. It is best not to try to cram yourself into tight jeans. To cope with the increased amount of blood circulating in your body and the baby's need for oxygen, your enlarged heart has increased its output by 20 per cent.

The hair on your baby's head and brows is becoming coarser. If it has a gene for dark hair, the pigment cells of the hair follicles are beginning to produce black pigment.

WEEK *16*

Your second doctor's visit is now due. Some clinics do a scan at this visit. You will be able to see the outline of the baby's head and body. You feel butterflies in your stomach that just *might* be the baby moving. Your waistline will be starting to disappear. If you have not already done so, book childbirth education classes. Sometimes an "early-bird" class is available to discuss diet, exercise, posture, emotions, and health.

Lanugo (fine down) is starting to form all over the baby, following the whorled pattern of the skin, and the baby has grown fingernails and toenails. It is 6¾ in (16 cm) long and weighs nearly 5 oz (135 g).

WEEK *17*

You may find that you are sweating more than usual (due to the extra blood in your system) and also that your nose feels congested. This is a common result of pregnancy and will end after delivery. Vaginal secretions may increase now.

The growing baby has pushed the top of the uterus to halfway between your pubic bone and your navel. From now on the baby weighs more than its placenta. It is probably aware of—and may be startled by—sounds outside your body.

WEEK *18*

If this is your first baby, this is the time when you may feel the first prod which is definitely nothing to do with indigestion! At last you know that there really is a baby in there! Trouble in sleeping at night will be helped by increasing the number of pillows supporting you.

Measuring about 8 in (20 cm) long, your baby is now testing out its reflexes. As well as kicking, it is grasping and sucking. Some babies find their thumbs and are confirmed thumbsuckers before they are born.

WEEK *19*

Now is not too early to start practicing deep relaxation and steady, rhythmic breathing. Keep aside some time each day for this. You may notice that you are putting on weight on your buttocks as well as your abdomen.

Buds for permanent teeth are forming behind those that have developed for the milk teeth.

WEEK *20*

You will notice your baby being more and more active, and may even be able to see some of its movements. The growing uterus is pushing up against your lungs and pushing your tummy outward. Your navel may suddenly pop out and stay that way until after delivery. Your chest (rather than breasts) has expanded and, if you do not already have an adjustable bra, now is the time to buy one.

Sebum from the sebaceous glands mixes with skin cells and begins to form the protective vernix which clings to the lanugo all over the skin, especially on the hairier parts and in the creases. The baby is now about 10 in (25 cm) long.

WEEK 21

You may start having heartburn—a burning sensation in the lower part of the chest—and may also bring up small amounts of acid fluid. Get your doctor to give you some antacid tablets.

The baby weighs just under 1 lb (450 g). It is still moving about freely in the amniotic fluid and can be felt kicking, sometimes high in your tummy, at other times down near your pubis.

WEEK 22

Your gums may be swelling because of the pregnancy hormones in your system. Do not forget that dental hygiene is important throughout pregnancy.

The baby is settling into a pattern of activity and sleep. It is probably at its most active while you are resting.

WEEK 23

The different parts of the baby can be felt (palpated) through your abdominal wall. You may feel a stitchlike pain at times down the side of your tummy; this is the uterine muscle stretching and the pain should go after you have had a rest.

At about this time the Braxton Hicks "rehearsal" contractions may become more pronounced, gripping and massaging the baby regularly.

WEEK 24

Your next doctor's visit—by now the doctor will be able to hear the baby's heart through a stethoscope. The top of your uterus (the fundus) now reaches to just above your navel.

The baby is growing rapidly—it is now about 13 in (32 cm) long and weighs over 1¼ lb (0·5 kg). Although its vital organs are quite mature by now, its lungs are not yet sufficiently developed for survival outside the uterus.

WEEK 25

You may get a cramp now and later. Avoid pointing your toes down. The baby may also be pressing against your bladder, causing you to go to the toilet little and often.

The baby's bone centers are beginning to harden.

WEEK 26

You should make arrangements for maternity leave and discover what benefits you are entitled to.

The baby's skin is beginning to change: instead of being paper-thin and transparent, it is gradually becoming opaque.

WEEK 27

You will be putting on weight fairly regularly now until about the 36th week. It may be a good idea to start thinking about what to get for the baby before you become so big that shopping becomes an unpleasant chore.

The baby's skin is very wrinkled, but is protected and nourished by the covering of vernix.

WEEK 28

Colostrum may leak from your breasts. From now on you will probably be visiting the doctor every two weeks. If you are Rhesus negative, an antibody check is done.

At this stage of development, the baby is considered legally viable, which means that if delivered it must be registered. It is about 14 in (38 cm) long and weighs around 2 lb (0·9 kg).

WEEK 29

You probably feel as if all your internal organs are being crowded out by the baby. There is pressure on your diaphragm, liver, stomach, and intestine.

By now the baby's head is more or less in proportion with the rest of its body.

WEEK 30

It is important to remember to maintain good posture when you are standing or sitting, even though the weight of the baby seems to be dragging you off balance.

The baby is probably very aware of the Braxton Hicks contractions, coming at regular intervals, even when you do not notice them.

WEEK 31

You may be getting very breathless when you climb stairs or exert yourself.

However breathless you feel, the baby is getting enough oxygen. It now weighs 4 lb (1·8 kg).

WEEK 32

At each doctor's visit the baby's position is felt, its rate of growth assessed and its heart checked.

The baby is 16 in (42 cm) long. It is perfectly formed but the fat reserves beneath its skin are only gradually laid down. Born at this time it would still need to be cared for in an incubator.

WEEK 33

You may be able to distinguish the baby's bottom from a foot or knee. You feel its movements more as prods and kicks—it may be too big now to swoop around in the amniotic fluid.

Your baby has probably adopted the most usual head down ("vertex" or "cephalic") position, in which it will now stay until delivery.

WEEK 34

You will be attending childbirth education classes by now.

The baby can differentiate between dark and light, and is bathed in a red glow when sunlight is on your tummy. Its skin is becoming pinker.

WEEK 35

You may have some backache at about this time, because the ligaments and muscles supporting the joints in the small of your back relax.

The fetus measures approximately 18 in (44 cm) in length and weighs around 5½ lb (2·5 kg).

WEEK 36

Doctor's visits will be every week from now on. If this is your first baby, it will probably engage some time this week or soon after, and may have done so already. Your lump will settle lower down and you should find that your breathing becomes easier, though you may also need to urinate more often.

The baby is almost fully mature and any time now the presenting part may drop into your pelvis ready for birth. It is about 18 in (49 cm) long.

WEEK 37

You may have a chance to tour the maternity floor and labor room of the hospital in which you are planning to give birth.

The baby may be rehearsing slight breathing movements, though there is no air in its lungs. In this way amniotic fluid passes into the baby's trachea, giving it hiccups!

WEEK 38

You may notice that the baby moves less now and that, instead of whole body movements, there are only jabs from the feet and knees, and the strange buzzing sensation inside your vagina of the baby's head moving against your pelvic floor muscles.

The baby may be putting on as much as 1 oz (28 g) in weight a day at this stage.

WEEK 39

Your cervix is ripening in preparation for labor. You may feel heavy and weary and be having quite strong Braxton Hicks contractions.

The amniotic fluid is renewed every 3 hours. The baby's bowel is filled with greenish-black meconium, excretions from the baby's alimentary glands mixed with bile pigment, lanugo, and cells from the bowel wall—its first stool after birth.

WEEK 40

The long-awaited day is near, and perhaps after the long wait you are now wishing that it had not come so quickly! You will soon hold your child in your arms.

The baby is about 20 in (55 cm) long. The presenting part is in the lower segment of your uterus and pressing through the softened, partially opened, cervix. It is about to leave the security it has always known and then it will need all your love and care.

Appendix 1

Health and hospitalization insurance

An amendment to Federal Law now makes it mandatory for all employers with 15 or more workers to provide equal benefits for male and female employees. This means that if you receive a health insurance benefit, it must cover pregnancy and birth in the same way as any other medical condition. This does not mean that the employer is required to give health insurance but if he does give it, it must not discriminate against the pregnant woman, whether married or not. Contact your insurance carrier for the precise details of your policy.

Most policies cover the hospital costs of a semiprivate room. If you wish to have a private room, you will be asked to pay a supplement. Your doctor will probably supply you with hospital registration forms or arrange to have them sent to you. At this time inquire about fees, deposits, and estimated costs. The obstetrician's fee does not usually include tests such as amniocentesis, nor does it include vitamins. Most health care policies do not cover the full cost of the obstetrician and may not cover any part of the cost of a midwife. In addition you may be asked to pay a standby fee for an anesthesiologist and a fee for a pediatrician. These may or may not be covered. The conditions of coverage for well baby care vary with the policy. Some insurance policies do not cover prenatal classes. It is worth while for women to group together to put pressure on the company to cover these costs. You should be aware that most policies do not pay until after the baby is born. Therefore it is important to make financial arrangements with your birth attendant regarding the time of payment, so that if possible you can pay when it is most convenient for you.

Childcare leave

Some employers allow a woman to have maternity leave without loss of benefits or seniority. It is now a Federal Law that companies that give maternity leave must not discriminate against fathers.

Disability benefits

These are determined by company policy. Federal Law states that if employees are covered by disability insurance, pregnancy and childbirth must be included. For further information, contact your State Department of Labor.

Union benefits

Contact your shop steward regarding union benefits since these vary widely.

Public assistance

If you have been receiving public assistance, visit the doctor or clinic as soon as you suspect you are pregnant. You will need a letter stating your expected date of delivery to qualify for an additional allowance for your expected baby. This will begin at the beginning of your fourth month of pregnancy and is equivalent to the allowance for an additional person. The expected baby is not entitled to food stamps or rent allowance. Contact your local Bureau of Public Assistance or Department of Social Services.

Medicaid

If you cannot afford prenatal care, contact your local Bureau of Medical Assistance or the Department of Social Services office at your local hospital or clinic. If your medical bills are excessive, you may qualify for Medicaid even though your income is otherwise adequate.

Free clinics

Contact your state or local Board of Health and local Women's Health Center for information about free or low cost clinics.

Women, Infants and Children's Supplementary Food Program (WIC)

This program supplies supplementary foods to women, infants and children at nutritional risk. Each state determines the standards for nutritional risk but two of the common criteria are inadequate weight gain and anemia. Women should apply through the appropriate state agency; in most instances this is the Department of Health or Department of Social Services. A woman is eligible as soon as her pregnancy is confirmed; she remains eligible until six months postpartum if she is bottlefeeding and twelve months postpartum if she is breastfeeding. The income regulations are standard throughout the 48 contiguous states. In 1989 a family of four may gross $21,553 a year and still be eligible. Nutritional risk is determined by a physician, registered nurse, dietician or nutritionist. Currently the supplementary foods include milk, cheese, eggs, juice, cereal, peanut butter, and dried beans for the pregnant and lactating woman, and infant formula, cereal and juice for the bottlefed baby.

Appendix 2

These research references relate to the asterisks in the main text. Where there is more than one asterisk on a page the references appear in order, with each entry on a new line relating to a different asterisk.

p. 32 Quoted by Pamela Nowicka, *Independent*, November 23, 1987.

p. 46 M. Enkin and I. Chalmers (eds), *Effectiveness and Satisfaction in Antenatal Care*, Spastics International Medical Publications, 1982. Ann Oakley, *The Captured Womb*, Blackwell Ltd, 1984.

p. 51 Sheila Kitzinger, *The Good Birth Guide*, Penguin 1983.

p. 52 Sheila Kitzinger, *Birth at Home*, Oxford University Press, 1979. Sheila Kitzinger, *Some Women's Experience of Induced Labour*, NCT, 1978.

p. 86 Sir Dugald Baird, *Journal of Biosocial Science*, I, 113, 1974.
☐ R. W. Smithells *et al.* "Maternal nutrition in early pregnancy", *British Journal of Nutrition*, 38, 3, 497–506, 1977. *Nutrition and Fetal Development* (ed. M. Winick), John Wiley & Sons, 1974. H. A. Kaminetzky and H. Baker, "Micronutrients in Pregnancy", *Clinical Obstetrics and Gynecology*, 20, 2, 363–380, 1977. R. M. Pitkin, "Nutritional support in obstetrics and Gynecology", *Clinical Obstetrics and Gynecology*, 19, 3, 489–513, 1976.

p. 87 P. J. Illingworth, R. T. Jung, P. W. Howie, T. E. Isles, "Reduction in postprandial energy expenditure during pregnancy", *British Medical Journal*, 294, 1573–1576, June 1987.
☐ Gary K. Oakes and Ronald A. Chez, "Nutrition in Pregnancy", *Contemporary Obstetrics and Gynecology*, 4, 147–150, 1974.
☐ M. D. G. Gillmer, "Obesity in pregnancy—physical and metabolic effects", in *Nutrition in Pregnancy: Proceedings of the Tenth Study Group of the Royal College of Obstetricians and Gynaecologists* 213–230, RCOG, London, 1983.

p. 88 Ellen Buchman Ewald, *Recipes for a Small Planet*, Ballantine, 1977.

p. 91 A. Malhotri and R. S. Sawers, *British Medical Journal*, 293, 465–466, 1986.
☐ M. Puig-Abuli *et al.*, "Zinc and uterine muscle contractivity", paper given at European Congress of Perinatal Medicine, Dublin, 1984.
☐ Jacqueline Gibson Gazella, *Nutrition for the Childbearing Year*, Woodland Publishing Co., Wayzata, Minn., 1979.
☐ R. W. Smithells *et al.*, *Lancet*, I, 8164, 339–340, 1980.

p. 92 M. Robinson, "Salt in Pregnancy", *Lancet*, I, 178–181, 1958.
☐ B. S. Worthington, J. Vermeersch and S. R. Williams, *Nutrition in Pregnancy and Lactation*, Mosby, 1977.
☐ B. S. Worthington *et al.*, *op. cit.*

p. 93 Jonathan Scher and Carol Dix, *Pregnancy*, Penguin, 1983.
☐ G. M. Stirrat, *Obstetrics*, Grant McIntyre Ltd, 1981.

p. 94 Federal Register, 43, 114, US Department of Health, Education and Welfare, 1978.

p. 95 *Perinatal Problems* (eds N. R. Butler and E. D. Alberman), Livingstone, 1969.
☐ M. B. Meyer, "How does maternal smoking affect birth weight and maternal weight gain?" *American Journal of Obstetrics and Gynecology*, 131, 888–893, 1978.
☐ J. Kline *et al.*, "Smoking: a risk factor for spontaneous abortion", *New England Journal of Medicine*, 297, 793–795, 1977. R. L. Naeye, "Relationship of cigarette smoking to congenital anomalies and perinatal death", *American Journal of Pathology*, 90, 289–297, 1978. M. B. Meyer and J. A. Tonascia, "Maternal smoking, pregnancy complications and perinatal mortality", *American Journal of Obstetrics and Gynecology*, 128, 494–502, 1977.

p. 97 I. J. Chasnoff *et al.*, "Cocaine Use in Pregnancy", *New England Journal of Medicine*, 313, 666–669, 1985.
☐ Cree *et al.*, *British Medical Journal*, 4, 251, 1973.
☐ J. V. Kelly, "Drugs used in the management of pregnancy", *Clinical Obstetrics and Gynecology*, 20, 395–410, 1977. See also G. M. Stirrat, *op. cit.*

p. 99 Peter Parish, *Doctors' & Patients' Handbook*, Knopf, 1977.

p. 100 Federal Register, 41, 115, 1976.

p. 101 Roger Hoag, "Perinatal psychology", *Birth and the Family Journal*, 113, 1974.
☐ Parish, *op. cit.*

p. 102 Studies of babies born in England and Wales between 1943 and 1965 revealed that the children of mothers who had had pelvic X-rays in pregnancy were almost twice as likely to develop leukemia before they were 10 years old as those whose mothers had had no X-rays. The greatest risk is in the earliest weeks, when the mother may not even know she is pregnant. The risk of cancer was increased 15 times when X-rays were done in the first three months of pregnancy. See A. Stewart and G. W. Kneale, "Radiation dose effects in relation to obstetric X-rays and childhood cancers", *Lancet*, I, 1495, 1970.
☐ David W. Smith, Sterling K. Clarren and Mary Ann Sedgwick Harvey, "Hyperthermia as a possible teratogenic agent", *Journal of Pediatrics*, 92, 6, 878–883, June, 1978. Peter Miller, David W. Smith and Thomas H. Shepard, "Maternal hyperthermia as a possible cause of anencephaly", *Lancet*, I, 8063, 519–521, 1978.

p. 105 *British Journal of Obstetrics and Gynaecology*, 91, 724–730, 1984.

p. 114 Aidan MacFarlane, *The Psychology of Childbirth*, Harvard UP, 1977.

p. 115 E. Noble, *Essential Exercises for the Childbearing Year*, John Murray, 1978.

p. 126 Christopher Redman, "Old-fashioned alertness is the key", *General Practitioner*, 1979.

p. 128 Pregnant women often have "physiological" anemia. There is a greater volume of blood circulating in their bodies; hence the red blood cells are dilated. This is normal and does not mean that they are suffering from anemia.
Having iron supplements when you do not need them may do more harm than good; excess iron enlarges the red blood cells (macrocytosis) until they are too big to pass through some of the capillaries in the mother's and the baby's circulatory systems. This deprives the baby of essential nutrients and can lead to its growth being retarded. See T. Lind, *British Journal of Obstetrics and Gynaecology*, 83, 760, 1976.

p. 162 Sherry L. Jimenez, Linda C. Jones and Ruth G. Jungman, "Prenatal classes for repeat parents", *MCN*, 4, 305–308, Sept./Oct., 1979.

p. 167 Grantly Dick-Read, *Childbirth Without Fear*, Harper & Row, 1972.

p. 168 Erna Wright, *The New Childbirth*, Pocket, 1969.

p. 170 Janet Balaskas, *Active Birth*, Unwin, London, 1983.

p. 187 Sheila Kitzinger, *Women as Mothers*, Random House, 1978.

p. 208 G. Kolata, "Fetuses Treated Through Umbilical Cords", *The New York Times*, March 29, 1988.

p. 210 T. J. Bassler, "Dietary practices of marathon runners", in *Health Aspects of Endurance Training, Medicine and Sport*, 12, Karger, 1978.

p. 215 F. Chenia and Ch. B. and C. A. Crowther, "Does advice to assume knee-chest position reduce the incidence of breech presentation at delivery? A randomized clinical trial", *Birth*, 14, 2, 75–78, June 1987.
☐ J. P. VanDorsten, B. S. Schifrin and R. L. Wallace, "Randomized controlled trial of external cephalic version with tocolysis in late pregnancy", *American Journal of Obstetrics and Gynecology*, 141, 417, 1981.

p. 219 J. F. Pearson and J. B. Weaver, *British Medical Journal*, I, 1305, 1976.
☐ J. F. Pearson, *op. cit.*

p. 232 Professor Mendez-Bauer discovered that dilatation of the cervix and the efficiency of contractions is much greater when a woman is standing up than when she is lying on her back. The uterus works nearly twice as well.[1]
Professor Caldeyro-Barcia, looking at the difference between contractions when a woman is lying on her left side and on her back, found that contractions were as frequent when a woman was standing as when lying flat on her back but that they were stronger. He concluded that for the uterus to work really effectively the woman should be standing.[2, 3]
Eleven hospitals in seven Latin-American countries joined in a study of the effects of the mother's position in labor. At each hospital half the mothers were told to lie in bed during the first stage and the other half were encouraged to get up or sit or lie in bed as they liked. Some 95 per cent of the women did not want to lie down. The membranes were not ruptured artificially, and the waters went at the end of the first stage or the beginning of the second in 85 per cent of the women. First-time mothers who stayed upright had shorter first stages than those who were lying down. The majority of the women said they were more comfortable when they stayed upright.
To find out whether an upright position could produce traumatic pressure on the

baby's head the researchers looked at the incidence of caput and also at the effect on the baby's heart and discovered that, when the membranes had not ruptured, there was no increased rate of caput if the mother was standing, nor was there an increase in deceleration of the fetal heart as recorded by an electronic monitor. They concluded that in normal labor an upright position is fine for the baby, shortens labor and reduces pain.[4]

Further research at the Queen Elizabeth Hospital, Birmingham, came up with the same results.[5]

See 1 Peter M. Dunn, "Obstetric delivery today", *Lancet*, I, 7963, 790–793, 1976.
2 R. Caldeyro-Barcia *et al.*, "Effects of position changes on the intensity and frequency of uterine contractions during labor", *American Journal of Obstetric Gynecology*, 80, 284, 1960.
3 Yuen Chou-liu, "Effects of an upright position during labor", *American Journal of Nursing*, December 1974.
4 R. L. Schwarcz *et al.*, "Fetal heart rate patterns in labors with intact and with ruptured membranes", *Journal of Perinatal Medicine*, 1, 153, 1973.
5 A. M. Flynn, J. Kelly, G. Hollins and P. F. Lynch, "Ambulation in labour", *British Medical Journal*, II, 591–593, 26 August, 1978.

p. 262 S. A. Huchcroft, M. P. Wearing and C. W. Buck, "Late results of cesarean and vaginal deliveries in cases of breech presentation", *Canadian Medical Association Journal*, 125, 726, 1982.

p. 264 J. G. B. Russel, "Moulding of the pelvic outlet", *Journal of Obstetrics and Gynaecology, British*

Commonwealth, 76, 817, 1967.
□ Michel Odent, *Birth Reborn*, Pantheon, 1984.

p. 265 Emanuel A. Friedman, MD, *Labor. Clinical Evaluation and Management*, Meredith Publishing Co., 1967.

p. 267 Marshall H. Klaus, John H. Kennel, Steven S. Robertson and Roberto Sosa, "Effects of social support during parturition and infant morbidity", *British Medical Journal*, 293, 585–587, 1986.

p. 278 Ronald Melzack, *The Puzzle of Pain*, Penguin 1973.

p. 279 Melzack, *op. cit.*
□ *ibid.*
□ *ibid.*

p. 282 Josephine A. Williamson, "Hypnosis in Obstetrics", *Nursing Mirror*, 27 November, 1975.

p. 283 Song Meiyu, "Acupuncture anaesthesia for caesarian section", *Midwives' Chronicle*, April 1985.
□ I. F. Skelton, "Acupuncture in labour", Society of Bio-physical Medicine, June 1985.
□ Christine Brown, "Therapeutic effects of bathing during labour", *Journal of Nurse-Midwifery*, 27, 1, 1982.

p. 284 M. Rosen, "Patient controlled analgesia", *British Medical Journal*, 289, 640–641, 1984.

p. 285 *Obstetrics*, a drug-information publication produced by Roche.
□ Dianne Houslow *et al.*, "Intrapartum drugs and fetal blood pH and gas status", *Journal of Obstetrics and Gynaecology, British Commonwealth*, 80, 1007–1012, 1973.

p. 286 Michael Rosen, "Pain

and its Relief", *Benefits and Hazards of the New Obstetrics*, (ed. T. Chard and M. Richards), William Heinemann, 1977.

p. 287 M. B. Wingate, "Effects of epidural analgesia on fetal and neonatal status", in *American Journal of Obstetrics and Gynecology*, 119, 1101–1106, 1974 and B. S. Schiffrin, "Fetal heart rate patterns following epidural anaesthesia and oxytocin infusion during labour", *Journal of Obstetrics and Gynaecology, British Commonwealth*, 79, 332, 1972.
□ Andrew Doughty, *Journal of Royal Society of Medicine*, December, 1978.

p. 288 Sheila Kitzinger, *Some Women's Experiences of Epidurals*, NCT, 1987.
□ A. D. Noble *et al.*, "Continuous lumbar epidural using bupivicaine", *Journal of Obstetrics and Gynaecology, British Commonwealth*, 78, 559, 1971.
□ Kay Standley *et al.*, "Local-regional anaesthesia during childbirth; effect on newborn behaviors", *Science*, 186, November 15, 1974.
□ Michael Rosen, *op. cit.*

p. 290 Kieran O'Driscoll and Declan Meagher, *Active Management of Labour*, W. B. Saunders, London, 1980.

p. 291 R. Caldeyro-Barcia *et al.*, "Adverse perinatal effects of early amniotomy during labour", *Modern Perinatal Medicine* (ed. L. Gluck), 431–439, Year Book Medical Publishers, Chicago, 1974.

p. 292 A. Huch *et al.*, "Continuous transcutaneous monitoring of fetal oxygen tension during labour", *British Journal of Obstetrics and Gynaecology*, 84, Suppl. 1, 1977.

☐ G. C. Gunn et al., "Premature rupture of the fetal membranes", *American Journal of Obstetrics and Gynecology*, 106, 469–477, 1970.

☐ P. J. Steer et al., "The effect of membrane rupture on fetal heart in induced labour", *British Journal of Obstetrics and Gynaecology*, 83, 454–459, June 1976.

p. 296 R. F. Harrison et al., "Is routine episiotomy necessary?", *British Medical Journal*, 288, 1971–1975, 1984.

☐ J. Sleep et al., "West Berkshire perineal management trial", *British Medical Journal*, 289, 587–590, 1984.

☐ S. Kitzinger and R. Walters, *Some Women's Experiences of Episiotomy*, National Childbirth Trust, 1981; S. Kitzinger and P. Simkin (eds), *Episiotomy and the Second Stage of Labor*, Pennypress, Seattle, 1984.

p. 300 "Caesarean Childbirth", Summary of a National Institute of Health statement, *British Medical Journal*, 1981.

p. 301 A. W. Linston and A. J. Campbell, "Danger of oxytocin-induced labour to fetuses", *British Medical Journal*, 3, 606–607, 1974.

p. 302 *Reducing the Risk*, Department of Health and Social Security, 1977.

p. 305 D. M. Okada and A. W. Chow "Neonatal scalp abscess following intrapartum fetal monitoring", *American Journal of Obstetrics and Gynecology*, 127, 875, 1977.

p. 306 G. S. Sykes et al., "Fetal distress and the condition of newborn infants", *British Medical Journal* 287, 943–945, October 1983. P. W. Howe, "Fetal monitoring in labour",

British Medical Journal, 292, 6518, 427–428, February 1986.

p. 309 Stuart Campbell, *Sharing*, Maternal Health Committee of Social Planning and Review Council of British Columbia, Summer 1979.

p. 316 Frederick Leboyer, *Birth Without Violence*, Knopf, 1975.

p. 321 Aidan MacFarlane, *Getting to Know Each Other*, Farley Products, 1979.

p. 324 Michel Odent, *Birth Reborn*, Pantheon, 1984, and *Entering the World: the Demedicalization of Childbirth*, Penguin, 1985.

☐ Johnson's Baby *Newsline*, Autumn 1978.

p. 328 Much of the original research was done with monkeys: Robert Hinde discovered that rhesus monkey babies separated from their mothers shortly after birth became very distressed and stayed hunched up in a corner of the cage. He suggested that separation from the mother might be bad for a newborn human baby too.[1] Other research has even gone so far as to indicate that mothers who had greater contact with their babies, and continued this contact through early childhood, produced children whose IQ, when tested at the age of five, was significantly higher than average.[2] Those who advocate bonding between mother and baby at birth also suggest that skin-to-skin contact between mother and child is important. Criticisms have been voiced that the child could become chilled, but a study of heat loss in warmed cribs as compared with that in the mother's arms showed that there was no significant difference between

the temperature of babies lying in heated cribs and others left with their mothers.[3]

See 1 Robert Hinde in *Proceedings of the Royal Society*, 196, 29, 1977.
2 F. S. W. Brimblecombe, *Separation and Special care Baby Units*, Heinemann, 1978.
3 C. N. Phillips, "Neonatal heat loss in heated cribs vs mother's arms", *Journal of Obstetrical, Gynecological and Neonatal Nursing*, 6, 11–15, 1974.

☐ Marshall Klaus and John Kennel, *Maternal-Infant Bonding*, Mosby, 1977.

p. 333 Klaus and Kennel, *op. cit.*

p. 334 L. Silverman, W. A. Silverman and J. C. Sinclair, *Pediatrics*, 41, 1033, 1969.

p. 337 P. A. and J. P. Davies, *Lancet*, 2, 1216, 1970.

p. 342 Cicely Williams and Derrick B. Jelliffe, *Mother and Child Health*, OUP, 1972.

p. 344 Harriet Sarnoff Schiff, *The Bereaved Parent*, G. K. Hall, 1977.

p. 359 Rudolph Schaffer, *Mothering*, Harvard UP, 1977.

p. 366 If a woman has never had German measles (rubella), the obstetrician may advise her to have a rubella vaccination after delivery. Since this vaccine could affect any baby conceived within the next three months, it is vitally important for her not to conceive during this time. If the woman is unsure about what kind of contraceptive to use, she may be offered an injection of a long-acting contraceptive called Depo Provera. Some women who intend to breastfeed are reluctant to have this injection which introduces hormones into the bloodstream.

Useful reading

Balaskas, J. *Active Birth*. New York: McGraw-Hill. 1983.

Balaskas, J. *The Active Birth Partners Handbook*. London: Sidgwick & Jackson. 1984.

Baldwin, R. and T. Palmarini. *Pregnant Feelings*. Berkeley: Celestial Arts. 1986.

Baldwin, R. *Special Delivery: The Complete Guide to Informed Birth*. Berkeley: Celestial Arts. 1989.

Blatt, R. *Prenatal Tests: What They Are, Their Benefits and Risks and How to Decide Whether to Have Them or Not*. New York: Vintage. 1988.

Brackhill, Y., J. Rice and D. Young. *Birth Trap*. New York: Warner. 1985.

Brewer, G. S. *The Very Important Pregnancy Program: A Personal Approach to the Art and Science of Having a Baby*. Emmaus, Pa.: Rodale Press. 1988.

Cohen, N. and L. Estner. *Silent Knife: Cesarean Prevention and Vaginal Birth After Cesarean*. South Hadley, Mass.: Bergin and Garvey. 1983.

Davis, E. *Heart and Hands: A Midwife's Guide to Pregnancy and Birth, 2nd ed*. Berkeley: Celestial Arts. 1987.

Inch, S. *Birthrights: What Every Parent Should Know About Childbirth in Hospitals*. New York: Pantheon. 1985.

Kitzinger, S. *Birth Over Thirty*. New York: Penguin. 1985.

Kitzinger, S. *Breastfeeding Your Baby*. New York: Knopf. 1989.

Kitzinger, S. *The Experience of Breastfeeding*. New York: Penguin. 1987.

Kitzinger, S. *Giving Birth: How it Really Feels*. New York: Farrar, Straus & Giroux. 1989.

Kitzinger, S. *Some Women's Experiences of Epidurals*. London: National Childbirth Trust. 1987.

Kitzinger, S. *Woman's Experience of Sex*. New York: Penguin. 1983.

Kitzinger, S. *Women as Mothers*. New York: Vintage. 1979.

Kitzinger, S. *Your Baby Your Way: Making Pregnancy Decisions and Birth Plans*. New York: Pantheon. 1987.

Kitzinger, S. and L. Nilsson. *Being Born*. New York: Putnam. 1986.

Kitzinger, S. and P. Simkin. *Episiotomy and the Second Stage of Labor, 2nd ed*. Seattle: Pennypress. 1986.

Korta, D. and R. Scaer. *A Good Birth: A Safe Birth*. New York: Bantam. 1984.

Leboyer. F. *Birth Without Violence*. New York: Knopf. 1975.

Lubic, R. W. and G. R. Hawes. *Childbearing: A Book of Alternatives*. New York: McGraw-Hill. 1987.

Odent, M. *Birth Reborn*. New York: Pantheon. 1986.

Olkin, S. K. *Positive Pregnancy Fitness: A Guide to a More Comfortable Pregnancy and Easier Birth Through Exercise and Relaxation*. New York: Avery Publishing. 1987.

Panuthos, C. *Transformation Through Birth: A Woman's Guide*. South Hadley, Mass.: Bergin and Garvey. 1984.

Richards, L. B. *The Vaginal Birth After Cesarean (VBAC) Experience: Birth Stories by Parents and Professionals*. South Hadley, Mass.: Bergin and Garvey. 1987.

Rothman, B. K. *In Labor: Women and Power in the Birthplace*. New York: W. W. Norton & Co. 1982.

Rothman, B. K. *The Tentative Pregnancy: Prenatal Diagnosis and the Future of Motherhood*. New York: Viking. 1986.

Simkin, P., J. Whalley and A. Keppler. *Pregnancy, Childbirth and the Newborn*. Deephaven, Minn.: Meadowbrook. 1984.

Useful addresses

American Academy of
Husband-Coached Childbirth
(AAHCC) (Bradley)
P.O. Box 5224
Sherman Oaks, CA 91413
(818) 788-6662

American College of Nurse
Midwives (ACNM)
1522 K Street N.W.
Suite 1120
Washington, D.C. 20005
(202) 347-5445

American College of
Obstetricians and
Gynecologists (ACOG)
409 12th Street S.W.
Washington, D.C. 2004-2188
(202) 638-5577

American Foundation for
Maternal Child Health
439 E. 51st Street
New York, NY 10022
(212) 759-5510

American Society for
Psychoprophylaxis in
Obstetrics (ASPO/Lamaze)
1840 Wilson Blvd., Suite 204
Arlington, VA 22201
(703) 524-7802

Association for Childbirth at
Home International (ACHI)
116 S. Louise
Glendale, CA 91205
(213) 663-4996

Birth & Life Bookstore
P.O. Box 70625
Seattle, WA 98107-0625
(206) 789-4444

Cascade Birthing Catalog
P.O. Box 12203
Salem, OR 97309
(503) 378-7545

Cesarean Prevention
Movement
P.O. Box 152
University Station
Syracuse, NY 13210
(315) 424-1942

Feminist Women's Health
Centers Federation
6221 Wilshire Blvd., Suite 419
Los Angeles, CA 90048
(213) 938-9838

Informed Birth and Parenting
P.O. Box 3675
Ann Arbor, MI 48106
(313) 662-6857

International Childbirth
Education Association (ICEA)
P.O. Box 20048
Minneapolis, MN 55420-0048
(612) 854-8660
Toll free # for book orders:
(800) 624-4939

La Leche League International
9616 Minneapolis Avenue
Franklin Park, IL 60131
(312) 455-7730

Moonflower Birthing Supply
P.O. Box 128
Louisville, CO 80027
(303) 665-2120

National Association of
Childbearing Centers
R.D. 1, Box 1
Perkiomenville, PA 18074
(215) 234-8068

National Association for
Parents and Professionals for
Safe Alternatives in Childbirth
(NAPSAC)
Route 1
Box 646
Marble Hill, MO 63764
(314) 238-2010

National Women's Health
Network
1325 G Street N.W.,
Lower Level
Washington, D.C. 20005
(202) 347-1140

Sibling Information Network
991 Main Street, Suite 3A
East Hartford, CT 06108
(203) 282-7050

VBAC Information
Nancy Wainer Cohen
10 Great Plain Terrace
Needham, MA 02192
(617) 449-2490

Women, Infants & Children's
Supplementary Food Program
Contact your State Department
of Health for local office.

*Sudden Infant Death
Syndrome* (SIDS)
Sudden Infant Death
Syndrome Alliance
330 North Charles Street
Baltimore, MD 21201
(800) 638-SIDS

Perinatal Bereavement
Compassionate Friends
P.O. Box 3696
Oak Brook, IL 60522-3696
(312) 990-0010

National Perinatal
Bereavement Coalition
1409 Willow Street
Suite 400
Minneapolis, MN 55403
(612) 870-1242

Pregnancy and Infant Loss
Center
1421 E. Wayzata Blvd.
Suite 40
Wayzata, MN 55391
(612) 473-9372

Glossary

Abdomen The part of the body containing the intestines, stomach, bowels, and uterus.

Abortion (Miscarriage) Either spontaneous or induced delivery of the fetus before the 28th week of development.

Abruptio placentae (Accidental hemorrhage) The peeling away of part of the placenta from the wall of the uterus in late pregnancy, which may result in bleeding.

Accelerated labor The artificial augmentation of contractions, after the cervix has started to dilate, by the injection of oxytocin through an intravenous drip. Often used to speed up a long labor or to get a "tired" or incoordinate uterus working more effectively.

Active birth An approach to childbirth which entails practicing stretching positions and movements and being in "open" and upright positions in labor.

Active management of labor The constant monitoring and technical control or induction of labor.

AFP See *Alphafetoprotein.*

AIDS Acquired immune deficiency syndrome – the collection of illnesses resulting from infection with the human immunodeficiency virus (HIV).

ALB See *Albumin.*

Albumin A protein present in all animal tissues. Albumin in the urine of a pregnant woman can be a sign of preeclampsia.

Alphafetoprotein (AFP) A substance produced by the embryonic yolk sac, and later by the fetal liver, which enters the mother's bloodstream during pregnancy. A very high level can indicate neural tube defects of the fetus—such as spina bifida or Down syndrome—but can also mean that the woman is carrying more than one child.

Alveoli Milk glands in the breasts which, when they are stimulated by prolactin, produce a flow of milk.

Amenorrhea The absence of menstrual periods.

Amino acids The main organic chemical constituents of proteins found in all foods produced from animals, but only in limited and varying combinations in vegetables.

Ammonium chloride See *Diuretics.*

Amnesia Loss of memory, usually short term, which can be a side effect of certain drugs, especially Valium.

Amniocentesis The surgical extraction of a small amount of amniotic fluid through the pregnant woman's abdomen. Usually done as a test for fetal defects or maturity.

Amnion The layer of membrane immediately enveloping the fetus and the amniotic fluid inside the uterus; it is also referred to as the amniotic sac, or bag of waters.

Amniotic fluid The fluid surrounding the fetus in the uterus.

Amniotic sac See *Amnion.*

Amniotomy The surgical rupture of the amniotic sac, sometimes done to speed up labor. Referred to as ARM (artificial rupture of the membranes).

Amytal See *Barbiturates.*

Anemia A condition in which there is an abnormally low proportion of red corpuscles in the blood, treated by iron (Fe) supplements.

Anesthetic Medication that produces partial or complete insensibility to pain.

Anesthetic, general Anesthetic that affects the whole body, usually with loss of consciousness.

Anesthetic, local Anesthetic that affects a limited part of the body. See also *Caudal; Epidural; Paracervical.*

Analgesics Painkilling agents not inducing unconsciousness.

Anencephaly The congenital absence of the brain.

Antepartum cardiotography Test during pregnancy to check fetal heartbeat.

Antepartum hemorrhage (APH) Bleeding from the vagina occurring after the 28th week of pregnancy. See also *Abruptio placentae; Placenta previa.*

Anterior position See *Occipito anterior.*

Antibacterials Chemical agents that limit the growth of, or destroy, bacteria. See also *Sulphonamides.*

Antibiotics Substances capable of destroying or limiting the growth of micro-organisms, especially bacteria.

Antibodies Protein produced naturally by the body to combat any foreign bodies, germs, or bacteria.

Anticholinergenic drugs Used in the treatment of nausea and vomiting, partly by limiting the impulses through the nervous system and partly by restricting the secretion of stomach acids.

Anticoagulants   Drugs that prevent the blood clotting.

Anticonvulsants   Drugs that combat convulsions, especially epilepsy.

Antihistamines   Tranquilizers used in the treatment of nausea, vomiting, and certain allergics.

Apgar scale   A general test of the baby's wellbeing given immediately after birth to ascertain the heart rate and tone, respiration, blood circulation, and nerve responses.

APH   See *Antepartum hemorrhage.*

Apnea   Interrupted breathing which may occur in preterm and low-birthweight babies.

Areola   The pigmented circle of skin surrounding the nipple.

Arhythmic contractions Irregular contractions.

ARM   See *Amniotomy.*

Aspirin (Salicylate)   A mild analgesic. Taken in pregnancy, it may interfere with the clotting of blood in the fetus and can cause neonatal jaundice.

Bag of waters   See *Amnion.*

Barbiturates   Powerful and highly addictive tranquilizers.

Bearing down   The pushing movement made by the uterus in the second stage of labor.

Bile pigment   See *Bilirubin.*

Bilirubin   Broken-down red blood cells, normally converted to nontoxic substances by the liver. Some newborn babies

have levels of bilirubin too high for their livers to cope with. See also *Jaundice, neonatal.*

Birth canal   See *Vagina.*

Blastocyst   An early stage of the developing egg when it has segmented into a group of cells.

Blighted ovum   An abnormal development of the egg in which the cells do not develop in the usual way to form a baby. It results in miscarriage.

Bradycardia   A slow heart rate. In the fetus and newborn baby, this is a rate of less than 120 beats a minute.

Braxton Hicks contractions (Rehearsal contractions) Contractions of the uterus which occur throughout pregnancy, but which may not be noticed until the ninth month.

Breast pump   Apparatus for drawing milk from the breasts.

Breech presentation   The position of a baby who is bottom down rather than head down in the uterus.

Brow presentation   The position of a baby who is head down in the uterus, but with chin up, so that the brow comes through the cervix first.

Cesarean section   Delivery of the baby through a cut in the abdominal and uterine walls.

Candida   See *Thrush.*

Caput   A small, temporary swelling on the crown of the baby's head caused by the head being pressed against an incompletely dilated cervix.

Carpal tunnel syndrome   A numbness and tingling of the hands arising from pressure on the nerves of

the wrist. In pregnancy it is caused by the body's accumulation of fluids.

Catheter   A thin plastic tube inserted into the body, through a natural channel to draw off urine from the bladder, or into a vein to maintain a constant input of fluids, or into the epidural space to introduce anesthetic.

Caudal (Caudal epidural block)   An anesthetic injected into the base of the spine. See also *Epidural.*

Cephalhematoma   A temporary swelling on the side of the baby's head caused by pressure during labor.

Cephalic presentation   The position of a baby who is head down in the uterus. This is the most common presentation.

Cephalopelvic disproportion A state in which the head of the fetus is larger than the cavity of the mother's pelvis. Delivery must be by cesarean section.

Certified Nurse Midwife   A graduate of an approved program who has passed National Boards and is licensed to practice by her state.

Cervical dilatation   See *Dilatation.*

Cervical erosion   Superficial inflammation of the cervix which sometimes occurs during early pregnancy, and may if infected produce irritation and yellow vaginal discharge.

Cervical incompetence   A disorder of the cervix, usually arising after a previous mid-pregnancy termination or damage to the cervix during a previous labor, in which the cervix opens up too soon, resulting in repeated mid-pregnancy miscarriages. It is sometimes treated by suturing to hold the cervix closed.

Cervix The lower entrance to the uterus, or neck of the womb.

Chloasma Skin discoloration during pregnancy, often facial.

Chloral drugs Non-barbiturate hypnotic tranquilizers.

Chlorpromazine (Thorazine) A powerful sedative often used in conjunction with hypnotics, analgesics and anesthetics.

Chorion The outer membranous tissue enveloping the developing fetus and placenta.

Chorionic gonadotrophin See *Human chorionic gonadotrophin (HCG).*

Chorionic villi The layer of tiny fronds which forms around the fertile ovum, allowing it to become embedded in the uterine wall.

Chorionic villus sampling A method of screening for genetic handicap by analysis of tissue from the small protrusions on the outer membrane enveloping the embryo, which later form the placenta. The sample is taken by inserting a needle through the vagina.

Chromosomes Rodlike structures containing genes occurring in pairs within the nucleus of every cell. Human cells each contain 23 pairs. *See* also *Gene.*

Circumcision An operation to cut the foreskin from the penis, usually performed soon after delivery if desired.

Cleft palate A congenital abnormality of the roof of the mouth.

Clitoris Sensitive small organ at the upper end of a woman's genitals, just under the pubic bone and between the folded external labia.

Club foot A congenital abnormality when the foot is twisted out of shape.

Codeine An addictive pain-killing agent derived from opium.

Colostrum A kind of milk, rich in proteins, formed and secreted by the breasts in late pregnancy and gradually changing to mature milk some days after delivery.

Conception The fertilization of the egg by the sperm and its implantation in the uterine wall.

Congenital abnormality An abnormality or deformity existing from birth usually arising from a damaged gene, the adverse effect of certain drugs, or the effect of some diseases during pregnancy.

Contractions The regular tightening of the uterine muscles as they work to dilate the cervix in labor and to press the baby down the birth canal.

Cordocentesis See *Umbilical vein sampling.*

Corpuscles Constituents of blood, divided into red and white varieties.

Corpus luteum A glandular mass which forms in the ovary after fertilization. It produces progesterone which helps to form the placenta, and is active for the first 14 weeks of pregnancy.

Cortisone A steroid produced by the adrenal gland which appears in the amniotic fluid immediately before labor.

Count to ten chart A log of the first 10 fetal movements felt by the mother over 12 hours some time at the end of pregnancy. Sometimes called "fetal movement" or "kick" chart.

Crowning The moment when the largest part of the baby's head appears in the vagina and does not slip back again.

CVS See *Chorionic villus sampling.*

Cystitis An inflammation of the bladder and urinary tract, producing a stinging sensation when water is passed.

D and C The surgical *dilatation* (opening) of the cervix, and *curettage* (removal of the contents) of the uterus.

Dehydration An excessive loss of body water.

Demerol See *Analgesics.*

Depression, respiratory Breathing difficulties in the newborn baby.

Dextrose A solution of glucose used to supplement the level of blood sugar, usually introduced by intravenous drip.

Dextrostix A test to assess the level of sugar in the urine.

Diabetes Failure of the system to metabolize glucose, traced by excess sugar in the blood and urine.

Diastolic pressure The blood pressure between heart beats. See also *Systolic pressure.*

Diazepam (Valium) See *Tranquilizers.*

Dilatation The progressive opening of the cervix, caused by uterine contractions during labor.

Distocia, shoulder A state in which the baby's shoulders get stuck during delivery.

Distress See *Fetal distress.*

Diuretics   Drugs which increase the amount of urine excreted.

Dizygotic   See *Twins*.

Doppler   A method of using ultrasound vibrations to listen to the fetal heart.

Down syndrome (Mongolism)   A severe congenital abnormality producing subnormal mentality.

Drip   See *Intravenous drip*.

Dura   The outer membrane protecting the spinal cord.

Eclampsia   The severe form of preeclampsia, characterized by extremely high blood pressure, headaches, visual distortion and flashes, convulsions and, in the worst cases, coma and death. The condition is now rare since the symptoms of preeclampsia are treated immediately.

Ectopic pregnancy   A pregnancy which develops outside the uterus, usually in the fallopian tube. The mother has severe pain low down at one side of the abdomen at any time from the 6th to 12th weeks of pregnancy. The pregnancy must be surgically terminated.

EDD   The estimated date of delivery.

Edema   Fluid retention, which causes the body tissues to be puffed out.

Elective induction   Induction done for convenience rather than for medical reasons. See also *Induction*.

Electrode   A small electrical conductor used obstetrically for monitoring the fetal heartbeat.

Electronic fetal monitoring   The continuous monitoring of the fetal heart by a transducer placed on the mother's abdomen over the area of the fetal heart or by an electrode inserted through the cervix and clipped to the baby's scalp.

Embryo   The developing organism in pregnancy, from about the 10th day after fertilization until about the 12th week of pregnancy, when it is termed a fetus.

Endocrinological changes   Changes in the secretion of the endocrine glands which occur in pregnancy or the four weeks after delivery (the puerperium).

Endometrium   The inner lining of the uterus.

Enema   The injection of fluids through the rectum to expel its contents.

Engaged (Eng/E)   The baby is engaged when it has settled with its presenting part deep in the pelvic cavity. This often happens in the last month of pregnancy.

Engorgement   The over-congestion of the breasts with milk. If long periods are left between feedings, painful engorgement can occur, and can be relieved by putting the baby to the breast or expressing the excess milk.

Epidural (Lumbar epidural block)   Regional anesthesia, used during labor and for cesarean sections, in which an anesthetic is injected through a catheter into the epidural space in the lower spine.

Episiotomy   A surgical cut in the perineum to enlarge the vagina.

Estriol   A form of estrogen. Its level in the urine or blood may be tested in late pregnancy to find if the placenta is working well.

Estrogen   A hormone produced by the ovary.

External version (External cephalic version, or ECV)   The manipulation by gentle pressure of the fetus into the cephalic position. This may be done by an obstetrician some time between the 32nd and 34th week of pregnancy if the baby is breech.

Face presentation   The position of a baby whose face is coming through the cervix first.

Fallopian tube (Oviduct)   The tube into which a ripe egg is wafted after its expulsion from the ovary, along which it travels on its way to the uterus.

False labor   Braxton Hicks (rehearsal) contractions that come so strongly and regularly that they are mistaken for the contractions of the first stage of labor.

Fertilization   The meeting of the sperm with the ovum to form a new life.

Fetal distress   A shortage in the flow of oxygen to the fetus which can arise from numerous causes.

Fetus   The developing child in the uterus, from the end of the embryonic stage, at about the 12th week of pregnancy, until the date of delivery.

FH   Fetal heart.

Fiber optics   The transmission of light along flexible bundles of glass. Sometimes inserted into the uterus to give a view of the fetus inside.

Fluid retention   See *Edema*.

FMF   Fetal movement felt.

Folic acid A form of Vitamin B essential to the constant production of blood cells and hemoglobin, the shortage of which can produce anemia in the fetus. It is sometimes supplemented during pregnancy.

Fontanelles The soft spots between the unjoined sections of the skull of the fetus.

Foremilk Milk which accumulates naturally in the ducts behind the nipple and precedes the main release of milk.

Fraternal twins See *Twins.*

Fundal palpation Feeling through the abdominal wall for the top of the uterus to assess its height.

Fundus The upper part of the uterus.

Gamma globulin A protein-based antibody.

Gene The part of every cell which stores genetic characteristics.

Genetic counseling Advice on the probability of recurrent hereditary abnormalities or diseases.

Gentle birth One term used for a method of delivery proposed by Frederick Leboyer in which the shock of birth upon the baby is minimized and the baby is welcomed by loving hands, skin contact, and soft lights and is able to discover itself in a warm bath.

German measles See *Rubella.*

Gestation The length of time between conception and delivery.

Glucose A natural sugar found in certain organic materials and in the blood: the main source of energy.

Glycogen The natural source of glucose; glycogen stores carbohydrate materials and is formed by the liver and muscles.

Gynecologist A doctor who specializes in female medicine.

Hemoglobin (Hb) A constituent of the red blood cells which contains iron (Fe) and stores oxygen.

Hemorrhage Excessive bleeding.

Hemorrhoids (Piles) Swelling of the veins around the rectum.

Hb See *Hemoglobin.*

HCG See *Human chorionic gonadotrophin.*

Hegar's sign The softening of the lower part of the uterus that gradually occurs during the first 6 weeks of pregnancy.

Hormone A chemical messenger in the blood which stimulates various organs to action.

Hormone accelerated labor See *Induction.*

Human chorionic gonadotrophin A hormone released into the woman's bloodstream by the developing placenta from about 6 days after the last period was due. Its presence in the urine means that a woman is pregnant.

Hyaline membrane disease Respiratory distress affecting some preterm babies resulting from a lack of surfactant which holds the lungs open.

Hydatidiform mole A rare abnormality in which the egg fails to develop after becoming implanted in the uterine wall, so there is no baby, although the placenta and chorionic villi go on developing. If the woman does not miscarry, the growth must be removed.

Hydrocephalus A congenital abnormality in which the baby's head is swollen with fluid.

Hyperemesis gravidarum Almost continuous vomiting during pregnancy.

Hypertension High blood pressure. In pregnancy this can reduce the fetal blood supply.

Hyperventilation Abnormally heavy breathing which flushes carbon dioxide out of the bloodstream, so that the normal chemical balance of the blood is lost.

Hypnosis A state of mental passivity with a special susceptibility to suggestion. This can be used as an anesthetic, and can be self-induced.

Hypnotics See *Tranquilizers.*

Hypoglycemia Low blood sugar sometimes apparent in babies who have suffered a difficult delivery, preterm babies, or those of diabetic mothers. It can be artificially produced by giving the mother intravenous glucose in labor, since this increases the release of insulin, which breaks the sugar down. The baby may have to be given extra sugar.

Hypotension Low blood pressure.

Hypothermia A very low body temperature.

ICEA International Childbirth Education Association.

Identical twins See *Twins.*

Implantation The embedding of the fertilized ovum within the wall of the uterus.

Incoordinate uterine action See *Uterine action, incoordinate.*

Induction The process of artificially starting off labor and keeping it going.

Insulin A hormone produced by the pancreas which regulates the level of carbohydrates and amino acids in the system. It may be used as a means of controlling the effects of diabetes. See also *Diabetes.*

Internal monitoring See *Electronic fetal monitoring.*

Intramuscular injection An injection into a muscle.

Intravenous drip The infusion of fluids directly into the bloodstream by means of a fine catheter introduced into a vein.

Intravenous injection An injection into a vein.

Invasive techniques Any medical technique which intrudes into the body.

Involution of the uterus The process by which the uterus returns to its normal state after pregnancy.

jaundice, neonatal A common complaint in newborn babies, caused by inability of the liver to break down successfully an excess of red blood cells. See also *Bilirubin.*

Ketosis The accumulation of lactic acid in various body tissues and fluids, often indicated by acetone in the urine.

Labia The folds (or lips) of skin at the mouth of the vagina.

Lanugo The fine soft body hair of the fetus.

Lateral position Transverse lie or horizontal position of a fetus in the uterus (sometimes occurring if the mother has a large pelvis), where the presenting part is either a shoulder or the side of the head.

Laxatives Purgative drugs.

Leboyer approach See *Gentle birth.*

Let-down reflex See *Milk ejection reflex.*

Lie The position of the fetus in the uterus.

Ligament A fibrous tissue binding and connecting bones.

Lightening The engagement of the fetus in the pelvis, with its presenting part fitting securely in the pelvic inlet like an egg in an egg cup.

Linea nigra A line of dark skin which appears down the center of the abdomen over the rectus muscle in some women during pregnancy.

Lithotomy position The standard position for delivery, the mother lying flat on her back, with her legs wide apart and raised, fixed in stirrups.

Lochia Postnatal vaginal discharge.

Longitudinal lie The position of the fetus in the uterus, in which the spines of the fetus and the mother are parallel.

Long L See *Longitudinal lie.*

Low-birthweight baby A baby who at birth is below the weight of $5\frac{1}{2}$ lb (2.5 kg).

Meconium The first contents of the bowel, present in the fetus before birth and passed during the first days after birth. The presence of meconium in the fluid before delivery is usually taken as a sign of fetal distress.

Milk ejection reflex The flow of milk into the nipple.

Miscarriage See *Abortion.*

Molding The shaping of the bones of the baby's skull as it passes through the birth canal.

Mongolism See *Down syndrome.*

Monilia See *Thrush.*

Monitoring See *Electronic fetal monitoring.*

Monozygotic See *Twins.*

Montgomery's tubercles Small bumps on the areola surrounding the nipple.

Morphine A narcotic opium derivative used as an analgesic.

Morula A stage in the growth of the fertilized egg when it has developed into 32 cells.

Mucus A sticky secretion.

Multigravida A woman in her second or subsequent pregnancy.

Multiple pregnancy The development of two or more babies. See also *Twins.*

Mutation A damaged genetic cell. This can occur naturally or, more commonly, as an effect of outside agents, such as radiation.

Narcotic A drug which induces a state of stupor.

Nasogastric tube A pliable catheter passed into the stomach through the nose.

Nembutal See *Barbiturates.*

Neural tube defects Abnormalities of the central nervous system. See also *Anencephaly; Hydrocephalus; Spina bifida.*

Nicotine A highly poisonous substance present in tobacco. During pregnancy it enters the bloodstream of a woman who smokes, and affects the efficiency of the placenta, usually producing a low birthweight baby.

Notochord The cells which form the primitive nervous system.

Nucleus The central part or core of a cell which contains genetic information.

Occipito anterior The position of the baby in the uterus when the back of its head (the crown or occiput) is toward the front (anterior).

Occipito posterior The position of the baby in the uterus when the back of its head (the crown or occiput) is toward the mother's back (posterior).

Ovary One of the two female glands, set at the entrance of the fallopian tubes, which regularly produce eggs.

Oviduct See *Fallopian tube.*

Ovulation The production of the ripe egg by the ovary.

Oxygenate To saturate with oxygen.

Oxytocin A hormone secreted by the pituitary gland which stimulates uterine contractions and the milk glands in the breasts to produce milk.

Oxytocin challenge test A way of assessing the condition of the fetus and of the placenta, by which oxytocin is introduced into the mother's bloodstream and the reactions of the fetal heart to uterine contractions are recorded.

Palpation Feeling the parts of the baby through the mother's abdominal wall.

Paracervical block Regional anesthesia sometimes used during labor, involving a series of local anesthetic injections around the cervix.

Pelvic floor The muscular structure set within the pelvis which supports the bladder and the uterus.

Pelvis The bones forming a girdle about the hips.

Perinatal The period from the 28th week of gestation to one week following delivery.

Perineum The area surrounding the vagina and between the vagina and the rectum.

PET See *Preeclampsia.*

Phenobarbital See *Barbiturates.*

Phenothiazine Strong tranquilizers used in the treatment of nausea and vomiting. See also *Tranquilizers.*

Phototherapy Treatment by exposure to light, used in the treatment of jaundice.

Pituitary gland A gland set just below the brain which, among other functions, secretes various hormones controlling the menstrual cycle. In late pregnancy it releases a hormone, oxytocin, into the bloodstream, which stimulates the milk glands.

Placenta The organ which develops on the inner wall of the uterus and supplies the fetus with all its life-supporting requirements and carries waste products to the mother's system.

Placental function tests Tests to assess the condition and efficiency of the placenta. See also *Estriol; Oxytocin challenge test.*

Placental insufficiency A condition in which the placenta provides inadequate life support for the fetus, resulting in a baby at special risk.

Placenta previa A condition in which the placenta lies over the cervix. This part of the uterus stretches in the last few weeks of pregnancy, but the placenta cannot stretch, so it may separate; the result is antepartum hemorrhage. A woman with a complete placenta previa is delivered by cesarean section.

Polyhydramnios An excess of amniotic fluid in the uterus.

Posterior See *Occipito posterior.*

Postmaturity The state of the fetus in an overdue pregnancy. The skin may be dry and peeling, and the fingernails may need cutting immediately after birth.

Postnatal After the birth.

Postpartum After delivery.

PP See *Presenting part.*

Preeclampsia (Preeclamptic toxemia) An illness in which a woman has high blood pressure, edema, albumin in the urine and often excessive weight gain. See also *Eclampsia.*

Premature See *Preterm.*

Prenatal Before delivery.

"Prepping" Procedures carried out to prepare the woman for delivery.

Presentation   The position of the fetus in the uterus before and during labor.

Presenting part   That part of the fetus which is lying directly over the cervix.

Preterm   A baby born before the 37th week of pregnancy and weighing less than $5\frac{1}{2}$ lb (2.5 kg).

Primigravida   A woman having her first pregnancy.

Progesterone   A hormone produced by the corpus luteum and then by the placenta.

Progestogen   A synthetic variety of the hormone progesterone used in oral contraceptives.

Prostaglandins   Natural substances, which stimulate the onset of labor contractions. Prostaglandin gel is used to soften the cervix and induce labor.

Psychoprophylaxis   A method of preparation for childbirth which is centered on techniques for breathing.

Pubis   The bones forming the front of the lower pelvis.

Pudendal block   Injection to numb the nerves in the perineum.

Puerperium   The four weeks following delivery.

Purse-string (Shirodkar) suture   Stitches passed through and around the cervix, and then drawn tight to support the uterus when the cervix is "incompetent".

Pyelitis   An infection of the kidneys. It is treated by a course of antibiotics.

Pyridoxine   Vitamin B6.

Quickening   The first noticeable movements of the fetus.

Rectus muscle   The muscles running up the center of the abdomen.

REM   Rapid eye movement in sleep, indicating mental activity.

Respiratory depression   See *Depression, respiratory.*

Rhesus factor   A distinguishing characteristic of the red blood corpuscles. All human beings have either Rhesus positive or Rhesus negative blood. If the mother is Rhesus negative and the fetus Rhesus positive severe complications and Rhesus disease (the destruction of the red corpuscles by antibodies) may occur unless prevented by anti-D gamma globulin.

Rooting   The baby's instinctive searching for the nipple.

Rubella (German measles)   A mild virus which may cause congenital abnormalities in the fetus if contracted by a woman during the first 12 weeks of pregnancy.

Sacrum   The big bone at the base of the spine, forming the back of the pelvis.

Salicylate   See *Aspirin.*

Scan (Screen)   A way of building up a picture of an object by bouncing high-frequency soundwaves off it. The sonar or ultrasound scan is used during pregnancy to show the development of the fetus in the uterus. See also *Transducer.*

Senna   Derivatives of the cassia plant, components of many laxatives.

Shirodkar   See *Purse-string suture.*

Shoulder distocia   See *Distocia, shoulder.*

Show   A vaginal discharge of bloodstained mucus occurring before labor, resulting from the onset of cervical dilatation. Sign of labor.

Small for dates   Babies who are born at the right time but for some reason have not flourished in the uterus. See also *Placental insufficiency.*

Sonargram   See *Doppler.*

Sperm (Spermatozoon)   The male reproductive cell which fertilizes the egg.

Spina bifida   A congenital neural tube defect, in which the fetal spinal cord forms incorrectly, outside the spinal column.

Spinal anesthesia   An injection of local anesthetic into the spinal cord.

Spontaneous abortion   See *Abortion.*

Stanislavsky technique Acting exercises for increasing body awareness and muscle control.

Stasis of milk   A reduction in the flow of breast milk.

Steroids   Drugs used in the treatment of skin disorders, asthma, hay fever, rheumatism, and arthritis. Because they alter the chemical balance of the metabolism they may cause fetal abnormalities if used extensively during pregnancy.

Stethoscope, fetal   A trumpet-shaped instrument placed against the pregnant woman's abdomen for the fetal heart to be heard.

Stillbirth   The delivery of a

dead baby after the 28th week of pregnancy.

Stool bulk producers Drugs to treat constipation.

Streptomycin A wide spectrum antibiotic which should not be taken in pregnancy. See also *Antibiotics.*

Stress tests Tests during pregnancy that cause stress to the fetus.

Stretch marks See *Striae.*

Striae Silvery lines that sometimes appear on the skin after it has been stretched during pregnancy.

Sulpha drugs See *Sulphonamides.*

Sulphonamides Chemicals sometimes used to combat infections. See also *Antibacterials.*

Supplementary feeding Additional bottles given to a breastfed baby.

Surfactant A creamy fluid which reduces the surface tension of the lungs so that they do not stick together when deflated. Preterm babies may have breathing difficulties because the surfactant has not developed sufficiently.

Suture The surgical stitching together of a wound or tear.

Syntocinon The synthetic form of oxytocin, used to induce or accelerate labor.

Systolic pressure The blood pressure built up in the arteries when the heart is beating. It is the upper figure on any record. See also *Diastolic pressure.*

Tachycardia An abnormally fast heart rate in the fetus and newborn baby. This is a rate of above 160 beats per minute.

Telemetry A method of monitoring, using radio waves. See also *Electronic fetal monitoring.*

Teratogenic A general term for drugs which cause physical defects in the embryo.

Term The end of pregnancy: 40 weeks from the last menstrual period.

Termination An artificially induced abortion before the end of the 28th week of pregnancy. Sometimes used as a synonym for induction.

Test weighing A method of assessing how much breast milk the baby is taking by weighing the baby immediately before and after a feeding.

Tetracycline A wide spectrum antibiotic which should be avoided during pregnancy, as it can affect the fetal teeth and bones. See also *Antibiotics.*

Thrombosis A blood clot in the heart or blood vessels.

Thrush A yeast infection which can form in the mucous membranes of the mouth or genitals.

Thyroid gland A gland in the throat which produces hormones that control the metabolic rate.

Tochodynamometer A pressure gauge attached by a belt to the mother's abdomen to record contractions.

Touch relaxation A means of releasing muscular tension by resting the hand on tense areas and drawing out the tension.

Toxemia See *Preeclampsia* and *Eclampsia.*

Toxoplasmosis, congenital Toxoplasmosis is a parasitic disease spread by cat faeces. If it crosses the placenta during the first 12 weeks of

pregnancy, it can cause blindness in the baby.

Tranquilizers Drugs used to calm a state of anxiety or tension without inducing unconsciousness. Mild tranquilizers, such as Valium, may be prescribed during pregnancy, but should be avoided during labor as they can cause fetal respiratory depression. Powerful tranquilizers (along with antihistamines and hypnotics, which are sometimes used for their tranquilizing properties) should be avoided during pregnancy. See also *Barbiturates.*

Transducer An instrument which is sensitive to the echoes of very high-frequency sound-waves bounced off the developing fetus, and which translates the information to build up an image on a television screen. This form of scan is known as ultrasound. See also *Scan.*

Transition A point between the first and second stages of labor when the cervix has dilated to between 7 and 8 cm.

Trial of labor A situation in which, although a cesarean section seems necessary, the mother is allowed to go into labor in order to see if a natural delivery is possible.

Twins The simultaneous development of two babies in the uterus, either as a result of the production of two eggs which are fertilized independently by two sperm—dizygotic or fraternal twins—or, more rarely, as a result of one fertilized egg dividing to produce monozygotic or identical twins.

Ultrasound See *Scan; Transducer.*

Umbilical cord The cord connecting the fetus to the placenta.

Umbilical vein sampling (Cordocentesis) A fine needle is passed through the mother's abdomen into the fetal vein in the umbilical cord. The technique allows fetal blood to be tested, facilitates intra-uterine blood transfusions, and enables drugs to be injected directly into the baby.

Undescended testicle A testicle which has failed to drop naturally from the lower abdomen into the scrotum.

Uterine action, incoordinate Irregular uterine contractions.

Uterine inertia Weak and ineffective uterine contractions.

Uterus (Womb) The hollow muscular organ in which the fertile egg becomes embedded, where it develops into the embryo and then the fetus.

Vacuum extractor An instrument, used as an alternative to forceps, which adheres to the baby's scalp by suction and, with the help of the mother's bearing-down efforts, can be used to pull the baby out of the vagina.

Vagina The canal between the uterus and the external genitals. It receives the penis during intercourse and is the passage through which the baby is delivered.

VE Vaginal examination.

Vernix A creamy substance which often covers the fetus whilst in the uterus.

Vertex presentation (VX) *See Cephalic presentation.*

Vulva The external part of the female reproductive organs, including the labia and clitoris.

Water birth Birth while the woman is lying or floating in water.

XX/XY chromosomes The chromosomes which genetically distinguish the female and male respectively.

Yolk sac The sac which stores the nutrients for the developing fertile egg.

Index

Acknowledgments

Dorling Kindersley would like to thank the following for their help: David Ashby, Susan Berry, Sue Burt, Giovanni Caselli, Mary Chesshyre, Penny Church, Kate Duffield, Helen Dziemidko, Eleanor Enkin, Dr Murray Enkin, Jean Flynn, Jeanette Graham, Daisy Hayes, Andrew Heritage, Ken Hone, Dr Meeks Joankins, Elaine and Jerry Kingett, Tess and Jon McKenney, Chris Meehan, Kevin Molloy, MS Filmsetting Limited, Helen Sampey, Spectrum Reproductions, W Photo, Steven Wooster.

Special thanks go to the team who prepared the first edition for publication: Sybil del Strother, Ginger Weatherley, Lindy Newton, Bob Gordon and Julia Harris; and in the US Janice Presser Greene.

Artists
David Ashby, Giovanni Caselli, Andrew Farmer, Nicholas Hall, Shian Hartshorn, Terri Lawlor, Miriam Mills, Kevin Molloy, Howard Pemberton, Andrew Popkiewicz, Les Smith.

Photographs
The photographs on page 211, between pages 232 and 257 and on page 319 were taken by Nancy Durrell McKenna. All other photographs of mothers, fathers and their children were taken by Camilla Jessel.

The photograph on page 57 is reproduced courtesy of Cornell Medical Center, New York.

The drawings on page 263 were based on photographs in *Birth Reborn* by Michel Odent (Pantheon 1984).

The photographers and the publishers would like to thank all the parents and parents-to-be who allowed themselves and their children to be photographed for this book – especially those who so generously agreed to share the experience of the birth of their babies. They are also deeply grateful to the nurses, doctors, and midwives concerned for their warm cooperation and advice. Special thanks go to all the staff of the Delivery Suite, the Special Care Unit, and the Antenatal Department of the West Middlesex Hospital, Isleworth, and to the Hounslow Community Midwife Service.